THE 45TH ANNUAL
BRIGHAM YOUNG UNIVERSITY
SIDNEY B. SPERRY SYMPOSIUM

Foundations of the Restoration

Foundations of the Restoration

FULFILLMENT OF THE COVENANT PURPOSES

Edited by
Craig James Ostler
Michael Hubbard MacKay
Barbara Morgan Gardner

THE 45TH ANNUAL
BRIGHAM YOUNG UNIVERSITY
SIDNEY B. SPERRY SYMPOSIUM

RSC
BYU

DESERET
BOOK

Frontispiece painting: Gary Smith, Jesus Christ Appearing to Joseph Smith and Oliver Cowdery in the Kirtland Temple. *Courtesy of Intellectual Reserve, Inc.*

Library of Congress Cataloging-in-Publication Data

Names: Sperry Symposium (45th : 2016 : Brigham Young University), author. | Ostler, Craig J., 1954- editor. | MacKay, Michael Hubbard, editor. | Morgan, Barbara E., editor.
Title: Foundations of the Restoration : fulfillment of the covenant purposes : the 45th annual Brigham Young University Sidney B. Sperry Symposium / edited by Craig James Ostler, Michael Hubbard MacKay, and Barbara E. Morgan.
Description: Provo, Utah : Religious Studies Center, Brigham Young University ; Salt Lake City : Deseret Book, [2016] | Includes index.
Identifiers: LCCN 2016020458 | ISBN 9781944394073
Subjects: LCSH: Restoration of the gospel (Mormon doctrine)--Congresses. | Church of Jesus Christ of Latter-day Saints--Doctrines--Congresses. | Mormon Church--Doctrines--Congresses.
Classification: LCC BX8635.3 .S64 2016 | DDC 230/.9332--dc23 LC record available at https://lccn.loc.gov/2016020458

Contents

Introduction

Religious educators around the world have begun teaching new curriculum focused on the Restoration of the gospel. Inspired by the new course "Foundations of the Restoration," this volume will support teachers and students as they study and teach key events and doctrines of the Restoration. Each article adds to our understanding of various aspects of the Restoration.

Robert L. Millet, former dean of Religious Education at Brigham Young University, who delivered the keynote address at the Sperry Symposium, introduces the Restoration and the Prophet Joseph Smith's role in restoring plain and precious truths. Colleagues Gerrit J. Dirkmaat, Michael MacKay, and Anthony Sweat examine how we evaluate doctrine and propose a model to assist students in their study of doctrinal topics and challenges. Craig Ostler and Lloyd Newell address the historical development of sustaining Church leaders as prophets, seers, and revelators and how these good yet imperfect individuals are inspired in directing the Lord's Church.

Other chapters provide answers to questions such as the following: What can the First Vision teach us about the learning process? How do we apply the truths in the Articles of Faith? What did the work of translating the Bible contribute to the Prophet Joseph Smith's understanding of the

Restoration? How does the law of consecration continue today? What did early Saints understand regarding Adam-ondi-Ahman, Zion, the gathering of Israel and their place regarding the Second Coming of Christ? What contributions did Church newspaper editor and hymn writer William W. Phelps and Hyrum Smith, the Prophet's brother, provide to our understanding of the Restoration? How did temples and temple ordinances develop in the Restoration? What correlations are found in historical understandings of Christian marriage and the doctrine of eternal family as we face new challenges to marriage in the culture of the twenty-first century? And how does restoration of true Sabbath worship affect our lives today?

We are happy to offer this volume to students of the Restoration. We trust that it will inspire and inform your understanding of the gospel of Jesus Christ and the history of the Saints that have accepted the Savior's call to gather to his fold.

Craig James Ostler
Michael Hubbard MacKay
Barbara Morgan Gardner
Patty Smith
Beverly Yellowhorse

2016 Sperry Symposium Committee

1

"The Morning Breaks"

THE GLORIOUS LIGHT OF RESTORATION

Robert L. Millet

Robert L. Millet is a professor emeritus of ancient scripture and former dean of
Religious Education at Brigham Young University.

Jesus and the Apostles spoke of the coming of the end of an age, the end
of the dispensation of the meridian of time. There would come a day,
they warned, when men and women would "not endure sound doctrine"
(2 Timothy 4:3), a day when malicious persons would seek to interject "dam-
nable heresies" (2 Peter 2:1) into the faith.

Though the political empire of Alexander the Great did not survive
his death in 323 BC, the cultural empire he founded lasted for nearly one
thousand years, until the rise of Islam and the Arab conquests in the seventh century. Greek or Hellenistic influence was profound—on the Roman
empire, on the world of Judaism, and, unfortunately, on the early Christian
Church. As Zenos had foreseen, for a time the grafting of branches from
the "wild olive tree" (Gentile influence) would result in a season of strength
for the Church (see Jacob 5:17). But it was only a matter of time before the
teachings of the prophets and ideas of the philosophers would come in conflict; those with eyes to see were aware that attempts to merge the doctrines
of the temple of God with the doctrines of Plato would be abortive to the

1

Christian faith. Ecumenism would lead to shared impotence. Philosophical error, mixed with truth, resulted in a heretical hybrid—a conceptual concoction foreign to the spiritually sensitive and certainly offensive to that God who delights in revealing himself to his children.

Certainly there were good and noble souls who enjoyed and hearkened to that influence we know as the Light of Christ; they strove to live according to the best light and knowledge they possessed. Having discussed the flickering and dimming of the flame of Christian faith, President Boyd K. Packer stated, "But always, as it had from the beginning, the Spirit of God inspired worthy souls. We owe an immense debt to the protesters and the reformers who preserved the scriptures and translated them. They knew something had been lost. They kept the flame alive as best they could."[1] On another occasion he taught: "The line of priesthood authority was broken. But mankind was not left in total darkness or completely without revelation or inspiration. The idea that with the Crucifixion of Christ the heavens were closed and they opened in the First Vision is not true. The Light of Christ would be everywhere present to attend the children of God; the Holy Ghost would visit seeking souls. The prayers of the righteous would not go unanswered."[2]

Elder Alexander B. Morrison of the Seventy wrote, "The view that changes in the early church resulted in the dissent of a blanket of stygian darkness over the entire earth such that humankind had no contact with God or the Spirit for nearly two millennia simply doesn't stand up to the scrutiny of modern scholarship. Scholars of today, benefiting from perspectives and information not readily available a century ago, understand that the 'Dark Ages' were not nearly so dark as previously had been thought."[3] John Taylor declared that there were persons during medieval times who "could commune with God, and who, by the power of faith, could draw aside the curtain of eternity and gaze upon the invisible world . . . , have the ministering of angels, and unfold the future destinies of the world. If those were dark ages I pray God to give me a little darkness, and deliver me from the light and intelligence that prevail in our day."[4]

Nevertheless, apostolic authority—divine direction on how to regulate the affairs of the Church of Jesus Christ and to proclaim and interpret true doctrine—was taken from the earth. That glorious luminary we know as revelation, that always comes institutionally through the ministry of apostles and prophets, was no longer enjoyed among the people of earth. The losses included the keys of the holy priesthood as well as the essential covenants and ordinances that lead to life eternal; plain and precious truths taken or kept back from the Bible (see 1 Nephi 13:24–29, 34); the true doctrine of God, the Godhead, and man's relationship to deity; and sacred insights into the means whereby mortals can have divine experience. These and a myriad of other treasures became mysteries to the masses and slipped into the realm of the unknowable and the unavailable.

The Dawning of a Brighter Day

The spring of 1820 heralded the dawn of a new day. The Sacred Grove in upstate New York was not to be the location of a complete restoration, a place and a time wherein God would make all things known and correct all the flaws of a faltering world. Rather, the First Vision began the era of restitution, the times of refreshing (see Acts 3:19–21), and the season of cleansing and purification and endowment that would reach a zenith in a millennial dispensation. Unable to walk fully in the light of the Lord, the people of earth had chosen their own paths and sought to direct their own destinies. The Lord's description of the spiritual condition of earth in the morn of restoration was given as follows: "They have strayed from mine ordinances, and have broken mine everlasting covenant; they seek not the Lord to establish his righteousness, but every man walketh in his own way, and after the image of his own god, whose image is in the likeness of the world, and whose substance is that of an idol, which waxeth old and shall perish in Babylon, even Babylon the great, which shall fall" (D&C 1:15–16). The pressing problem was idolatry—devotion and dedication to anything other than the true and living God. The problem was one we observe frequently in our day: distraction from those things of greatest worth. Man had fashioned unto himself a god, an unknown god, the unreachable and the unknowable Essence, that Wholly Other. Whether Catholic or Protestant, Jew or Muslim, the religious leaders of the nineteenth century, with their congregants—even the most sincere among them, and surely there were many—had lost their way.

The Lord then set forth the medicine for earth's malady: "Wherefore, I the Lord, knowing the calamity which should come upon the inhabitants of the earth,"—the spiritual calamity should the people of earth continue as they were and the perilous times that lay ahead even for those whose faith was fully centered on their Redeemer—"called upon my servant Joseph Smith, Jun., and spake unto him from heaven, and gave him commandments; And also gave commandments to others, that they should proclaim these things"—the glad tidings of the Restoration—"unto the world; and all this that it might be fulfilled, which was written by the prophets—The weak things of the world shall come forth and break down the mighty and strong ones, that man should not counsel his fellow man" (D&C 1:17–19). That is, the children of God need no longer place their trust in or rely on the limited wisdom of the unilluminated, those who are not truly men and women of God (see Mosiah 23:14).

Indeed, God would call upon the weak and the simple to bring forth his great and marvelous work, "those who are unlearned and despised" (D&C 35:13), those who are teachable, who are willing to unlearn falsehood and strip themselves of pride and duplicity, whose minds and hearts are open to the will of the Almighty. The Restoration heralded a day wherein men and women could come unto God, press forward through the mists of darkness, and then fall down and worship the true and living God, in the name of the Son, by the power of the Holy Ghost. The days in which only the chosen few could come unto God, those times when only a priestly hierarchy could perform the sacraments and commune with Deity, were no more. The gospel of God, the new and everlasting covenant, was restored to earth "that every man might speak in the name of God the Lord, even the Savior of the world; that faith also might increase in the earth" (D&C 1:20–21).

The Restoration would begin by a revelation, a re-revelation of doctrine and principles and precepts. It would of necessity start with the First Vision, the beginning of the revelation of God to man. It would be followed by the coming forth of the Book of Mormon: Another Testament of Jesus Christ. Through the truths contained in this sacred volume—including verities long lost on such vital matters as the Creation, the Fall, and the Atonement—the fulness of the gospel could be had again. Revelation upon revelation would come to and through Joseph Smith, including the restoration of those plain and precious truths once taken away or kept back from the Bible.

But there was more, more to come by way of truth, more than theology. The Restoration was destined to be a significant revolution. It must have been a mighty vision that filled the mind of Joseph Smith the Seer when he announced, "I calculate to be one of the instruments of setting up the kingdom [of God envisioned by] Daniel by the word of the Lord, and I intend to lay a foundation that will revolutionize the whole world."[5]

Joseph Smith's vision of the kingdom of God, and of the power and ultimate reach of the Restoration, was cosmic. It consisted of more than preaching and study and Sabbath services; it entailed the entire renovation of the order of things on earth, the transformation of mankind and the elevation of society. The Restoration was to be as broad and as deep as had been the long season when apostles and prophets were not on earth. Eventually the people of Zion would know and acknowledge the truth, discern and dispel error, and teach and live the truth in all they said and did, in all facets of human endeavor—intellectual, moral, and spiritual. "Behold, I, the Lord, have made my church in these last days like unto a judge sitting on a hill, or in a high place, to judge the nations. For it shall come to pass that the inhabitants of Zion shall judge all things pertaining to Zion" (D&C 64:37–38).

"'Mormonism' is destined to revolutionize the world," President George Q. Cannon observed.

> But how many are there who realize the truth of this saying? Some, no doubt, but not nearly all who have heard it, and yet that very revolution is going on, and they are helping to promote it; it commenced many years ago—the very moment the first revelation was given to the Prophet Joseph Smith.
>
> But to revolutionize a world, with religions, political and social systems, the outgrowth of nearly six thousand years' experience is a slow process. . . .
>
> For this reason the Kingdom of God upon the earth will not be characterized by a wonderfully rapid growth, . . . but, grappling ever with, and never ceasing the strife until it is victor over, error and evil of every kind, its foundations will be securely laid in the hearts and affections of those who love and live by truth and righteousness only.[6]

A Window to the Past

Of Joseph Smith and all those who are called as President of the Church, the Savior said, "And again, the duty of the President of the office of the High Priesthood is to preside over the whole church, and to be like unto Moses—Behold, here is wisdom; yea, to be a seer, a revelator, a translator, and a prophet, having all the gifts of God which he bestows upon the head of the church" (D&C 107:91–92; see also 124:125). Joseph Smith would not only stand as the head of this final dispensation but preside as the "choice seer" among the fruit of the loins of Joseph (2 Nephi 3:7). A seer, Ammon explained to King Limhi, is a prophet and a revelator also (see Mosiah 8:16). "A gift which is greater can no man have," he went on to say, "except he should possess the power of God, which no man can; yet a man may have great power given him from God. But a seer can know of things which are past, and also of things which are to come, and by them shall all things be revealed, or, rather, shall secret things be made manifest, and hidden things shall come to light, and things which are not known shall be made known by them. . . . Thus God has provided a means that man, through faith, might work mighty miracles; therefore he becometh a great benefit to his fellow beings" (Mosiah 8:16–18).

I am particularly interested in the seer's role in making known *things past*. Ponder for a moment on what we have come to know about the past as a result of the ministry of seers in these last days. Through what has been revealed by means of the Book of Mormon, the revelations in the Doctrine and Covenants, the Prophet's translation of the King James Bible (Joseph Smith Translation), the Book of Abraham, and other inspired prophetic commentary, we sit as it were with a great Urim and Thummim before us, gazing upon the scenes of days gone by. It just may be that the Lord revealed to Joseph Smith as much or more pertaining to the past as he did in regard to the future.

Surely there could be no truth of greater worth, no insight from the Restoration of more precious value—and yet so mysterious and strange to others in the religious world—than the idea of an eternal gospel. Because of the supplementary scriptures of the Restoration, we know that Christian prophets have declared Christian doctrine and administered Christian ordinances since the dawn of time. Adam and Eve were taught the gospel. They prayed to the Father in the name of the Son, repented of their sins, were baptized by immersion, received the gift of the Holy Ghost, were married for eternity, and entered into the order of the Son of God. They knew and they taught their children and their grandchildren the plan of salvation and the eternal fact that redemption would be wrought through the shedding of the blood of the Son of Man (see Moses 5:1–9; 6:51–68). And what was true of our first parents was true of Abel and Seth and Enoch and Melchizedek and Abraham. They had the gospel. They knew the Lord, taught his doctrine, and officiated as legal administrators in his earthly kingdom. Isaac, Israel, Joseph, Ephraim, and all the patriarchs enjoyed personal revelation and communion with their Maker. Samuel, Nathan, and those from Isaiah to Malachi in the Old World and from Nephi to Moroni in the New—all these prophets held the Melchizedek Priesthood.[7]

"We cannot believe," Joseph Smith stated, "that the ancients in all ages were so ignorant of the system of heaven as many suppose, since all that were ever saved, were saved through the power of this great plan of redemption, as much before the coming of Christ as since; if not, God has had different plans in operation (if we may so express it), to bring men back to dwell with Himself; and this we cannot believe, since there has been no change in the constitution of man since he fell."[8] Further, "Now taking it for granted that the scriptures say what they mean, and mean what they say, we have sufficient grounds to go on and prove from the Bible that the gospel has always been the same; the ordinances to fulfill its requirements, the same; and the officers to officiate, the same; and the signs and fruits resulting from the promises, the same."[9]

In one of the most informative statements in our literature on this principle—that the gospel message and ordinances are forever the same—Elder Bruce R. McConkie declared:

> The everlasting gospel; the eternal priesthood; the identical ordinances of salvation and exaltation; the never-varying doctrines of salvation; the same Church and kingdom; the keys of the kingdom, which alone can seal men up unto eternal life— all these have always been the same in all ages; and it shall be so everlastingly on this earth and all earths to all eternity. These things we know by latter-day revelation.

Once we know these things, the door is open to an understanding of the fragmentary slivers of information in the Bible. By combining the Book of Mormon, the Doctrine and Covenants, and the Pearl of Great Price, we have at least a thousand passages that let us know what prevailed among the Lord's people in the Old World.

Did they have the fulness of the everlasting gospel at all times? Yes. There was not a period of ten minutes from the days of Adam to the appearing of the Lord Jesus in the land Bountiful when the gospel—as we have it in its eternal fullness—was not on earth.

Do not let the fact that the performances of the Mosaic law were administered by the Aaronic Priesthood confuse you on this matter. Where the Melchizedek Priesthood is, there is the fulness of the gospel, and all the prophets held the Melchizedek Priesthood. . . .

Was there baptism in the days of ancient Israel? The answer is in the Joseph Smith Translation of the Bible . . . and in the Book of Mormon. The first six hundred years of Nephite history is simply a true and plain account of how things were in ancient Israel from the days of Moses downward.

Was there a Church anciently, and, if so, how was it organized and regulated? There was not so much as the twinkling of an eye during the whole so-called pre-Christian Era when the Church of Jesus Christ was not on earth, organized basically in the same way it now is. Melchizedek belonged to the Church. . . . Laban was a member. . . . So also was Lehi, long before he left Jerusalem.

There was always apostolic power. . . . The Melchizedek Priesthood always directed the course of the Aaronic Priesthood. All of the prophets held a position in the hierarchy of the day. Celestial marriage has always existed. Indeed, such is the heart and core of the Abrahamic covenant. . . . Elias and Elijah came to restore this ancient order and to give the sealing power which gives it eternal efficacy. . . .

People ask, Did they have the gift of the Holy Ghost before the day of Pentecost? As the Lord lives they were so endowed; such is part of the gospel; and those so gifted wrought miracles and sought and obtained a city whose builder and maker is God. . . .

I have often wished the history of ancient Israel could have passed through the editing and prophetic hands of Mormon. If so, it would read like the Book of Mormon; but I suppose that was the way it read in the first instance anyway.[10]

". . . Save Jesus Only"

It is not difficult to catch an occasional glimpse of the singular role of Joseph Smith in this final age. In a spirit of tribute, a spirit of gratitude and praise, Elder John Taylor, a man not prone to hyperbole, wrote, "Joseph Smith, the Prophet and Seer of the Lord, has done more, save Jesus only, for the salvation of men in this world, than any other man that ever lived in it" (D&C 135:3). We ask, More than Enoch? More than Abraham? More than Jacob? More than Moses? What did Elder Taylor mean? Here are a few points to ponder:

1. Joseph Smith serves as the legal administrator associated with that period of time prophesied by Joel: "And it shall come to pass afterward, that I will pour out my spirit upon all flesh; and your sons and your daughters shall prophesy, your old men shall dream dreams, your young men shall see visions: and also upon the servants and upon the handmaids in those days will I pour out my spirit" (Joel 2:28–29). When Moroni first appeared in September 1823, he quoted these verses and said "that this was not yet fulfilled, but was soon to be" (Joseph Smith—History 1:41). The Spirit of God would certainly prove to be the driving influence behind the dissemination of eternal truth and the spiritual transformation of those who submitted to the terms and conditions of the gospel of Jesus Christ. But what of others outside the faith? Would not this Spirit affect them? President Joseph Fielding Smith, after having quoted the prophecy of Joel, explained:

Now, my brethren and sisters, *I am not going to confine this prophecy to the members of the Church.* The Lord said he would pour out his Spirit upon all flesh. That does not mean that upon all flesh the Holy Ghost should be sent, and that they should be participants in the blessings which those are privileged to receive who have been baptized and endowed and become members of the Church; but *the Lord would pour out his blessings and his Spirit upon all people and use them to accomplish his purposes.* . . .

There has never been a step taken . . . , in discovery or invention, where the Spirit of the Lord (that is, the Spirit of which Joel spoke, the Light of Christ, not the Holy Ghost!) was not the prevailing force, resting upon the individual, which caused him to make the discovery or the invention. The world does not understand that, but it is perfectly clear to me; *nor did the Lord always use those who have faith, nor does he always do so today. He uses such minds as are pliable and can be turned in certain directions to accomplish his work, whether they believe in him or not.*

President Smith then provided the following insight: "There have been a great many discoveries. In fact, since the establishment of the gospel, these discoveries and inventions have been increasing more rapidly and we have seen more, perhaps . . . than was seen during all the years from the days of the revival of learning and the Reformation down to the visitation of Moroni to the Prophet Joseph Smith."[11] (It is interesting to note that these words were spoken some time before 1954.) In short, the Spirit of God—meaning the Light of Christ—has been behind the rapid intellectual, scientific, and technological developments from the time of the Industrial Revolution to our own Information Age. The modern seer presides over this age of enlightenment and expansion.

2. Though we thrill in the knowledge that God continues to guide his Church and kingdom and continues to make known his mind and will to his chosen servants, we conclude that most of what we know today in the form of doctrine—thousands of pages of revelations and instructions and prophetic direction—has come to us through the instrumentality of Joseph Smith. His call initiated the "times of restitution of all things, which God hath spoken by the mouth of all his holy prophets since the world began" (Acts 3:21), a day of restoration that will continue throughout the

Millennium. It is the final period in which the gospel will be delivered to earth, an era that will not end in apostasy. It is called the dispensation of the fulness of times, or the dispensation of the fulness of dispensations. Joseph Smith wrote the following inspired words from Liberty Jail: "God shall give unto you knowledge by his Holy Spirit, yea, by the unspeakable gift of the Holy Ghost, [knowledge] that has not been revealed since the world was until now; which our forefathers have awaited with anxious expectation to be revealed in the last times, which their minds were pointed to by the angels, as held in reserve for the fulness of their glory; a time to come in the which nothing shall be withheld" (D&C 121:26–28). In a revelation received in January of 1841 dealing with the ordinances of the temple, the Lord stated: "I deign to reveal unto my church things which have been kept hid from before the foundation of the world, *things that pertain to the dispensation of the fulness of times*" (D&C 124:41; emphasis added). Joseph Smith was raised up to make known "those things which never have been revealed from the foundation of the world, but have been kept hid from the wise and prudent, [things that] shall be revealed unto babes and sucklings in this, the dispensation of the fulness of times" (D&C 128:18).

3. With the visit of the disembodied Savior to the postmortal spirit world, the work of the redemption of the dead began. We know from Paul's epistle to the Corinthians that the early Christians had begun vicarious labors (1 Corinthians 15:29), and we can assume that such work continued until the priesthood was taken from the earth. That may have been no more than seventy or eighty years after the death of Christ. Thus, persons who died without a knowledge of the gospel from the beginning of time will fall within the purview of the dispensation of the fulness of times. After the period of falling away, who would have performed the appropriate saving ordinances for all humankind, ordinances not only for those after the meridian of time, but also for people from the earliest ages of the world? Other than the brief period wherein the first-century Christian Church made vicarious salvation available to some, it would appear that the responsibility for gospel ordinances for the residue of earth's inhabitants rests with our dispensation.

Think on it! Joseph Smith and his successors are responsible for the teaching of the gospel in the world of spirits and the performance of saving ordinances for literally billions of our Father's children. My colleague Larry E.

Dahl has written, "Without diminishing in the least the importance of the work done by earlier prophets and others of the Lord's servants, clearly in terms of the numbers of souls to whom the saving principles and ordinances of the gospel have been made available, a monumental work has been effected through the instrumentality of 'Joseph Smith, the Prophet and Seer of the Lord' (D&C 135:3)."[12] President Joseph F. Smith taught, "The work in which Joseph Smith was engaged was not confined to this life alone, but it pertains as well to the life to come, and to the life that has been. In other words, it relates to those who have lived upon the earth, to those who are living and to those who shall come after us. It is not something which relates to man only while he tabernacles in the flesh, but to the whole human family from eternity to eternity. Consequently, . . . Joseph Smith is held in reverence."[13]

Being Loyal to the Restoration

Largely because of the repeated emphasis by President Ezra Taft Benson during his administration (1985–94), we have become very much aware of the condemnation, scourge, and judgment that rest upon the members of The Church of Jesus Christ of Latter-day Saints because of our near neglect of the Book of Mormon and modern revelation. The Lord's censure has come because we have "treated lightly the things [we] have received." The solution for ridding ourselves of this curse is quite simple: "They shall remain under this condemnation until they repent and remember the new covenant"—or the new testament—"even the Book of Mormon and the former commandments which I have given them, not only to say, but to do"—to incorporate, to inculcate, to live—"according to that which I have written." The Master also explains, "I will forgive you of your sins with this commandment—that you remain steadfast in your minds in solemnity and the spirit of prayer, in bearing testimony to all the world of those things which are communicated unto you" (D&C 84:54, 57, 61).

About six centuries before the coming of Jesus in the flesh, Nephi offered a haunting warning. Speaking of those in the last days, he prophesied, "They wear stiff necks and high heads; yea, and because of pride, and wickedness, and abominations, and whoredoms, they have all gone astray save it be a few, who are the humble followers of Christ; nevertheless, they are led"—many of the humble followers of Christ —"that in many instances they do err because they are taught by the precepts of men" (2 Nephi 28:14). In a modern revelation, a similar warning is sounded: "And when the times of the Gentiles is come in, a light shall break forth among them that sit in darkness, and it shall be the fulness of my gospel; but they receive it not; for they perceive not the light, and they turn their hearts from me because of the precepts of men" (D&C 45:28–29). It should be clear to most of us that this prophecy will not be fulfilled solely through the rejection of Mormonism by persons of other faiths. Sadly, it will find its fulfillment also in the lives of those baptized members who choose to live beneath their privileges, who exist in twilight when they could bask in the glorious light of noonday sun (see D&C 95:5–6). The doctrines of the Restoration assist us immeasurably in sifting and sorting through the views and philosophies of men and riveting ourselves to that which is true and enduring.

Being loyal to the Restoration entails being ready and willing to bear witness of the truths made known to us in this latter day. We love the Bible. We cherish its truths, treasure its marvelous stories of faith, and seek to live according to its precepts. But the scriptures of the Restoration carry a spirit all their own, particularly the Book of Mormon. There is a light and an endowment of spiritual power that come into our lives through searching Restoration scripture that can come in no other way. Being loyal to the Restoration entails giving careful attention to and teaching from the things that have been delivered to Joseph Smith and his successors.

In a modern revelation, Thomas B. Marsh was instructed, "Lift up your heart and rejoice, for the hour of your mission is come; and your tongue shall be loosed, and you shall declare glad tidings of great joy unto this generation." And what were those glad tidings? What, specifically, was Brother Marsh to declare? Was he to go forth and restate the truths of the New Testament? Was he to bear witness in the words of Peter, Paul, or John the Beloved? Was he to teach the Sermon on the Mount or repeat the words of the Master concerning the bread of life? No, he was to "*declare the things which have been revealed to my servant, Joseph Smith, Jun.*" (D&C 31:3–4; emphasis added). Likewise, Leman Copley was specifically instructed how to teach the gospel to those of his former faith, the Shakers. He was to "reason with them" —the Shakers—"not according to that which he has received of them, but according to that which shall be taught him by you my servants." And note this important detail: "By so doing I will bless him, otherwise he shall not prosper" (D&C 49:4).

Modern revelation provides an interpretive lens and a hermeneutical key to the Bible. Much of what we understand about the Testaments is clear to us because of the Book of Mormon, the Joseph Smith Translation, the Doctrine and Covenants, and the Pearl of Great Price. There are those, however, who hesitate to accept what we know from modern revelation and who feel that to do so is to somehow compromise the integrity or unique contribution of the Bible itself. In response to this posture, let me suggest an analogy. If one were eager to locate a valuable site, should that person use a map that is deficient in detail or inaccurate in layout simply because the map had been in the family for generations and was highly prized? Should one choose to ignore the precious information to be had on a more reliable or complete map, if such were available? Of course the whole matter is inextricably tied to the question of whether the traveler sincerely desires to reach his destination; maps have real value only to the degree that they guide us to a desired location. Furthermore, would a scholar in any discipline choose to maintain a position or defend a point of view when subsequent and current research had shed further (and perhaps clarifying) light on the subject? To do so would represent, at best, naiveté, and, at worst, shoddy and irresponsible scholarship.

In that spirit, and knowing what we do about the everlasting nature of the gospel, the Church and kingdom, and the principles and ordinances pertaining thereto, it is perfectly appropriate and perhaps even incumbent upon us to make doctrinal inferences about personalities in scripture when recorded details may be lacking. For example, I know that Eve and Sarah and Rebekah were baptized, that Jacob received the temple endowment, and that Micah and Malachi stood in the prophetic office by divine call. I know that Nephi, son of Lehi, was baptized by water and received the gift of the Holy Ghost as well as the high priesthood, although an account of the same is not stated directly in the Nephite record. These are valid inferences, based on principles of doctrine and priesthood government. Because of what has been made known through Joseph Smith, we know what it takes to operate the kingdom of God and what things the people of God must do to comply.

There is a final matter that deserves our attention, something that unfortunately is not understood by some today. As members of the Church at the beginning of the twenty-first century, we can be loyal to Joseph Smith only to the degree that we are loyal to the leaders of the Church in our own day. Those who criticize or find fault with the present Church or its constituted authorities in the name of being true to Brother Joseph know not what they do. The spirit of Joseph is with the leaders of this Church. Of that I have no question. President Joseph F. Smith testified:

> I feel quite confident that the eyes of Joseph the Prophet, and of the martyrs of this dispensation, and of Brigham and John and Wilford, and those faithful men who were associated with them in their ministry upon the earth, are carefully guarding the interests of the Kingdom of God in which they labored and for which they strove during their mortal lives. I believe they are as deeply interested in our welfare today, if not with greater capacity, with far more interest, behind the veil, than they were in the flesh. I believe they know more; I believe their minds have expanded beyond their comprehension in mortal life, and their interests are enlarged in the work of the Lord to which they gave their lives and their best service. . . . I have a feeling in my heart that I stand in the presence not only of the Father and of the Son, but in the presence of those whom God commissioned, raised up, and inspired, to lay the foundations of the work in which we are engaged.[14]

It is vital that members of the Church pay heed to the words and counsel of the living oracles. Just as Noah's revelation to build an ark was not sufficient to instruct Abraham in his duties, so what the God of heaven made known to Joseph Smith is not sufficient to lead this Church today. We do well to follow the inspired counsel directed to the early missionaries of this dispensation to declare "none other things than that which the prophets and apostles have written" (D&C 52:9, 36). If the leaders of the Church do not feel the need to stress a given point that seems to be an obsession with some—to warn of coming economic crises or the eminent overthrow by foreign nations or the need to leave our present culture and reestablish an agrarian society—then we would be wise to ask ourselves why such things are not being spoken of by our leaders. Are they unaware? Are they aware but unwilling to reveal these things to us?

President Harold B. Lee passed away suddenly and unexpectedly on 26 December 1973 after serving as President of the Church for less than a year and a half. In January 1974, Elder Bruce R. McConkie delivered a remarkably insightful sermon to the students at Brigham Young University regarding principles of apostolic succession:

> The Lord, in his infinite wisdom and goodness, knows what ought to be done with his servants. The other thing to note is that when the Lord calls a new prophet he does it because he has a work and a labor and a mission for the new man to perform. I can imagine that when the Prophet Joseph Smith was taken from this life the Saints felt themselves in the depths of despair. To think that a leader of such spiritual magnitude had been taken from them! . . . And yet when he was taken the Lord had Brigham Young. Brigham Young stepped forth and wore the mantle of leadership. With all respect and admiration and every accolade of praise resting upon the Prophet Joseph, still *Brigham Young came forward and did things that then had to be done in a better way than the Prophet Joseph could have done them.*[15]

Though as a people we have miles to go before we rest and we have much spiritual development ahead of us, I bear witness that the Church is in excellent hands, is in the line of its duty, and is preparing a people for the Second Coming of the Son of Man. What is spoken by the General Authorities of the Church is what we need to hear and what the Lord would have his Saints know; those messages should become, as President Harold B. Lee once said, "the guide to [our] walk and talk."[16] If the Lord desires to warn his people and to provide appropriate interpretation of difficult prophetic passages, then that warning will surely come, but it will come through the channels he has established. It is wonderful to be able to raise our hands to sustain the prophets, seers, and revelators. I would suggest that one very practical way to sustain them is to take ourselves off their "worry list" through staying in the mainstream of the Church, living a sane and balanced life, and serving and loving our brothers and sisters in a manner befitting the Saints of the Most High God.

In March 1844, the Prophet Joseph Smith gave an unusual assignment to a group of Church leaders: they were asked to amend the Constitution of the United States, so as to make it "the voice of Jehovah." Later in the week, Elder John Taylor, as a representative of a special committee of three, responded that no progress had been made toward the preparation of a constitution for the kingdom of God. The Prophet acknowledged their failure, indicating that he knew "they could not draft a constitution worthy of guiding the Kingdom of God." He himself had gone before the Lord, seeking that such a constitution be made known by revelation. The answer came: "Ye are my Constitution and I am your God and ye are my spokesmen, therefore from henceforth keep my commandments."[17] In a revelation given to President John Taylor on 27 June 1882, the Savior said, "Verily, thus saith the Lord, I have instituted my Kingdom and my laws, with the keys and power thereof, and have appointed you as a spokesman and my Constitution, with President John Taylor at your head, whom I have appointed to my Church and my Kingdom as Prophet, Seer and Revelator." Later in the same revelation the Lord affirmed, "Ye are my Constitution, and I am your God."[18] In short, this Church is to be governed by revelation—current, daily, modern, and ongoing divine direction—and not by written documents alone (D&C 46:2). All of God's purposes for his children cannot be codified. Nothing is more fixed, set, and established than the fact that among the people of God the canon of scripture is open, flexible, and expanding.

Reading the Signs of the Times

On one occasion the Pharisees came to Jesus demanding a sign—some physical proof of his messiahship. The Lord took that opportunity to contrast their ability to read the face of the sky (and thus discern "signs" associated with weather patterns) with their marked inability to read the "signs of the times" (and thus discern the true meanings of messianic prophecies and testimonies). The greatest evidence that the leaders of the Jews in Jesus' day could not read the vital signs of eternity is the simple fact that they missed the Messiah when he came among them. The Hope of Ages had arrived and was ignored or rejected, and those who thus spurned the Lord of Life were left hopeless (see Matthew 16:1–6). We face a future that is, like the Second Coming, both great and terrible. There are those things that lie in futurity that frighten us and cause us to quake and tremble. And yet there are remarkably wonderful things that lie ahead for those who prove true and faithful. How we fare in days to come will be determined largely by how well we are able to read the signs of the times.

Reading the signs of the times not only enables one to recognize and adjust to the events of the present but also to foresee and prepare for coming events. Those outside the Church who reject its teachings and doctrines are not in a position to fully perceive and properly adapt to the present and future social, economic, and spiritual challenges. Even those within the Church who have not been wise and thus have not "taken the Holy Spirit for their guide" (see D&C 45:57) lack that discernment necessary to sense the urgency of the messages of the Lord's servants.

To read the signs of the times is to perceive the unfolding of God's divine drama in these last days and to have the broad perspective of the plan of life and salvation and a special appreciation for the scenes incident to its consummation. It is to understand that this is the day long awaited by the prophets of old, when God would pour out knowledge and power from on high "by the unspeakable gift of the Holy Ghost" (D&C 121:26).

On the other hand, to read the signs of the times in our day is to read the signs of wear and tear in the faces of those who have chosen to love and give devoted service to either questionable or diabolical causes. Error and wickedness take terrible tolls on the hearts and countenances of those who pursue divergent paths; the wheels of waywardness grind away slowly but inexorably to produce a character that is devoid of spirituality. To read the signs of the times is in part to recognize that Alma spoke a profound truth when he declared that "wickedness never was happiness" (Alma 41:10).

Reading the signs of the times in our day does not mean seeking signs in our day. The Savior taught that a wicked and adulterous generation may be recognized by its tendency to demand physical proof as evidence of the veracity of the Lord's work (see Matthew 12:39; 16:4). Interestingly enough, those who are not spiritually mature enough to read the signs of the times are so often those who demand signs. "Show us the golden plates," they cry out. "Call down the angel Moroni, and while you're at it, furnish the complete text for the Book of Abraham." Those who truly seek to be in tune with the divine will, on the other hand, become witnesses and recipients of those wonders and miracles that a gracious Lord always bestows upon his faithful flock. "Faith cometh not by signs," the holy word declares, "but signs follow those that believe" (D&C 63:9).

To read the signs of the times is to make a decision in favor of the society of Zion and the Church of the Lamb of God (see 1 Nephi 14:10). This is in contrast to a decision to enter or perpetuate Babylon. Each city—Zion and Babylon—makes definite demands of its citizens, and as the Millennium approaches, each of these communities will insist upon the complete consecration of its citizenry. To read the signs of the times is to recognize that in the future there will be fewer and fewer "lukewarm" Latter-day Saints; the myopic and the misguided of the religious world will grow in cynicism and confusion; the ungodly will, as time goes by, sink ever deeper into despair; wickedness will widen and malevolence will multiply until the congregants in Babylon seal themselves to him who is the father of all lies.

Finally, to read the signs of the times is also to know that "Zion must arise and put on her beautiful garments" (D&C 82:14) and that the restored Church will continue to require the time, talents, and means of its members as an integral part of their growth toward perfect faith. Through consecrating all they have and are to the Lord, the Saints of the Most High will establish a heaven on earth and receive the precious assurance of exaltation in the highest degree of glory.

As to the destiny of the Church, as well as the specific directions to be taken by it, these matters are the responsibility of apostles and prophets. Thankfully, at the head of this Church are men of vision, true seers, those who, like Enoch, discern and behold "things which [are] not visible to the natural eye" (Moses 6:36). The Church and kingdom in this final dispensation is led by those who can see "afar off" (D&C 101:54) and can discern and expose the enemies of Christ around the corner. Thus, they prepare the Latter-day Saints and the world for what lies ahead. Speaking to the leaders of the Church in 1831—who later became members of the first Quorum of the Twelve Apostles—the Lord promised, "And he that believeth shall be blest with signs following, even as it is written. And unto you it shall be given to know the signs of the times, and the signs of the coming of the Son of Man" (D&C 68:10–11).

While each member of the Church has the sobering responsibility to cultivate the gifts of the Spirit and thereby come to see things as they really are and as they really will be (Jacob 4:13; D&C 93:24), the Almighty has his own way of directing and preparing and readying the Saints as a body. In a revelation given to President John Taylor on 14 April 1883 concerning the organization of the priesthood and the Church, the word of the Lord came as follows:

> Thus saith the Lord unto the First Presidency, unto the Twelve, unto the Seventies, and unto all my holy Priesthood, let not your hearts be troubled, neither be ye concerned about the management and organization of my Church and Priesthood and the accomplishment of my work. *Fear me and observe my laws and I will reveal unto you, from time to time, through the channels that I have appointed, everything that shall be necessary for the further development and perfection of my Church,* for the adjustment and rolling forth of my Kingdom, and for the building up and establishment of my Zion. For ye are my Priesthood, and I am your God. Even so, Amen.[19]

Conclusion

There are few things about which the membership of the Church need to be anxious. We need to learn the gospel. We need to live the gospel and put on Christ and put off the works of the flesh. We need to become more Christlike. We need to be anxiously engaged in publishing the message of the Restoration to all the world. We need to be worthy to receive the ordinances of salvation and then make the same available to our kindred dead. We need to rivet ourselves, our children, and our children's children to the redemption that is in Christ, that we and they might know to what source to look for a remission of our sins (see 2 Nephi 25:26). Further, and most importantly, we need to look to the presidency of this Church and heed the counsel of those called and appointed to direct its destiny. We must follow the Brethren as they point the way to eternal life. Though there will be individual casualties from the faith as we move toward the end, we need not be anxious about the future of the Church and kingdom of God. We need not be concerned about the leadership of the Church; we need only cultivate the little plot of ground assigned to us and leave the government of the kingdom to the King. The Lord does not ask us to magnify other people's callings.

Because of the knowledge, keys, and powers associated with latter-day revelation, salvation will come to men and women who live in this final age of the earth's history. Most of what we know about God's dealings with humanity in the past, about his work and purposes in this day, and about the end of times, we know because the heavens have been opened and the Lord Jehovah has restored ancient records for the benefit and blessing of those who live in a modern time. He has spoken again through prophets and apostles, has given vision to seers, and has brought light, inspiration, and holiness to a world that had been travelling in darkness.

Where once darkness reigned, love, light, and pure religion are found. Where ignorance, doubt, and superstition were the order of the day, now hope, knowledge, and the quiet rest of spiritual certitude prevail among the faithful. Joseph Smith the Prophet laid the foundation. By revelation he set in motion a revolution whose foreordained effects will not be fully realized until that day when the Lord reigns in the midst of his Saints and evil and wickedness are done away, and when, as Isaiah foresaw, the knowledge of God covers the earth as the waters cover the sea (see Isaiah 11:9). President Spencer W. Kimball said, "Never again will the sun go down; never again will all men prove totally unworthy of communication with their Maker; never again will God be totally hidden from his children on earth. Revelation is here to remain. Prophets will follow each other in a never-ending succession, and the secrets of the Lord will be revealed without measure."[20] Our charge as people of the covenant is to help these promised blessings be realized by us and by the world. That we may do so is my earnest hope and prayer.

Notes

1. Boyd K. Packer, in Conference Report, April 2000, 7.

2. Boyd K. Packer, "The Light of Christ," *Ensign*, April 2005, 11.

3. Alexander B. Morrison, *Turning from Truth: A New Look at the Great Apostasy* (Salt Lake City: Deseret Book, 2005), 2.

4. John Taylor, in *Journal of Discourses*, 26 vols. (Liverpool: F. D. Richards & Sons, 1851–86), 16:197.

5. *Teachings of Presidents of the Church: Joseph Smith* (Salt Lake City: The Church of Jesus Christ of Latter-day Saints, 2007), 512; cited hereafter as *Joseph Smith*.

6. George Q. Cannon, *Gospel Truth*, ed. Jerreld L. Newquist (Salt Lake City: Deseret Book, 1987), 322–23.

7. *Joseph Smith*, 109.

8. *Joseph Smith*, 48–49.

9. *Joseph Smith*, 93.

10. Bruce R. McConkie, "The Bible: A Sealed Book," in *Doctrines of the Restoration: Sermons and Writings of Bruce R. McConkie*, ed. Mark L. McConkie (Salt Lake City: Bookcraft, 1989), 292–93.

11. Joseph Fielding Smith, *Doctrines of Salvation*, 3 vols., comp. Bruce R. McConkie (Salt Lake City: Bookcraft, 1954–56), 1:176–78, 179; emphasis added.

12. Larry E. Dahl, "The Theological Significance of the First Vision," in *Studies in Scripture*, ed. Robert L. Millet and Kent P. Jackson, 8 vols. (Salt Lake City: Randall Book, 1985), 2:321.

13. Smith, *Gospel Doctrine* (Salt Lake City: Deseret Book, 1971), 481.

14. Joseph F. Smith, "In the Presence of the Divine," in *Messages of the First Presidency*, ed. James R. Clark, 6 vols. (Salt Lake City: Bookcraft, 1965–75), 5:6.

15. Bruce R. McConkie, "Succession in the Presidency," in *1974 BYU Speeches of the Year* (Provo: BYU Publications, 1975), 24; emphasis added.

16. Harold B. Lee, in Conference Report, April 1946, 68.

17. Joseph Smith Diary, 10 March 1844, Church History Library, Salt Lake City; cited in Andrew F. Ehat, "'It Seems Like Heaven Began on Earth': Joseph Smith and the Constitution of the Kingdom of God," *Brigham Young University Studies* 20, no. 3 (Spring 1980): 259.

18. Joseph F. Smith, Minutes of the Council of Fifty, 21 April 1880, as quoted in Ehat, "'It Seems Like Heaven Began on Earth,'" 259.

19. *Unpublished Revelations of the Prophets and Presidents of the Church of Jesus Christ of Latter Day Saints*, ed. Fred C. Collier (Salt Lake City: Colliers Publishing Company, 1979), 132, 134; emphasis added.

20. *Teachings of Spencer W. Kimball*, ed. Edward L. Kimball (Salt Lake City: Bookcraft, 1982), 433.

2

Evaluating Latter-day Saint Doctrine

Anthony R. Sweat, Michael Hubbard MacKay, and Gerrit J. Dirkmaat

Anthony R. Sweat, Michael Hubbard MacKay, and Gerrit J. Dirkmaat
are assistant professors of Church history and doctrine at BYU.

In early 1833, the presiding elder of a small branch in Benson, Vermont, wrote to his brother living at Church headquarters in Kirtland, Ohio, hoping to receive guidance from Joseph Smith on a very important question: How do I know what teachings in my branch I should accept as doctrine? He was writing because Jane Sherwood, a woman in his congregation, asserted that she had seen visions of angels and of God that had given her revelation "concerning that which must come hereafter, p[u]rporting indeed that the power of God's Judgment has come & astonishing things soon are to take place."[1]

In response to the inquiry, Joseph Smith wrote back and related an important truth regarding the way true doctrine is disseminated in the Church. Joseph explained, "As it respects the vision you speak of we do not consider ourselves bound to receive any revelation from any one man or woman without being legally constituted and ordained to that authority and given sufficient proof of it." The Prophet further taught, "I will inform you that it is contrary to the economy of God for any member of the Church or any one to receive instruction for those in authority higher than themselves, therefore you will see the impropriety of giving heed to them." Succinctly, Joseph Smith had laid out essential principles for understanding doctrine in the Lord's restored Church. If a revelation or doctrine was to be given to the Church, it would come from the designated Church authorities, "for the fund[a]mental principals, government and doctrine of the church is invested in the keys of the kingdom."[2]

Questions about Church doctrine did not originate, nor did they cease, in 1833 in Benson, Vermont. Many yet wonder and have pressing questions related to Latter-day Saint "doctrine," such as, "If God is unchanging and truth is eternal, then why does Church doctrine sometimes change?" or "Why don't we still teach some of the doctrines that were taught in the early Church? Were they wrong, or are we?" When discussing the Latter-day Saint faith, some imply or assume that everything ever spoken by any Church authority past or present constitutes eternally binding Church doctrine. Additionally, upon hearing an idea brought up in the Church, some want to know, "Is that teaching an *official* doctrine? How can I know?" These questions and many others have caused difficulty for many, both within and outside the Church, who desire to accurately understand and articulate what is and is not considered Church doctrine.

The purpose of this chapter is to open a dialogue about the nuances and complexities of Mormon doctrine by proposing two models: the first to evaluate varying *types* of doctrine and the second to evaluate *official sources* of doctrine. We begin by defining and understanding the word *doctrine*. Next we explore various aspects of the word, including concepts such as "eternal doctrine," "supportive doctrine," "policy doctrine," and "esoteric doctrine." We conclude by considering categories that may help us evaluate "official doctrine," and the power vested in the prophetic keys to declare and expand doctrine.

Understanding "Doctrine"

Some of the current confusion surrounding Latter-day Saint doctrine may derive from how it has been variously defined over time, which is primarily a question of semantics. Commonly today, many Latter-day Saints define the word *doctrine* as those things which are eternal or unchanging gospel truths.[3] However, the term was much more loosely applied by past prophets to also include other types of non-eternal, authoritative teachings.

In its most basic definition, dictionaries state that *doctrine* simply means "something that is taught"[4] or "teaching, instruction."[5] This broader understanding of the term is often the way the word is used in scripture as well. For example, when Jesus finished the Sermon on the Mount, Matthew records that "the people were astonished at his doctrine: For he taught them as one having authority" (Matthew 7:28–29; see also Matthew 22:33). The word *doctrine* in this verse derives from the Greek *didachē*, meaning "teaching" or "the act of teaching."[6] In the Sermon on the Mount, Jesus taught eternal, timeless truths of the plan of salvation, such as the command to be perfect like God our Father, but he also taught timely cultural applications specific mainly to his hearers, such as not to appear sad faced while fasting and how to respond to lawsuits. All of these teachings, whether eternal or dispensation-specific, were part of the Lord's doctrine because they each encompassed part of what he taught (see also Mark 2:27; Mark 11:17–18; Mark 12:38; Luke 4:32).

Historically, Joseph Smith often used the word *doctrine* more in line with this biblical usage of "something that is taught" or "teaching, instruction." The Prophet and his associates, when printing the *Lectures on Faith* from the School of the Prophets, classified them as "Theology," and subtitled them "On the Doctrine of the Church of the Latter Day Saints."[7] In the preface to the 1835 Doctrine and Covenants, Joseph articulated that the volume "contains in short, the leading items of the religion which we have professed to believe. The first part of the book will be found to contain a series of Lectures as delivered before a Theological class in this place, and in consequence of their embracing the important doctrine of salvation, we have arranged them into the following work."[8] Thus, the *Lectures on Faith* defined Church doctrine to such an extent that Church leaders included these lectures in the 1835 printing of Joseph's canonized revelations as the Doctrine and Covenants, rather than the earlier title, the Book of Commandments. Part 1 of the Doctrine and Covenants, the lectures, was "The Doctrine," and part 2, Joseph's revelations, was "The Covenants." Because the lectures became part of the canonized scripture, they were taught authoritatively as doctrine. These lectures, however, covered a vast array of topics that included not only eternal, unchanging, simple truths of the gospel but also history, rational theology, elaborative ideas, and pedagogical precepts.[9]

Since Latter-day Saint prophets continually reveal new teachings and interpret doctrines of the past, what is taught in the Church has changed over time. Currently, the Church teaches many things through its official avenues that are different and novel when compared to what was taught when the Church was founded in April of 1830. For example:

1. We emphasize that "exaltation in the highest degree of the celestial kingdom can be attained only by those who have faithfully lived the gospel of Jesus Christ and are sealed as eternal companions."[10]

2. Youth are taught not to "disfigure [themselves] with tattoos or body piercings."[11]

3. We declare that God "saves all the works of his hands, except those sons of perdition" into a kingdom of heavenly glory (D&C 76:43).

4. We teach that in the interim between his death and resurrection, Jesus did not go personally to the ungodly and wicked in spirit prison, but that "from among the righteous, he organized his forces and appointed messengers, clothed with power and authority, and commissioned them to go forth and carry the light of the gospel to them that were in darkness" (D&C 138:30).

5. Regarding missionary service, "worthy young women who have the desire to serve may be recommended for missionary service beginning at age 19."[12]

6. Faithful members are not to gather to a central location, but to "build up Zion wherever we live."[13]

God did not reveal all of his doctrines to Joseph Smith, especially as early as 1830. In fact, many of the doctrines revealed to Joseph, like baptisms for the dead, came to him at the end of his ministry. And unlike many other Christian churches, Latter-day Saints do not believe that all doctrines can be found in scripture. Because we believe in living prophets and continuing revelation, our doctrine is not static, and we will constantly receive new authoritative teachings. The ninth article of faith declares, "We believe all that God has revealed, all that He does now reveal, and we believe that He will yet reveal many great and important things pertaining to the Kingdom of God." This does not mean that doctrines cannot be eternal or immovable, but that some of them have yet to be revealed, and that some of the things

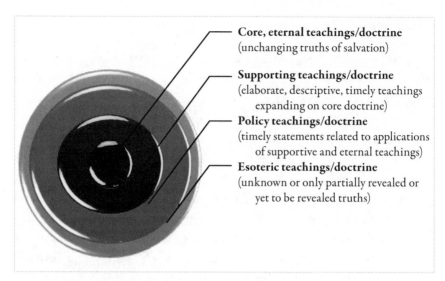

Figure 1. Types of LDS doctrine.

from the past will be less authoritative—perhaps even no longer taught. Therefore, it is deeply important that we understand those core doctrines that are eternal and recognize those that are timely, descriptive, or no longer taught.

Figure 1 provides a model for discussing this broader concept: making core, eternal doctrines the center, yet allowing for us to evaluate additional types of teachings of authoritative statements by General Authorities. This model follows the Church's 2007 statement on doctrine, which explains that "some doctrines are more important than others" and that central among these various doctrines are those that "might be considered core doctrines."[14] To analyze LDS doctrine, we explore each part of this model and discuss potential implications for our understanding and application. The model encourages the evaluation of each doctrine and requires careful historical and theological thought to understand the meaning of doctrines past, present, and future, rather than basic acceptance of all declarative statements as being eternally binding.

Core, Eternal Doctrine

There are teachings that could be termed "core doctrines" or "eternal doctrines." In the words of Elder David A. Bednar, these are "gospel doctrines [that] are eternal, do not change, and pertain to the eternal progression and exaltation of Heavenly Father's sons and daughters."[15] Elder B. H. Roberts of the Seventy said that "the great framework of the plan of salvation" has "certain truths that are not affected by ever-changing circumstances; truths which are always the same, no matter how often they may be revealed; truths which are elementary, permanent, fixed; from which there must not be, and cannot be, any departure without condemnation."[16] Such eternal truths that do not change may include the nature of God, the eternal makeup of the spirit, the universal resurrection, and the work and the glory of God to bring to pass the immortality and eternal life of his children (see Moses 1:39). The Church's founding "Articles and Covenants," found in Doctrine and Covenants 20, contain a succinct declaration of core, timeless doctrines, beginning in verse 17 with "there is a God in heaven, who is infinite and eternal," who "created man, male and female, after his own image" (v. 18) and "gave unto them commandments" (v. 19). However, by departing from his ways, humankind "became fallen" (v. 20). "Wherefore, the Almighty God gave his Only Begotten Son" (v. 21) so that through belief in the Savior's divine sacrifice and through the covenant of baptism mankind "should be saved" (v. 25). Those that "worship the Father in his name, and endure in faith on his name to the end" (v. 29) will receive both "justification" (v. 30) and "sanctification through the grace of our Lord and Savior Jesus Christ" (v. 31). Such truths are at the heart of what has been taught, is taught, and will yet be taught in all dispensations. Such plan-of-salvation truths are what Elder Boyd K. Packer referred to when he said there are "doctrines" that "will remain fixed, eternal."[17]

As emphasized in Doctrine and Covenants 20, the apex of these timeless, eternal, and unchanging doctrines is what is sometimes referred to as *the doctrine of Christ*—that Jesus is the Savior of the world and salvation is found through his name alone (see Mosiah 3:17). The Lord said, "This is my doctrine, . . . that the Father commandeth all men, everywhere, to repent and believe in me. And whoso believeth in me, and is baptized, the same shall be saved; and they are they who shall inherit the kingdom of God. And whoso believeth not in me, and is not baptized, shall be damned. Verily, verily, I say unto you, *that this is my doctrine*" (3 Nephi 11:32–35; emphasis added; see also 2 Nephi 31:21; 3 Nephi 27:13–21; D&C 33:11–12). The doctrine of Christ and the centrality of his redeeming Atonement will never change, being a fixed and permanent focal point to the plan of God.

Although eternal truths do not vary, what is understood and officially taught can vary as prophets come to comprehend core doctrines more clearly (2 Nephi 28:30).[18] Many modern Latter-day Saints assume that because the gospel of Christ is eternal that God's prophets have all known the end from the beginning and understand all truths not only that have been revealed but those that will yet be revealed. But Brigham Young taught that Joseph Smith did not know everything about the plan of salvation, or his role in the Restoration as he walked out of the Sacred Grove following his experience with God and Jesus. Instead, truths were revealed to him point by point as he learned over many years. Brigham Young explained:

> The Lord can't reveal to you and I that we can't understand; . . . for instance when Joseph first received revelation the Lord could not tell him what he was going to do. He didn't tell him he was going to call him to be a prophet, seer, revelator, high priest, and founder of [the] kingdom of God on earth. Joseph would have said . . . "just what does that mean? You are talking that I can't understand." He could merely reveal to him that the Lord was pleased to bless him and forgive his sins and there was a work for him to perform on the earth and that was about all he could reveal. The first time he sent [an] angel to visit him he could then lead his mind a little further. He could reveal to him there was certain records deposited in the earth to be brought forth for the benefit of [the] inhabitants of the earth. He could reveal after this that Joseph could get them; then he could reveal he should have power to translate the records from the language and characters in which it was written and give it to the people in the English language, but this was not taught him first. . . . He could then tell him he was to be called a prophet. He could then reveal to Joseph that he might take Oliver Cowdery into water and baptize him and ordain him to [the] priesthood.

After this he could tell him he could receive the high priesthood to organize the church and so on. . . . This is the way the Lord has to instruct all people upon the earth. I make mention of this to show you that . . . the Lord can't teach all things to people at once. He gives a little here [a] little there, revelation upon revelation, on revelation after revelation, a precept today, tomorrow another, next day another. If the people make good use of it and improve upon what the Lord gives them, then he is ready to bestow more.[19]

"New" eternal truths revealed to Joseph Smith, such as the universal resurrection and salvation of the human family in degrees of heavenly glory (D&C 76), have always existed, even prior to "The Vision" in February of 1832. As scholar Robert J. Matthews pointed out, "Through the experience of translating the Bible, Joseph Smith was to come into possession of knowledge he did not previously have."[20] As the Apostle Paul taught, the Lord's prophets "know in part, and we prophesy in part" because, although they are seers, they do not see all; "for now we see through a glass, darkly" (1 Corinthians 13:9, 12). As seers continue to see, and new eternal truths are revealed more fully, former perceptions distorted by the lenses of mortality will be clarified, expanded, adapted, and changed as they come to learn and teach "that which is perfect" and then "that which is in part shall be done away" (1 Corinthians 13:10).

Supporting Doctrine

Many doctrines strengthen our belief in and elaborate on the core doctrines. Some are timely answers, and others are authoritative interpretations by prophets. For example, if a core doctrine is that God exists, understanding his corporality will help us better comprehend his nature, and in turn, deepen our faith in him. Additionally, since we were created in God's bodily image, knowing how God obtained his form and image can expand our understanding and faith even further. Christ's Atonement is core and essential, but teachings that discuss how he suffered and what he suffered serve to expand upon the core concept of Atonement and redemption. Supporting doctrines can be eternal truths, but knowledge of them, unlike core doctrines, are not necessarily essential for salvation. In other words, supporting doctrines help us understand and elaborate on the eternal doctrines of salvation. They expand upon our understanding of core doctrines, often providing explanation of "how" such teachings function.

An example of an eternal doctrine is that Jesus Christ will return to earth and reign as its rightful king and lawgiver. It has been further revealed as a supporting doctrine that a righteous city of New Jerusalem will be built and Christ's people gathered to prepare for his return. Other supporting doctrines related to the Second Coming are that there will be a great gathering in Adam-ondi-Ahman to prepare for Christ's millennial rule, that when Jesus returns to the earth the Mount of Olives will split, that the Jewish people will recognize the Lord as the Messiah (see D&C 45:51–53), that Satan will be bound, and that there will be a thousand-year period of peace. These teachings may not be essential for salvation, but they elaborate upon, expand our understanding about, increase our faith in, and provide potential "hows" to the core doctrine of Christ's return to earth. This supporting ring of doctrine has the potential to include many doctrines of the Church. Although knowledge of supporting doctrines may not be essential for salvation, the truths in them have an eternal element that make them distinct from doctrines that may be termed as policy or procedure.

Policy Doctrine

Church policy is always authoritative, but it inevitably changes as the Church forms new policies that adjust, expand, and react to the situations of the membership. Policy doctrines are formed as the Church addresses issues in each generation to help bring to pass the eternal life of mankind. These are "the organization, programs, and procedures [that] will be altered as directed by Him whose church this is."[21] Or as President Dieter F. Uchtdorf taught, "Procedures, programs, policies, and patterns of organization are helpful for our spiritual progress here on earth, but let's not forget that they are subject to change. In contrast, the core of the gospel—the doctrine and the principles—will never change."[22]

Policy doctrines are based on eternal, essential truths and supporting doctrines. They can include such teachings as ordaining worthy young men to the priesthood at age twelve, standards for dress and grooming, placing baptismal fonts under the ground, not drinking wine, and changes in Church structure, such as the role of the Seventies or who attends Church council meetings. Surely such teachings as these have not existed in all dispensations and are therefore subject to change based on inspiration and revelation by those who hold the keys to establish laws for the Church. Joseph Smith wrote, "Whatsoever those men [priesthood leaders] did in authority, in the name of the Lord, and did it truly and faithfully, and kept a proper and faithful record of the same, it became a law on earth in heaven" (D&C 128:9).

Policy doctrine exists because God reveals different behavioral applications and policies to his children based on their temporal circumstances. The Word of Wisdom is a modern example of policy doctrine. Restrictions on tea, coffee, and wine have not been in effect in all dispensations, yet because the Lord foresaw "evils and designs which do and will exist in the hearts of conspiring men in the last days" (D&C 89:4), he provided a new doctrine for the "benefit" (D&C 89:1) of the Saints. This doctrine, in particular, has taken many shifts in policy, and eventually by 1933 the Church handbook of instruction required members to strictly follow the Word of Wisdom to be able to enter into the temple. Similarly, the doctrinal teachings restricting multiple piercings were not authoritatively taught prior to President Gordon B. Hinckley's prophetic counsel for women to have only one pair of earrings.

Policy doctrines are likely to change and be given different emphasis depending upon the needs and direction of Church leadership during the time—with each era being commanded and inspired in order to guide the Church to accomplish its mission in varied circumstances over time.

Esoteric Doctrine

The word *esoteric* implies teachings that are only understood by a small group of people. Its synonyms are words such as *obscure* and *ambiguous*. Not all doctrines have been revealed, and there are also doctrines no longer taught that may be true, but not necessary for our understanding now. The Prophet Joseph Smith explained that "it is not always wise to relate all the truth. Even Jesus, the Son of God, had to refrain from doing so, and had to restrain

His feelings many times for the safety of Himself and His followers, and had to conceal the righteous purposes of His heart in relation to many things pertaining to His Father's kingdom."[23] M. Gerald Bradford and Larry E. Dahl succinctly stated about "doctrine" in the *Encyclopedia of Mormonism*:

> Many individuals write or preach their views. Some, by study and obedience, may learn truths that go beyond the stated position of the Church, but this does not authorize them to speak officially for the Church or to present their views as binding on the Church. There are many subjects about which the scriptures are not clear and about which the Church has made no official pronouncements. In such matters, one can find differences of opinion among Church members and leaders. Until the truth of these matters is made known by revelation, there is room for different levels of understanding and interpretation of unsettled issues.[24]

The Prophet Joseph lamented, "I could explain a hundred fold more than I ever have, of the glories of the Kingdoms manifested to me in the vision, were I permitted, and were the people prepared to receive it."[25]

Joseph Smith revealed in April 1829 to Oliver Cowdery that "other records have I, that I will give unto you power that you may assist to translate" (D&C 9:2). During that same period, Joseph protected the gold plates, which included a large sealed portion, translated by Moroni, that God would reveal to them later. The book of Ether declared, "Touch them not in order that ye may translate; for that thing is forbidden you, except by and by it shall be wisdom in God" (Ether 5:1). Moroni testified after he had translated the brother of Jared's vision as the sealed portion of the gold plates that "never were greater things made manifest than those which were made manifest to the brother of Jared" (Ether 4:4). Moroni and the brother of Jared were not the only people who were privileged enough to know the things that were sealed in the gold plates. In fact, Moroni explained that "after Christ truly had showed himself unto his people [3 Nephi 11; 24; 26] he commanded that [the things the brother of Jared saw] should be made manifest" to them (Ether 4:2). Therefore, there are greater doctrines that were known to them that are not known to us. These esoteric doctrines are true but are not declared openly. These examples demonstrate that there are doctrines that are not currently taught, but that are valid. This opens an avenue for us to evaluate doctrines that are no longer taught but were at some time taught authoritatively. This does not mean that all things taught in the past will eventually be revealed as core, eternal truth, but it does suggest that we should evaluate authoritative statements of the past with vigor and hope for more doctrines in the future.

In some cases, esoteric doctrines are referred to as "deep doctrines" in a somewhat negative tone. Yet, we are told that one day we will read the sealed portion of the gold plates in hopes that it will bring us closer to Christ (see Ether 4; 5). The Lord promises that to the obedient he will "give the mysteries of my kingdom" (D&C 63:23), even to the point of giving "things which have never been revealed" (Alma 26:22). Generally, we discuss and search for esoteric doctrines in private rather than in public. These teachings are esoteric because we do not proclaim them publically nor officially, although they may be true and have been taught or known in the past or will yet be given in the future.

Baptism: An Example of Types of Doctrine

As a potential example of the four types of doctrine in our model, we will analyze the doctrines of baptism. As an example of "core" doctrine, Doctrine and Covenants 20 indicates the essential nature of baptism for the salvation of all humankind. However, how everyone was to have access to the ordinance of baptism was not always understood at the inception of this dispensation. In 1836, Joseph received a vision of the celestial kingdom in the Kirtland temple that showed him his beloved brother Alvin residing there, and Joseph "marveled how it was that he had obtained an inheritance in that kingdom, seeing that he had departed this life before the Lord had set his hand to gather Israel the second time, and had not been baptized for the remission of sins" (D&C 137:6). Joseph himself seemed surprised, given the strictness of the teaching that baptism was essential for salvation in the celestial kingdom. The voice of the Lord further instructed him, "All who have died without a knowledge of this gospel, who would have received it if they had been permitted to tarry, shall be heirs of the celestial kingdom of

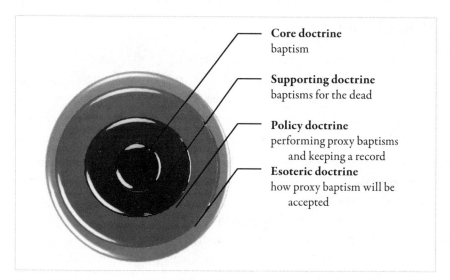

Core doctrine
baptism

Supporting doctrine
baptisms for the dead

Policy doctrine
performing proxy baptisms
and keeping a record

Esoteric doctrine
how proxy baptism will be
accepted

Figure 2. Baptism as an example of types of doctrine.

God; also all that shall die henceforth without a knowledge of it, who would have received it with all their hearts, shall be heirs of that kingdom" (D&C 137:7–8). Still, the apparent contradiction stood without explanation until Joseph Smith revealed, in the funeral sermon of Seymour Brunson in August 1840, that members could perform proxy baptisms for their deceased relatives, a doctrine on which he further elaborated over successive years.[26] Initially, baptisms for the dead were performed in rivers without proper record keeping, with very little instruction about proper procedures. Joseph Smith later revealed a policy that there would come a time when baptisms for the dead would have to be performed in sacred temples where witnesses and recorders were present (D&C 124; 127).

Baptism is a core doctrine of salvation.

Baptism for the dead is a supportive, essential doctrine revealed to explain the process by which every soul will have the opportunity to be baptized.

How and where proxy baptisms can legitimately be performed has been established by the policy of the Church.

Precisely how these proxy baptisms will be accepted by the deceased in the spirit world has not been fully revealed and may be considered an esoteric doctrine.

Helpful Tools to Evaluate Doctrine

Because we have a lay membership that is required to teach each other the doctrines of the kingdom (D&C 88:77), members will, inevitably, need to evaluate the Church's authorized teachings. How can we know if the Church stands behind a particular teaching as one of its authorized doctrines? Although a variety of things are taught in the Church (and thus may be considered part of Latter-day Saint doctrine), the following four[27] questions are designed to help point us in the right direction when we are looking for official teachings.

1. Is it repeatedly found in the scriptures?

2. Is it proclaimed by the united voice of the current Brethren?

3. Is it consistently taught by current General Authorities and general officers acting in their official capacity?

4. Is it found in recent Church publications or statements?

Let's briefly analyze each of these four potential sources of official Latter-day Saint Church doctrine.

The harmonized scriptures. The officially accepted Latter-day Saint scriptures (the Bible, the Book of Mormon, the Doctrine and Covenants, and the Pearl of Great Price) are primary sources that members should address when identifying doctrine. Indeed, these books are often colloquially called the "standard" works, implying "accepted," or a benchmark criterion for doctrine. Elder B. H. Roberts of the Seventy taught, "The Church has confined the sources of doctrine by which it is willing to be bound before the world to the things that God has revealed, and which the Church has officially accepted, and those alone. . . . These have been repeatedly accepted and endorsed by the Church in general conference assembled, and are the only sources of absolute appeal for our doctrine."[28] Professor Robert L. Millet wrote, "In determining whether something is a part of the doctrine of the Church, we might ask, 'Is it found within the four standard works?'"[29] Elder D. Todd Christofferson said, "The scriptures are the touchstone for measuring correctness and truth."[30]

It should be noted, however, that simply because something is found within the pages of canonized scripture does not mean that it represents the Church's official doctrine (see Articles of Faith 1:8). When using scripture to define official doctrines we are also to seek truths that are often repeated and internally self-consistent. Although it is found in the New Testament, for example, we would not proclaim as our doctrine that "no man hath seen God at any time" (1 John 4:12), because this singular verse sits outside many other harmonized examples of those who have seen God face-to-face (see Exodus 24:9–10, 33:11; Genesis 32:30; Acts 7:55–56, Joseph Smith—History 1:16–17). Elder Russell M. Nelson taught, "In the Bible we read this important declaration: 'In the mouth of two or three witnesses shall every word be established' (2 Corinthians 13:1). This assures God's children that divine doctrines are confirmed by more than one scriptural witness. . . . Scriptural witnesses authenticate each other."[31] Similarly, Elder Boyd K. Packer taught that "essential truths are repeated over and over again [in the scriptures]. . . . Every verse, whether oft-quoted or obscure, must be measured against other verses. There are complementary and tempering teachings in the scriptures which bring a balanced knowledge of truth."[32]

Additionally, some doctrines in scripture, like the required ordinance of circumcision for males or the performances of the law of Moses, or policy doctrines such as requiring missionaries to leave without purse (money) or scrip (food) (see Matthew 10:9–10; D&C 24:18), have been superseded by later revelation or prophetic direction (see Galatians 6:15; 3 Nephi 9:17; 3 Nephi 15:8). Thus we should look to see if a scriptural teaching is confirmed by modern revelation or supplanted by it.

The united voice of the current Brethren. Because the words of the Lord never cease, we look to the Brethren to declare his current voice and will to his Church and people. We do not believe in *sola scriptura* (by scripture alone), but in *sola prophēta* (by prophet alone).[33] One of the roles of the prophet, as President Gordon B. Hinckley said when he was President of the Church, is to "declare doctrine."[34] Those who also hold all the keys of the kingdom, namely the First Presidency (D&C 81:2), "receive the oracles for the whole church" (D&C 124:126). Sustained by the key-holding Quorum of the Twelve Apostles (D&C 112:30), "with divine inspiration" these two highest governing bodies of the Church "counsel together to establish doctrine."[35]

In a recent *Ensign* article titled "How Is Doctrine Established?," LaRene Porter Gaunt of Church magazines wrote, "When revelation is doctrine for the whole Church, it comes to only the First Presidency and Quorum of the Twelve Apostles. . . . The prophet and President of the Church can receive revelation individually that becomes doctrine when it is sustained by the united voice of the First Presidency and Quorum of the Twelve Apostles."[36] This is consistent with the scriptural injunction to the Quorum of the Twelve Apostles and the Seventy in Doctrine and Covenants 107:27 that "every decision made by either of these quorums must be by the unanimous voice of the same; that is, every member in each quorum must be agreed to its decisions, in order to make their decisions of the same power or validity one with the other" (D&C 107:27).

President Hinckley expounded on the point of prophetic unanimity, relating that "any major questions of policy, procedures, programs, or doctrine are considered deliberately and prayerfully by the First Presidency and the Twelve together. . . . No decision emanates from the deliberations of the First Presidency and the Twelve without total unanimity among all concerned."[37] Recently, Elder M. Russell Ballard taught, "When the First Presidency and the Quorum of the Twelve speak with a united voice, it is the voice of the Lord for that time."[38] Although "the objective is not simply consensus among council members but revelation from God,"[39] as Elder Christofferson reminded, prophetic unanimity cannot be lightly overlooked, as without it there is not the "same power or validity" (D&C 107:27) in united doctrinal pronouncements.

Examples of doctrine proclaimed by the united voice of the current First Presidency and Twelve Apostles can include statements such as letters from the First Presidency, official declarations and proclamations, and official handbooks of instruction. There are other books, manuals, publications, or documents released under the approval or sanction of the united voice of the current prophets, such as *Preach My Gospel*.[40] Additionally, there are official announcements made or released under the united voice of the prophets. For example, in the press conference after announcing the change of the mission ages for males and females in October 2012, Elder Nelson said of the age change, "This has been the subject of much study and prayer. We as a First Presidency and Quorum of the Twelve are united in our decision to make these important adjustments."[41]

Repeated teachings from the current General Authorities and officers. An additional source to evaluate whether something may be considered part of official Latter-day Saint doctrine is if something is being taught collectively by the current general Church authorities and officers acting in their official capacity. For example, currently many in Church leadership are making a pronounced effort to increase devotion to the Sabbath day and meaning to the ordinance of the sacrament, with Church leaders sending training videos and other materials to Church leaders for dissemination in their wards and branches. In another example, a supportive doctrine of Christ's Atonement—his "enabling power" or "strengthening power"—has been oft-repeated in official Church settings by Church officers acting in their capacity.[42] However, the phrase "enabling power" is not found in the standard works, nor is it found in any known official united statement by the First Presidency and Quorum of the Twelve Apostles.[43] Undoubtedly, however, Jesus Christ's enabling power is an official, supportive doctrine of the Church as it is oft-repeated and taught collectively by numerous Church officers acting in their official capacity. Venues of delivering authorized Church doctrine by Church officers include general conference addresses, worldwide leadership trainings and broadcasts, regional conferences, and trainings and seminars for ecclesiastical leaders.

There is safety in the cumulative teachings of general Church officers. Though many doctrines are emphasized, those that have staying power and find their way into the talks and statements delivered to the membership of the Church by numerous authorities can be trusted more than individual statements. As the LDS Newsroom article "Approaching Mormon Doctrine" reminds, "A single statement made by a single leader on a single occasion often represents a personal, though well-considered, opinion, but is not meant to be officially binding [doctrine] for the whole Church."[44] As Elder Neil L. Andersen said, "The doctrine of the Church . . . is not hidden in an obscure paragraph of one talk. True principles are taught frequently and by many. Our doctrine is not difficult to find."[45]

Current/recent publications of the Church. While not carrying the weight of harmonized scripture or the united voice of the Brethren, official doctrine for the Church is also taught via the Church's authorized publications. The LDS Newsroom statement reminds us that "[Church doctrine] is consistently proclaimed in official Church publications." While much of the content contained within official Church publications is written by curriculum personnel, scholars, and lay members alike, "All of the [Church publications] . . . are reviewed and cleared . . . before they are published and issued to the Church," said Elder Dean L. Larsen of the First Quorum of

Seventy while acting as the managing director of Curriculum Resources. He also stated, "Official publications of the Church carry messages that are sound in doctrine and fully in harmony with currently approved policies and procedures."[46]

Examples of authorized doctrine coming from official Church publications include current Church magazines such as the *Ensign* or *New Era*, seminary/institute manuals, priesthood/relief society manuals, items published by © Intellectual Reserve/Corporation of the President of The Church of Jesus Christ of Latter-day Saints such as the *Addiction Recovery Program*, scholarly publications such as *The Joseph Smith Papers* from the Church Historian's Press, and web content on official Church spaces such as mormon.org, lds.org, and the LDS Newsroom. While these publications are not the ultimate source for appeal of eternal, supportive, policy, or esoteric doctrine, they can be considered trustworthy sources that represent teachings of authorized Church doctrine.

Conclusion: Expanding Doctrine

In Mormonism, the current prophets identify the authentic and authoritative doctrines of The Church of Jesus Christ of Latter-day Saints. Though scripture, personal experience, tradition, and our own reason are constantly part of our evaluation of doctrine, prophetic declaration reigns supreme. The concept of continuing revelation, expressed in the ninth article of faith, has allowed for prophets to address each generation and the Church to build "line upon line, precept upon precept" with a certain kind of flexibility that is limited when doctrine can only be found within the pages of the Bible, or to being only that which is eternal and unchanging. All of this implies that new ideas, altered concepts, expanded teachings, and additional knowledge will be given, thus requiring what we teach—our doctrine—to also be expandable. The very notions of a living Church and continuing revelation suggest that any statement on doctrine is not a declaration of eternal finality, but temporary understanding or expediency.

When doctrine becomes too fixed, it loses its inert potential for revelation. The Prophet Joseph Smith opposed the idea of too strict a definition of the tenants of the Latter-day Saint faith, even after he published his own "Articles of Faith" in a letter to John Wentworth in March of 1842. As Joseph told a Mr. Butterfield who interviewed him in 1843, "The most prominent point of difference in sentiment between the Latter Day Saints [*sic*] and Sectarians was, that the latter were all circumscribed by some peculiar creed, which deprived its members the privilege of believing any thing not contained therein: Whereas the Latter Day Saints have no creed, but are ready to believe all true principles that exist, as they are made manifest from time to time."[47]

We are not ignorant to the contradictions of our own positions within this paper—that we are encouraging a more flexible and expansive understanding of Latter-day Saint doctrine, all the while drawing circles and lines to confine it. Defining Church doctrine is much like trying to identify humility: the moment you proclaim it, you have lost its very essence. Thus, although we have proposed delineations of Latter-day Saint doctrine, our model proposed herein—like the nature of doctrine itself—is meant to be flexible and aid in coming to a clearer understanding of truth. To do anything contrary is opposed to the very concept of revelation and living oracles. We anticipate that readers of this article may question whether something is an eternal doctrine or a supportive doctrine, or whether something is considered policy or esoteric doctrine. We expect that persons will come to differing conclusions not only about which category of doctrine a certain teaching may be placed but that they may even disagree with the categorical definitions and delineations we have proposed in this paper. We hope this is the case and that this model will act as a springboard for not only helping to answer questions or concerns related to Latter-day Saint doctrine but also further discussing and debating about how doctrine is explained.

Although understanding Latter-day Saint doctrine requires believers to turn to the prophets, it also requires personal evaluation and rigorous study. The declarative nature of doctrine may seem rigid, but its flexibility is also paramount. To be too rigid in defining doctrine goes against the very concept Joseph Smith articulated about creeds: it closes us to new and expansive ways of seeing, understanding, believing, and teaching. Latter-day Saint doctrine is that which we teach—eternal, supportive, policy, esoteric, among others—guided and revealed and officially proclaimed by authorized, key-holding prophets, seers, and revelators. That which tries to confine the Lord and his servants from receiving and teaching anything that is not eternally expansive in nature simply is not Latter-day Saint doctrine.

Notes

1. John Sims Carter, Journal, 10 March and 5 April 1833, Church History Library, Salt Lake City.

2. Gerrit J. Dirkmaat, Brent M. Rogers, Grant Underwood, Robert J. Woodford, and William G. Hartley, eds. *Documents, Volume 3: February 1833–March 1834*, vol. 3 of the Documents series of *The Joseph Smith Papers*, ed. Ronald K. Esplin and Matthew J. Grow (Salt Lake City: Church Historian's Press, 2014), 59–61.

3. The current Seminaries and Institutes of Religion's *Gospel Teaching and Learning* manual uses the following definition of doctrine: "A doctrine is a fundamental, unchanging truth of the gospel of Jesus Christ." Church Educational System, *Gospel Teaching and Learning: A Handbook for Teachers and Leaders in Seminaries and Institutes of Religion* (Salt Lake City: The Church of Jesus Christ of Latter-day Saints, 2012), 26.

4. Dictionary.com, s.v. "doctrine."

5. *Merriam-Webster's Collegiate Dictionary*, 11th ed., s.v. "doctrine."

6. *Strong's Concordance* G1321 rendering "doctrine" as *didachē*, meaning "1. Teaching" and "2. The act of teaching."

7. Doctrine and Covenants, 1835 ed., http://josephsmithpapers.org/paperSummary /doctrine-and-covenants-1835#!/paperSummary/doctrine-and-covenants-1835&p=13.

8. Preface, Doctrine and Covenants, 1835 ed.

9. The authoritative power of these lectures goes from one prophet simply teaching something to a declaration voted upon by the Church and published as scripture. These profound lectures on "doctrine" cover a vast array of topics, from eternal truths such as the creation of the world and the Fall of man in Lecture First; to historical dates, ages, and lists of righteous men in Lecture Second to elaborative and supportive theology such as the three necessary components to have true faith in God in Lecture Third; to esoteric and arcane concepts in Lecture Fifth such as "there are two personages" that make up the Godhead: "The Father being a personage of spirit . . . the Son, who was in the bosom of the Father, a personage of tabernacle." *Lectures on Faith* (Salt Lake City: Deseret Book, 1985), 5:2. All of these ideas, some of which may not be eternal and unchanging, were part of "something that is taught" or "teaching, instruction" and thus represented part of the doctrine of the Latter-day Saints at that time.

10. *Handbook 2: Administering in the Church* (Salt Lake City: The Church of Jesus Christ of Latter-day Saints, 2010), 3.

11. "Dress and Appearance," in *For the Strength of Youth* (Salt Lake City: The Church of Jesus Christ of Latter-day Saints, 2010), 7.

12. Thomas S. Monson, "Welcome to Conference," *Ensign*, November 2012, 5.

13. "Zion," in *True to the Faith* (Salt Lake City: The Church of Jesus Christ of Latter-day Saints, 2004), 189.

14. LDS Newsroom, "Approaching Mormon Doctrine," 4 May 2007.

15. David A. Bednar, *Increase in Learning* (Salt Lake City: Deseret Book, 2011), 151. On another occasion, before he was a member of the Quorum of the Twelve Apostles, then BYU–Idaho president David A. Bednar taught, "Doctrine refers to the eternal, unchanging, and simple truths of the gospel of Jesus Christ." "Teach Them to Understand," Ricks College Campus Education Week devotional, 4 June 1998, 4.

16. *Improvement Era*, May 1900, 576–77.

17. Boyd K. Packer, in Conference Report, October 1989, 18–19.

18. The prophet Mormon provides an interesting example of how new and additional doctrinal understanding comes to the Lord's prophets. As Mormon edited 3 Nephi 28, he discussed the three Nephite disciples who were translated. Mormon mentioned that he did not know if the three Nephites "were mortal or immortal" (3 Nephi 28:17) after they were translated. Later, in the same chapter, Mormon says in verse 37 that after he had recorded his uncertainty of the three Nephites's mortality or immortality, Mormon had asked God about it and the Lord "made it manifest unto me that there must needs be a change wrought upon their bodies" (v. 37), but that the change "was not equal to that which shall take place at the last day" as immortal beings in the resurrection (v. 39). Mormon's knowledge on the doctrinal matter of translated and resurrected beings was expanded and improved upon in front of the reader's very eyes within a single chapter of scripture.

19. Brigham Young, Discourse, 25 March 1855, Papers of George D. Watt, MS 4534, box 3, disk 1, images 142–53, transcribed by LaJean Purcell Carruth, punctuation and capitalization added.

20. Robert J. Matthews, *"A Plainer Translation": Joseph Smith's Translation of the Bible—A History and Commentary* (Provo, UT: Brigham Young University Press, 1975), 53.

21. Boyd K. Packer, "Revelation in a Changing World," *Ensign*, November 1989, 19.

22. Dieter F. Uchtdorf, "Christlike Attributes—the Wind Beneath Our Wings," *Ensign*, November 2005; emphasis added.

23. As cited in Robert L. Millet, "What Is Our Doctrine?," *Religious Educator* 4, no. 3 (2003): 17.

24. M. Gerald Bradford and Larry E. Dahl, "Doctrine: Meaning, Source, and History of Doctrine," in *Encyclopedia of Mormonism*, ed. Daniel H. Ludlow (Macmillan: New York, 1992), 1:395.

25. History, 1838–1856, volume D-1 [1 August 1842–1 July 1843], Joseph Smith Papers.

26. Joseph Smith to the Council of the Twelve, 15 December 1840, Letterbook 2, Church History Library. See D&C 124, 127, and 128 for further elaborations of this doctrine.

27. These four categories are similar to those that Robert L. Millet identified: "In determining whether something is a part of the doctrine of the Church, we might ask, Is it found within the four standard works? Within official declarations

or proclamations? Is it discussed in general conference or other official gatherings by general Church leaders today? Is it found in the general handbooks or approved curriculum of the Church today? If it meets at least one of these criteria, we can feel secure and appropriate about teaching it." Millet, "What Is Our Doctrine?," 19.

28.   B. H. Roberts, sermon of 10 July 1921, delivered in Salt Lake Tabernacle, printed in *Deseret News*, 23 July 1921, 7, as cited in Stephen E. Robinson, *Are Mormons Christians?* (Salt Lake City: Deseret Book, 1991), 15.

29.   Millet, "What Is Our Doctrine?," 16, 19.

30.   D. Todd Christofferson, "The Blessings of Scripture," *Ensign*, May 2010, 34.

31.   Russell M. Nelson, "Scriptural Witnesses," *Ensign*, November 2007.

32.   Boyd K. Packer, "The Pattern of Our Parentage," *Ensign*, November 1984, 66.

33.   See the forthcoming work of Michael Hubbard MacKay, *Sola Prophēta: The Radical Origins of Mormon Priesthood in the Burned-Over District*.

34.   Gordon B. Hinckley, "What Are People Asking about Us?," *Ensign*, November 1998, 70.

35.   LDS Newsroom, "Approaching Mormon Doctrine."

36.   LaRene Porter Gaunt, "How Is Doctrine Established?," *Ensign*, September 2013, 39.

37.   Gordon B. Hinckley, "God Is at the Helm," *Ensign*, May 1994, 53.

38.   M. Russell Ballard, "Stay in the Boat and Hold On!," *Ensign*, November 2014, 90.

39.   D. Todd Christofferson, "The Doctrine of Christ," *Ensign*, April 2012, 88.

40.   Elder M. Russell Ballard said of *Preach My Gospel*, "Under the direction of the First Presidency and the Quorum of the Twelve Apostles, *Preach My Gospel* has been produced. . . . Every word has been studied by the full First Presidency and the Quorum of the Twelve; this has their complete and total blessing and endorsement." In "Preach My Gospel: Introduction for Leaders," Missionary Training Satellite Broadcast, 15 October 2004, DVD. See also Benjamin White, "The History of *Preach My Gospel*," *Religious Educator* 14, no. 1 (2013): 129–58.

41.   Transcribed from Mormon Newsroom video of press conference for new missionary age service requirements, 7 October 2012, https://www.youtube.com/watch?v=3Uwe9nz2w8k.

42.   See examples in recent general conference addresses of the phrase "enabling power," used in Linda K. Burton, "We'll Ascend Together," April 2015; Kevin W. Pearson, "Stay by the Tree," April 2015; Cheryl A. Esplin, "The Sacrament—a Renewal for the Soul," October 2014; David A. Bednar, "Bear Up Their Burdens with Ease," April 2014; Rosemary Wixom, "Keeping Covenants Protects Us, Prepares Us, and Empowers Us," April 2014.

43.   Perhaps the nearest approximation to this is in *True to the Faith*, which has the First Presidency's endorsement (see "Grace").

44.   LDS Newsroom, "Approaching Mormon Doctrine"; see this exact statement repeated in Elder D. Todd Christofferson, "The Doctrine of Christ," *Ensign*, April 2012, 88.

45.   Neil L. Andersen, "Trial of Your Faith," *Ensign*, November 2012, 41.

46.   Dean L. Larsen, "I Have a Question," *Ensign*, August 1977, 38.

47.   History, 1838–1856, volume D-1 [1 August 1842–1 July 1843], 1433.

3

"Here Is Wisdom; Yea, to Be a Seer, a Revelator, . . . and a Prophet"

Craig James Ostler and Lloyd D. Newell

Craig James Ostler and Lloyd D. Newell are professors of Church history and doctrine at Brigham Young University.

One of the most distinctive tenets of The Church of Jesus Christ of Latter-day Saints is the belief that living prophets, seers, and revelators continue to make known the mind and will of God in our day. Today there are renewed attacks on and questions regarding the place of ecclesiastical leaders being sustained as prophets, seers, and revelators. Modern cultural changes, such as those regarding same-sex marriage and challenges to Church practice regarding women and priesthood, as well as historical items concerning plural marriage and priesthood restrictions on black members, have brought to the forefront the need to clarify and understand the historical development and doctrinal implications of sustaining members of the First Presidency and Quorum of the Twelve Apostles as prophets, seers, and revelators.

This chapter provides historical overview, discussion, and references with regard to understanding and answering questions regarding this unique aspect of The Church of Jesus Christ of Latter-day Saints. We define the calling of prophets, seers, and revelators and identify their biblical precedence.

45

In addition, we review the historical development of the Lord designating the President of the Church, his counselors, members of the Quorum of the Twelve Apostles, and others as prophets, seers, and revelators. Further, we discuss the necessary counseling, collaboration, and harmony among these individuals as they seek the mind and will of the Lord in making administrative decisions and declaring doctrine. Lastly, we consider the implications of imperfections in those that make administrative and revelatory decisions as prophets, seers, and revelators.

The Roles of Prophets, Seers, and Revelators

Prophets are God's mouthpiece to his people. That is, they speak in behalf of the Lord and are called upon to keep sacred records of the revelations from God as well as an account of the people's history in choosing to hearken to or reject the words of God as given them by his prophets.[1] In the Bible, the word *prophet* comes from the Hebrew word *nabi*, meaning spokesperson. Another Hebrew word, *ro'eh*, literally means one who sees—a seer. In Greek, the word is *prophētēs*, meaning "one who *speaks forth* by the inspiration of God."[2]

It naturally follows that a prophet has the spirit of prophecy. "The institution of prophecy is founded on the basic premise that God makes his will known to chosen individuals in successive generations. A prophet is a[n] . . . individual endowed with the divine gift of both receiving and imparting the message of revelation."[3] The prophets or patriarchs from Adam to Enoch "were preachers of righteousness, and spake and prophesied, and called upon all men everywhere, to repent" (Moses 6:23).

Much of our understanding of the role of prophets in the Restoration is founded upon knowledge of biblical prophets. "The Hebrew word [nabi] for 'prophet' is a common noun appearing more than three hundred times in the O[ld] T[estament]."[4] Moses is the great prototype for prophets, and all succeeding prophets have been expected to follow the pattern that the Lord set with his calling of Moses.[5] First, prophets will intimately know the Lord, and second, prophets will receive and declare the word of the Lord to the people.[6] The Lord likened Old Testament prophets to watchmen on mounts, walls, and towers who warned the people of the approaching enemy and declared repentance to sinners.[7] The New Testament Church continued the use of the term *prophet* in that day to refer to those called of God to teach his message or to those that had the spirit of prophecy.[8] However, it is not clear from the Bible if prophets are the administrative leaders of the Church of Christ or if prophets fulfill a role of advising the Church. For example, Luke recorded that "in these days came prophets from Jerusalem unto Antioch. And there stood up one of them named Agabus, and signified by the Spirit that there should be a great dearth throughout all the world" (Acts 11:27–28). In addition, in the Old Testament, the high priest, as well as priests and Levites, are most often completely separate from those recognized as prophets.

Similar to our understanding of a prophet, our understanding of the term *seer* hearkens to Old Testament times. While not as common in use as the term *prophet*, the term *seer*, from the Hebrew *ro'eh* and *chozeh*, referring to one who sees a vision, occurs in the Old Testament at least twenty times.[9] The term is closely associated with that of *prophet*.[10] For example, we read that "beforetime in Israel when a man went to inquire of God, thus he spake, Come, and let us go to the *Seer*: for he that is now called a *Prophet* was beforetime called a *Seer*" (1 Samuel 9:9; emphasis added). A further biblical example is in the time of King David: "The word of the LORD came unto the *prophet* Gad, David's *seer*" (2 Samuel 24:11; emphasis added). In addition, Isaiah placed the terms in parallel poetic verse:

> The LORD has poured out upon you
> a spirit of deep sleep,
> and has closed your eyes, the *prophets*,
> and covered your heads, the *seers*.
> (Isaiah 29:10; emphasis added)

At the dawn of the Restoration the term *seer* was also closely associated with seer stones. It appears that reference to the Prophet Joseph Smith as a seer most likely also referred to his use of seer stones in translating the Book of Mormon and receiving revelation. Referring to the stones deposited with the Book of Mormon plates, Joseph explained that "the possession and use of these stones were what constituted 'seers' in ancient or former times" (Joseph Smith—History 1:35; see also Mosiah 28:13–16).[11]

We are indebted to the Book of Mormon for further understanding of a seer. In the record of King Limhi and Ammon's discussion, Limhi declared,

"A seer is greater than a prophet. And Ammon said that *a seer is a revelator and a prophet also*; and a gift which is greater no man can have. . . . But a seer can know of things which are past, and also of things which are to come, and by them shall all things be revealed" (Mosiah 8:15–17; emphasis added). They conclude, "Thus God has provided a means that man, through faith, might work mighty miracles; therefore he becometh a great benefit to his fellow beings" (Mosiah 8:18).

The third term, *revelator*, continues the linking of prophets and seers. As noted in the passage above from the Book of Mormon, a seer is a revelator. However, unlike the terms *prophet* and *seer,* an ancient equivalent word for *revelator* is not found in the Bible. On the other hand, the concept of a revelator is present in the understanding of the callings of prophets and seers. Elder John A. Widtsoe taught, "In the sense that a prophet is a man who receives revelations from the Lord, the titles 'seer and revelator' merely amplify the larger and inclusive meaning of the title 'prophet.' . . . A revelator makes known, with the Lord's help, something before unknown. It may be new or forgotten truth, or a new or forgotten application of known truth to man's need."[12] Although the term *revelator* does not occur in the Bible, the Apostle John is commonly distinguished as the Revelator due to the vision he received and revealed, giving name to the book of Revelation in the New Testament.[13] Thus, the expectation is that revelators will receive revelation from the Lord and then convey it to others.

In summary, President Russell M. Nelson explained, "Prophets see ahead. They see the harrowing dangers the adversary has placed or will yet place in our path. Prophets also foresee the grand possibilities and privileges awaiting those who listen with the intent to obey."[14]

Joseph Smith as the Prophet, Seer, and Revelator of the Church

How did early members of the Church learn of the place of a prophet and seer as well as the meaning of sustaining Church leaders as prophets and seers for the Church? The first reference to members of the restored Church of Christ sustaining a prophet and seer occurred on the day that the Church was organized, 6 April 1830. About fifty individuals had gathered in the Peter and Mary Whitmer home in Fayette, New York, to fulfill the Lord's command that Joseph Smith and Oliver Cowdery be ordained elders in the Church of Christ (after receiving the sanction of those willing to be baptized and confirmed members of the newly organized church). Joseph and Oliver were to "have them decide by vote whether they were willing to accept us as spiritual teachers or not."[15]

The Lord instructed those gathered to call Joseph Smith "a seer, a translator, a prophet, an apostle of Jesus Christ, an elder of the church" (D&C 21:1). These designations were not necessarily new to the little flock gathered to organize Christ's church. Most likely they understood that Apostles were "to take the lead of all meetings" and elders were "to conduct the meetings" (D&C 20:44–45). In addition, prior to that day, Joseph Smith was looked upon as a prophet and translator as he had received several revelations and translated the Book of Mormon. Early followers saw in him the fulfillment of the prophecy of Joseph who was sold into Egypt, that "a seer shall the Lord my God raise up, who shall be a choice seer unto the fruit of my loins. ... And his name shall be called after me; and it shall be after the name of his father" (2 Nephi 3:6, 15). However, the revelation received the day that the Church was organized formalized the practice for Church members to officially sustain Joseph in those roles. The Lord's commandment connected the spiritual callings of a prophet, seer, and translator with that of the administrative office of an elder of the Church as well as to that of an Apostle. That is, the spiritual gifts of prophecy, seeric endowment, and translation were associated with ordained priesthood offices in the Church and the apostleship.[16] The office of an Apostle, even at that early day, may have already carried with it a sense of duality in that it referred to those that governed over both spiritual and administrative matters. Based on the Saints' knowledge of the callings of the New Testament Apostles, it could be understood that Apostles were also prophets and served as both spiritual witnesses of the divinity of Jesus Christ as well as the administrative leaders of the new Christian church.[17]

The Presiding Priesthood Officer to Receive Revelations for the Church

Comprehending the place and appointment of prophets, seers, and revelators in the Restoration incurred some mistakes, correction, and even divine chastening. The meaning and ramifications of sustaining Joseph in these spiritual and administrative positions were not clear in the early days of this dispensation. A few months after the Church was organized, two events helped to further clarify the importance and connection between Joseph's administrative office to serve as the presiding elder of the Church and his calling as the prophet and seer for the Church. Joseph Smith received a letter from Oliver Cowdery, who also was an Apostle and an elder of the Church. Joseph Smith explained:

> He wrote to inform me that he had discovered an error in one of the Commandments, Book of "Doctrine and Covenants" Sect, 2nd Par. 7th [D&C 20:37] "and truly manifest by their works that they have received of the Spirit of Christ unto a remission of their sins."
>
> The above quotation he said was erroneous, and added; "I command you in the name of God to erase those words, that no priestcraft be amongst us."
>
> I immediately wrote to him in reply, in which I asked him, by what authority he took upon him to command me to alter, or erase, to add or diminish to or from a revelation or commandment from Almighty God.[18]

Joseph explained that the second incident occurred when "Brother Hyrum [Hiram] Page had got in his possession, a certain stone, by which he had obtained to certain, concerning the upbuilding of Zion, the order of the Church, &c &c, all of which were at entirely at variance with the order of Gods house, as laid down in the new Testament, as well as in our late revelations. . . . Finding however that many (especially the Whitmer family and Oliver Cowdery) were believing much in the things set forth by this stone, we thought best to enquire of the Lord concerning so important a matter, and before conference convened, we received the following . . ."[19]

In response to these two challenges and to correct the order of his kingdom the Lord revealed, "No one shall be appointed to receive commandments and revelations in this church excepting my servant Joseph Smith, Jun., for he receiveth them even as Moses" (D&C 28:2).[20] Later, these commandments and revelations referred to were published as the Doctrine and Covenants. In essence, the Lord established that new revelation to be included in the scriptures, or standard works of the Church, would come through Joseph, the prophet and seer for the Church. To Oliver, the Lord further explained, "If thou art led at any time by the Comforter to speak or teach, or at all times by way of commandment unto the church, thou mayest do it. But thou shalt not write by way of commandment, but by wisdom; and thou shalt not command him who is at thy head, and at the head of the church; for I have given him the keys of the mysteries, and the revelations which are sealed, until I shall appoint unto them another in his stead" (D&C 28:4–7). That is, the Lord had appointed Joseph to be a prophet and a seer to the Church holding the keys of revelation, and they were a function of Joseph's calling as the presiding elder and Apostle.

Confusion most likely occurred due to the original penning of the Articles and Covenants of the Church of Christ (see D&C 20; 22). "The designation of Joseph and Oliver as 'first' and 'second' elders of the Church was added to the original document which simply read 'elders.' This denomination helped clarify their role as the presiding officers in the Church during its early years when its size did not justify the organizational structure known to us today."[21] This later revelation further clarified Joseph's presiding position ahead of Oliver Cowdery in receiving revelations for the Church. Thus, Oliver and any elders were distinct from Joseph Smith in their offices in the Church in that, as the first elder, the Lord had appointed Joseph alone to receive commandments or revelations for the Church. Early revelations emphasized and clarified that other individuals could receive revelations and inspiration; however, these revelations were not for the Church, but for their personal lives and ministry.[22] With reference to Hiram Page's revelations for the Church, the Lord commanded and explained, "Tell him that those things which he hath written from that stone are not of me and that Satan deceiveth him; for, behold, these things have not been appointed unto him, neither shall anything be appointed unto any of this church contrary to the church covenants" (D&C 28:11–12).

A few months later, in February 1831, members of the Church in Ohio were disturbed by a woman, who "came making pretensions of revealing commandments, laws and other curious matters."[23] John Whitmer identified the intruder as "a woman by the name of Hubble [Laura Fuller Hubble] who professed to be a prophetess of the Lord and professed to have many revelations, and knew that the Book of Mormon was true; and that she should become a teacher in the Church of Christ."[24]

Joseph inquired of the Lord, and the Lord reiterated to his Saints this clarifying principle:

> Ye have received a commandment for a law unto my church, through him whom I have appointed unto you to receive commandments and revelations from my hand.
>
> And this ye shall know assuredly—that there is none other appointed unto you to receive commandments and revelations until he be taken, if he abide in me.
>
> But verily, verily, I say unto you, that none else shall be appointed unto this gift except it be through him; for if it be taken from him he shall not have power except to appoint another in his stead.
>
> And this shall be a law unto you, that ye receive not the teachings of any that shall come before you as revelations or commandments; and this I give unto you that you may not be deceived, that you may know they are not of me. (D&C 43:2–5)

The President of the Church as Presiding High Priest and Prophet, Seer, and Revelator

Change and growth in the kingdom of God are constant. This includes development of Church priesthood offices and those sustained as prophets, seers, and revelators. A little more than a year after the organization of the Church, the first individuals were ordained to the high priesthood or to the office of high priest.[25] Later, on 25 January 1832, at a conference held in Amherst, Ohio, Joseph Smith was sustained and ordained as President of the High Priesthood.[26] In later instructions regarding the standing of the President of the High Priesthood, Joseph explained, "And again, the duty of the President of the office of the High Priesthood is to preside over the whole church, and to be like unto Moses—behold, here is wisdom; yea, to be a seer, a revelator, a translator, and a prophet, having all the gifts of God which he bestows upon the head of the church" (D&C 107:91–92).

Line upon line, precept upon precept, the Lord revealed his laws to his Saints as he further directed the organization of his Church. The calling of prophet, seer, and revelator was not centered in the person of Joseph Smith. Rather, it is wisdom that the President of the High Priesthood, whoever he may be, exercises those gifts of prophecy, seeric endowment, and revelation. Today the President of the High Priesthood is more commonly referred to as the President of the Church, in harmony with Joseph's explanation above. This understanding is reflected in presentation of Official Declaration 2. The letter presented to those attending general conference declared that President Spencer W. Kimball received a revelation to extend the priesthood to all worthy men. President N. Eldon Tanner explained, "Recognizing Spencer W. Kimball as the prophet, seer, and revelator, and president of The Church of Jesus Christ of Latter-day Saints, it is proposed that we as a constituent assembly accept this revelation as the word and will of the Lord" (Official Declaration 2).

Sustaining Additional Prophets, Seers, and Revelators

Moses exclaimed, "Would God that all the Lord's people were prophets and that the Lord would put his spirit upon them!" (Numbers 11:29). The next clarification regarding others to be sustained as prophets, seers, and revelators required as much, if not more time, to unfold. Today, we also sustain members of the First Presidency and the Quorum of the Twelve Apostles as prophets, seers, and revelators. Expansion of the organizational structure of Christ's Church preceded expansion of others being called as prophets, seers, and revelators. Sustaining Joseph as the President of the High Priesthood and of the Church, along with two counselors as fellow presidents occurred a little over two months after Joseph had been first sustained and ordained President. In March 1832 the Lord called Sidney Rigdon and Jesse Gause to serve as counselors to Joseph and to be "given the keys of the kingdom, which belong always unto the Presidency of the High Priesthood" (D&C 81:2). A year later Frederick G. Williams was called to replace Jesse Gause and the Lord clarified that he and Sidney Rigdon were "accounted as equal with [Joseph] in holding the keys of this last kingdom" (D&C 90:6).[27] Within three years of the organization of the First Presidency, individuals were called to serve as members of the Quorum of Twelve Apostles on 14 February 1835.[28] However, neither the counselors to Joseph nor the apostles were formally recognized as prophets, seers, and revelators until later.

On 27 March 1836, during the dedicatory session of the Kirtland Temple, the Prophet Joseph Smith first "called upon the several quorums commencing with the presidency, to manifest by rising up, their willingness to acknowledge me as a prophet and seer and uphold me as such by their p[r]ayers of faith."[29] Following an intermission, Joseph "made a short address, and called upon the several quorums, and all the congregation of saints to acknowledge the Presidency as Prophets and Seers, and uphold them by their prayers, they all covenanted to do so by rising; [he] then called upon the quorums and congregations of saints to acknowledge the 12 Apostles who were present as Prophets and Seers <Revelators> and special witnesses to all the nations of the earth, holding the keys of the kingdom, to unlock it or cause it to be done among them; and uphold them by their prayers, which they assented to by rising."[30] Beginning with this dedicatory session, it appears that members of the First Presidency and the Quorum of the Twelve Apostles have continually been sustained as prophets, seers, and revelators.

Earlier, on 5 December 1834, Oliver Cowdery had been ordained as "assistant-president to the high and holy priesthood."[31] At a meeting held two days later, "the propriety of ordaining others to the office of Presidency of the high priesthood was also discussed, after which High Counsellor Hyrum Smith was ordained <to> the Presidency under the hands of President Smith, and High Counsellor Joseph Smith sen. under the hands of President Rigdon."[32] It appears that these individuals were included among the presidency that were sustained as prophets, seers and revelators during the dedication of the Kirtland Temple.[33] In 1841, when Hyrum Smith was called to take Oliver Cowdery's place as assistant president and as Joseph Smith Sr.'s place as patriarch of the Church, he was again appointed as a prophet, seer, and revelator (D&C 124:94). In addition, at various times, individuals were called as counselors to or in the First Presidency that were also sustained as prophets, seers, and revelators. For example, at the April 1968 General Conference three additional counselors in the First Presidency—Joseph Fielding Smith, Thorpe B. Isaacson, and Alvin R. Dyer—were sustained along with the members of the First Presidency, the

Quorum of the Twelve Apostles, and the Patriarch to the Church as prophets, seers, and revelators.[34]

During other times, counselors were called to the Quorum of the Twelve Apostles who also were sustained as prophets, seers, and revelators. Such was the case in 1877 with John W. Young and Daniel H. Wells, who both previously served as counselors in the First Presidency with Brigham Young. Following Brigham Young's death, they were released since a new First Presidency was not organized and the Quorum of the Twelve Apostles was the presiding quorum of the Church. They were instead called as counselors to the Twelve and were presented by President John Taylor for a sustaining vote as prophets, seers, and revelators.[35]

In 1902, John Smith, older brother of President Joseph F. Smith and the Presiding Patriarch of the Church, was sustained as a prophet, seer, and revelator, as were, for a time, individuals subsequently called to serve as Patriarch to the Church.[36] This practice ended in November 1979 with the designation of the Church Patriarch to emeritus status.[37] Thus, recognizing and sustaining individuals as prophets, seers, and revelators of the Church has been expanded in the past. It may be wise to have an open mind as to what the Lord might reveal in the future regarding his will concerning those he would have sustained as prophets, seers, and revelators in his Church.[38]

Prophets, Seers, and Revelators Counsel Together

Having more than one individual sustained as a prophet, seer, and revelator necessitated clarification regarding how revelation is received for the Church and who may receive that revelation. A little over a year following the dedication of the Kirtland Temple, on 6 April 1837, Joseph explained that "the Presidents, or Presidency, are over the church, and revelations of the mind and will of God to the church are to come through the presidency."[39] The First Presidency and the Twelve Apostles form two separate administrative quorums (see D&C 107:22–24). However, they have conferred upon them the same keys of the kingdom with regard to administrative keys of the priesthood as well as keys of revelation for the Church. Even so, the Twelve have a president that presides over that quorum; the First Presidency presides over the Twelve; and the President of the High Priesthood is sustained as the President of the Church and presides over the First Presidency. This includes presiding over both the administrative and revelatory affairs of the Church. As Elder Jeffrey R. Holland explained, "The First Presidency and Quorum of the Twelve are commissioned by God and sustained by you as prophets, seers, and revelators, with the President of the Church sustained as *the* prophet, seer, and revelator, the *senior* Apostle, and as such the only man authorized to exercise all of the revelatory and administrative keys for the Church."[39] President J. Reuben Clark Jr. wrote, "Some of the General Authorities [the Apostles] have had assigned to them a special calling; they possess a special gift; they are sustained as prophets, seers, and revelators, which gives them a special spiritual endowment in connection with their teaching of the people. They have the right, the power, and authority to declare the mind and will of God to his people, subject to the over-all power and authority of the President of the Church." He then added, "Only the President of the Church, the Presiding High Priest, is sustained as Prophet, Seer, and Revelator for the Church, and he alone has the right to receive revelations for the Church, either new or amendatory, or to give authoritative interpretations of scriptures that shall be binding on the Church."[41]

Unlike many biblical or Book of Mormon prophets, whose ministry was relatively solitary, today Latter-day Saints recognize and sustain several individuals as prophets. The Lord directed that these prophets sit in council together in making decisions. The quorum of the First Presidency and the Quorum of the Twelve are often referred to as the Council of the First Presidency and the Council of the Twelve. The Prophet Joseph Smith explained that "every decision made by either of these quorums must be by the unanimous voice of the same; that is, every member in each quorum must be agreed to its decisions. . . . Unless this is the case, their decisions are not entitled to the same blessings which the decisions of a quorum of three presidents were anciently" (D&C 107:27–29).

President Nelson recently explained the revelatory process of the First Presidency and the Quorum of the Twelve Apostles in making decisions as prophets, seers, and revelators:

> Some may question why the Church does some of the things that it does. . . . We sustain 15 men, who are ordained as prophets, seers, and revelators. When a thorny problem arises—and

they only seem to get thornier each day—these 15 men wrestle with the issue, trying to see all the ramifications of various courses of action, and they diligently seek to hear the voice of the Lord. After fasting, praying, studying, pondering, and counseling with my Brethren about weighty matters, it is not unusual for me to be awakened during the night with further impressions about issues with which we are concerned. And my Brethren have the same experience.

The First Presidency and Quorum of the Twelve Apostles counsel together and share all the Lord has directed us to understand and to feel individually and collectively. And then we watch the Lord move upon the President of the Church to proclaim the Lord's will.[42]

This principle is perfectly illustrated in the occasion of President Spencer W. Kimball's receiving the revelation declaring that all worthy men may receive the priesthood:

On Thursday, June 1, 1978, President Spencer W. Kimball, while meeting with his counselors in the First Presidency and the Twelve in the Salt Lake Temple, indicated that for months he had been giving prayerful consideration to the matter of conferring the priesthood upon those of all races and that he felt the need for divine guidance. He explained that he had spent many hours in the upper room in the temple pleading with the Lord for counsel and direction. He indicated his hope that the Lord would give a revelation and resolve the matter. He further stated that if it was the mind and will of the Lord that the Church continue in the present course, he was willing to sustain and support that decision and defend it to the death. He said he hoped for a clear affirmation so there would be no question in anyone's mind.

All present were invited to express their views on the matter, which they did. A strong spirit of unity existed. At the conclusion of this discussion, President Kimball asked his counselors in the presidency and the Quorum of the Twelve to join with him in prayer. President Kimball then importuned the

Lord with great fervor and faith. The prayer offered by President Kimball was dictated by the Holy Ghost.

"On this occasion," recalled one of those who was present, "because of the importuning and the faith, and because the hour and the time had arrived the Lord in his providences poured out the Holy Ghost upon the First Presidency and the Twelve in a miraculous and marvelous manner, beyond anything that any then present had ever experienced. The revelation came to the President of the Church; it also came to each individual present. There were ten members of the Council of the Twelve and three of the First Presidency there assembled. The result was that President Kimball knew, and each one of us knew, independent of any other person, by direct and personal revelation to us, that the time had now come to extend the gospel and all its blessings and all its obligations, including the priesthood and the blessings of the house of the Lord, to those of every nation, culture, and race, including the black race. There was no question whatsoever as to what happened or as to the word and message that came."[43]

Mortal Men Called of God

The education of prophets is founded upon the inspiration of the Holy Ghost and study of earlier prophetic writings and revelations. Three months following the organization of the Church, the Lord further clarified Joseph's role as a prophet: "Thou shalt continue in calling upon God in my name, and writing the things which shall be given thee by the Comforter, and expounding all scriptures unto the church" (D&C 24:5). Thus, prophets, seers, and revelators not only receive the word of the Lord but also expound and clarify scripture that has already been given. The Lord commanded Joseph, "Let your time be devoted to the studying of the scriptures, and to preaching" (D&C 26:1).

The Lord only has imperfect individuals whom he can choose from to call as prophets, seers, and revelators. The qualification is that they are appointed, commissioned, and admonished to do as the sons of Mosiah, whom Mormon described as individuals who "had waxed strong in the knowledge of truth; for they were men of sound understanding and they had searched the scriptures diligently, that they might know the word of God. But this is not all; they had given themselves to much prayer, and fasting; therefore they had the spirit of prophecy, and the spirit of revelation, and when they taught, they taught with power and authority of God" (Alma 17:2–3).

It is evident that the Lord expects those called as presiding officers to know and understand those inspired words he previously gave to earlier prophets and that they often cite the teachings of former prophets in their own messages. Their inspired understanding of the Lord's will is built upon their study of the scriptures, teachings of earlier prophets and apostles, and the inspiration of the Spirit. Examples of this principle are the documents "The Family: A Proclamation to the World" and "The Living Christ." Each as proclaimed by the First Presidency and the Quorum of the Twelve Apostles and each were built upon scripture previously revealed as well as inspiration to those penning the documents. In addition, personal experiences and application of the scriptures provide each prophet, seer, and revelator with unique insights. This allows for the different strengths and weaknesses that each brings to his calling and the inspired synergy that results from their actions and deliberations.

Prophets are no more than mortal men, but they are also no less than prophets of God. Far from diminishing prophets in our view, knowing that God has called mortals to move his work forward ought to give us a deep sense of gratitude and hope. With the eyes of faith, prophets' mortal weaknesses can be seen as evidence that their wise counsel and powerful witness come not from the strength of a man but from the power of God. Elder David A. Bednar bore his testimony of this truth in these words: "The Lord's revealed pattern of governance by councils in His Church provides for and attenuates the impact of human frailties. Interestingly, the mortal limitations of these men actually affirm the divine source of the revelations that come to and through them."[44]

Elder M. Russell Ballard explained, "During my nearly 40 years of close association, I have been a personal witness as both quiet inspiration and profound revelation have moved to action the prophets and apostles, the other General Authorities, and the auxiliary leaders. While neither perfect nor infallible, these good men and women have been perfectly dedicated to

leading the work of the Lord forward as He has directed."[45] President Dieter
F. Uchtdorf bore a similar witness:

> I suppose the Church would be perfect only if it were run by
> perfect beings. God is perfect, and His doctrine is pure. But
> He works through us—His imperfect children—and imper-
> fect people make mistakes. . . . As an Apostle of the Lord Jesus
> Christ and as one who has seen firsthand the councils and
> workings of this Church, I bear solemn witness that no deci-
> sion of significance affecting this Church or its members is
> ever made without earnestly seeking the inspiration, guidance,
> and approbation of our Eternal Father. This is the Church of
> Jesus Christ. God will not allow His Church to drift from its
> appointed course or fail to fulfill its divine destiny."[46]

We can have confidence that while not perfect or infallible, those that
we sustain as prophets, seers, and revelators are called and inspired of God.
They declare the truth as a united voice.

Hearkening to Prophets, Seers, and Revelators

The Lord does not intend for his people to be lulled into such a sense of security or blind obedience regarding the teachings and counsels of apostles and
prophets that they cease to grow and have individual conscience. President
Brigham Young declared, "I am more afraid that this people have so much
confidence in their leaders that they will not inquire for themselves of God
whether they are led by Him. I am fearful they settle down in a state of
blind self-security, trusting their eternal destiny in the hands of their leaders
with reckless confidence that in itself would thwart the purposes of God. . . .
Let every man and woman know, by the whispering of the Spirit of God to
themselves, whether their leaders are walking in the path the Lord dictates,
or not."[47] We must come to know for ourselves to gain an unshakeable testimony of their prophetic calling. President Nelson explained, "You may not
always understand every declaration of a living prophet, but when you know
a prophet is a prophet, you can approach the Lord in humility and faith and
ask for your own witness about whatever his prophet has proclaimed."[48]

Conclusion

Prophets and seers have been part of the Lord's kingdom since Old Testament times. As part of the foundation of the Restoration, the Lord called on Joseph Smith to be a prophet, seer, and revelator. Today, in addition to the President of the Church, we also sustain members of the First Presidency and Quorum of the Twelve Apostles as prophets, seers, and revelators. Even so, it is recognized that only the President of the Church is appointed to receive revelations for the Church as *the* Prophet, rather than as *a* prophet.

The Lord clarified the uniting of administrative priesthood officers and spiritual gifts in this dispensation. That is, he appointed those in presiding priesthood positions to also be prophets, seers, and revelators for his Church. He and the Saints recognize that these appointed individuals are not perfect nor infallible. However, the Lord is not an absentee master and continues today to guide his kingdom through his appointed servants. These individuals counsel together, teach the gospel, and administer its principles accordingly. Thus, like the Church in the meridian of time, The Church of Jesus Christ of Latter-day Saints is "built upon the foundation of the apostles and prophets, Jesus Christ himself being the chief corner stone" (Ephesians 2:20).

Notes

1.   See Exodus 24:4; Revelation 1:19; Ether 4:1; D&C 21:1; Moses 1:40; 6:4–6; Abraham 1:28, 31.

2.   Bible Hub, "4396. prophétés," http://biblehub.com/greek/4396.htm.

3.   *Illustrated Dictionary & Concordance of the Bible*, ed. Geoffrey Wigoder (New York: Sterling Publishing, 2005), 790.

4.   B. D. Napier, "Prophet, Prophetism," in *The Interpreter's Dictionary of the Bible* (New York: Abingdon Press, 1962), 3:896, http://biblehub.com/hebrew/5030.htm.

5.   See D&C 107:91–92; 103:16; 28:2.

6.   See Exodus 4:10–16; 33:11.

7.   See Isaiah 62:6; Jeremiah 6:17, 31:6; Ezekiel 3:16–21, 33:7–16.

8.   See Acts 11:27, 13:1, 15:32, 19:6, 21:10.

9.   Bible Hub, "7203. ro'eh," http://biblehub.comhebrew/7203.htm and "2374. chozeh," http://biblehub.com/hebrew/2374.htm.

10.   For a detailed discussion of the connection between the terms *prophet* and *seer*, see Napier, "Prophet, Prophetism," 3:897–98.

11. For a discussion on the connection between seer stones and the Prophet Joseph Smith as a seer, see Richard E. Turley Jr., Robin S. Jensen, and Mark Ashurst-McGee, "Joseph the Seer," *Ensign*, October 2015, https://www.lds.org/ensign/2015/10/joseph-the-seer?lang=eng. In addition, it should be noted that Joseph Smith was a type of natural seer. That is, he was a seer before receiving seer stones with the Book of Mormon plates and had exercised that gift before he translated as well as in conjunction with the gift of translation.

12. John A. Widtsoe, *Evidences and Reconciliations*, vols. 1–3, comp. G. Homer Durham (Salt Lake City: Bookcraft, 1960), 258.

13. See D&C 77:2; apparently, the first use of the term *revelator* was in 1764 and most likely was familiar to the early members of the Church. http://www.merriam-webster.com/dictionary/revelator.

14. Russell M. Nelson, "Becoming True Millennials," worldwide devotional, 10 January 2016, https://www.lds.org/broadcasts/article/worldwide-devotionals/2016/01/becoming-true-millennials?lang=eng.

15. Joseph Smith, History, ca. June 1839–ca. 1841, handwriting of James Mulholland and Robert B. Thompson, in Joseph Smith History, 1838–1856, vol. A-1, CHL, http://josephsmithpapers.org/paperSummary/history-circa-june-1839-circa-1841-draft-2?p=33.

16. See Joseph Smith—History 1:72; D&C 20:1, 21:10–11, 27:12–13, 65:2, 128:20.

17. In this regard, Richard L. Bushman has noted that "the most startling feature of the organization Joseph formed was its merger of the charismatic and the bureaucratic." Richard L. Bushman, "Joseph Smith and Power," in *A Firm Foundation: Church Organization and Administration*, ed. David J. Whitaker and Arnold K. Garr (Provo, UT: Religious Studies Center; Salt Lake City: Deseret Book, 2011), 4. Paul indicated that the Church was "built upon the foundation of the apostles and prophets, Jesus Christ himself being the chief corner stone" (Ephesians 2:20).

18. Karen Lynn Davidson, David J. Whittaker, Mark Ashurst-McGee, and Richard L. Jensen, eds., *Histories, Volume 1: Joseph Smith Histories, 1832–1844*, vol. 1 of the Histories series of *The Joseph Smith Papers*, ed. Dean C. Jessee, Ronald K. Esplin, and Richard Lyman Bushman (Salt Lake City: Church Historians Press, 2012), 426.

19. *JSP*, H1:436–38.

20. Alexander Baugh noted that "the Doctrine and Covenants contains 138 sections. All but four sections bear the revelatory stamp of Joseph Smith (see D&C 134, 135, 136, 138)." https://speeches.byu.edu/talks/alexander-l-baugh_joseph-smith-seer-translator-revelator-prophet/. Additionally, as a brief note of explanation regarding the wording of the revelation, one of the challenges for the modern reader is the use of the word *commandment*. At this time in the Restoration, commandments also referred to revelations and inspired instructions that the Lord gave. This meaning was later reflected in the title for each in the manuscripts printed in the *Book of Commandments*.

21. Joseph Fielding McConkie and Craig J. Ostler, *Revelations of the Restoration* (Salt Lake City: Deseret Book, 2000), 156. See also "Articles and Covenants," Fayette Township, Seneca Co., NY, ca. April 1830. http://josephsmithpapers.org/paperSummary/?target=x4904.

22.   See D&C 21:4, 24:5, 28:2–6.

23.   JS, History, A-1:101; http://josephsmithpapers.org/paperSummary/history -1838-1856-volume-a-1-23-december-1805-30-august-1834?p=107.

24.   John Whitmer, History, 1831–ca. 1847, *The Joseph Smith Papers, Histories, Volume 2: Assigned Histories, 1831–1847,* ed. Karen Lynn Davidson, Richard L. Jensen, David J. Whittaker (Salt Lake City: Church Historians Press, 2012), 29.

25.   Minutes, Geauga Co., OH, ca. 3–[4] June 1831, CHL. http://josephsmithpapers .org/paperSummary/minutes-circa-3-4-june-1831?p=1#!/paperSummary/minutes -circa-3-4-june-1831&p=2. For consideration of the office of high priest, see McConkie and Ostler, *Revelations of the Restoration,* 597–602.

26.   Minutes, Independence, Jackson Co., MO, 26–27 April 1832, CHL, http:// josephsmithpapers.org/paperSummary/?target=X4041.

27.   Also see D&C 107:21–22.

28.   JS, History, 1838–1856, vol. B-1, created 1 October 1843–24 February 1845, CHL, http://josephsmithpapers.org/paperSummary/history-1838-1856-volume-b-1-1 -september-1834-2-november-1838?p=18&highlight=14%20february%201835.

29.   Dean C. Jessee, Ronald K. Esplin, and Richard Lyman Bushman, eds., *The Joseph Smith Papers,* vol. 1 of the Journals series (Salt Lake City: The Church Historian's Press, 2008), 203; JS, History, September 1834–2 November 1838, vol. B-1,   http://josephsmithpapers.org/paperSummary/history-1838-1856-volume-b-1-1 -september-1834-2-november-1838?p=170&highlight=prophets%20seers%20 revelators.

30.   http://josephsmithpapers.org/paperSummary/history-1838-1856-volume -b-1-1-september-1834-2-november-1838?p=170.

31.   JS, History, December 1834–May 1836, 19, CHL, http://josephsmithpapers.org /paperSummary/history-1834-1836?p=19#!/paperSummary/history-1834-1836&p=19.

32.   Ibid., 22, CHL.

33.   Note that the seating of presidents in the Melchizedek Priesthood pulpits of the Kirtland Temple may have caused some later confusion regarding the distinction of the First Presidency and those serving in other capacities as presidents and counselors. Along with the forenamed presidents, the stake presidency of the Church in Missouri, David Whitmer, William W. Phelps, and John Whitmer, were also seated in those pulpits. Further research may clarify whether these individuals were also sustained as prophets, seers, and revelators at this time.

34.   Conference Report, 5–7 April 1968, 70. Those that have served as counselors are John C. Bennett (1841–42), Amasa M. Lyman (1843–44), Joseph F. Smith (1866–77), Lorenzo Snow (1873–77), Brigham Young Jr. (1873–77), Albert Carrington (1873–77), John W. Young (1873–76), George Q. Cannon (1873–77), Hugh B. Brown (1961), Joseph Fielding Smith (1965–70), H. Thorpe B. Isaacson (1965–70), Alvin R. Dyer (1968–70), Gordon B. Hinckley (1981–82). See *1999–2000 Church Almanac,* 16, 47–55.

35.   *Deseret News Weekly,* 10 October 1877, 569, http://udn.lib.utah.edu/cdm /compoundobject/collection/deseretnews3/id/152487/rec/41. See also Conference Report, April 1880, 68. At the death of Brigham Young an epistle was sent to the members of the Church from the Twelve and Counselors. In that epistle they explained

that "the two Counselors of President Young—Presidents John W. Young and Daniel H. Wells—were unanimously sustained as one with, counselor to, and associated in action with the Twelve Apostles." "Epistle of the Twelve Apostles and Counselors, to the Church of Jesus Christ of Latter-day Saints in all the World," in *Messages of the First Presidency*, comp. James R. Clark (Salt Lake City: Bookcraft, 1965), 2:300.

36.   Conference Report, October 1902, 83. The previous conference John W. Taylor taught, "Patriarchs have the gift of being prophets, seers and revelators, to reveal the mind and will of God and portray unto the faithful their future lives." Conference Report, April 1902, 44.

37.   See "The Sustaining of Church Officers," general conference, April and October 1979, https://www.lds.org/general-conference/1979/04/the-sustaining-of -church-officers?lang=eng. President N. Eldon Tanner made the following announcement: "Before presenting the authorities for the vote of the confer- ence, President Kimball has asked me to read the following statement: Because of the large increase in the number of stake patriarchs and the availability of patri- archal service throughout the world, we now designate Elder Eldred G. Smith as a Patriarch Emeritus, which means that he is honorably relieved of all duties and responsibilities pertaining to the office of Patriarch to the Church." "The Sustaining of Church Officers," general conference, October 1979, https://www.lds .org/general-conference/1979/10/the-sustaining-of-church-officers?lang=eng.

38.   Note that a group of early members met in an upper room of the Newel K. Whitney store in Kirtland, Ohio, under the title of School of the Prophets.

39.   JS, History, 1838–1856, vol. B-1, CHL, http://josephsmithpapers.org /paperSummary/history-1838-1856-volume-b-1-1-september-1834-2-november-1838 ?p=209&highlight=april%206%201837#!/paperSummary/history-1838-1856-volume -b-1-1-september-1834-2-november-1838&p=210.

40.   Quoted in Jeffrey R. Holland, "Prophets, Seers, and Revelators," general con- ference, October 2004, https://www/lds.org/general-conference/2004/10/prophets -seers-and-revelators?lang=eng.

41.   "When Are Church Leaders' Words Entitled to Claim of Scripture?," *Church News*, 31 July 1954, 9–10.

42.   Nelson, "Becoming True Millennials."

43.   McConkie and Ostler, *Revelations of the Restoration*, 1154–55.

44.   David A. Bednar, "Chosen to Bear Testimony of My Name," general con- ference, October 2015, https://www.lds.org/general-conference/2015/10/chosen -to-bear-testimony-of-my-name?lang=eng.

45.   M. Russell Ballard, "God Is at the Helm," general conference, October 2015, https://www.lds.org/general-conference/2015/10/god-is-at-the-helm?lang=eng.

46.   Dieter F. Uchtdorf, "Come, Join with Us,'" general conference, October 2013, https://www.lds.org/general-conference/2013/10/come-join-with-us?lang=eng.

47.   Brigham Young, in *Journal of Discourses*, 26 vols. (Liverpool: Latter-day Saints' Book Depot, 1854–86), 9:150.

48.   Nelson, "Becoming True Millennials."

4

"Unless I Could Get More Wisdom, I Would Never Know"

THE FIRST VISION, A PATTERN FOR SPIRITUAL LEARNING

Barbara Morgan Gardner

Barbara Morgan Gardner is an assistant professor of Church history and doctrine at BYU and is the LDS higher education chaplain-at-large.

Joseph Smith's vision in 1820 of God the Eternal Father and his Son Jesus Christ initiated the Restoration and today is the foundation of the Latter-day Saint faith. President David O. McKay related, "That one revelation answers all the queries of science regarding God and his divine personality. . . . What God is, is answered. His relation to his children is clear. His interest in humanity through authority delegated to man is apparent. The future of the work is assured. These and other glorious truths are clarified by that glorious first vision."[1] To President McKay's list could be added the understanding that God answers prayers, Satan has real power, the nature of the Godhead is distinct, and other truths.

There is more, however, to be learned from this experience than even these wonderful insights. In regard to the First Vision, Joseph Fielding McConkie asserted: "The prophetic efforts of Joseph Smith did not center in sharing his spiritual experiences but rather in the effort to qualify us to have our own spiritual experiences. The emphasis of his ministry was not on what he had seen but on what we could see. . . . Joseph invited us to check him by having our own Sacred Grove experience. The validity of an experience is if it can be repeated. A good seed not only bears good fruits but it always bears the same fruits—regardless of who plants it."[2] By examining the various accounts of the First Vision through the framework of one seeking to help others learn for themselves, a clear pattern emerges. Each account sheds unique light on Joseph's experience but also solidifies critical principles of a spiritual learning pattern all honest seekers of truth must follow. While most Latter-day Saints turn to accounts of the First Vision to learn historical and doctrinal truths, this paper will show how one can turn to the First Vision to discover something entirely different—the pattern for spiritual learning leading to wisdom. The principles encompassed in this spiritual learning pattern include the following: personal perplexity, cognitive dissonance, or both great effort required for personal learning; dependence and recognition that all truth comes from a divine source; and the acknowledgment of personal responsibility to learn and act.

First Vision Accounts

Before we can gain insights into the process of spiritual learning, we must understand something of what Joseph shared in different accounts of the First Vision.[3] Although the First Vision occurred in 1820 when Joseph was a young boy of fourteen, his first attempt at documenting this significant theophany actually occurred much later. During a ten-year period from 1832 to 1842, Joseph wrote or dictated various accounts of the First Vision on at least four different occasions. These accounts vary based on audience, experience, purpose, and circumstance. Recent scholars typically ascribe five additional accounts indirectly to Joseph.[4] This paper, however, will focus on those four directly attributed to the Prophet Joseph Smith.

The 1832 account. The earliest known recording of the First Vision was written in 1832, when Joseph was twenty-seven. It was written in his own hand as part of a short autobiography. At this stage in his life, Joseph had received more than half of the revelations now found in the Doctrine and Covenants. In this raw and personal account, Joseph vividly relates his insatiable concern for the welfare of his soul as a youth. He also describes his confusion with religion in general because he found a great discrepancy between what he read in the scriptures and what he saw taught and practiced in different religious groups. In this account, Joseph shared the historical events of the Restoration through the personal, heart-wrenching eyes of one who was being "chastened for his transgressions" and feeling the "affliction of soul" as he was divinely tutored and prepared by the Lord to bring forth a marvelous work on the earth. In so doing, Joseph learned for himself the purposes of the Lord and felt of his love. Clearly Joseph sought personal reprieve and answers to his soul's sincere desire.[5]

The 1835 account. Three years later, in Kirtland, Ohio, Joseph related another account of his vision to a visitor—the self-proclaimed prophet Robert Matthews. Joseph's scribe, Warren Parrish, recorded this 1835 retelling. Unlike what he did in the previous account, Joseph emphasized the adversarial influence prior to his prayer and his struggle as he fought the evil force that seemingly did not want him to succeed in calling upon God. He later said, the "powers of darkness strove hard against me." Determined to follow through with his plan, Joseph recalled, "I kneeled again[,] my mouth was opened and my tongue liberated, and I called on the Lord in mighty prayer." The contrast Joseph portrayed between the adversary and the feeling following this prayer is stark: "A pillar of fire appeared above my head, it presently rested down upon me, and filled me with joy unspeakable."[6]

The 1838 account. Joseph Smith originally dictated the 1838 account as part of a longer history of the Church. Rewritten by James Mullholland in 1839 as part of the first volume of the 1838–56 history and published in the *Times and Seasons* in 1842, this account is the most recognizable among Latter-day Saints today because it is the version published in the Pearl of Great Price as Joseph Smith—History. Joseph stated the objective of this account was to "disabuse the public mind, and put all inquirers after truth in possession of the facts, as they have transpired, in relation both to myself and the Church, so far as I have such facts in my possession" (Joseph Smith—History 1:1). It is significant to note that at the time of this most recognizable version, Joseph and the Saints had completed their Kirtland years; in Kirtland they had received revelations and life experiences in connection with the School of the Prophets, they had built and dedicated the house of the Lord, and they had received the keys of the priesthood. Thus, the writing of this version of the First Vision was authored by a seasoned, tried, and divinely tutored prophet of God. In this account as well, Joseph described a clear, matter-of-fact, step-by-step process he followed in preparation for his divine vision according to the knowledge he had obtained. This process will be elaborated on later in the paper.

The 1842 account. The final account, written in response to a request by John Wentworth, editor of the *Chicago Democrat*, was published in the *Times and Seasons* on 1 March 1842, and is known as the Wentworth letter. This straightforward account, written for a non-Mormon audience, was a response to an inquiry regarding the "rise, progress, persecution and faith of the Latter-day Saints."[7] With minor modifications, Joseph Smith sent the account to historian Israel Daniel Rupp, who published it in his book, "He Pasa Ekklesia [The Whole Church]: An Original History of the Religious Denominations at Present Existing in the United States." This 1842 account contains a more personal historical touch by the prophet, relating how, at a young age, he "began to reflect upon the importance of being prepared for a future state," and finding, as he visited a variety of faiths, "a great clash in religious sentiment" which caused him "much confusion." He recognized that "if God had a church" he would not teach worshiping, administering of ordinances, and principles in such ways that were so "diametrically opposed." While "fervently engaged in supplication," Joseph saw "two glorious personages who exactly resembled each other in features, and likeness." They told him "that all religious denominations were believing in incorrect doctrines," and he was "expressly commanded to 'go not after them.'"

In all of these accounts, Joseph made it clear that he was in a deep and desperate search for knowledge, information, or wisdom and that he was willing to do all he needed to in order to obtain it.

Pattern for Spiritual Learning

Opinions regarding what constitutes real learning are varied and are at times controversial. For some, learning may be defined by cognitive growth or additional information, where for others, learning is based on behavior outcomes. According to Robert Gagne, a highly acclaimed educational psychologist, "Learning is a change in human disposition or capability, which can be retained, and which is not simply ascribable to the process of growth."[8] Elder Dallin H. Oaks aptly instructs that the process of religious learning requires more than the acquisition of knowledge. "It is not even enough," he instructs, "for us to be *convinced* of the gospel; we must act and think so that we are *converted* by it." Therefore, he continues, "In contrast to the institutions of the world, which teach us to *know* something, the gospel of Jesus Christ challenges us to *become* something."[9] In Ephesians, the Apostle Paul taught that teachings and teachers of the Lord were given to help all attain "the measure of the stature of the fulness of Christ" (Ephesians 4:13). Therefore, in secular learning, and more specifically in spiritual learning, the purpose is not merely for an individual to know something but rather to do and become something.

Recognizing this critical pattern and desired outcome associated with learning, Elder David A. Bednar boldly declared, "The Prophet Joseph Smith was the greatest learner in the dispensation of the fullness of times." Continuing, he related, "He was a sincere and eager student, his teachers were members of the Godhead and angels, and his curriculum was focused upon the truths of eternity. Joseph is the quintessential example of a humble and diligent learner."[10] Although applying the pattern Joseph Smith exemplified may not lead to a duplication of the First Vision, the principles of learning distilled from Joseph Smith's accounts of the First Vision will lead one to the same fruit: gaining wisdom and becoming a new person.

Personal perplexity and/or cognitive dissonance. A preliminary factor in the learning process is personal perplexity and what educational psychologists term *cognitive dissonance* (an inconsistency between beliefs and behaviors), which motivates an individual to seek a resolution or answer, thus instigating true learning. J. T. Dillon clarified, "The main event at the start of [learning] is the experience of perplexity. That is the precondition of questioning and thus the prerequisite for learning. Questioning still might not follow, nor learning; without perplexity [questioning or learning] cannot follow."[11] Although Joseph related that he "sought information" in the 1832 account, Joseph was seeking more than a dissemination of knowledge. He clearly yearned for the truth that could resolve his perplexity and dissonance. In addition, Joseph also recounted his struggle with inconsistencies between the beliefs and teachings of various religious sects and their actions. Personal perplexity and cognitive dissonance stimulated Joseph's desire for resolution, which in turn led to intense pondering and questioning required for learning. A closer examination of each of Joseph's four First Vision accounts further illustrates this primary principle of perplexity and cognitive dissonance.

In his 1832 account, Joseph related that at the age of twelve, his "mind became seriously impressed with regard to the all-important concerns for the welfare of my immortal soul." Having a firm belief in the truths declared in the scriptures, Joseph began searching the word of God, but he began to "marvel exceedingly" as he compared what he read with what he saw in his "intimate acquaintance with those of different denominations." He became aware that those of religious traditions "did not adorn their profession by a holy walk and Godly conversation agreeable to what [he] found contained in that sacred depository." He expressed, "This was a grief to my soul." As a result of this personal perplexity and cognitive dissonance, he continued, "My mind became exceedingly distressed for I become convicted of my sins." It appears that the recognition of the seeming hypocrisy of the ungodly walk of others caused him to reflect on his own conduct, perhaps recognizing the same tendency in himself, which therefore likely led to his personal need for repentance.

Joseph's private struggle is plainly and succinctly revealed in each of the accounts. In the 1835 account, he described being "perplexed in mind" and "being wrought up in my mind, . . . I knew not who was right or who was wrong." In the 1838 account, Joseph further portrayed his perplexity that "the seemingly good feelings of both the priests and the converts were more pretended than real." This dissonance became a catalyst for even greater perplexity and restlessness regarding the decision of which church to join. "During this time of great excitement my mind was called up to serious reflection and great uneasiness." He continued, "So great were the confusion and strife among the different denominations, that it was impossible for a person young as I was, and so unacquainted with men and things, to come to any certain conclusion who was right and who was wrong."

In the Wentworth letter of 1842, Joseph expressed his confusion concerning the "great clash in religious sentiment" regarding the "plan of salvation." Each religious sect taught its plan to be the "summum bonum of perfection." Joseph indicated that he believed that all of the various plans could not be right at the same time; he felt that "God could not be the author of so much confusion" and that "if God had a church it would not be split up into factions, and that if he taught one society to worship one way, and administer in one set of ordinances, he would not teach another principles which were diametrically opposed."

Joseph described in these four accounts what Gagne referred to as a possible "learning event" and a "stimulus situation."[12] However, having a learner and a stimulus does not necessarily lead to learning. Learning is dependent on the desire and effort exerted by the learner. Hence, Joseph's accounts reflected this first principle or precondition of learning, but what he did with this stimulus situation determined if learning would actually occur.

Effort required for personal learning. As Dillon poignantly expressed, perplexity is a precondition to learning but does not necessarily lead to it. In Joseph's case, however, his insatiable need for resolution and understanding indeed led him to further inquiry. Perhaps it was the very personal nature of the perplexity that necessitated resolution. "Only when learning becomes personal, when the learner makes choices and the spirit and body unite," Russell Osguthorpe explained, "will learning find lasting place in one's soul."[13] In fact, in the 1832 account, Joseph acknowledged that it was the concern for the "welfare of my immortal soul which led me to searching the scriptures. . . . I pondered many things in my heart." His continued search for truth as he pondered, questioned, and studied is eventually what led him to "[cry] unto the Lord for mercy."

In the 1835 account, Joseph acknowledged that it was in his search of the Bible that he found the critical principle with the promise, "Ask, and it shall be given you; seek, and ye shall find; knock, and it shall be opened unto you" (Matthew 7:7), as well as the more widely reported admonition, "If any of you lack wisdom, let him ask of God, that giveth to all men liberally, and upbraideth not" (James 1:5). It was James's admonition in the scriptures that led to Joseph's determination to retire "to the silent grove and [bow] down before the Lord." In his 1838 account, Joseph elaborated even more on the questioning and searching process that followed his perplexity: "In the midst of this war of words and tumult of opinions, I often said to myself: What is to be done? Who of all these parties are right; or, are they all wrong together? If any one of them be right, which is it, and how shall I know it?"

Joseph's questioning process was not casual, nor out of mere curiosity for information. Joseph described this state of being in the 1838 account (a prime example of what educators would call cognitive dissonance): "I was laboring under the extreme difficulties caused by the contests of these parties of religionists." It was this searching, laboring, and heartfelt experience that led him to read the passage from James as sighted above. In this 1838 account, however, Joseph described his feelings following the reading of this passage: "Never did any passage of scripture come with more power to the heart of man than this did at this time to mine," he declared. "It seemed to enter with great force into every feeling of my heart. I reflected on it again and again, knowing that if any person needed wisdom from God, I did; for how to act I did not know, and unless I could get more wisdom than I then had, I would never know."

This search for truth, as Osguthorpe instructed, requires a different search than does traditional sectarian learning. "It demands that we have faith, that we ponder and pray, and that we open ourselves to guidance from others and from God. There must be no pretense that such a search will be easy. Exercising faith, pondering, praying and listening for guidance require our utmost commitment, our maximum energy, our whole being. . . . Once we have taken our first step on the path, we must follow it to its conclusion."[14] Pondering, praying, listening, exercising faith—these are not words for the lazy or passive learner but rather are the requirements necessary for one ready to wrestle for that which is of great worth.

A later lecture attributed to Joseph Smith states, "We understand that when a man works by faith he works by mental exertion instead of physical force: it is by words instead of exerting his physical powers, with which every being works when he works by faith."[15] On this assertion Robert Millet, expanded, "We are not to understand . . . that exercising faith is merely an intellectual exercise or that those with unusual mental capacities necessarily have more faith. Rather, the mental exertion of which the Prophet spoke seems to be the rigor and strenuous labor, the soul searching and personal denial associated with coming to know the mind and will of God and then acting upon it."[16] Joseph had not only pondered and prayed, but he personally attended "their several meetings as often as occasion would permit" (Joseph Smith—History 1:8). He literally seemed to have done all he could to find the truth he so desperately desired.

Later, while in the sacred tutoring environment of the Liberty Jail (often described as a "temple prison"), Joseph taught the critical relationship between individual effort and spiritual learning. "The things of God are of deep import," he declared, "and time, and experience, and careful and ponderous and solemn thoughts can only find them out." Then, perhaps in his desire to expand on how far this searching must go, he continued, "Thy mind, O man! If thou wilt lead a soul unto salvation, must stretch as high as the utmost heavens, and search into and contemplate the darkest abyss, and the broad expanse of eternity."[17]

Thus, for an individual to expect revelation on the things of eternity, one must understand the wrestle required to obtain it. Joseph Smith instructed his brethren, "After your tribulations, if you do these things, and exercise fervent prayer and faith in the sight of God always, He shall give unto you knowledge by His Holy Spirit, yea by the unspeakable gift of the Holy Ghost."[18] It is interesting to note, among other things in this statement, the inclusion of tribulations for one trying to learn the things of God. In his own endeavors, even as described in his First Vision accounts, Joseph acknowledged "tribulation" as part of the learning experience. Tribulation itself does not ensure spiritual learning but rather, as was demonstrated in the 1835 account, the ability to push through the tribulation and rely on the Lord. Joseph did not cease to call upon God in the presence of the adversary but rather "kneeled again . . . and called on the Lord in mighty prayer."

In the popular 1838 account, Joseph described the attacks of the adversary as he attempted to cry to the Lord and attempted to endure in seeking the will of God. "I had scarcely done so, when immediately I was seized upon by some power which entirely overcame me, and had such an astonishing influence over me as to bind my tongue so that I could not speak. Thick darkness gathered around me, and it seemed to me for a time as if I were doomed to sudden destruction, . . . not to an imaginary ruin, but to the power of some actual being from the unseen world, who had such marvelous power as I had never before felt in any being."

As part of the pattern required for all spiritual learners, Joseph, through great effort on his own, fought through the darkness, the confusion, and the tribulation and continued to call upon the Lord. Although Joseph became starkly aware of the reality of the adversary in a very personal way, this did not impede him from his continued search for truth. He humbly acted in accordance with the prescriptive truth he found in the Bible and in so doing was given even greater light. Among other things, he learned the eternal truth that God is more powerful than Satan. He witnessed the existence of them both as a direct result of taking upon himself the personal responsibility to endure to the end—giving, in a sense, whatever it took.

Dependence and recognition that all truth comes from the divine. Recognizing as a young man that he was unable to make a decision based on his personal discussions with family and religious community leaders, Joseph went to the Bible, believing it to be the word of God. Through his struggle to obtain truth, however, he learned that even the Bible itself could not be interpreted by him alone, "for the teachers of religion of the different sects understood the same passages of scripture so differently as to destroy all confidence in settling the question by an appeal to the Bible." With this acknowledgment, he came to the conclusion that rather than finding the answer in the study of the Bible itself, he must do as the Bible taught and ask God.

It is critical to note here that Joseph trusted the Bible to be the word of God and believed it was literally from a divine source, and thus he was willing to obey its precepts. Mary Boys and Thomas Groome indicate various categories of perceptions of the Bible that in turn lead to a variety of implications. These categories of perception include, first, a "collection of ancient & diverse literature"; second, "reflection and telescoping of beliefs and experiences of communities"; third, "a classic text"; fourth, the "Word of God in human language"; and fifth, "Scripture." Only when the Bible is perceived as scripture, according to Boys and Groome, does the reader "allow [the] text to nurture, shape [their] identity or transform [them]."[19]

Feeling similar sentiments to those expressed by Timothy in the Bible, Joseph found himself in a category of those who were "ever learning, but never able to come to a knowledge of the truth" (2 Timothy 3:7). Thus Joseph, having learned of and considered upon the true nature of God's invitation to ask any question, and desiring to "seek" those who "worship him in spirit and truth" decided to cry unto the Lord, for he came to the conclusion that "there was none else to whom I could go" (1832 account).

In the 1835 account, he explained, "Information was what I most desired at this time, and with a fixed determination to obtain it, I called upon the Lord for the first time." In the 1838 account, Joseph similarly explained that he "came to the conclusion that I must either remain in darkness and confusion, or else I must do as James directs, that is, ask of God." In the 1842 account, Joseph specifically states that he "believ[ed] the word of God" and "had confidence in the declaration of James." In fact, he believed and had enough confidence to take the scriptural admonition at face value and "retired to a secret place in a grove and began to call upon the Lord."

George Albert Smith echoed the previous notion that Joseph spoke of his sacred experiences not merely to show what he had done but rather to invite others to have similar experiences. "Joseph Smith taught that every man and woman should seek the Lord for wisdom, that they might get knowledge from Him who is the fountain of knowledge."[20] Note in this quote that Joseph did not merely invite others to seek wisdom; he emphasized how to receive wisdom from God. Although Joseph received an answer directly from God, it is important to note that in the 1832 addition Joseph acknowledged, "I was filled with the spirit of God." Even though he had a personal visitation with God the Father and the Son, he still acknowledged the role of the Holy Ghost in the learning process.

On 7 April 1844, after years of spiritual learning and instruction from the Divine, Joseph expanded his explanation of the role of the Holy Ghost in his spiritual learning. "I have an old edition of the New Testament in the Latin, Hebrew, German and Greek languages. . . . I thank God that I have got this old book; but I thank him more for the gift of the Holy Ghost. I have got the oldest book in the world; but I have got the oldest book in my heart, even the gift of the Holy Ghost." He continued, "The Holy Ghost . . . is within me, and comprehends more than all the world; and I will associate myself with him."[21] President Harold B. Lee, a prophet himself and thus one of the most qualified people to write on the subject of spiritual learning, agreed: "A prophet . . . does not become a spiritual leader by studying books about religion, nor does he become one by attending a theological seminary. One becomes a prophet, a divinely called religious leader, by actual spiritual contacts. He gets his diploma, as it were, directly from God."[22]

The critical role of the Holy Ghost in confirming and teaching truth cannot be overlooked. In fact, the Lord himself declared in what later would become section 50 of the Doctrine and Covenants, "He that receiveth the word of truth, doth he receive it by the Spirit of truth or some other way? If it be some other way it is not of God" (D&C 50:19–20). Or in other words, eternal learning—any learning that applies to the salvation of the soul—comes only through a member of the Godhead. Joseph recognized that God's thoughts were higher than man's thoughts and his ways higher than man's ways. The closer Joseph seemed to draw to the Lord, the more he recognized his complete dependence on him and the immense gap between human and divine. In Liberty Jail, for example, Joseph meekly mused, "How much more dignified and noble are the thoughts of God, than the vain imaginations of the human heart!"[23] As is the case with all humble seekers of religious truth, the more they know about God, the more they recognize their complete dependence on him.

Acknowledgment of personal responsibility to learn and act. For this reason, as Elder David A. Bednar instructed, "Spiritual knowledge cannot be given by or borrowed from another person. Shortcuts to the desired destination do not exist. Cramming for the ultimate final examination on the day of judgment is not an option."[24] Perhaps one of the most critical principles of spiritual learning is that of taking responsibility for one's own learning and acting in accordance with newfound truth. Groome indicated that Jesus's whole intent as a teacher "was to empower people to become agents of their faith rather than dependents."[25] Thus, as Joseph Fielding McConkie asserted, "Real learning begins at the point that we assume personal responsibility for our learning. If there is a single moment of maturity, it is the moment at which we realize that the burden is ours to learn and not the teacher's to teach."[27] Not only had Joseph, at a young age, taken upon himself the responsibility of finding resolution to his perplexity through his intense search for truth, but he also recognized the importance of acting on the truth he had learned in order to find more truth. In so doing, his spiritual capacity expanded as he exercised his spirituality.[27]

In all of Joseph's accounts of the First Vision, it is clear that he searched for truth—eternal truth—with the intent to act upon what he had learned. In the 1832 account, Joseph simply recorded, "I cried unto the Lord." In the 1835 account, Joseph indicated after his study of the Bible that he "called upon the Lord for the first time." In the 1842 account, Joseph once again declared that he "began to call upon the Lord."

In the 1838 account, Joseph explained in greater detail the actions he took in preparation to ask. "After I had retired to the place where I had previously designed to go, having looked around me, and finding myself alone, I kneeled down and began to offer up the desires of my heart to God." This account provides additional understanding regarding Joseph's intent to act in faith. "My object in going to inquire of the Lord was to know which of all the sects was right, that I might know which to join. No sooner, therefore, did I get possession of myself, so as to be able to speak, than I asked the Personages who stood above me in the light, which of all the sects was right (for at this time it had never entered into my heart that all were wrong)—and which I should join." In this account, Joseph makes it clear that he was not merely asking for an opinion or guidance but rather that he desired to know the will and mind of God in order to then act in faith by joining one of the churches. As James A. Sanders, an American scholar of the Old Testament, summarized, when the scriptures are perceived as the literal word of God to man, they typically lead to two questions: *Who are we?* and *What are we to do?*[28] Not only then is Joseph told what to do (or rather, what not to do) at that moment, but in the 1832 account, Joseph was told who he was: "I saw the Lord and he spake unto me saying Joseph *my son* thy sins are forgiven thee." According to this account, the first thing the Lord communicates to Joseph is his divine identity as God's son.

Indeed, after the vision, when asked by his mother about his well-being, Joseph replied, "I have learned for myself" (Joseph Smith—History 1:20). Although he was surrounded by religious leaders at the time, so many that the area of his residence became known as the "burned-over district," Joseph was not content with borrowed light, nor did he settle for the opinions of others. Although he could have easily joined one of the religions of the day, succumbed to their teachings, and placed the responsibility for his salvation on the teacher, Joseph took responsibility for his own salvation. Elder Boyd K. Packer counseled, "There are too many in the Church who seem to be totally dependent, emotionally and spiritually, upon others. They subsist on some kind of emotional welfare. They are unwilling to sustain themselves. They become so dependent that they endlessly need to be shored up, lifted up, endlessly need encouragement, and they contribute little of their own."[29]

Joseph's determination to act upon the will of God did not end with his prayer but clearly continued as he acted upon, testified of, and defended his new found truth, even when persecuted until death. The object of the Lord's divine tutoring for Joseph was not merely for him to know something but for him to *do* something and, as a result, lead himself and others to *become* something. Validating this observation, Joseph later penned, "The object with me is to obey and teach others to obey God in just what He tells us to do. It mattereth not whether the principle is popular or unpopular, I will always maintain a true principle, even if I stand alone in it."[30]

It is this very attribute of obedience to God that made Joseph Smith a fruitful ground for divine tutoring and thus made him a self-reliant learner. By 1834, Joseph taught, "We consider that God has created man with a mind capable of instruction, and a faculty which may be enlarged in proportion to the heed and diligence given to the light communicated from heaven to the intellect."[31] Joseph was a great learner not because of a formal education or an uncommon IQ but instead because of his obedient, humble nature and compelling desire to know and do the will of God. In each of Joseph's First Vision accounts, he portrayed himself as a humble learner, willing to accept the teachings of God over his own findings and act accordingly. In the 1838 account, for example, he explained that he came to the determination to ask God, "concluding that if he gave wisdom to them that lacked wisdom, and would give liberally, and not upbraid, I might venture." Joseph put himself, therefore, in the category of one who lacked wisdom and recognized his complete, childlike dependence on the Lord. In so doing, he allowed the Lord to fill him with truth, line upon line, as he was able to bear.

Conclusion

Joseph was not one who wanted a monopoly on all things spiritual but rather desired that all would become self-reliant in this realm. In fact, he and his counselors in the First Presidency affirmed, "God hath not revealed anything to Joseph, but what He will make known unto the Twelve, and even the least Saint may know all things as fast as he is able to bear them, for the day must come when no man need say to his neighbor, Know ye the Lord; for all shall know Him . . . from the least to the greatest."[32] Thus, not only did Joseph Smith desire to instruct the Saints on the doctrines and truths associated with the First Vision but also desired to "qualify us to have our own spiritual experiences."[33] Therefore, all who follow Joseph's pattern of spiritual learning, by recognizing personal perplexity and cognitive dissonance, putting forth the necessary effort required to receive divine truth, and acting as an agent in responsibly applying the eternal truths, will also come to know for themselves, and having acted on the truth, become wise and, like Joseph, no longer lack wisdom.[34]

Notes

1. *Teachings of the Presidents of the Church: David O. McKay* (Salt Lake City: The Church of Jesus Christ of Latter-day Saints, 2011), 93.

2. Joseph Fielding McConkie, "The God of Joseph Smith," in *Regional Studies in Latter-day Saint Church History: Illinois*, ed. H. Dean Garrett (Provo, UT: Brigham Young University, Department of Church History and Doctrine, 1995), 206–7.

3. For a more in-depth discussion on these accounts, see Gospel Topics, "First Vision Accounts," www.lds.org/topics/first-vision-accounts?lang=eng. See also the works of Steven Harper, Milton Backman, and James B. Allen.

4. Gospel Topics, "First Vision Accounts."

5. History, circa Summer 1832, http://josephsmithpapers.org/paperSummary/history-circa-summer-1832?p=1. Although the quotes were taken directly from the accounts of Joseph Smith, spelling for these statements and all to follow have been standardized for ease in reading and understanding.

6. Journal, 1835–1836, http://josephsmithpapers.org/paperSummary/journal-1835-1836?p=24.

7. "Church History," 1 March 1842, http://josephsmithpapers.org/paperSummary/church-history-1-march-1842?p=1; Dean C. Jessee, "The Earliest Documented Accounts of Joseph Smith's First Vision," in *Opening the Heavens: Accounts of Divine Manifestations, 1820–1844*, ed. John W. Welch (Provo, UT: Brigham Young University Press; Salt Lake City: and Deseret Book, 2005), 17.

8. Robert M. Gagne, *The Conditions of Learning* (New York: Holt, 1965), 5.

9. Dallin H. Oaks, "The Challenge to Become," general conference address, October 2000, www.lds.org/general-conference/2000/10/the-challenge-to-become?lang=eng.

10. David A. Bednar, *Increase in Learning* (Salt Lake City: Deseret Book, 2011), 5.

11. James T. Dillon, *Questioning and Teaching: A Manual in Practice* (Eugene: Dillon, 2004), 18.

12. Gagne, *The Conditions of Learning*, 5.

13. Russell T. Osguthorpe, *The Education of the Heart: Rediscovering the Spiritual Roots of Learning* (American Fork, UT: Covenant Communications, 1996), 44.

14. Osguthorpe, *Education of the Heart*, 43–44.

15. Joseph Smith, comp., *Lectures on Faith* (Salt Lake City: Deseret Book, 1985), 7:3.

16. Robert L. Millet, "Line Upon Line" (unpublished document in author's possession, used by permission, April 2016), 236.

17. *Teachings of Presidents of the Church: Joseph Smith* (Salt Lake City: The Church of Jesus Christ of Latter-day Saints, 2007), 267.

18. *Teachings of Presidents of the Church: Joseph Smith*, 268; see Bednar, *Increase in Learning*, 7.

19. Mary C. Boys and Thomas H. Groome, "Principles and Pedagogy in Biblical Study," *Religious Education* 77, no. 5 (1982): 488–89.

20. George A. Smith, *Deseret News: Semi-Weekly*, 29 November 1870, 2.

21. *Teachings of Presidents of the Church: Joseph Smith*, 132.

22. Harold B. Lee, "He Lighted the Lamps of Faith," *Improvement Era*, February 1970, 94.

23. *Teachings of Presidents of the Church: Joseph Smith*, 267.

24. Bednar, *Increase in Learning*, 16.

25. Thomas H. Groome, *Will There Be Faith? A New Vision For Educating and Growing Disciples* (New York: Harper One, 2011), 31.

26. Joseph Fielding McConkie, *Teach and Reach* (Salt Lake City: Bookcraft, 1975), 48.

27. "Spiritual Exercise Increases Spiritual Capacity." Russell M. Nelson, "Twenty Questions," CES address to religious educators, Temple Square Assembly Hall, 13 September 1985, https://si.lds.org/library/talks/evening-with/twenty-questions?lang=eng.

28. James A. Sanders, "Torah and Christ," *Interpretation: A Journal of Bible and Theology* 29, no. 4 (1975): 378. See also his *God Has a Story Too: Sermons in Context* (Philadelphia: Augsburg Fortress, 1979), 1–27.

29. Boyd K. Packer, "Self-Reliance," fireside address delivered at Brigham Young University, 2 May 1975, https://speeches.byu.edu/talks/boyd-k-packer_self-reliance/.

30. *Teachings of Presidents of the Church: Joseph Smith*, 161.

31. *Teachings of Presidents of the Church: Joseph Smith*, 210.

32. *Teachings of Presidents of the Church: Joseph Smith*, 268.

33. McConkie, "The God of Joseph Smith," 206–7.

34. For more insights and reflection on this topic, see Elder Dieter F. Uchtdorf's testimony in "Truth Restored," a BYU Education Week address, 22 August 2006, *BYU Speeches*, https://speeches.byu.edu/talks/dieter-f-uchtdorf_truth-restored/.

5

The Articles of Faith

A FRAMEWORK FOR TEACHING THE RESTORATION

Ryan S. Gardner

Ryan S. Gardner is a professor of Religious Education
at Brigham Young University–Idaho.

Speaking at the 1993 Parliament of the World's Religions in Chicago, Illinois, then Elder Russell M. Nelson of the Quorum of the Twelve Apostles asserted that institutional integrity and religious tolerance would be "enhanced as we teach clearly and courteously the tenets of our religions."[1] To do this, President Nelson introduced his international, interfaith audience to the Articles of Faith. In his speech, he modeled how these thirteen statements could be employed to convey concisely and clearly the foundational beliefs, history, and practices of The Church of Jesus Christ of Latter-day Saints. While the Articles of Faith were never intended as a comprehensive statement of LDS beliefs or practices,[2] this essay endeavors to make a case for the Articles of Faith as an apostolically endorsed organizing framework[3] for helping students systematically deepen their understanding of the history and doctrine of the restored gospel of Jesus Christ.[4] As they do so, students will be better prepared to articulate their beliefs "clearly and courteously," as President Nelson suggested, thus providing an environment in which the Spirit of the Lord can attend their teaching and conversations.

81

Modern Apostolic Endorsement

Five years after Elder Nelson's address in Chicago, Elder L. Tom Perry reflected on the sesquicentennial celebration of the westward migration of the Mormon pioneers as "a grand opportunity . . . for the peoples of the world to learn more about who we are." He then challenged members of the Church to "determine whether we will just let it [the celebration] stand as a great media event or whether it will be an opportunity to better fulfill our charge to take the gospel to every nation, kindred, tongue, and people." Considering his own ability "to make a contribution to the kingdom," Elder Perry reported, "I reached the conclusion that if I *studied the content of each of the Articles of Faith*, I could explain and defend every gospel principle I might have the opportunity to expound to someone searching for the restored truth."[5] He then issued the following invitation and encouragement:

> What a great blessing it would be if every member of the Church memorized the Articles of Faith and *became knowledgeable about the principles contained in each.* We would be better prepared to share the gospel with others. . . . I encourage each of you to *study the Articles of Faith and the doctrines they teach*. . . . If you will *use them as a guide to direct your studies of the Savior's doctrine*, you will find yourselves prepared to declare your witness of the restored, true church of the Lord.[6]

Elder Perry's challenge clearly indicates that memorizing the Articles of Faith to gain familiarity with them is a good start, but it is not enough. Members of the Church should also diligently study the Articles of Faith to deepen their understanding of the truths connected therewith and use them to clearly and concisely teach the fundamental truths of the Restoration to others.[7]

Almost a decade after Elder Perry's apostolic admonition, Elder M. Russell Ballard offered the following assessment of our efforts to clearly teach our beliefs to others: "The many misunderstandings and false information about the Church are somewhat our own fault for not clearly explaining who we are and what we believe. The Public Affairs Committee, on which I serve, has learned that there is a great need for clear, simple statements that present those who are curious with the basics about the Church as it is today."[8] To prevent the spread of misinformation, misunderstanding, and prejudice concerning the Church, Elder Ballard recommended twice that members of the Church use the Articles of Faith in their conversations with people from other religious traditions.[9] Eighteen months after this recommendation, Elder Perry reported in the October 2009 general conference that "over one-half of the people in the United States and Canada have little or no awareness of our practices and beliefs." Elder Perry reiterated that when such persons are "exposed to clear and accurate information regarding Church beliefs and doctrines, their attitudes become positive and open."[10] Prophets, seers, and revelators have been indicating that we still have work to do in clearly communicating the message of the Restoration to others.

Perhaps this was one factor that led Elder Perry to speak again about the Articles of Faith in general conference in October 2013. After recounting his own experience of memorizing the Articles of Faith in Primary and illustrating how they teach core truths of the Restoration, Elder Perry taught:

> The Articles of Faith supply us with key doctrines of the Restoration. Each article of faith adds unique value to our understanding of the gospel of Jesus Christ.
>
> My Primary teacher . . . taught me to *seek the deep meaning contained in these simple Articles of Faith.* She promised me that if I would invest in learning these sacred truths, the knowledge I acquired would change my life for the better, and I testify to you that it has. . . .
>
> I encourage you to use your bright minds to study and learn the Articles of Faith *and the doctrines they teach.* They are among the most important and certainly the most concise statements of doctrine in the Church. *If you will use them as a guide to direct your studies of the gospel of Jesus Christ, you will find yourself prepared to declare your witness of the restored truth to the world.* You will be able to declare in simple, straightforward, and profound ways the core beliefs you hold dear as a member of The Church of Jesus Christ of Latter-day Saints.[11]

While memorizing the Articles of Faith would mean nothing more than a lot of words unless we understood the doctrines and principles contained in them, Elder Perry's injunction promises that members of the Church who anchor themselves in the core doctrines found in the Articles of Faith will have greater clarity and power as they teach the truths of the Restoration to others.

Historical Background

Modern exhortations from Apostles and other General Authorities[12] reminding Church members of the value and impact of the Articles of Faith are rooted in their prophetic origin and historic durability. In 1842, the Prophet Joseph Smith penned thirteen statements—known later as the Articles of Faith—as the conclusion to the Wentworth Letter, in which he proposed to provide a brief summary of "the rise, progress, persecution, and faith of the Latter-day Saints."[13] From 1842 to 1857, the Articles of Faith were published numerous times in the United States and throughout the world as a concise statement of the fundamental beliefs of the Latter-day Saints.[14] The most notable of these publications was Elder Franklin D. Richards's inclusion of the Articles of Faith in his 1851 booklet, *The Pearl of Great Price*. In the October 1880 general conference of the Church, a revised form of Richards's document was accepted by the membership of the Church as part of the standard works of the Church.[15] Thus, the Articles of Faith entered the LDS canon.[16] While the Saints were gathered in what would become a historic general conference in October 1890, Orson F. Whitney again presented the Articles of Faith by themselves for a sustaining vote just prior to reading a revelation from President Wilford Woodruff, known as "the Manifesto," to end the Church's practice of plural marriage. Perhaps this was to remind the Saints of certain core beliefs that would fortify their commitment to follow their current prophet's counsel in "being subject to kings, presidents, rulers and magistrates, in obeying, honoring, and sustaining the law" (A of F 1:12).[17]

On the eve of the twentieth century in 1899, Elder James E. Talmage of the Quorum of the Twelve Apostles published a series of lectures commissioned and reviewed by the First Presidency of the Church and other General Authorities, "delivered before Theology classes of the Church University and at other schools."[18] This work, titled *A Study of the Articles of Faith*, has been translated into thirteen different languages and been through more than fifty English editions. For many decades, it was part of the approved library for missionaries of the Church. As the twentieth century moved toward its close, another Apostle, Elder Bruce R. McConkie, prepared the manuscript for *A New Witness for the Articles of Faith*, which would be published post-humously in 1985. As is evident from the titles, both books use the Articles of Faith as a framework for studying and expounding the key doctrines and events relative to the Restoration of Jesus Christ's gospel and Church on the earth, similar to what I am proposing here.

The value of the Articles of Faith as "a guide in faith and conduct"[19] is further supported in the modern era by their frequent use in general conference by General Authorities and other general auxiliary leaders of the Church. Table 1 shows how often the Articles of Faith have been cited—singly, in various combinations, or as a whole—in general conference from 1950 to 2014.

Table 1. Articles of Faith Citations in General Conference, 1950–2014 (by Decade)[20]

1950s	1960s	1970s	1980s	1990s	2000s	2010–14
108	127	84	48	103	77	53

Throughout the last seven decades, the Articles of Faith have been cited at least six hundred times in general conference. In addition to the way the Articles of Faith were promulgated, canonized, and utilized throughout the latter half of the nineteenth century and into the first half of the twentieth century, the frequency with which leaders of the Church have turned to the Articles of Faith in their public discourses in the second half of the twentieth century and into the twenty-first century attests to their importance and practical use in communicating the truths of the restored gospel of Jesus Christ.

Articulating Our Beliefs

This historical background provides a powerful backdrop for examining just a few anecdotal examples in which Church leaders have extolled the value and impact of using the Articles of Faith to share our beliefs with others. After inquiring whether those in attendance at the priesthood session of the October 1975 general conference had the Articles of Faith memorized "word perfect," President Spencer W. Kimball related a story about a young Primary boy on a train from Utah to Los Angeles. When a fellow passenger found out the young man was a Mormon from Utah, he inquired about Mormon beliefs. As President Kimball recounted the story, the boy did more than just repeat the Articles of Faith "word perfect" in response. The recitation of each article led to a discussion about specific doctrines of the gospel and practices of the Church which inspired the man to inquire more diligently about the Restoration. He was astonished "not only at the ability of this young boy to outline the whole program of the Church, but at the very completeness of its doctrine." From this experience, President Kimball proposed, "You are always prepared with a sermon when you know the Articles of Faith."[21]

While serving as the second counselor in the Primary general presidency, Susan L. Warner related the following experience regarding the usefulness of the Articles of Faith:

> Not long ago our granddaughter Susie received a copy of the scriptures. She lives in an area where her classmates and teacher are not members of the Church, so she wanted to share with them the Articles of Faith that were recorded in her new scriptures. She decided it would be appropriate to do this at school during the time that was scheduled for sharing something newsworthy. When the time came, eight-year-old Susie stood before her classmates and began, "We believe in God, the Eternal Father, and in His Son, Jesus Christ, and in the Holy Ghost" (A of F 1:1). She continued, but when she got to the seventh article of faith, one classmate loudly complained, "This isn't a current event!" The teacher quickly responded, "Well, it's news to me!"
>
> Each of us can share the good news of the gospel and give words to our convictions. If we are sensitive to the whisperings of the Spirit, we can find opportunities to humbly express our beliefs. Even a shy, eight-year-old child felt the desire to share the articles of her faith.[22]

Many members of the Church may be unwilling to share their beliefs with others because they are unsure about what they should say. They might not initiate conversations about religion with others because they worry that someone will ask a question that they aren't sure how to answer. For example, one recent study affirmed that a large sample of LDS seminary students in Utah may lack confidence in sharing the gospel with others.[23] Even for those who may be shy or unsure about sharing their beliefs with others, knowing the Articles of Faith and understanding more deeply the truths connected with them can give individuals a place to begin as they trust in the Lord's promise that those who open their mouths to declare the truth will have them filled with the words of the Lord (see D&C 33:8–10).

During the 2006 worldwide leadership training broadcast, President Thomas S. Monson reported that his Primary teacher helped him develop a "knowledge of the Articles of Faith [which] was most helpful" during the difficult assignment to supervise the work of the Church in East Germany.[24] President Monson then recounted the conversion of a friend, which came as a result of a young girl who discussed the Articles of Faith with him on a bus ride from Salt Lake City to San Francisco. This man was so impressed and inspired by the little girl's knowledge of her faith that he further investigated the Church and later joined it, along with his wife and their six daughters. Considering the ramifications of this encounter, President Monson said, "Countless are those who have been brought to a knowledge of the gospel by the members of this family—all because a young child had been taught the Articles of Faith and had the ability and the courage to proclaim the truth to one who was seeking the light of the gospel."[25] These three experiences demonstrate how "the weak things of the world shall come forth" as ambassadors of the Restoration, "that every man [and woman] might speak in the name of God the Lord, even the Savior of the world . . . that the fulness of my gospel might be proclaimed by the weak and the simple unto the ends of the world" (D&C 1:19–20, 23).

The Articles of Faith as a Study Guide

The Articles of Faith can only be a useful resource in preparing disciples to fulfill the divine injunction from Doctrine and Covenants section 1 as we move beyond merely having the Articles of Faith memorized "word perfect," though that may be a useful beginning. As Elder Perry suggested, we will need to help students accomplish the following: (1) "study the Articles of Faith and the doctrines they teach," (2) "[become] knowledgeable about the principles contained in each," (3) "seek the deep meaning contained in these simple Articles of Faith," and (4) "use them as a guide to direct [their] studies of the gospel of Jesus Christ, [so they] will find [themselves] prepared to declare [their] witness of the restored truth to the world."[26]

While Elder James E. Talmage proposed that the Articles of Faith "suggest themselves as a convenient outline for a study of the theology of The Church of Jesus Christ of Latter-day Saints,"[27] there may be many ways to approach and utilize the Articles of Faith. I will outline one approach that can help students learn how to study and use the Articles of Faith in a way that can empower them to teach and testify of the truths and practices of the Church with greater concision and clarity, both within the household of faith and in the broader arena of public discourse.

Tables 2–4[28] provide a basic outline for how the Articles of Faith might help us study the history and doctrine of the Restoration. Since not all potential doctrinal subjects associated with each Article of Faith could be listed here, only a few have been noted as examples. Likewise, there are many more texts that could be used to teach the gospel truths associated with a particular Article of Faith. The few examples listed here focus on passages from Restoration scriptures (Book of Mormon, Doctrine and Covenants, Pearl of Great Price) that have relevant doctrinal value or represent key events of the Restoration associated with that Article of Faith. For example, the First Vision (JS—History 1:10–26) has significant impact on the LDS view of the Godhead; Joseph Smith and Sidney Rigdon's vision (D&C 76) plays a critical role in the LDS view of salvation; and JS—History 1:68–75, D&C 27:12–13, D&C 110, and D&C 128:20–24 all mention key events relative to the restoration of priesthood authority and keys.

In table 2, the first four articles of faith seem to deal primarily with matters of theology and soteriology. Broadly speaking, theology deals with the study of God and the relationship between humans and the divine. Assuming the existence of God, theological inquiries focus on the nature of God, the role of God in the world, the relationship between God and the existence of evil, and other like matters. As a branch of theology, soteriology focuses on the nature of salvation, how salvation is made possible, who can be saved, and the roles of God and man in the process of salvation. Studying and discussing the following doctrinal subjects associated with the first four articles of faith, as they were restored through key events and revelations of the Restoration, can help students understand key theological and soteriological truths.

Table 2. Articles of Faith 1–4: Theology and Soteriology[29]

Article of Faith	Doctrinal Subjects	Key Events and Revelations
1. We believe in God, the Eternal Father, and in His Son, Jesus Christ, and in the Holy Ghost.	Godhead Fatherhood of God Man as a child of God Divine Sonship of Jesus Christ Mission of the Holy Ghost	D&C 76:1–24 D&C 93:1–21 Moses 1 JS—H 1:10–26
2. We believe that men will be punished for their own sins, and not for Adam's transgression.	Agency and accountability The Fall Salvation of little children	2 Nephi 2 D&C 29:36–50 Moses 4:1–31 Moses 6:48–57
3. We believe that through the Atonement of Christ, all mankind may be saved, by obedience to the laws and ordinances of the Gospel.	Atonement of Jesus Christ Grace Obedience Ordinances of salvation Redemption of the dead	2 Nephi 9:3–26 Mosiah 3:4–13 Alma 7:7–13 D&C 19:15–21 D&C 76 D&C 84:17–28 D&C 131; 132:5–24 D&C 138
4. We believe that the first principles and ordinances of the gospel are: first, faith in the Lord Jesus Christ; second, Repentance; third, Baptism by immersion for the remission of sins; fourth, Laying on of hands for the gift of the Holy Ghost.	Faith in Jesus Christ Repentance Baptism and confirmation The gift of the Holy Ghost	2 Nephi 31 3 Nephi 27:13–22 D&C 20:20–27, 37 Moses 5:57–59; 6:58–68

As students come to better know the nature of God, their relationship to God, and God's plan for the salvation of his children, they will have a solid foundation from which to share the truths of the Restoration with others. As they seek to live according to these truths, they will have an increased measure of the Spirit of God to guide them in their own lives and to bear witness of these doctrines and principles to others.

As outlined in table 3, articles of faith 5–9 give primary emphasis to matters of ecclesiology and canon. Ecclesiology is the study of the Church and striving to seek to understand its role in the lives of God's followers and in establishing his kingdom on the earth. Ecclesiology explores the need for a Church, the need for divine authority, church organization, the role of the Church in God's work of salvation, and the place of spiritual gifts in the Church. Just as the Church is one resource God has established for the guidance of his children in the journey of salvation, the scriptures are another. The canon, which Latter-day Saints usually refer to as the standard works, refers to "the authoritative collection of the sacred books used by the true believers in Christ."[30] However, Latter-day Saints have a unique view of the canon in contrast with traditional Christianity, believing in an open canon that can be adjusted and added to by authorized prophets and apostles. Members of the Church should, therefore, be especially prepared to explain the Latter-day Saint attitude toward the Bible, the need and benefit of additional scripture, and the role of revelation in connection with scripture.

The importance of these doctrines cannot be overestimated. Priesthood authority and ongoing revelation are key to the Restoration and the reorganization of the Church in the last days.[31] And the gift of the Holy Ghost with its attendant spiritual gifts is a distinguishing feature of the true Church of Christ.[32] Especially in an era when increasing numbers of people doubt the need to belong to any church,[33] the holy scriptures are often neglected,[34] and the words of prophets are rejected as either unenlightened or outdated, there is an increased need for Latter-day Saints who can clearly articulate the importance and impact of the Church, the gift of the Holy Ghost, the scriptures, and ongoing revelation.

The final four articles, as shown in table 4, deal primarily with matters of eschatology and morality. Eschatology is a specific branch of theology that focuses on the final events in the history of the world and the fate of humankind. Within the Christian faith particularly, eschatology seeks to better understand the signs of Jesus Christ's return to the earth, the role of the Church and its members in preparing for the return of the Savior, and the ultimate destiny of the earth. The very name of the Church indicates our special interest in the events of the last days, and our belief that we live in the

Table 3. Articles of Faith 5–9: Ecclesiology and Canon

Article of Faith	Doctrinal Subjects	Key Events and Revelations
5. We believe that a man must be called of God, by prophecy, and by the laying on of hands by those who are in authority, to preach the Gospel and administer in the ordinances thereof.	Priesthood authority Priesthood keys	3 Nephi 12:1–2 Moroni 3 D&C 22 D&C 27:12–13 D&C 110 D&C 128:20–24 JS—H 1:68–72
6. We believe in the same organization that existed in the Primitive Church, namely, apostles, prophets, pastors, teachers, evangelists, and so forth.	Organization of the Church Church Structure Blessings of Church membership	3 Nephi 27:1–12 Moroni 6 D&C 10:52–56, 62–70 D&C 20:1–4, 38–60 D&C 90:1–5 D&C 107: 1–15, 22–26, 33–38, 58–67, 91–97
7. We believe in the gift of tongues, prophecy, revelation, visions, healing, interpretation of tongues, and so forth.	Gifts of the Spirit Role of spiritual gifts in the Church Gifts of the Spirit discerned by priesthood authority	Moroni 10:8–33 D&C 28:9–14 D&C 46 D&C 50
8. We believe the Bible to be the word of God as far as it is translated correctly; we also believe the Book of Mormon to be the word of God.	Bible Book of Mormon Standard works (Canon)	1 Nephi 13:20–41 D&C 20:6–12 D&C 35:20; 45:60–62 JS—H 1:9–13
9. We believe all that God has revealed, all that He does now reveal, and we believe that He will yet reveal many great and important things pertaining to the Kingdom of God.	Revelation for the Church Revelation for individuals Role of prophets	D&C 6 D&C 8 D&C 9 D&C 21 D&C 28:1–7 D&C 43:1–7 D&C 76:1–10 D&C 101:32–35

final dispensation of the gospel of Jesus Christ before his triumphant return and global reign—we are *Latter-day* Saints.[35] One who accepts the literality of Jesus Christ's return to earth as Judge and King also accepts the obligation to live in such a way that he or she will be prepared to meet him, either in this life or in the next. This leads to the topic of morality, which is much broader in scope than pertaining to sexual purity alone.

Morality has to do with right and wrong behavior required for establishing and living in the kingdom of God. Disciples of Jesus Christ deal with issues of morality every day as they determine how to follow the light in a darkening world, and how to seek for, recognize, and live according to truth amidst error, confusion, and persecution. Together, the eleventh and twelfth articles of faith have interesting relevance to morality: "Members of the Church seek to live according to the moral values taught by Jesus Christ and His servants and to be an influence for sound moral values in society and government. . . . Freedom is inextricably linked to our morality, and religious believers and institutions are essential to preserving morality."[36] Further, speaking of the thirteenth article of faith as a guide for morality and discipleship, Elder Perry taught: "The thirteenth article of faith provides special insight into how we should conduct our lives and present ourselves." And, finally, regarding the Articles of Faith as a whole, Elder Perry declared, "All of us should aspire to embody these attributes and lead lives that exemplify them."[37]

In a world of increasing doubt, despair, and discouragement, striving for a better understanding of and belief in our destiny as a Church under the influence of the Holy Ghost will lead to the kind of "redemptive faith" that Elder Jeffrey R. Holland said must be "exercised toward experiences in the future—the unknown, which provides an opportunity for the miraculous."[38] For example, Helaman connected the strong faith of his stripling warriors "in the prophecies concerning that which is to come" with their ability to "stand fast in that liberty wherewith God has made them free . . . [to be] strict to remember the Lord their God from day to day; yea, . . . [and to] observe to keep his statutes, and his judgments, and his commandments continually" (Alma 58:40). Likewise, not only must Latter-day Saints know and have faith in the truth regarding our future, but they must live according to it. Orthodoxy must align with orthopraxy in order for discipleship to

Table 4. *Articles of Faith 10–13: Eschatology and Morality*

Article(s) of Faith	Doctrinal Subjects	Key Events and Revelations
10. We believe in the literal gathering of Israel and in the restoration of the Ten Tribes; that Zion (the New Jerusalem) will be built upon the American continent; that Christ will reign personally upon the earth; and, that the earth will be renewed and receive its paradisiacal glory.	Gathering of Israel Zion/New Jerusalem Second Coming of Jesus Christ Millennium Destiny of the earth	1 Nephi 22:3–12 3 Nephi 21:22–29 D&C 29:1–23 D&C 37; 38:31–33 D&C 45:16–75 D&C 57 D&C 88:17–20 D&C 101:22–36 D&C 133 Moses 7:17–21, 61–64
11. We claim the privilege of worshiping Almighty God according to the dictates of our own conscience, and allow all men the same privilege, let them worship how, where, or what they may. 12. We believe in being subject to kings, presidents, rulers, and magistrates, in obeying, honoring, and sustaining the law.	Religious freedom Civic responsibility Citizenship	D&C 98:1–18 D&C 101:76–95 D&C 134 OD 1; "Excerpts from Three Addresses by President Wilford Woodruff Regarding the Manifesto"
13. We believe in being honest, true, chaste, benevolent, virtuous, and in doing good to all men; indeed, we may say that we follow the admonition of Paul—We believe all things, we hope all things, we have endured many things, and hope to be able to endure all things. If there is anything virtuous, lovely, or of good report or praiseworthy, we seek after these things.	Honesty and integrity Chastity Benevolence and service Virtue Hope Enduring to the end Conversion Discipleship Sanctification	Mosiah 24:8–15 3 Nephi 27:19–22 Moroni 7:5–19 Moroni 10:32–33 D&C 11:12–14 D&C 42:18–29, 40–42 D&C 58:2–4, 26–29 D&C 59 D&C 88:25–29, 36–40, 67–69 D&C 93:40–50 D&C 136:10–11, 17–30

lead to exaltation. In other words, in the end, it will be of little use or benefit to us to be *right* if we are not also *good*. As we seek to live in harmony with our vision of the glorious kingdom of God to come, the Holy Spirit will guide us as we invite others, by word and example, to make that vision a reality with the grace of God attending us.

A brief example of using the Articles of Faith in the classroom will illustrate how this structure for using them as a study guide for the Restoration can be helpful for students. After briefly introducing students in some of my classes to this approach to the articles of faith, I invited them to write down a question that someone who is not a member of the Church might sincerely ask them about the beliefs or practices of the Church. Students then considered which category (i.e., theological, soteriological, ecclesiological, moral, and so forth) that question most closely matches. They then took a few moments to consider how they might use articles of faith from that corresponding category as a starting point to begin a response to the question. They didn't just recite the article of faith or relevant parts as the answer to the question. Rather, I encouraged them to use the article of faith as a "springboard" into key revelations or historical events that explain the doctrines or practices of the Church relative to the question. As students then discussed their questions and responses with a partner or in small groups, they found that the articles of faith provide a solid starting point for their conversation and increase their confidence when explaining or defending the truths of the Restoration to others.

Conclusion

For over 170 years, the Articles of Faith have stood as a succinct summary of the most basic tenets of The Church of Jesus Christ of Latter-day Saints. They can be a powerful organizing framework for helping students deepen their understanding of and ability to teach the doctrine and history of the Restoration. Moreover, Elder McConkie's closing exhortation in *A New Witness for the Articles of Faith* encourages teachers and students to not only study the truths associated with the Articles of Faith, but incorporate the saving doctrines and principles therein into their lives:

It is the hope and prayer of this disciple that the doctrines announced and the truths taught in the Articles of Faith may live in the hearts of the Latter-day Saints and of all who will yet join with them in striving to gain that eternal life which is the greatest of all the gifts of God. There is no salvation in an unused truth; it is only when men conform to the truth and make it a part of their very being that they advance and progress and finally qualify to return to the Eternal Presence.[39]

Studying and living according to the truths contained in and connected to these thirteen simple statements will provide us with a sure foundation for both faith and conduct as we carry forward the message and work of the Restoration of the gospel throughout the earth.

Notes

1.   Russell M. Nelson, "Combatting Spiritual Drift—Our Global Pandemic," *Ensign*, November 1993, 103.

2.   While acknowledging that Latter-day Saints have no creed "as a complete code of faith," Elder Talmage recognized the Articles of Faith as "an epitome of the tenets of the Church" and "a convenient outline for a study of the theology of The Church of Jesus Christ of Latter-day Saints." James E. Talmage, *A Study of the Articles of Faith: Being a Consideration of the Principal Doctrines of The Church of Jesus Christ of Latter-day Saints*, 12th ed. (Salt Lake City: The Church of Jesus Christ of Latter-day Saints, 1924), 6–7. Similarly, Elder Bruce R. McConkie noted that while the Articles of Faith do not "mention all the basic doctrines" of salvation, "when we have mastered what is in them, we will be in a position to go forward in the University of the Universe, studying and believing until we believe and know all things." Bruce R. McConkie, *A New Witness for the Articles of Faith* (Salt Lake City: Deseret Book, 1985), 16, 42.

3.   An organizing framework provides a structure to guide the development and learning of content, concepts, beliefs, etc. President Boyd K. Packer suggested a similar idea when he encouraged religious educators to create a one-page summary of the plan of salvation. See "The Great Plan of Happiness," *CES Symposium on the Doctrine and Covenants/Church History*, 10 August 1993, Brigham Young University. Not all of the doctrines of salvation can be included on one page, but a one-page summary provides a framework to which all of the truths of the gospel can be connected. Likewise, the Articles of Faith can serve as an organizing framework for studying the history and doctrine of the Restoration.

4.   For a simple example showing how the Articles of Faith can provide a framework for simultaneously teaching the doctrines of the gospel and events from Church history, see John W. Welch, "The Articles of Faith and the Life of Joseph Smith," *Ensign*, December 2013, 70–75. Another model for teaching the doctrine of the restored gospel

within the history of the Restoration can be found in D&C 20:1–37. Verse 17 reminds us that it is "by these things" (i.e. the historical events alluded to in verses 1–12) that "we know" the doctrines set forth in verses 17–37.

5.   Perry, "The Articles of Faith," *Ensign*, May 1998, 22–23; emphasis added.

6.   Perry, "Articles of Faith," 23–24; emphasis added.

7.   Steven P. Sondrup discusses the value of the Articles of Faith for use within the Church and in proselyting efforts in "On Confessing Belief: Thoughts on the Language of the Articles of Faith," in *Literature of Belief: Sacred Scripture and Religious Experience*, ed. Neal E. Lambert (Provo, UT: Religious Studies Center, 1981), 197–216. His examination of the rhetorical power and deeper implications of the formulaic statement, "we believe," demonstrates both the unifying power of the Articles of Faith for believers and their practical benefits when declaring these fundamental truths to others.

8.   M. Russell Ballard, "Faith, Family, Facts, and Fruits," *Ensign*, November 2007, 25.

9.   Ballard, "Faith, Family, Facts, and Fruits," 25, 27.

10.   L. Tom Perry, "Bring Souls unto Me," *Ensign*, May 2009, 110.

11.   L. Tom Perry, "The Doctrines and Principles Contained in the Articles of Faith," *Ensign*, November 2013, 46, 48; emphasis added.

12.   In addition to examples already cited, see Marion G. Romney, "Maintaining Spirituality," *Ensign*, November 1979, 16; Thomas S. Monson, "Preparing the Way," *Ensign*, May 1980, 6–7; Neal A. Maxwell, "Answer Me," *Ensign*, November 1988, 31; Joseph B. Wirthlin, "Seeking the Good," *Ensign*, May 1992, 86; Robert D. Hales, "Gaining a Testimony of God the Father; His Son, Jesus Christ; and the Holy Ghost," *Ensign*, May 2008, 30; and William R. Walker, "Three Presiding High Priests," *Ensign*, May 2008, 38. The *New Era* also ran a series of articles from July 2005 to July 2006 that included prophetic messages, personal experiences, and suggestions for application related to each of the Articles of Faith.

13.   "The Wentworth Letter," *Ensign*, July 2002, 27; the original letter to John Wentworth was published in *Times and Seasons* 3, no. 9, 1 March 1842, 706–10. For more on the background of the Wentworth Letter, see "Church History, 1 March 1842," http://josephsmithpapers.org/paperSummary/church-history-1-march-1842. For more on the historical development of the Articles of Faith specifically, John W. Welch and David J. Whittaker have explored the origins and development of the Articles of Faith in commendable detail in "'We Believe. . . . ': Development of the Articles of Faith," *Ensign*, September 1979, 51–55. RoseAnn Benson has also discussed the Articles of Faith within the theological context of nineteenth-century America in "The Articles of Faith: Answering the Doctrinal Questions of the 'Second Great Awakening'" in *Joseph Smith and the Doctrinal Restoration* (Provo, UT: Religious Studies Center, 2005), 46–64.

14.   See Ed Brandt, "The Origin and Importance of the Articles of Faith," in *Studies in Scripture,* vol. 2: *The Pearl of Great Price*, ed. Robert L. Millet and Kent P. Jackson (Salt Lake City: Randall Book, 1985), 411–20.

15.   More on the canonization process of the Pearl of Great Price can be found in H. Donl Peterson, "The Birth and Development of the Pearl of Great Price," in *Studies*

in Scripture, vol. 2, 11–23; Richard D. Draper, S. Kent Brown, and Michael D. Rhodes, *The Pearl of Great Price: A Verse-by-Verse Commentary* (Salt Lake City: Deseret Book, 2005), 1–11; and in *Encyclopedia of Mormonism*, s.v. "Pearl of Great Price," 1070–72.

16. While some had reservations about including the Articles of Faith in the Pearl of Great Price, this question was settled in the October 1890 general conference of the Church; see Draper, Brown, and Rhodes, *Pearl of Great Price*, 9; and Peterson, "Birth and Development," 20.

17. See "The Manifesto and the End of Plural Marriage," in LDS Gospel Topics, https://www.lds.org/topics/the-manifesto-and-the-end-of-plural-marriage?lang=eng#22.

18. Talmage, *Articles of Faith*, iii.

19. Talmage, *Articles of Faith*, 6–7.

20. At the current rate for the present decade (roughly 13.25 citations per year), total citations for the first decade of the twenty-first century could total more than 130, making this opening decade the one in which the Articles of Faith were cited the most in the last 70 years. At any rate, barring a sudden cessation of the usage of the Articles of Faith, it will likely have the highest number of citations of any decade in the last fifty years. Data was collected using http://scriptures.byu.edu/.

21. Spencer W. Kimball, "The Privilege of Holding the Priesthood," *Ensign*, November 1975, 79.

22. Susan L. Warner, "Bear Record of Him," *Ensign*, November 1998, 66.

23. See Anthony R. Sweat, "Student Oral Participation and Perceived Spiritual Experiences in Latter-day Saint Seminary" (PhD diss., Utah State University, 2011), 84. Of the twenty survey items students were asked to evaluate in regards to their in-class spiritual experiences, "I felt confidence in speaking to others about the gospel" was ranked the lowest. Latter-day Saints aren't the only youth who have this challenge. When this survey was administered to a sample of Evangelical youth in Canada, they likewise ranked this same item last in regards to their comparable in-class religious education experience; see also Arch Wong, Anthony R. Sweat, and Ryan S. Gardner, "Pedagogy of the Spirit: Comparing Evangelical and Latter-day Saint Youth Self-Reported In-Class Spiritual Experiences," *Religious Education* (2017), article accepted for publication.

24. Thomas S. Monson, "Examples of Great Teachers," *Ensign*, June 2007, 109.

25. Monson, "Examples of Great Teachers," 110.

26. L. Tom Perry, "The Articles of Faith," *Ensign*, May 1998, 22–24.

27. Talmage, *Articles of Faith*, 7.

28. While I alone am responsible for the content of tables 2–4, I express thanks to Dale Sturm, John Thomas, Tomm Chapman, Greg Venema, John Parker, Greg Palmer, and Gary Purse for their excellent contributions.

29. Gerald E. Smith has recently explored the contribution of the Book of Mormon to the development of the Prophet Joseph Smith and the theology of Mormonism in *Schooling the Prophet: How the Book of Mormon Influenced Joseph Smith and the Early Restoration* (Provo, UT: Neal A. Maxwell Institute for Religious

Scholarship, 2015). As a major revelation of the Restoration, it seems entirely appropriate to include Book of Mormon passages when studying key doctrines of the restored gospel of Jesus Christ.

30.   LDS Bible Dictionary, s.v. "Canon," 630.

31.   See Jeffrey R. Holland, "Our Most Distinguishing Feature," *Ensign*, May 2005, 43–45.

32.   See David A. Bednar, "Receive the Holy Ghost," *Ensign*, November 2010, 94–97.

33.   "The Christian share of the population [in the United States] is declining and the religiously unaffiliated share is growing in all four major geographic regions of the country. Religious 'nones' now constitute 19% of the adult population in the South (up from 13% in 2007), 22% of the population in the Midwest (up from 16%), 25% of the population in the Northeast (up from 16%) and 28% of the population in the West (up from 21%). In the West, the religiously unaffiliated are more numerous than Catholics (23%), evangelicals (22%) and every other religious group." Pew Research Center, "America's Changing Religious Landscape," http://www.pewforum.org/2015/05/12/americas-changing-religious-landscape/.

34.   While 82 percent of Americans in a 2014 sample survey considered themselves somewhat to highly knowledgeable about the Bible, 26 percent of the sample reported that they never read the Bible. Only 15 percent of those surveyed reported that they read the Bible daily; only 43 percent could correctly name the first five books of the Old Testament; and 55 percent could name the four Gospels. Jennifer Barry Hawes, "Studies show many Americans not reading the Bible, lack basic knowledge," *The Post and Courier*, http://www.postandcourier.com/article/20141101/PC1204/141109965/1005/biblical-illiteracy.

35.   Grant Underwood has done exceptional work on the eschatological worldview of Mormonism, most notably in his book *The Millenarian World of Early Mormonism* (Chicago: University of Illinois Press, 1993). He explains: "Millennialism . . . is far more than simply believing that the millennium is near. It is a comprehensive way of looking at human history as an integrated system of salvation. . . . Mormon eschatology deals with more than just what Latter-day Saints [think] about the Second Coming or how they [envision] the millennium. It probes many related aspects of their mental universe." *Millenarian World of Early Mormonism*, 2.

36.   "Citizenship," in LDS Gospel Topics, https://www.lds.org/topics/citizenship?lang=eng. This is an especially relevant topic considering the efforts of the Church recently to promote the protection of religious freedom; see "Religious Freedom," in LDS Newsroom, http://www.mormonnewsroom.org/official-statement/religious-freedom.

37.   Perry, "Doctrines and Principles," 48.

38.   Jeffrey R. Holland, *Christ and the New Covenant* (Salt Lake City: Deseret Book, 1997), 18.

39.   McConkie, *New Witness for the Articles of Faith*, 702.

6

The Education of a Prophet

THE ROLE OF THE NEW TRANSLATION
OF THE BIBLE IN THE LIFE OF JOSEPH SMITH

David A. LeFevre

David A. LeFevre is an independent scholar in the Seattle area.

From June 1830 to July 1833, Joseph Smith labored on a new translation of the Bible, commonly known today as the Joseph Smith Translation (JST). During this time, the majority of the doctrines of the Church and the sections of the Doctrine and Covenants were first revealed or understood. The work on the JST and the receipt of these doctrines and revelations were not only overlapping in time but were directly related—the Lord used the work on the JST to reveal to the young Prophet "many great and important things pertaining to the Kingdom of God" (Articles of Faith 1:9).[1]

Joseph Smith's view of the Bible was influenced by his day but was also unique. He believed in "the literality, historicity, and inspiration of the Bible."[2] But unlike others, he didn't believe the Bible alone was adequate to resolve important questions (see Joseph Smith—History 1:8–12). "Instead, he produced more scripture, scripture which echoed biblical themes, reinforced biblical authority, interpreted biblical passages, was built with biblical language, shared biblical content, corrected biblical errors, filled biblical gaps, and restored biblical methods. . . . Smith put himself inside the Bible story."[3] That is the achievement of the JST.

The work on the Joseph Smith Translation was beneficial to the Church and especially to Joseph Smith, serving as his personal spiritual tutorial. Joseph Smith's role "did include scriptural study, but it was grounded in direct revelation."[4] His translation of the Bible was revelation, and revelation was how he learned the things of God.[5] This article examines the correlation between concepts revealed to Joseph Smith through the work on the JST with those of his other revelations and teachings.

Beginning the Work

The Book of Mormon first went on sale at the end of March 1830.[6] A few days later, the Church was organized on 6 April 1830 (see D&C 20, heading). Shortly after those events, Joseph returned to Harmony, Pennsylvania, where he was living with his wife Emma. On 9 June 1830, the Prophet traveled to a Church conference held in Fayette.[7] At the end of June, he was in Colesville, New York, with Emma, Oliver Cowdery, and John and David Whitmer to baptize and confirm members there (including Emma) when he was arrested and tried.[8] Between the conference and the Colesville visit, he was in Harmony.[9] It is likely that during this period at Harmony that Joseph Smith received a new revelation, recorded in the hand of Oliver Cowdery, that begins, "A Revelation given to Joseph the Revelator June 1830."[10] This revelation related encounters Moses had with God and Satan after the burning bush incident but before he delivered the children of Israel out of bondage in Egypt.[11]

With that revelation, the work on the translation of the Bible began.[12] There is no recorded directive compelling the Prophet to do the work, though many subsequent revelations demonstrate that it was a divinely sanctioned part of his mission.[13] What is very clear from the beginning is that Joseph saw the translation as an important learning experience and a critical part of his calling. In the first mention of the JST work in a revelation, the Lord told Joseph in early July 1830, shortly after the vision of Moses in June, "& thou shalt continue in calling upon [God] in my name & *writing the Things which shall be given thee by the Comforter & thou shalt expound all scriptures* to unto the church & it shall be given thee in the very moment what thou

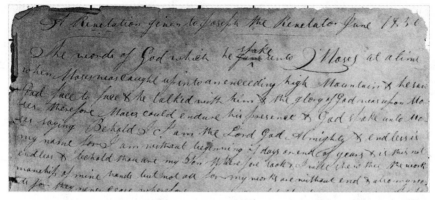

Figure 1: The vision of Moses, the start of the translation of the Bible. (Courtesy of Community of Christ Archives.)

shalt *speak & write & they [the church] shall hear it . . . & in temporal labo[rs]*
thou shalt not have strength for this is not thy calling attend to thy calling &
thou shalt have wherewith to magnify thine Office, & to expound all scrip-
tures."[4] Though the Prophet was receiving other revelations, the inspired
translation of Genesis he was doing at this time was an important part of
his writing of things given by the Comforter and led directly to his ability to
"expound all scriptures" to the Church, which the Lord identified as a core
part of his office.

It is interesting to note that in this effort, he was given "in the very
moment" what to speak and to write, indicating that the work on the Bible
was not so much an intense intellectual study as knowledge and understanding that flowed from the Spirit as they considered each passage. This "in
the very moment" experience was similar to his efforts with the Book of
Mormon translation, which was also completed "by the gift and power of
God."[5] This revelatory experience was surely why the Prophet considered
his work on the Bible also a "translation," even though no language but
English was involved.[16] Another revelation reinforced this, given to Joseph
Smith, Oliver Cowdery, and John Whitmer, who worked together on the
Bible translation, just a few days later: "Behold I say unto you that ye shall
let your time be devoted to *the studying the Scriptures & to preaching & to*
confirming the Church."[17]

Frederick G. Williams was called as a scribe to Joseph Smith as early as
February or March of 1832.[18] His writing began in the JST in the book of
Revelation, about 20 July 1832.[19] On 5 January 1833, as the translation was

progressing through the Old Testament, Frederick G. Williams was called as a counselor to Joseph Smith and asked to continue his work as scribe. In that revelation not in the Doctrine and Covenants, the Lord declared, "My Servant Joseph is called to do a great work and hath need that he may do the work of translation for the salvation of souls."[20] This was a work that was fully supported by the Lord.

Spiritual Lessons Learned

As the Prophet Joseph Smith worked his way through the Bible between June 1830 and July 1833, he was consistently tutored by the Spirit and taught eternal truths for his personal benefit and for the Church as a whole. Here are examples where Joseph Smith personally learned new truths that impacted his life and triggered additional revelations that were often recorded in the Doctrine and Covenants.

The nature of Satan. Joseph Smith had learned about Satan in a very personal way in his First Vision.[21] Early sections of the Doctrine and Covenants also mentioned "Satan" and "the devil" several times.[22] But D&C 29, given about 26 September 1830, revealed seemingly new information about Satan that is not found in the Bible nor understood by anyone in Joseph Smith's day. In the revelation, the Lord explained that he made man "an agent unto himself" with commandments given to provide direction, but the devil "rebelled against me saying give me thine honour which is my Power" so that Satan might take away the agency of man. This rebellion was the cause of him and "a third part of the host of Heaven" being "thrust down" and thereby allowed to "tempt the children of men or they could not be agents unto themselves."[23]

If all we had was the Doctrine and Covenants, we might view this information as new and unique. But this wasn't the first time Joseph Smith had heard it. He had learned about Satan in June 1830 with the initial Visions of Moses,[24] but even more directly, what is now Moses 4:1–6 has the same concepts and similar wording as D&C 29—and it was translated from Genesis 3 prior to the revelation. The exact date Moses 4:1–6 was recorded is not known, but dates on the manuscript give us a range between June 1830 and 21 October 1830.[25] However, the text for that entire section is

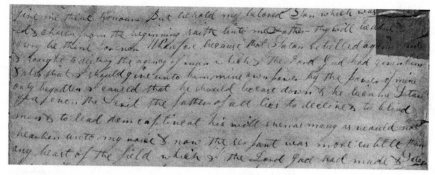

Figure 2: Close-up of page 6 of Old Testament Revision 1, showing Satan's rebellion. (Courtesy of Community of Christ Archives.)

in Oliver Cowdery's handwriting, so we can narrow that range by looking at when Joseph and Oliver were together and likely to write. Oliver left Harmony and returned to live with the Whitmers in Fayette in mid-July,[26] while Joseph moved back to Fayette in early September.[27] After the Prophet arrived in Fayette, and until just before the 26 September conference, he and Oliver were at odds over the Hiram Page incident (D&C 28), making it unlikely they would work on the translation that month. October saw Oliver preparing to leave on his mission to the Lamanites. So the most likely date for all the material in Oliver's handwriting (everything up to Moses 5:43a) is June–mid-July 1830, weeks before D&C 29.[28]

In the New Translation, Satan says, "Behold I send me I will be thy son and I will redeem all mankind that one soul shall not be lost, and surely I will do it Wherefore give me thine honour."[29] However, because Satan's action was a rebellion to "destroy the agency of man" and an effort that God "should give unto him mine [God's] own power," Satan was "cast down," becoming "the Devil the father of all lies to deceive & to blind men & to lead them captive at his will even as many as would not hearken" to the Lord's voice.[30] The Prophet learned about Satan through the Bible translation, and the Lord made that information directly relevant to the latter-day Church in D&C 29.

On several occasions, Joseph Smith taught from this understanding of the role of Satan in God's plan. He said, "The devil has no power over us only as we permit him; the moment we revolt at anything which comes from God the Devil takes power."[31] Furthermore, he explained, "Satan Cannot Seduce us by his Enticements unles we in our harts Consent & yeald—our organization such that we can Resest [resist] the Devil If we were Not organized so we would Not be free agents."³² In abbreviated notes, he was recorded to have taught, "The plans the devil laid to save the world.—Devil said he could save them all—Lot fell on Jesus."³³ Applying this understanding to the Saints in an 1841 discourse, Joseph said, "Satan was generally blamed for the evils which we did, but if he was the cause of all our wickedness, men could not be condemned. The devil cannot compel mankind to evil, all was voluntary.—Those who resist the spirit of God, are liable to be led into temptation, and then the association of heaven is withdrawn from those who refuse to be made partakers of such great glory—God would not exert any compulsory means and the Devil could not; and such ideas as were entertained by many were absurd."³⁴

Zion and the New Jerusalem. Joseph Smith's understanding of the terms "Zion" and "New Jerusalem" clearly changed and deepened with the translation work and related revelations. From the Book of Mormon's forty-five references and others in the Bible, he would have understood that Zion generally referred to Jerusalem or was "a holy community, a fortification of the Saints against evil,"³⁵ while "New Jerusalem" referred to a city that will be built as the gathering place of the righteous³⁶ and another city of unknown origin which will come again.³⁷ References to "Zion" in the Prophet's early revelations take that same meaning; several Saints in 1830 were called to "seek to bring forth and establish the cause of Zion" (D&C 6:6; see also 11:6; 12:6; 14:6; 24:7). The first hint that Zion was a different place than Jerusalem was in a revelation to Oliver Cowdery in late September 1830. In relation to things Hiram Page had falsely said, Oliver was told, "Now Behold I say unto you that it is not Revealed & no man knoweth where the City shall be built But it shall be given hereafter."³⁸ The city was the New Jerusalem or Zion.³⁹

There is no immediate explanation for a shift in revelatory meaning of "Zion"—the Lord simply started referring to it as a new city starting with D&C 28. But like Adam, who first sacrificed and then had it explained to him (see Moses 5:5–8), the details soon came to the Prophet through the work on the Bible and the revelations it triggered. In early December 1830, after Sidney Rigdon's arrival in Fayette to meet Joseph Smith, they recorded what is now Moses 7:13–21, where they learned about Enoch's people and city, how the people were called Zion as was the city, and that the city was taken up into heaven. On 2 January 1831, an almost casual reference is made to Enoch's Zion as the Lord described himself: "I am the same which hath taken the Zion of Enoch into mine own bosom."[40] Without the context of Moses 7, that remark would make little sense—in the Bible, there is no mention of Enoch with a city called Zion. On 7 March 1831, another revelation spoke of the righteous gathering to Zion and the wicked being afraid of it (D&C 45:67–71), which echoes what Joseph Smith had already learned the previous December, that all nations greatly feared Enoch's Zion because Enoch "spake the word of the Lord and the earth trembled and the Mountains fled even according to his command and the rivers of water were turned <out> of their course and the roar of the Lions was heard out of the willderness."[41]

In terms of the "New Jerusalem," the work in Genesis built upon what was in the Book of Mormon. In December 1830, Joseph and Sidney Rigdon learned that Zion was equated with the New Jerusalem: "a place which I shall prepare an holy City that my people may gird up their loins and be looking fourth for the time of my coming for there shall be my tabernicle and it shall be called Zion a New Jerusalem."[42] That city would be the abode of God during the "thousand years the earth shall rest" (Moses 7:64). The first mention of the term "New Jerusalem" in the Doctrine and Covenants is about two months later, on 9 February 1831 in D&C 42:9 (also vv. 35, 62, and 67). "Mount Zion" and "New Jerusalem" are first mentioned together even later, on 3 November 1831 (see D&C 133:56) and not equated until 22–23 September 1832 (see D&C 84:2). In other words, Joseph Smith learned these concepts through his work on the Bible at least a year before they were made clear in the Doctrine and Covenants.

On 20 July 1831, the Prophet revealed to the Church the promised location of Zion, the New Jerusalem, in the last days—Independence, Missouri (see D&C 57:1–2). There the Saints would gather and build a temple (see D&C 57:3). Subsequent revelations throughout 1832–1834 developed and directed this activity, including the attempt to redeem Zion with an army (see D&C 103). As the Saints were driven from Jackson County into Clay and Caldwell counties, and eventually out of Missouri entirely, the Prophet's definition of "Zion" enlarged, finally coming to take in all of North and South America.[43]

The importance of Zion to Joseph Smith is reflected in an 1839 discourse—after their failure to establish a city in Missouri—when Joseph Smith said, "We ought to have the building up of Zion as our greatest object.—when wars come we shall have to flee to Zion, the cry is to make haste."[44] However, his most expansive definition of "Zion" came before the Saints had even gone to Missouri: "The Lord called his people Zion because they were of one heart and of one mind and dwelt in righteousness and there was no poor among them."[45] Later, before Joseph knew of the troubles just beginning in Missouri, in a revelation he received just one month after he finished the work on the Bible, the Lord said simply, "Zion [is] the pure in heart."[46]

One historian noted, "The City of Zion occupied a central place in Joseph Smith's design for world renewal. He conceived the world as a vast funnel with the city at the vortex and the temple at the center of the city. Converts across the globe would be attracted to this central point to acquire knowledge and power for preaching the gospel. Trained and empowered in the temple, the missionary force would go back into the world and collect Israel from every corner of the earth. The city, the temple, and the world, existed in a dynamic relationship. Missionaries flowed out of the city and converts poured back in. The exchange would redeem the world in the last days."[47]

The law of consecration. Closely related to the concept of Zion is the revelation on "the law" (D&C 42:2). The growing understanding and application of this law spanned several years, with the Bible translation experiences playing a major role in its advancement.

As mentioned above, after Sidney Rigdon's arrival in Fayette in December 1830, he began to scribe for Joseph Smith on the translation work. The first thing they worked on was what is now Moses 7, where they learned about Enoch protecting his people with miraculous priesthood power (Moses 7:13); that his people and their city were called Zion because "they were of one heart and of one mind, and dwelt in righteousness; and there was no poor among them" (v. 18); and that Zion was taken (v. 69). Just a few days later, a revelation was received in which the Lord identified himself as "the same which have taken the Zion of Enoch into mine own bosom" (D&C 38:4). Following Zion's example, the Saints were counseled to "let evry man esteem his Brother as himself . . . I say unto you be one & if ye are

Figure 3: Old Testament Revision 1, page 16, showing the reference to Zion and no poor among them. (Courtesy of Community of Christ Archives.)

not one ye are not mine." The Church was also commanded to "look to the poor & the needy & administer to their relief that they shall not suffer."[48]

After a cold trip in late January/early February to Kirtland, Ohio, Joseph met with newly baptized members, including Isaac Morley and Leman Copley, who had already been attempting to live a communal life style they called "the family" or "common stock," in emulation of Acts 2:44–45 and 4:32–35.[49] Recognizing several problems with their implementation, Joseph received a revelation on 4 February 1831, promising "by the prayer of your faith ye shall receive my law that ye may know how to govern my Church Church & have all things right before me."[50]

Just five days later, 9 February 1831, the first revelation on that law was received, titled "The Laws of the Church of Christ" by John Whitmer.[51] This document answered five questions posed to Joseph Smith by twelve elders, the second of which concerned "The Law." After reciting a number of commandments (don't kill, steal, commit adultery, or speak evil of a neighbor; do love your wife), the Lord stated, "If thou lovest me thou shall serve & keep all my commandments & Behold thou shalt consecrate all thy property properties that which thou hast unto me with a covena[n]t and Deed which cannot be broken & they Shall be laid before the Bishop of my church & two of the Elders such as he shall appoint & set apart for that purpose."[52] Unlike the communal efforts of the Kirtland Saints previously, this system relied on a bishop to make "every man a Steward over his own property or that which he hath received . . . that every man may receive according as he stands in need."[53] The remainder would be managed by the bishop in a storehouse to take care of the poor and needy.[54] This was the latter-day implementation of the doctrines of Zion and caring for the poor taught to the Prophet through the Enoch chapters, which information prepared him to receive and teach this law.

On 6 June 1831, another revelation was given on the second day of a conference held in Kirtland. The brethren were told that their next conference was to be in Missouri, and they were to travel there two by two, preaching as they went. Missouri was "the land which I will consecrate unto my People,"[55] and they were to "assemble yourselves together to rejoice upon the land of your inheritance which is now the land of your enemies but behold I the lord will hasten the City in its time."[56]

Finally, once all had arrived in Missouri, Joseph Smith pondered the question of where the holy city of Zion should be built. The brethren were in Independence, on the western border of Missouri, when the revelation was given on 20 July 1831: "Wherefore, this is the land of promise & the place for the City of Zion. . . . Behold the place which is now called Independence is the centre place, & the spot for the Temple is lying westward upon a lot which is not far from the court-house."[57]

The history of the Saints in Missouri is well-documented in the Doctrine and Covenants and an abundance of books of the Church history of the period. Trying to make Zion flourish in Missouri became a core focus of Joseph Smith and many others in the Church for several years. The effort that started all the questions and triggered the revelations was the Prophet's experience and learning gained through translating the Bible. This is surely one of the great reasons the Lord directed Joseph Smith to perform the labor of the translation in the first place, for even today "The Law" of consecration and stewardship forms a foundational structure upon which the entire ability of the Church to function and be successful is based.

The age of accountability. One of the most widely noticed chains of learning experiences related to the Bible translation is with the age of accountability.[58] The Book of Mormon has nearly an entire chapter devoted to the idea that "little children need no repentance, neither baptism" (Moroni 8:11), but the age when they do need repentance and baptism is not given. In June 1829, as the brethren were finishing up the translation of the Book of Mormon, the Prophet received a revelation directing that "all men must repent and be baptized; and not only men, but women and children, which have arriven to the years of accountability,"[59] but again, the age of account-ability was not given.

In the period of February–March 1831, Joseph Smith and Sidney Ridgon were working through the Genesis chapters about Abraham.[60] In Genesis 17 they learned that people had turned away from the ordinances of "anointing and the buriel or baptism wherewith I commanded them." Instead, they were washing children and sprinkling blood. The Prophet must have rejoiced when in Abraham's discussion with the Lord, Abraham was instructed to make a covenant of circumcision with the Lord, part of which was designed to teach "that children are not accountable before me till eight years old."[61] This was a very practical and needed piece of informa-tion to correctly apply the doctrine of accountability.

Later that year, at a Church conference held in Hiram, Ohio, on 1 November 1831, the Lord was instructing parents in the Church in their responsibilities toward their children: "And again inasmuch as parents have children in Zion that teach them not to understand the doctrine of repen-tance faith in Christ the Son of the living God & of baptism & the gift of the Holy Spirit by the laying <on> of the hands *when eight years old* the sin be upon the head of the parents for this shall be a Law unto the inhabitants of Zion & their children shall be baptised for the remission of their sins *when eight years old* & receive the laying on of the hands & they also shall teach their children to pray & to walk uprightly before the Lord."[62] The informa-tion about the age of eight is noted not as new information but as something already understood—which it was to the Prophet and others with whom he shared it after the Genesis translation. The emphasis in the revelation is rather on how parents prepare their children for baptism and the laying on of hands when they arrive at eight years old.

Joseph Smith had several children die before the age of eight.[63] In 1836, while in the Kirtland Temple, he received a vision that included the amaz-ing discovery that "all children who die before they arrive at the years of accountability are saved in the celestial kingdom of heaven" (D&C 137:10). Knowing that their small children were not accountable and would be exalted must have brought great comfort to him and Emma, as it does to millions today.

The degrees of glory. One of the clearest links between the translation work and significant new knowledge occurred on 16 February 1832. Joseph

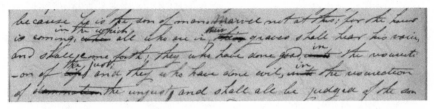

Figure 4: New Testament Revision 2, part 4, page 114, showing John 5:29 revisions. (Courtesy of Community of Christ Archives.)

Smith and Sidney Rigdon were living at Hiram, Ohio, and had progressed in the translation work to John chapter 5. When they first encountered John 5:29, Rigdon wrote it in the manuscript fundamentally the same as it appeared in the King James Bible they were using as a reference: "And shall come forth; they who have done good, unto the resurection of life and they who have done evil, unto the resurection of damnation."[64] Then the men paused, being "in the spirit . . . and through <by> the power of the spirit our eyes were opened and our understandings were enlarged so as to see and understand the things of God."[65] In this state, they understood a change needed to be made to the verse, and they recorded it so: "And shall come forth; they who have done good, unto <in> the resurection of life <the just;> and they who have done evil, unto <in> the resurection of damnation the unjust."[66] The bracketed words were inserted above the crossed out words, showing they had to squeeze them in above the already-written verse, but the phrase "the unjust" was added after the crossed-out "damnation," indicating the pause before the edits, as they had room to write the final phrase on the same line.[67] The men wrote that this small change of six words "caused us to marvel for it was given <unto> us of the spirit."[68] Then they had a lengthy visionary experience where they saw and conversed with Jesus Christ, who was on the right hand of the Father, and witnessed angels and others before the throne of God. They saw the fall of Lucifer, learned about "sons of perdition," then learned about those saved in three different kingdoms of glory—celestial, terrestrial, and telestial.

This vision had a powerful impact on Joseph Smith. After receiving it, he used the language of D&C 76 in sermons, letters, prayers, and more.[69] In his history, he is recorded to have said, "Nothing could be more pleasing to the Saint, upon the order of the kingdom of the Lord, than the light which burst upon the world, through the foregoing vision. . . . [It] witnesses the fact that that document is a transcript from the Records of the eternal world.

The sublimity of the ideas; the purity of the language; the scope for action; the continued duration for completion, in order that the heirs of salvation, may confess the Lord and bow the knee; The rewards for faithfulnes & the punishments for sins, are so much beyond the narrow mindedness of men, that every honest man is constrained to exclaim; It came from God."[70]

Wheat and tares. This parable in Matthew 13 was first recorded in the translation effort probably in April or May 1831, and was first written fundamentally as it stands in the King James Version.[71] The key verse (30) had no changes: "Let both grow till <untill> the harvest and in the time of harvest I will say to the reapers gather ye together first the tares and bind them in bundles to burn them but gather the wheat into my barn."[72] Shortly after that, John Whitmer made a copy of the first New Testament manuscript and kept the wording exactly the same.[73] After the brethren completed the work on the New Testament at the end of July 1832, they turned their attention back to the Old Testament.[74] However, Joseph and Sidney continued to make revisions in the New Testament manuscript until 2 February 1833.[75] Sometime during this review, the words "gather ye together first the tares & bind them in bundles to burn them but gather the wheat into my Barn" were crossed out in the New Testament and a note was pinned over the text as follows: "Gather ye together first the *wheat into my barns, and the tares are bound in bundles to be burned.*"[76]

On 6 December 1832, Joseph Smith personally wrote in his own journal, "December 6th translating and received a Revelation explaining the Parable the wheat and the tears [tares] &c."[77] The resulting revelation (D&C 86) gives a marvelous latter-day interpretation of the parable, including the same reversal of the order of the harvest expressed on the pinned note. Both the pinned note and the original revelation were in the handwriting of Sidney Rigdon, especially significant because Frederick G. Williams was the principal scribe for the translation in December 1832.[78] Though we don't know the date of the pinned note with certainty, the journal entry for the revelation gives the impression of cause and effect—"translating and received a Revelation." It is reasonable then, that, like section 76 and similar experiences, the change was first made to the biblical text by inspiration, which then triggered the larger revelation recorded in the Doctrine and Covenants.

The reversal of the order was significant to the message of the Restoration. About a year previous, the Lord had told the Church to "flee unto Zion" and "flee unto Jerusalem." They were to come "out from among the nations" and "from the midst of wickedness," separating themselves from the wicked, "which is spiritual Babylon" (D&C 133:12–14; see also verses 4–5, 36–38, all of which focus on the Church's mission and message to gather the righteous out of the wicked world). This then became a main mission of the Church and drove the Prophet to send missionaries abroad and men to preach the gospel in many nations. Changing the parable to gather the wheat first aligned with that vision and mission and was good doctrine. D&C 86 put the interpretation squarely in a latter-day context: "But behold in the last days, even now while the Lord is begining to bring forth his <the> word, and the blade is springing up and is yet tender," the angels are anxiously waiting to start the harvest. But the Lord refrains them: "Pluck not up the tears while the blade is yet tender (for verily your faith is weak) least you distroy the wheat also, therefore let the wheat and the tears grow together untill the harvest is fully ripe then ye shall first gather out the wheat."[79]

A couple of years later, Joseph Smith explained it this way: "We understand that the work of the gathering together of the wheat into barns, or garners, is to take place while the tares are being bound over and preparing for the day of burning."[80] The wheat may be first, but both types of harvest are the work of the latter-days.

Israel and the priesthood. Joseph Smith had been learning about the priesthood since his ordination by John the Baptist in May 1829 (see D&C 13) and through the early 1830s. The work on the Bible translation was an important avenue for his increased understanding. While translating Genesis 14 (probably in February 1831), he learned significant new information about Melchizedek, including that Melchizedek "was ordained a high priest after the order of the covenant which God made with Enock it being after the order of the Son of God."[81] About a year later, while working through Hebrews 7, it was revealed: "For this Melchisedec was ordained a priest after the order of the son of God, who was <which order was> without father, without mother, without descent, having neither begining of days, nor end of life; and all those who are ordained unto this Priesthood, are made like unto the son of God, abiding a Priest continually."[82]

Then in September 1832, after returning from Missouri and resuming the work on the Old Testament, two similar passages were changed to instruct how the priesthood was handled among the Israelites in Moses' day.

The first was in the opening verses of Exodus 34: "And the Lord said unto Moses, hew thee two other tables of stone, like unto the first, and I will write upon them also, the words of the Law, according as they were writen at the first, on the tables which thou breakest; but it shall not be according to the first, for I will take away the priest-hood out of there midst; therefore my holy order; <and the ordinances thereof,> shall not go before them; for my pressence shall not go up in there midst Least I distry [destroy] them,<.>"[83]

The second was Deuteronomy 10:1–2 that reinforced his learning from Exodus: "At that time the Lord said unto me, hewe thee two other tables of stone, like unto the first, and come up unto me upon the mount, and make thee an ark of wood,<.> And I will write on the tables the words that were on the first tables which tho breakest, save the words of the <everlasting> covenant of the holy Priesthood, and thou shalt put them in the ark,<.>"[84]

The culminating revelation from all this work was given on 22 September 1832, just after these changes, today section 84.[85] Joseph Smith learned that Moses received "the holy Priesthood" from his father-in-law, Jethro,[86] who received it through a chain of ordinations that originated with Abraham, who "received the Priesthood from Melchesedec who received it through the lineage of his fathers even till Noah, and from Noah till Enoch, through the lineage of thare fathers,"[87] who could trace his priesthood lineage back to Adam. The priesthood "continueth in the church of God in all generations."[88] Compared to the priesthood of Aaron, this "holiest order of God" is the "greater Priesthood" and without it and its associated ordinances, "the power of Godliness is not manifest unto man in the flesh."[89] Referring back to Joseph's recent translation work in Exodus and Deuteronomy, the Lord clarified, "Now this Moses plainly taught to the children of Israel in the wilderness and saught diligently to sanctify his people that they might behold the face of God, but they hardened ther hearts and could not endure his presence," so the Lord took the holy priesthood away from them.[90]

Priesthood offices and authority were largely unknown concepts in Joseph Smith's day.[91] The Prophet had to be tutored so that he could understand the authority he had received from divine messengers and then administer that throughout the Church. Matthew C. Godfrey argued:

> The Lord taught these truths to Joseph through a variety of
> means, including providing inspiration as Joseph worked on his

translation of the Bible and giving Joseph additional revelations
that clarified priesthood doctrine and responsibilities. Joseph,
in turn, conveyed these teachings through his revelations and
through conferences of elders and high priests. . . . In the years
that followed, the Lord would reveal more to the Prophet about
priesthood; by 1835, for example, the greater priesthood, or the
umbrella under which all offices of the priesthood exist, was
known as the Melchizedek Priesthood, and the lesser priesthood
was called the Aaronic Priesthood. But the doctrines revealed
in the Church's initial years provided the foundation for this
understanding, making what Joseph taught about the priesthood in the early years of the Church even more significant.[92]

Conclusion

The Prophet Joseph Smith was a man who thoroughly engaged with the
scriptures. He studied them intensely and sought revelation as he did so.
His translation of the Bible, which was done by the Spirit of God, like the
Book of Mormon translation, is a model for how the study of the scriptures
can stimulate revelation in our own lives. As Joseph pondered the words on
those sacred pages and asked questions that thereby came to his mind, the
Lord revealed answers to him. In his role as the Prophet of the Restoration,
many of his answers impacted not only his own life but the entire path of
the Church in the last days. While our own revelations may not have the
same scope, they are nevertheless personally significant. Studying scripture
is a catalyst to personal revelation, an effort we make to show the Lord that
we seriously seek his voice, need his guidance, and desire to be "a greater follower of righteousness, and to possess a greater knowledge" (Abraham 1:2).
Joseph Smith demonstrated through his work on the translation of the Bible
that such an effort is well rewarded.

Notes

1.   Robert J. Matthews, in his groundbreaking work on the translation, called
the abundance of revelations in the Doctrine and Covenants during the work on the
Joseph Smith Translation "not coincidental but consequential." Robert J. Matthews,

"A Plainer Translation": Joseph Smith's Translation of the Bible—A History and Commentary (Provo, UT: Brigham Young University Press, 1975), 265.

2. Philip L. Barlow, "Before Mormonism: Joseph Smith's Use of the Bible, 1820–1829," *Journal of the American Academy of Religion* 57, no. 4 (Winter 1989), 741.

3. Barlow, "Before Mormonism," recognizing that Barlow is speaking mostly of the Book of Mormon and revelations in the Doctrine and Covenants, given the time period of his article, but what he says applies equally to the translation of the Bible.

4. Barlow, "Before Mormonism," 763.

5. Richard Lyman Bushman, *Joseph Smith: Rough Stone Rolling* (New York: Vintage Books, 2005), 388.

6. Michael Hubbard MacKay and Gerrit J. Dirkmaat, *From Darkness unto Light: Joseph Smith's Translation and Publications of the Book of Mormon* (Provo, UT: Religious Studies Center, 2015), 215.

7. Michael Hubbard MacKay, Gerrit J. Dirkmaat, Grant Underwood, Robert J. Woodford, and William G. Hartley, eds., *Documents, Volume 1: July 1828–June 1831,* vol. 1 of the Documents series of *The Joseph Smith Papers,* ed. Dean C. Jessee, Ronald K. Esplin, Richard Lyman Bushman, and Matthew J. Grow (Salt Lake City: Church Historian's Press, 2013), 139.

8. Karen Lynn Davidson, David J. Whittaker, Mark Ashurst-McGee, and Richard L. Jensen, eds., *Histories, Volume 1: Joseph Smith Histories, 1832–1844,* vol. 1 of the Histories series of *The Joseph Smith Papers,* ed. Dean C. Jessee, Ronald K. Esplin, and Richard Lyman Bushman (Salt Lake City: Church Historian's Press, 2012), 390–412; see also page 552 in the same volume that gives the date of Joseph Smith's arrest and trial at Colesville that occurred at this time as 28 June–1 July 1830.

9. History Drafts, 1838—Circa 1841, Draft 1 and Draft 2, in *JSP,* H1:390.

10. Visions of Moses, June 1830, in *JSP,* D1:152.

11. Moses 1:17 shows that it was after the burning bush encounter recorded in Exodus 3, and Moses 1:26 proves that the deliverance from Egypt was yet to happen.

12. It's not clear that the initial "Visions of Moses" revelation was immediately linked to the translation process in the minds of Joseph and Oliver, or how long it was after that revelation that they turned to the first chapter of Genesis. But the same document used to record the initial revelation became the one used for the translation, and the copies made later all included the vision. That some time passed between what is now Moses 1 and the work on Genesis seems evident by the formatting (strong lines dividing the vision from the rest of the text) and a note at the start of Genesis chapter 1: "A Revelation given to the Elders of the Church of Christ On the first Book of Moses given to Joseph the Seer." Old Testament Revision 1, p. 3, in Scott H. Faulring, Kent P. Jackson, and Robert J. Matthews, *Joseph Smith's New Translation of the Bible: Original Manuscripts* (Provo, UT: Religious Studies Center, 2004), 86.

13. For example, D&C 45:60–61 directs the Prophet to start the translation of the New Testament with this counsel, showing the Lord gave him the work: "And now, behold, I say unto you, it shall not be given unto you to know any further concerning this chapter, until the New Testament be translated, and in it all these things shall be made known; Wherefore *I give unto you that ye may now translate it, that ye may be prepared for the things to come*" (emphasis added).

14. Revelation, July 1830-A [D&C 24], in *JSP*, D1:158–59 (emphasis added); see D&C 24:5–6, 9.

15. The Church of Jesus Christ of Latter-day Saints, "Book of Mormon Translation," https://www.lds.org/topics/book-of-mormon-translation?lang=eng.

16. D&C 76:15 and chapter heading to that section quoting from *History of the Church;* see also D&C 45:60–61. The work is referred to as the "new translation" in many documents, such as D&C 124:89 and a verse originally in the revelation that is now D&C 104 (the deleted section would be after verse 59 today) with the Lord telling the brethren to seek "the copy right to the new translation of the scriptures" so "that others may not take the blessings away from you which I conferred upon you." Robin Scott Jensen, Robert J. Woodford, and Steven C. Harper, eds., *Manuscript Revelation Books*, facsimile edition, vol. 1 of the Revelations and Translations series of *The Joseph Smith Papers*, ed. Dean C. Jessee, Ronald K. Esplin, and Richard Lyman Bushman (Salt Lake City: Church Historian's Press, 2009), 369. The latter quote significantly shows the Lord's attitude that the work on the translation was a great blessing to Joseph and the early Church.

17. Revelation, July 1830-B [D&C 26], in *JSP*, D1:160 (emphasis added); see D&C 26:1.

18. Letter to William W. Phelps, 31 July 1832, in Matthew C. Godfrey, Mark Ashurst-McGee, Grant Underwood, Robert J. Woodford, and William G. Hartley, eds., *Documents, Volume 2: July 1831–January 1833*, vol. 2 of the Documents series of *The Joseph Smith Papers*, ed. Dean C. Jessee, Ronald K. Esplin, Richard Lyman Bushman, and Matthew J. Grow (Salt Lake City: Church Historian's Press, 2013), 267n337.

19. Faulring, Jackson, and Matthews, *Joseph Smith's Translation of the Bible*, 47; Revelation, 5 January 1833, in *JSP*, D2:357.

20. Revelation, 5 January 1833, in *JSP*, D2:361.

21. See Joseph Smith—History 1:15–17; see also History, circa June 1839–circa 1841 [Draft 2], in *JSP*, H1:212–214.

22. E.g. D&C 10:5, 10, 12, 14, 20, 22–27, 29, 32–33; 18:20; and 19:3.

23. Revelation, September 1830-A [D&C 29], in *JSP*, D1:181.

24. See Moses 1:12–24.

25. Faulring, Jackson, and Matthews, *Joseph Smith's Translation of the Bible*, 57.

26. See History Drafts, 1838—Circa 1841, Draft 1 and Draft 2, in *JSP*, H1:424; and Revelation, July 1830-A [D&C 24], Historical Introduction, in *JSP*, D1:157n220.

27. See Chronology, in *JSP*, H1:552.

28. My examination of the handwriting on the manuscripts also supports continuous work for the entire section, with similar ink flow and color right up to the point where the handwriting changes to John Whitmer's handwriting.

29. Old Testament Revision 1, p. 6, in Faulring, Jackson, and Matthews, *Joseph Smith's New Translation of the Bible*, 90. The phrase in Moses 4:1 today is, "Behold, here am I, send me," with the words "here am" being added by James E. Talmage in the 1902 edition of the Pearl of Great Price that he prepared. Kent P. Jackson, *The Book of Moses and the Joseph Smith Translation Manuscripts* (Provo, UT: Religious Studies Center, 2005), 43.

30. Old Testament Revision 1, p. 6, in Faulring, Jackson, and Matthews, *Joseph Smith's New Translation of the Bible*, 90.

31. 5 January 1841 (Tuesday), Old Homestead, Extracts from William Clayton's Private Book, in Ehat and Cook, *The Words of Joseph Smith*, 60.

32. 16 March 1841 (Tuesday), McIntire Minute Book, in Ehat and Cook, *The Words of Joseph Smith*, 65.

33. 7 April 1844 (Sunday afternoon), at the temple, Joseph Smith Diary, by Willard Richards, in Ehat and Cook, *The Words of Joseph Smith*, 342.

34. 16 May 1841 (Sunday morning), at meeting ground, *Times and Seasons 2* (1 June 1841): 429–430, in Ehat and Cook, *The Words of Joseph Smith*, 72.

35. Arnold K. Garr, Donald Q. Cannon, and Richard O. Cowan, eds., *Encyclopedia of Latter-day Saint History* (Salt Lake City: Deseret Book, 2000), 1397. The Book of Mormon references they give in support are 1 Nephi 13:37; 2 Nephi 10:11–13; 26:29–31; 28:20–21, 24.

36. E.g., 3 Nephi 20:22; 21:23–24; and Ether 13:5.

37. E.g., Ether 13:3–4, 10; it has a similar meaning in Revelation 3:12 and 21:2.

38. Revelation, September 1830-B [D&C 28], in *JSP*, D1:185–86; see D&C 28:9.

39. Revelation, September 1830-B [D&C 28], in *JSP*, D1:186n361.

40. Revelation, 2 January 1831 [D&C 38], in *JSP*, D1:230; see D&C 38:4.

41. Old Testament Revision 1, p. 16, in Faulring, Jackson, and Matthews, *Joseph Smith's New Translation of the Bible*, 104; see Moses 7:13.

42. Old Testament Revision 1, p. 19, in Faulring, Jackson, and Matthews, *Joseph Smith's New Translation of the Bible*, 109; see Moses 7:62.

43. Glossary, "Zion," in *JSP*, D1:505.

44. Before 8 August 1839 (1), Willard Richards Pocket Companion, in Ehat and Cook, *The Words of Joseph Smith*, 11.

45. Old Testament Revision 1, p. 16, in Faulring, Jackson, and Matthews, *Joseph Smith's New Translation of the Bible*, 105; see Moses 7:18.

46. Revelation, 2 August 1833-A [D&C 97], in Gerrit J. Dirkmaat, Brent M. Rogers, Grant Underwood, Robert J. Woodford, and William G. Hartley, eds., *Documents, Volume 3: February 1833–March 1834*, vol. 3 of the Documents series of *The Joseph Smith Papers*, ed. Ronald K. Esplin and Matthew J. Grow (Salt Lake City: Church Historian's Press, 2014), 202; see D&C 97:21.

47. Bushman, *Joseph Smith: Rough Stone Rolling*, 220–21.

48. Revelation, 2 January 1831 [D&C 38], in *JSP*, D1:232–33; see D&C 38:4, 25–27, 24–25.

49. Stephen E. Robinson and H. Dean Garrett, *A Commentary on the Doctrine and Covenants*, vol. 2 (Salt Lake City: Deseret Book, 2000), 1–2; Revelation, 4 February 1831 [D&C 4], Historical Introduction, in *JSP*, D1:241–242.

50. Revelation, 4 February 1831 [D&C 41], in *JSP*, D1:244; see also D&C 41:3.

51. Revelation, 9 February 1831 [D&C 42:1–72], in *JSP*, D1:249.

52. Revelation, 9 February 1831 [D&C 42:1–72], in *JSP*, D1:251.

53. Revelation, 9 February 1831 [D&C 42:1–72], in *JSP*, D1:252.

54. Revelation, 9 February 1831 [D&C 42:1–72], in *JSP*, D1:252.

55. Revelation, 6 June 1831 [D&C 52], in *JSP*, D1:328.

56. Revelation, 6 June 1831 [D&C 52], in *JSP*, D1:332.

57. Revelation, 20 July 1831 [D&C 57], in *JSP*, D2:7–8.

58. For example, see Matthews, "A Plainer Translation," 260, 317; Joseph Fielding McConkie and Craig J. Ostler, *Revelations of the Restoration* (Salt Lake City: Deseret Book, 2000), 492–93; Revelation, 1 November 1831-A [D&C 68], in *JSP*, D2:102n179.

59. Revelation, June 1829-B [D&C 18], in *JSP*, D1:73; see D&C 18:42.

60. On 10 December 1830, Sidney Rigdon began to write at what is now Moses 7:2. Faulring, Jackson, and Matthews, *Joseph Smith's Translation of the Bible*, 57 and 103; see D&C 35:20. On 30 December 1830 they stopped the translation process at the Lord's direction, shortly after receiving the Enoch material in the Book of Moses. Revelation, 30 December 1830 [D&C 37], in *JSP*, D1:226–27. The translation did not resume until the brethren relocated to Kirkland, Ohio, on 4 February 1831. Revelation, 4 February 1831 [D&C 41], in *JSP*, D1:241. The work on the Old Testament ended temporarily at Genesis 24:41a on 7 March 1831 when they were commanded to begin work on the New Testament (D&C 45:60–61). Thus the chapters on Abraham in Genesis 12:1–24:41a were the focus in February–March 1831.

61. Old Testament Revision 1, p. 41, in Faulring, Jackson, and Matthews, *Joseph Smith's New Translation of the Bible*, 131–32.

62. Revelation, 1 November 1831-A [D&C 68], in *JSP*, D2:102 (emphasis added); see D&C 68:25–28.

63. Five of the Smith's children died in infancy; see, Bushman, *Joseph Smith: Rough Stone Rolling*, 425.

64. New Testament Revision 2, part 4, p. 114, in Faulring, Jackson, and Matthews, *Joseph Smith's New Translation of the Bible*, 454.

65. Revelation Book 2, 16 February 1832 [D&C 76], in *JSP*, MRB:414–17; see D&C 76:11–12.

66. New Testament Revision 2, part 4, p. 114, in Faulring, Jackson, and Matthews, *Joseph Smith's New Translation of the Bible*, 454.

67. Rigdon drew a bold line down across two lines just after the word "unjust," which later was written over by a semicolon and a letter in the line below it, further emphasizing the dramatic pause they experienced.

68. Revelation Book 2, 16 February 1832 [D&C 76], in *JSP*, MRB:417; see D&C 76:18.

69. For example, see http://josephsmithpapers.org/searchNew?query=Celestial kingdom&sort=Relevance&page=1&perpage=10&startdate=&enddate=&tra nscripts=false&issuggestion=true&types=documents-papers|documents-papers -documents|documents-papers-histories|documents-papers-revelations-and -translations|documents-papers-journals for a list of references just to "celestial kingdom."

70. History, 1838–1856, volume A-1 [23 December 1805–30 August 1834], page 192, *The Joseph Smith Papers*, http://josephsmithpapers.org/paperSummary /history-1838-1856-volume-a-1-23-december-1805-30-august-1834#!/paperSummary/ history-1838-1856-volume-a-1-23-december-1805-30-august-1834&p=198.

71.   There were some minor changes that do impact the meaning of the text, such as changing "which" to "who" in verse 24 and dropping the word "was" from verse 26 to smooth out the reading.

72.   New Testament Revision 1, p. 34, in Faulring, Jackson, and Matthews, *Joseph Smith's New Translation of the Bible*, 192.

73.   New Testament Revision 2, part 1, p. 25, in Faulring, Jackson, and Matthews, *Joseph Smith's New Translation of the Bible*, 267.

74.   Joseph Smith declared the translation work on the New Testament done in his letter to W. W. Phelps, dated 31 July 1832: "We have finished the translation of the New testament great and marvilous glorious things are revealed, we are making rapid strides in the old book [Old Testament]." Letter to William W. Phelps, 31 July 1832, in *JSP*, D2:267.

75.   Minute Book 1 has an entry dated 2 February 1833 by Frederick G. Williams that states, "This day completed the translation *and the reviewing* of the New testament and sealed up no more to be broken till it goes to Zion." Minute Book 1, page 8, *The Joseph Smith Papers*, http://josephsmithpapers.org/paperSummary/minute-book-1#!/paperSummary/minute-book-1&p=12 (emphasis added).

76.   New Testament Revision 2, part 1, p. 25, in Faulring, Jackson, and Matthews, *Joseph Smith's New Translation of the Bible*, 267; emphasis added.

77.   Dean C. Jessee, Mark Ashurst-McGee, and Richard L. Jensen, eds., *Journals, Volume 1: 1832–1839*, vol. 1 of the Journals series of *The Joseph Smith Papers*, ed. Dean C. Jessee, Ronald K. Esplin, and Richard Lyman Bushman (Salt Lake City: Church Historian's Press, 2008), 11.

78.   New Testament Revision 2, part 1, p. 25, in Faulring, Jackson, and Matthews, *Joseph Smith's New Translation*, 267n1 explains that the pinned note was "in Sidney Rigdon's handwriting." Though we don't have the original copy of D&C 86, the early copy made by Frederick G. Williams affirms that it was "written by Sidney [Rigdon] the scribe an[d] Counsellor." Revelation, 6 December 1832 [D&C 86], in *JSP*, D2:327. Williams was the scribe for the Old Testament work then going on and some of the New Testament revisions, but Rigdon did much of the revision writing. Faulring, Jackson, and Matthews, *Joseph Smith's New Translation of the Bible*, 59.

79.   Revelation, 6 December 1832 [D&C 86], in *JSP*, D2:326; see D&C 86:4–7.

80.   *Messenger and Advocate*, December 1835, 226–29, cited in Kent P. Jackson, ed., *Joseph Smith's Commentary on the Bible* (Salt Lake City: Deseret Book, 1994), 95.

81.   Old Testament Revision 1, p. 34, in Faulring, Jackson, and Matthews, *Joseph Smith's New Translation of the Bible*, 127.

82.   New Testament Revision 2, part 4, p. 139, in Faulring, Jackson, and Matthews, *Joseph Smith's New Translation of the Bible*, 539.

83.   Old Testament Revision 2, p. 70, in Faulring, Jackson, and Matthews, *Joseph Smith's New Translation of the Bible*, 701.

84.   Old Testament Revision 2, p. 72, in Faulring, Jackson, and Matthews, *Joseph Smith's New Translation of the Bible*, 709.

85.   The revelation was received over two days, 22–23 September 1832, but the section containing the information about the priesthood is in the beginning verses and was thus confined to 22 September.

86. Revelation, 22–23 September 1832 [D&C 84], in *JSP*, D2:293; see D&C 84:6.

87. Revelation, 22–23 September 1832 [D&C 84], in *JSP*, D2:295; see D&C 84:14–15.

88. Revelation, 22–23 September 1832 [D&C 84], in *JSP*, D2:295; see D&C 84:17.

89. Revelation, 22–23 September 1832 [D&C 84], in *JSP*, D2:295; see D&C 84:19–21.

90. Revelation, 22–23 September 1832 [D&C 84], in *JSP*, D2:295–96; see also D&C 84:23–25.

91. Matthew C. Godfrey, "A Culmination of Learning: D&C 84 and the Doctrine of the Priesthood," in *You Shall Have My Word: Exploring the Text of the Doctrine and Covenants*, ed. Scott C. Esplin, Richard O. Cowan, and Rachel Cope (Provo, UT: Religious Studies Center, 2012), 170–71.

92. Godfrey, "Culmination of Learning," in *You Shall Have My Word: Exploring the Text of the Doctrine and Covenants*, 178.

7

"A Covenant and a Deed Which Cannot Be Broken"

The Continuing Saga of Consecration

Casey Paul Griffiths

Casey Paul Griffiths is an assistant professor of
Church history and doctrine at Brigham Young University.

Among modern Latter-day Saints there is a tendency to use past-tense or future-tense language when speaking of the law of consecration, as if consecration is either something that Church members *used* to live or something the Saints *will come* to live in the future. Not only is this an inaccurate reading of the early revelations of the Restoration, but it also directly ignores standard practice in the Church today. Consecration was introduced by the Lord as "a covenant and a deed which cannot be broken" to fulfill his command to "remember the poor" (D&C 42:30).[1] This study serves to provide a broad overview of the practice of consecration within the Church, from 1831 to the present. While it is impossible to fully explore consecration in all its forms in a work as brief as this one, historical examples from every period of Church history show a consistent series of attempts by the leader of the Church to understand the principles of consecration and adapt them to current circumstances. The few examples mentioned here demonstrate that, while the means and methods of the *practice* of consecration underwent alterations throughout the history of the Church, the *doctrines* and

121

principles of consecration have never been rescinded. The attempts to implement the principles form a golden thread of charity running throughout the entire history of the Church and even into the present day.[2]

Church Practice and Principles

One of the misunderstandings surrounding the law of consecration surrounds the operation introduced by the Lord in an early revelation given to the Prophet Joseph Smith (D&C 42).[3] Part of the tendency to refer to the law of consecration as a practice of the past grows out of a belief that this revelation, given in 1831, represents the only way consecration can be fully carried out. This view ignores the continual alterations made to the methodology of consecration found throughout the revelations of Joseph Smith. Consecration is perhaps best thought of as a set of guiding principles and doctrines introduced throughout the Doctrine and Covenants, and not a strict set of rules. The practice of consecration, like many Church practices, has been continually altered to fit the needs of the changing Church. The way consecration was practiced in 1831 Kirtland, 1838 Missouri, or 1870s Utah does not necessarily represent the best way for it to operate in the global Church of the twenty-first century. President Boyd K. Packer explained, "Changes in organization or procedures are a testimony that revelation is ongoing. . . . The doctrines will remain fixed, eternal; the organizations, programs, and procedures will be altered as directed by Him whose church this is."[4] The first step toward understanding consecration is to identify the key doctrines and principles found in the revelations of Joseph Smith.

Principles of Consecration

The most basic approach to understanding consecration is to examine the meaning of the word itself and how it was used in the time frame of the early Restoration. An 1828 dictionary defined "consecration" as "the act or ceremony of separating from a common to a sacred use." The entry further adds, "Consecration does not make a person or a thing *holy*, but declares it to be *sacred*, that is, devoted to God or to divine service."[5] This is a broad definition of the term but is perhaps the most useful in order to comprehend the wide range of practical applications of the law of consecration. Throughout the history of the Church, the terms "law of consecration" and "United Order" both refer to attempts to devote the temporal and spiritual resources of the Church to assist the poor and needy. In practice, these attempts took many forms. While the law of consecration for the early Saints in Kirtland or Nauvoo was markedly different than today's present practice, Saints in all ages make the covenant to offer their resources to the sacred use of God's kingdom.

A cursory reading of the revelations of Joseph Smith provides insight to the importance of consecration. Speaking conservatively, at least twenty-four revelations in the Doctrine and Covenants deal directly with consecration and different methods of implementing it.[6] The earliest mention of an organized form of caring for the poor is found in a January 1831 revelation, in which the Lord commands the Saints that certain men should be appointed among them to "look to the poor and the needy, and administer to their relief that they shall not suffer" (D&C 38:35).[7] A few weeks later, after Joseph Smith arrived in Kirtland, Ohio, a revelation was given and was labeled in its earliest forms as "The Laws of the Church of Christ."[8] This revelation provided the first specifics about how to provide for the poor.

The portion of the revelation detailing consecration begins, "Behold thou shalt consecrate *all* thy properties that which thou hast unto me with a covenant and deed which cannot be broken and they shall be laid before the Bishop of my church."[9] Inclusion of the word "all" leads the reader to believe that every single item of property possessed by an individual must be submitted to the priesthood leaders. The Prophet and his associates clarified this in later editions of the revelation, most significantly in the 1835 edition of the Doctrine and Covenants, which changed the passage to instruct the Saints to "consecrate *of* thy properties."[10] Consecration of properties denotes a sacrifice of resources to benefit the poor but leads away from a completely communal interpretation of the law which would require all property to be given to the Church.

This is further bolstered by the next instruction given in the revelation, when the Lord provides instructions for the priesthood leaders administering the law. They must provide a stewardship, allowing participants to be stewards over their "own property, or that which he has received by consecration, as much as is sufficient for himself and family" (D&C 42:32).[11] Additional revelations confirmed that while unity was a primary goal of the law, equality was a relative term. Following the Lord's counsel in the earliest copies of the revelation, stewardships were provided not just according to the needs and wants of an individual or family. When the revelation was first published in the 1835 edition of the Doctrine and Covenants, the Prophet was inspired to add the phrase "according to his circumstances" (D&C 51:3).[12] Provisions were also added, which clarified that, if an individual chose to no longer participate in the law, they retained their stewardship but could not reclaim what was consecrated (D&C 42:37; 51:5).[13] Private ownership of property and voluntary participation served as key principles of the law from the start. Joseph Smith and other Church leaders wrote in an 1833 letter, "Every man must be his own judge how much he should receive and how much he should suffer to remain in the hands of the Bishop. . . . The matter of consecration must be done by mutual consent of both parties."[14]

Another key component of the law consisted of the use of surpluses to provide for a "storehouse, to administer to the poor and the needy" and also for purchasing land, "building houses of worship," and "building up of the New Jerusalem" (D&C 42:34–35).[15] Other revelations instruct that the storehouse be directed under the hands of a bishop or church agents "appointed by the voice of the church" (D&C 51:12–13).[16] The storehouse was "common property of the whole church," with every individual improving on their "talents"—a word denoting both the New Testament currency and the gifts and abilities given by the Lord (D&C 82:18).[17] An undergirding motivation for the law was the need for the Saints to sacrifice in order to build a faithful community with the New Jerusalem on their spiritual horizons.[18]

Finally, the Lord commanded the Saints to avoid pride, be modest in dress, and be clean (D&C 42:40–41). The revelation also commanded the Saints to avoid idleness, warning, "He that is idle shall not eat the bread nor wear the garments of the laborer" (D&C 42:42).[19] (By no means do these statements represent a comprehensive treatment of all of the Lord's commandments to early Saints concerning consecration. Our aim here is simply to provide a summary of the key principles of the law.) Throughout the history of the Church these principles remained consistent. Since 1831, successive generations of Church leadership have applied them in a wide variety of circumstances. This is logical given the varied circumstances the Saints have found themselves in, from times when the entire membership of the Church consisted of a small handful of people to today, when millions of Saints live in diverse circumstances around the globe. In an effort to illustrate the different applications of the law of consecration, we will now embark on a brief overview of the history of consecration in the Church from its founding to the present day.

Consecration in the Early Restoration, 1831–44

One of the key evidences that the law of consecration was not intended to strictly follow the mode of operation explained in Doctrine and Covenants 42 is found in the versatile ways Joseph Smith directed the practice of the law. In some ways, consecration began in the Church as a grassroots effort. When Joseph Smith arrived in Kirtland, Ohio, he already found members trying to implement a form of communal living on their own. One outside observer from the time noted, "Isaac Morley had contended that in order to restore the ancient order of things in the Church of Christ, it was necessary that there should be a community of goods among the brethren; and accordingly a number of them removed to his house and farm, and built houses and worked and lived together, and composed what is here called the 'Big Family,' which at this time consisted of 50 or 60, old and young."[20]

The new converts in Kirtland began the effort out of a sincere desire to adhere to the scriptures, but a lack of specific direction caused problems to emerge immediately. Church historian John Whitmer later recorded, "The disciples had all things in common, and were going to destruction very fast as to temporal things. . . . Therefore they would take each other's clothes and other property and use it without leave, which brought on confusion."[21] When Joseph Smith arrived in Kirtland in February 1831, a number of members clamored to know the Lord's will concerning the practice of communal living. In response to these requests, the Lord provided the revelations that revealed the foundational principles of consecration (D&C 42; 51).

The first attempt to practice the principles of the law in Kirtland was short lived. The first signs of trouble appeared in June 1831, when Leman Copley, a recent convert, rescinded an offer to allow Church members arriving from Colesville, New York, to settle on his land. In a revelation the Lord informed the Colesville Saints that "the covenant which they made unto me has been broken, even so it has become void and of none effect" (D&C 54:4).

The Lord condemned Copley for breaking his oath but assured blessings for those who "kept the covenant and observed the commandment, for they shall obtain mercy" (D&C 54:5–6).[22]

The episode involving Leman Copley and the Colesville Saints serves as a dramatic example of some of the challenges facing consecration, but it was not the end of attempts at consecration among the early members of the Church. Through Joseph Smith's Presidency the Lord offered a number of different ways to adapt the principles of consecration to meet the needs of the young Church. In a revelation given in November 1831, the Lord commanded Joseph Smith and five others to create an organization to manage the publication of Church materials, including the scriptures and other supplies. Funds raised through the work of this firm could be used to provide for the temporal needs of its members, with the Lord directing that the surplus "be given into my storehouse and the benefits thereof shall be consecrated unto the inhabitants of Zion and unto their generations" (D&C 70:7–8).[23] In the minutes of this organization it was referred to as the Literary Firm.[24] In March 1832 another revelation directed Church leadership to organize several Church-owned businesses, such as Newel K. Whitney's store in Kirtland, Ohio, and A. Sidney Gilbert's store in Independence, Missouri, to serve as a "storehouse for the poor" (D&C 78:3). These businesses, along with the Literary Firm and other Church interests, were brought together in a new organization referred to by its members as the United Firm (D&C 78:8).[25] This organization, at times referred to by the code name "United Order" has been referred to as the Church's "first master plan of business and finance."[26] The United Firm continued to play a key role in the financial affairs of the Church until 1834, when it was divided into two separate orders, one in Ohio and the other in Missouri, partially because of the persecution faced by Church members in Missouri but also because of the transgressions and covetousness of the Saints (D&C 104:51, 78–86).[27]

The United Firm was only one of several examples where the principles of consecration were applied in different ways to meet the needs of the Church. In August 1833 Joseph Smith received a revelation directing the organization of a committee to oversee the construction of the House of the Lord, later known as the Kirtland Temple, along with a "house for the presidency" and a "house for the printing of the translation of my scriptures" (D&C 88:119; 94:3,10).[28] When the Lord dissolved the United Firm, he commanded Church leaders to create two treasuries. The first was designated as "exclusive of the sacred things, for the purpose of printing these sacred things," a reference to the scriptures (D&C 104:60–66). At the same time the Lord set up "another treasury" for the purpose of "improving upon the properties which I have appointed unto you" (D&C 104:67–68).[29] These moves demonstrated the importance of disseminating revelations as widely as possible.

Throughout the majority of the 1830s, the Saints made various attempts to practice the law of consecration. One of the most important revelations in its development was given in Far West, Missouri, in July 1839. The revelation came in answer to the Prophet's question, "O! Lord, show unto thy servants how much thou requires of the properties of thy people for a Tithing?" The reply came, "I require all their surplus property to be put into the hands of the bishop of my church in Zion, for the building of mine house, and for the laying of the foundation of Zion and for the priesthood, and for the debts of the Presidency of my Church. And this shall be the beginning of the tithing of my people. And after that, those who have thus been tithed, shall pay one tenth of all their interest annually; and this shall be a standing law unto them forever" (D&C 119:1–4).[30] From the text it is clear that the law of tithing was not intended to replace the law of consecration. All the principles of consecration remained intact, with the added command for the Saints to contribute an additional tithe of ten percent.[31]

A mistaken impression has arisen within the Church that the law of tithing, given in 1838, replaced the law of consecration. In many ways the law of tithing required a greater sacrifice than the law of consecration: consecration required members to give their surplus *after* their needs were satisfied, but tithing required ten percent *before* any of their needs were met.[32] However, the requirement to give a surplus did not end. After section 119 was given, Brigham Young asked Joseph Smith, "Who shall be the judge of what is surplus property?" to which the Prophet responded, "Let them be the judge for themselves."[33]

The extreme trials of 1838–40, as the Prophet Joseph and other Church leaders languished in Liberty Jail and the Saints sought refuge in Illinois, caused a further suspension in attempts for the Saints to live the law of consecration. Recognizing the suffering of the Saints, the Prophet continued to urge them to comply to the principles of the law, writing to Saints, "For a man to consecrate his property . . . is nothing more nor less than to feed the hungry, clothe the naked, visit the widow and the fatherless, the sick and the afflicted, and do all he can to administer to their relief in their afflictions, and for him and his house to serve the Lord."[34]

In the midst of the difficulties surrounding the move to Illinois and the creation of the city of Nauvoo out of the malarial swamps on the banks of the Mississippi River, Joseph Smith steered a conservative course, freeing the people from their obligation to comply with all facets of the law. Elias Smith recorded a discourse given by the Prophet in 1840: "He said that the law of consecration could not be kept here and that it was the will of the Lord we should desist from trying to keep it . . . and that he assumed the whole responsibility of not keeping it until proposed by himself."[35]

Historians have at times referred to the Nauvoo era as a fallow period for consecration, but more recently documentary evidence has emerged demonstrating attempts to implement a more regimented practice of the doctrine during this time. A meeting recorded in Wilford Woodruff's journal from 18 June 1842 notes that "Joseph commanded the Twelve to organize the Church more according to the Law of God," a likely reference to a renewed attempt to implement consecration.[36] Only a few days later Brigham Young preached a sermon on "the law of consecration, and union of action in building up the city and providing labor for the city and providing labor and food for the poor."[37] Recently, historians Mitchell K. Schaefer and Sherilyn Farnes identified and published twenty affidavits of consecration dating from June 1842, the same period as when Joseph made this request of the Twelve.[38] Lewis Ziegler, a Saint from the period, wrote in his affidavit, "I for my part feel willing to lay what little is Committed to what is my trust at the Apostle[s'] feet . . . asking the hand of my heavenly Father to strengthen their hands abundantly."[39]

These attempts to renew earlier practices of consecration do not appear to have been fruitful, but doctrine of consecration remained at the core of the Saints' relationships with the Lord. As evidence of this, a covenant to commit to live the law of consecration was included in the sacred rites of the temple when they were revealed to Joseph Smith during his ministry in Nauvoo.[40]

The United Order in the West, 1846–85

The emergency conditions surrounding the exodus from Nauvoo and the eventual migration of the main body of the Church to the Salt Lake Valley made it difficult to set a uniform system for the practice of consecration. Nevertheless, the principles of the law remained a vital part of the beliefs of the Saints. In October 1845, Brigham Young proposed a covenant "that we take all the saints with us to the extent of our ability, that is, our influence and property."[41] The Lord reiterated the need for consecration in a revelation given at Winter Quarters, declaring, "Let each company bear an equal proportion, according to the dividend of their property, in taking the poor, the widows, the fatherless" and that "every man use all his influence and property to remove this people to the place where the Lord shall locate a stake of Zion" (D&C 136:8,10). As the settlements of the Saints spread throughout the Intermountain West, cooperation in irrigation and agricultural projects became essential for their survival. As the Saints became more settled, Brigham Young made attempts to launch a more formal program of consecration in the 1850s, though the conflict with the federal government of the United States in 1857 brought a practical end to most of these efforts.[42]

A more spirited effort to bring to practice the principles of consecration began in 1874 and lasted until roughly 1885.[43] Failure to live the law of consecration had long lingered in the minds of Church leaders, and Brigham Young spearheaded an effort to return the Saints to the ideals of consecration. According to reports of a meeting held in April 1874, "President Young showed very clearly that it [the united order] was not a personal speculation; that himself with the rest would put in all he possessed for the accomplishment of the work he was engaged in. . . . The intention was to elevate the poor, and make them as comfortable and happy as well as the rich. He wanted no poor in our midst, nor would there be any when the Order got fully established."[44] Spurred by the encouragement of Church leaders, new united orders sprang up throughout the Intermountain West. In initiating these efforts, Church leaders did not follow the exact same procedures given in the Doctrine and Covenants. Instead they taught the principles of the law and allowed the leaders in each individual settlement to work out procedures for the implementation of consecration. Thus, the systems of consecration varied from place to place, with consecration working slightly differently in

St. George than it did in Kanab, Orderville, or any of the locations where the Saints organized their efforts. The entire Church-wide effort was loosely labeled "the United Order" or the "Order of Enoch," though it differed in many respects from the united order of Joseph Smith's day.[45]

Interlude: The Transitional Period and the Law of Tithing, 1885–1935

Success varied in each of these efforts, but most ended when the Church became embroiled in the battle with the government of the United States over plural marriage. This battle financially exhausted the Church, making any new attempts to practice the law of consecration out of the question.[46] In the wake of fiscal devastation left by the Anti-polygamy crusades, Church leaders worked to place the Church back on stable footing. As part of this effort, leaders emphasized the law of tithing as the most practical means of accomplishing their goals. It is during this period that the belief that the law of tithing had replaced consecration became more prevalent. For instance, in April 1900 Joseph F. Smith, then a counselor in the First Presidency taught, "The Lord revealed to his people in the incipiency of His work a law [consecration] which was more perfect than the law of tithing. It comprehended larger things, greater power and a more speedy accomplishment of the purposes of the Lord. But the people were unprepared to live by the it, and the Lord, out of mercy to the people, suspended the more perfect law, and gave the law of tithing."[47]

While there was no revelation officially suspending the law of consecration, President Smith was correct in stating that during this period, when the Church was transitioning from its relative isolation in the West and moving closer to the mainstream of society, the practices of consecration received less emphasis, and the more clear-cut guidelines of tithing, a subset of the entire law, were given emphasis. At the same time, the Church did not abandon its charge to assist the poor and needy. During this period bishops were still given instruction to use fast offerings and Relief Society contributions to care for the poor. Church handbooks from the period instructed local leaders to send their surplus to Church headquarters to assist more needy wards and branches, though it was rare at the time for Church units to use less than their members contributed.[48]

These offerings allowed leaders to care for the immediate needs of the poor, but a larger overarching structure to implement consecration did not exist. Furthermore, a general perception lingered that consecration was a future goal. In 1931 Elder Orson F. Whitney taught, "The Lord withdrew the Law of Consecration, and gave his people a lesser law, one easier to live, but pointing forward, like the other, to something grand and glorious in the future."[49] While Elder Whitney's comments implied a distant promise of future consecration, they came on the eve of the most successful and long-lasting implementation of consecration practices within the Church.

The Church Welfare Program, 1935–Present

Ironically, the most enduring practical implementation of the law of consecration was born out of one of the worst economic catastrophes in history. In the depths of the Great Depression, Harold B. Lee, the president of the Pioneer Stake in Salt Lake City, launched an innovative series of programs designed to provide work and support for the struggling members of the stake. A storehouse where food and commodities could be gathered and distributed to the needy was built. Lee and his counselors purchased warehouses, a farm, and other enterprises, and the men of the stake were given opportunities to work for what they would receive from the storehouse. The particulars of the plan were new to the Church, but President Lee was quick to point out that the principles behind were not. In an article explaining the plan, Lee wrote, "The Church security plan is not something new to the Church; neither does it contemplate a new organization in the Church to carry out its purposes; but rather it is an expression of a philosophy that is as old as the Church itself, incorporated into a program of stimulation and cooperation to meet the demands of Church members in the solution of present day economic problems."[50]

While Harold B. Lee and other stake presidents worked from the ground up to care for the poor, leaders in the top echelons of Church government also began to reexamine consecration. J. Reuben Clark Jr., a newly called Counselor in the First Presidency, began to make an extensive study of the revelations in the Doctrine and Covenants pertaining to consecration.[51] As President Clark and other Church leaders observed the success of these programs, a plan began to develop to apply the principles of consecration on a wider level. On 18 April 1936, the First Presidency met with Harold B. Lee, who later wrote, "President [Heber J.] Grant said he wanted to take a 'leaf out of the Pioneer Stake's book in caring for the people of the Church. . . . He said that nothing was more important for the Church to do than to take care of its needy people and that so far as he was concerned, everything else must be sacrificed [so that] proper relief [could be] extended to our people."[52] Harold B. Lee was named as the managing director of the new program, and at the October general conference the following fall, the First Presidency announced the launch of the Church welfare plan. At a meeting for stake presidents, the First Presidency declared, "The real long term objective of the Welfare Plan is the building of character in the members of the Church, givers and receivers, rescuing all that is finest down deep inside of them, and bringing to flower and fruitage the latent richness of the spirit, which after all is the mission and purpose and reason for being of this Church."[53]

During the infancy of the Church welfare program, Church leaders downplayed the similarities between the new program and the early efforts of Church members. Speaking of the Church welfare system and the law of consecration, President J. Reuben Clark Jr. noted, "We have all said that the Welfare Plan is not the United Order and was not intended to be." He then added, "However, I should like to suggest to you that perhaps, after all, when the Welfare Plan gets thoroughly into operation—it is not so yet—we shall not be so very far from carrying out the great fundamentals of the United Order."[54]

Consecration in Our Time and Beyond

Is the Church welfare program the same thing as the United Order? Church members do not follow the exact methodology first mentioned in the revelations of Joseph Smith, but the principles of consecration have endured. Consecration, stewardships, storehouses, and nearly every component of the early revelations eventually found its way into the structure of the Church welfare systems. In 1943, J. Reuben Clark Jr. presented a plan to the Quorum of the Twelve Apostles where he noted, "I took it upon myself to make a study of the financial operations of the Church from the beginning down through and until after the death of the Prophet [Joseph Smith]."[55] At a ten-year anniversary of the Welfare Plan, President Clark reflected, "The Lord has always been mindful of the poor and of the unfortunate, and He has always charged His Church and its members to see to it that none of their brethren and their sisters suffer."[56]

Church leaders of the founding generation never became comfortable identifying the Church Welfare Plan as the same thing as the law of consecration, but the ensuing generations began to recognize the fulfillment of the principles of the law in the new plan. In a 1966 general conference address, Elder Marion G. Romney of the Quorum of the Twelve Apostles (who later became President of the Quorum of the Twelve) exhorted priesthood holders to "live strictly by the principles of the United Order insofar as they are embodied in present church practices such as the fast offering, tithing, and the welfare activities." He then added, "Through these practices we could as individuals, if we were of a mind to do so, implement in our own lives all the basic principles of the United Order."[57] In 1975 Elder Romney said, "The procedural method for teaching Church welfare has now changed, but the objectives of the program remain the same. *Its principles are eternal.* It is the gospel in its perfection—the united order, toward which we move."[58]

As time progressed Church leaders became more comfortable in seeing the Church welfare program as another iteration of consecration. In an address given in 2011, President Henry B. Eyring stated that the Lord's "way of helping has at times been called living the law of consecration. In another period His way was called the united order. In our time it is called the Church welfare program." Providing a summary of the evolution of the law, President Eyring added, "The names and the details of the operation are changed to fit the needs and conditions of people. But always the Lord's way to help those in temporal need requires people who out of love have consecrated themselves and what they have to God and to His work."[59]

There is nothing past tense about the law of consecration. It remains a vital part of the work of the Lord's kingdom on the earth. The doctrines of consecration are eternal and will always have a place in the Church. The eternal components of the law—love for God, love for neighbor, agency, stewardship, and accountability—are a vital part of the gospel of Jesus Christ. The temporal applications of the law, deeds, economic practices, and building and publishing projects are subject to frequent change. Until the return of the Savior we shall have the poor with us always (see Matthew. 26:11), and as long as the poor are with us we also have a charge to provide care and solace to them. The law of consecration is not an ideal or a command-ment; it is a covenant entered into by every worthy member of the Church. President Eyring taught, "He has invited and commanded us to participate in His work to lift up those in need. We make a covenant to do that in the waters of baptism and in the holy temples of God. We renew the covenant on Sundays when we partake of the sacrament."[60] Though often misunder-stood, overlooked, or forgotten, the covenant of consecration will always be a foundational part of the Restoration and the operation of the Lord's true Church.

Notes

1. The admonition to "remember the poor" and to consecrate properties "for their [the poor's] support" was first added in the 1835 edition of the Doctrine and Covenants. See Michael Hubbard MacKay, Gerrit J. Dirkmaat, Grant Underwood, Robert J. Woodford, and William G. Hartley, eds., *Documents, Volume 1: July 1828–June 1831*, vol. 1 of the Documents series of *The Joseph Smith Papers*, ed. Dean C. Jessee, Ronald K. Esplin, Richard Lyman Bushman, and Matthew J. Grow (Salt Lake City: Church Historian's Press, 2013), 251, also *The Parallel Doctrine and Covenants: The 1832–33, 1833, and 1835 editions of Joseph Smith's Revelations* (Salt Lake City: Smith-Petit Foundation, 2009), 68.

2. I am indebted to many authors who have argued this point before me, chiefly Lyndon W. Cook in *Joseph Smith and the Law of Consecration* (Provo, UT: Grandin Book Company, 1985), viii; Craig James Ostler, "The Laws of Consecration, Stewardship, and Tithing," in *Sperry Symposium Classics: The Doctrine and Covenants*, ed. Craig K. Manscill (Salt Lake City: Deseret Book, 2004); and Steven C. Harper, "'All Things are the Lord's': The Law of Consecration in the Doctrine and Covenants," in *The Doctrine and Covenants: Revelations in Context* (Salt Lake City: Deseret Book, 2008).

3. Revelation, 9 February 1831, in *JSP*, D1:245–56 (D&C 42).

4. Boyd K. Packer, "Revelation in a Changing World," *Ensign*, November 1989, 14–16.

5. http://webstersdictionary1828.com/Dictionary/consecration, accessed 6 February 2016.

6. Craig James Ostler, "Consecration," in *Doctrine and Covenants Reference Companion* (Salt Lake City: Deseret Book, 2012), 106. The sections focusing primarily on consecration are D&C 38, 42, 44, 48, 51, 54, 56, 58, 70, 72, 78, 82–85, 92, 96–97, 104–6, 119–20, and 136.

7. Revelation, 2 January 1831 [D&C 38], in *JSP*, D1:233.

8. Revelation, 9 February 1831 [D&C 42:1–72], in *JSP*, D1: 245–56.

9. *JSP*, D1:251; spelling, punctuation, and deletions have been removed, and emphasis added.

10. Robin Scott Jensen, Richard E. Turley Jr., and Riley M. Lorimer, eds., *Revelations and Translations, Volume 2: Published Revelations,* vol. 2 of the Revelations and Translations series of *The Joseph Smith Papers,* ed. Dean C. Jessee, Ronald K. Esplin, and Richard Lyman Bushman (Salt Lake City: Church Historian's Press, 2011), 105, 218, 433. The change in wording first appeared in *The Evening and Morning Star,* July 1832. It has remained consistent in every published version of the revelation down to the present day (2015).

11. Revelation, 9 February 1831 [D&C 42:1–72], in *JSP,* D1: 251–52.

12. Revelation, 20 May 1831 [D&C 51], in *JSP,* D1:314–16, Book of Commandments, in *JSP,* R&T2:127.

13. 1835 Doctrine & Covenants, Section XXIII, 156, in *JSP,* R&T2:460; revelation, 9 February 1831 [D&C 42:1–72], in *JSP,* D1: 252.

14. Letter to Church Leaders in Jackson County, Missouri, 25 June 1833, in *JSP,* D3:153.

15. Revelation, 9 February 1831 [D&C 42:1–72], in *JSP,* D1: 252.

16. Revelation, 20 May 1831 [D&C 51], in *JSP,* D1:316.

17. Revelation, 26 April 1832 [D&C 82], in *JSP,* D2:236.

18. See Ostler, "Consecration," 158.

19. Revelation, 9 February 1831 [D&C 42:1–72], in *JSP,* D1: 252.

20. Josiah Jones, "History of the Mormonites," *The Evangelist* 9 (1 June 1831): 132, quoted in Mark Lyman Staker, *Hearken, O Ye People: The Historical Setting for Joseph Smith's Ohio Revelations* (Salt Lake City: Greg Kofford Books, 2009), 45.

21. Karen Lynn Davidson, Richard L. Jensen, and David J. Whittaker, eds., *Histories, Volume 2: Assigned Historical Writings, 1831–1847,* vol. 2 of the Histories series of *The Joseph Smith Papers,* ed. Dean C. Jessee, Ronald K. Esplin, and Richard Lyman Bushman (Salt Lake City: Church Historian's Press, 2012), 22–23.

22. Revelation, 10 June 1831 [D&C 54], in *JSP,* D1:335–36.

23. Revelation, 12 November 1831 [D&C 70], in *JSP,* D2:140.

24. Minutes, 30 April 1832, in *JSP,* D2:238, spelling corrected.

25. Minutes, circa 1 May 1832, in *JSP,* D2:244.

26. Staker, *Hearken, O Ye People,* 231; Max H Parkin, "Joseph Smith and the United Firm: The Growth and Decline of the Church's First Master Plan of Business and Finance, Ohio and Missouri, 1832–1834," *BYU Studies* 46, no. 3 (2007): 56–60.

27. Revelation, 23 April 1834 [D&C 104], http://josephsmithpapers.org/paperSummary/revelation-23-april-1834-dc-104#!/paperSummary/revelation-23-april-1834-dc-104&p=5.

28. Revelation, 2 August 1833-B [D&C 94], in *JSP,* D3:206.

29. Revelation, 23 April 1834 [D&C 104], in Book of Commandments Book C, [pp. 19–43], http://josephsmithpapers.org/paperSummary/revelation-23-april-1834-dc-104#!/paperSummary/revelation-23-april-1834-dc-104&p=17.

30. Revelation, 8 July 1838-C [D&C 119], in JS, Journal, March–September 1838, 56, http://josephsmithpapers.org/paperSummary/revelation-8-july-1838-c-dc-119.

31. Ostler, "Consecration," 172.

32. See Joseph Fielding McConkie and Craig J. Ostler, *Revelations of the Restoration* (Salt Lake City: Deseret Book, 2000), 936.

33. *The Complete Discourses of Brigham Young*, ed. Richard S. Van Wagoner (Salt Lake City: Smith-Petit Foundation, 2009), 970.

34. Letter to the Church in Caldwell County, Missouri, 16 December 1838, http://josephsmithpapers.org/paperSummary/letter-to-the-church-in-caldwell -county-missouri-16-december-1838#!/paperSummary/letter-to-the-church-in -caldwell-county-missouri-16-december-1838&p=5.

35. Discourse, 6 March 1840, as reported by Elias Smith, http://josephsmith papers.org/paperSummary/discourse-6-march-1840-as-reported-by-elias-smith. Another witness recorded the Prophet saying, "Thus saith the Lord you need not observe the Law of Consecration until our case was decided in congress." Discourse, 6 March 1840, as reported by John Smith, http://josephsmithpapers.org/paper Summary/discourse-6-march-1840-as-reported-by-john-smith.

36. *The Words of Joseph Smith*, comp. Andrew F. Ehat and Lyndon W. Cook (Provo, UT: Religious Studies Center, 1980), 124–25.

37. *The Complete Discourses of Brigham Young*, 1:20.

38. Mitchell K. Shaefer and Sherilyn Farnes, "Myself . . . I Consecrate to the God of Heaven," *BYU Studies* 50, no. 3 (2011): 101.

39. Shaefer and Farnes, "Myself . . . I Consecrate to the God of Heaven," 132, spelling and punctuation in original. Shaefer and Farnes note that this affidavit of consecration is the only known documentation of Lewis Ziegler.

40. Cook, *Joseph Smith and the Law of Consecration,* 90.

41. *The Complete Discourses of Brigham Young*, 102; see also Leonard J. Arrington, Feramorz Y. Fox, and Dean L. May, *Building the City of God: Community and Cooperation Among the Mormons* (Salt Lake City: Deseret Book, 1976), 42.

42. Arrington et al., *Building the City of God*, 48, 63, 77–78.

43. Edward J. Allen, *The Second United Order Among the Mormons* (New York: AMS Press, 1967), 10.

44. Quoted in *Deseret News*, 22 April 1874, from *Beaver Enterprise.*

45. See Arrington et al., *Building the City of God,* which provides a detailed analysis of consecration systems in Brigham City, St. George, Richfield, Kanab, and Orderville, along with Mormon settlements in Utah Valley, Cache Valley, Bear Lake Valley, and other LDS settlements in Arizona, Nevada, and Mexico.

46. See Arrington et al., *Building the City of God,* 311–37.

47. Joseph F. Smith, in Conference Report, April 1900, 47.

48. Bruce D. Blumell, "Welfare before Welfare: Twentieth Century LDS Church Charity before the Great Depression," *Journal of Mormon History* 6 (1979): 92.

49. Orson F. Whitney, in Conference Report, April 1931, 63.

50. Harold B. Lee, "Church Security, Retrospect, Introspect, Prospect," *Improvement Era,* April 1937, 204.

51. Two unpublished documents in Clark's papers, "Notes on Church Finances," produced in June 1942, and "Study of the United Order," from March 1943, demonstrate Clark's serious intent to reform Church finances in line with the revelation in the Doctrine and Covenants. J. Reuben Clark Papers, MS 303, box 188, L. Tom Perry Special Collections, BYU.

52. Glen L. Rudd, *Pure Religion: The Story of Church Welfare Since 1930* (Salt Lake City: The Church of Jesus Christ of Latter-day Saints, 1995), 39–40. Garth Mangum and Bruce Blumell, *The Mormons' War on Poverty* (Salt Lake City: University of Utah Press, 1993), 130–32.

53. Rudd, *Pure Religion*, 45.

54. J. Reuben Clark Jr., in Conference Report, October 1942, 58.

55. "General Principles Underlying Church Finances," box 188, J. Reuben Clark Papers, BYU.

56. J. Reuben Clark Jr. address, ca. 1946, box 158, Clark Papers, 1.

57. Marion G. Romney, "Socialism and the United Order," *Improvement Era*, June 1966, 537.

58. Quoted in Arrington et al., *Building the City of God*, 361; emphasis added.

59. Henry B. Eyring, "Opportunities to Do Good," *Ensign*, May 2011, 22–26.

60. Eyring, "Opportunities to Do Good," 22–26.

8

"Her Borders Must Be Enlarged"

Evolving Conceptions of Zion

Taunalyn F. Rutherford

Taunalyn F. Rutherford is an adjunct instructor of religion at Brigham Young University and a PhD candidate at Claremont Graduate University.

The establishment of Zion in preparation for Christ's Second Coming has always been a vital part of the "ongoing process" of the Restoration of the gospel.[1] It was central to the work of Joseph Smith and has continued to be so with each of his successors from Brigham Young to Thomas S. Monson; however, conceptions of Zion and its establishment have passed through an "ongoing process" of change as well. When the Lord "consecrated the land of Kirtland . . . for a stake to Zion," he declared, "For Zion must increase in beauty, and in holiness; her borders must be enlarged; her stakes must be strengthened."[2] It is clear that through revelation, Joseph foresaw the "enlarged" borders of Zion beyond Missouri. We can see in the foundations laid by Joseph Smith a pattern for a global church—an ever-enlarging Zion. Scholars point to secular influences that have caused changes in LDS understandings of Zion and changes in policies of gathering. While it is important to be aware of and understand such explanations, it is crucial in a study of the "Foundations of the Restoration" to see the hand of the Lord as well as his foreknowledge of modern events as having brought to fruition modern conceptions of Zion. Early revelations can seem to be at odds with the modern globalization of the Church unless viewed through the lens of the Lord's foreknowledge. As the title suggests, this chapter will show how the Lord revealed and prepared a way for a much larger Zion than was sometimes initially conceived of by Latter-day Saints.

Foundational Concepts of Zion Established Through Joseph Smith: Zion and the Book of Mormon

The coming forth of the Book of Mormon was a significant part of the establishment of foundational concepts of Zion in the Restoration. According to Joseph's account, during Moroni's first appearance, he quoted Joel's prophecy of events of the "great and the terrible day of the Lord" that "in mount Zion and in Jerusalem shall be deliverance."[3] The Book of Mormon contains numerous references to Zion in addition to the many times Isaiah quotations mention Zion. For instance, the angel tells Nephi, "Blessed are they who shall seek to bring forth my Zion at that day (when he brings forth the plain and precious gospel) for they shall have the gift and the power of the Holy Ghost."[4] Nephi writes, "All who fight against Zion shall be destroyed."[5] Jacob adds his witness: "he that fighteth against Zion shall perish."[6] Abinadi testifies of a coming Zion[7] as does the Savior himself in his teachings to the Nephites.[8] Finally, at a crowning moment in the Book of Mormon, a Zion society was established after the ministry of Christ to the Nephites,[9] and Moroni's final words admonish, "Put on thy beautiful garments, O daughter of Zion; and strengthen thy stakes and enlarge they borders forever, that thou mayest no more be confounded."[10]

The Book of Mormon is evidence that in the very early stages of the Restoration the concept of Zion was significant. As Joseph and his followers began to read and internalize the message of the Book of Mormon, Ether's prophecy of a New Jerusalem on "this land"[11] became a particular interest, as was the prophecy by the Savior to the Nephites of a gathering of his people to Zion in America.[12] This interest brought about an inquiry of "Six Elders of the Church and three members" who seemed to believe "that the Book of Mormon prophecy about Zion would soon be fulfilled."[13] The Lord responded by calling the elders "to bring to pass the gathering of [his] elect" and specified that they would "be gathered in unto one place upon the face of this land" in preparation for his return.[14] Revelations had come previously through Joseph Smith calling followers to "seek to bring forth and establish the cause of Zion."[15] This revelation marked an important conceptual change from Zion as simply a cause to a specific, central gathering place for Zion.

The Location of Zion

I acknowledge the conceptual complexity of Zion in Joseph's understanding and revelations. Zion was simultaneously threefold: a cause; a geographical location or center to which those who fled Babylon could gather; and a condition or internal state of righteousness. A pivotal process of revelation that expanded latter-day understandings of Zion was Joseph Smith's translation of the Bible, particularly the narrative of Enoch, which from a mere 5 verses in Genesis extended to 110 verses in the Book of Moses.[16] A definition of Zion is proclaimed in the narrative of Enoch: "And the Lord called his people Zion because they were of one heart and one mind, and dwelt in righteousness, and there was no poor among them."[17] The quest for just such a Zion became central to all that the Prophet did. The concept of consecration was also an important aspect of the project of Zion. It is impossible to fully separate the cause of Zion, the internal conditions of Zion, and the location of Zion as a gathering place; however, because of the constraints of this chapter, I will focus primarily on the changing conceptions of Zion as a geographical location and the accompanying doctrine of gathering.

As noted earlier, a September 1830 revelation had spoken of the gathering of the Lord's elect "unto one place upon the face of this land."[18] In a follow-up to this revelation, the Lord called Oliver Cowdery to preach to the "Lamanites" and promised that the location of the "city Zion" would "be given hereafter." A clue was also added: the location of Zion would "be on the borders by the Lamanites."[19] That Joseph's concept of Zion encompassed more than just the much-anticipated geographic location for the city is evidenced in a letter he wrote to members in Colesville from Fayette, New York, dated 2 December 1830, in which he reports, "Zion is prospering here."[20] The anticipation of the location of the city of Zion, the New Jerusalem, increased in March 1831 as revelations encouraged the Saints to prepare to "gather out of the eastern lands" and "gather up" their riches to be prepared to "purchase

an inheritance" in Zion, the location of which had still not been revealed.[21]
In July of 1831 the Lord declared Missouri as the land "for the gathering of
the saints" and as "the place for the city of Zion."[22] Furthermore, the Lord
declared "the place which is now called Independence" as "the center place,"
and specified "a spot for the temple" which was "lying westward, upon a lot
which is not far from the courthouse."[23]

Stakes of Zion

While Joseph Smith's revelations established Independence, Missouri, as the
center place and the location of the future city of Zion, the concept of gathering to Zion in the revelations was always more expansive. For instance, as
early as November 1831, Joseph received a revelation in which the voice of
the Lord declared, "Send forth the elders of my church unto the nations
which are afar off." These elders were to cry, "Go ye forth unto the land of
Zion, that the borders of my people may be enlarged, and that her stakes
may be strengthened and that Zion may go forth unto the regions round
about."[24] By April 1832, the concept of a stake had been further solidified
when Kirtland was designated as the first "stake to Zion."[25] The reason for
the consecration of the stake in Kirtland was given by the Lord: "For Zion
must increase in beauty, and in holiness; her borders must be enlarged; her
stakes must be strengthened; yea, verily I say unto you, Zion must arise and
put on her beautiful garments."[26] Independence, and later other surrounding cities where the Saints were driven in Missouri, were seen as Zion—the
center place for the metaphorical tent, and outlying areas became stakes of
this central Zion. The importance of stakes in the conception of the expansion of Zion and of gathering was thus established early in the foundations
that Joseph Smith restored. Isaiah's metaphor of Zion's stakes, cords, tents,
and borders were quoted in the Book of Mormon and in the revelations that
came in the process of establishing the Church. In 1836, Joseph pleaded in
the dedicatory prayer of the Kirtland Temple that the Lord would "appoint
unto Zion other stakes besides this one which thou hast appointed, that the
gathering of thy people may roll on in great power and majesty."[27]

The Redemption of Zion by Power

The Prophet's initial dream of Zion in Missouri "abruptly turned to nightmare"[28] in 1833, when in the midst of violence the Saints in Independence were driven from their Zion, and the designation of Independence as the center place became problematic. Some of the greatest ambiguity for Joseph and these early saints came because of the elusive nature of building Zion in Jackson County, Missouri. For instance, the Lord cautioned Joseph, "Zion shall be redeemed, although she is chastened for a little season."[29] Yet, for Joseph, this "little season" spanned his lifetime. In a state of perplexity Joseph wrote, "I know that Zion, in the own due time of the Lord will be redeemed, but how many will be the days of her purification, tribulation, and affliction, the Lord has kept hid from my eyes; and when I enquire concerning this subject the voice of the Lord is, Be still, and know that I am God!"[30] As we witness the struggles and disappointments of Joseph Smith associated with the tenuous nature of building Zion, we can gain strength for our own efforts. In December 1833, a revelation promised, "Zion shall not be moved out of her place, notwithstanding her children are scattered." Then the Lord specified that "there is none other place appointed than that which I have appointed; neither shall there be any other place appointed than that which I have appointed, for the work of the gathering of my saints."[31] President Harold B. Lee interpreted this verse in 1973 explaining, "In the early years of the Church specific places to which the Saints were to be gathered together were given, and the Lord directed that these gathering places should not be changed."[32] In other words, "none other place than that which I have appointed" referred not only to Jackson County but to all subsequent gathering places designated by the Lord through his prophet. Church history reflects this interpretation as latter-day prophets established gathering places in other areas in Missouri, then Illinois, Winter Quarters, and eventually the valley of the Great Salt Lake and the surrounding territory.

Independence, Missouri, was not forgotten however, and the uncertainty of this elusive Zion deepened with the seemingly failed attempt to redeem Zion with an army. In what has been called a "purposefully ambiguous" revelation that led to the establishment of an army called Zion's Camp, the Lord states, "the redemption of Zion must needs come by power," but without any clear articulation of what kind of power.[33] The efforts of redeeming Zion through temporal power in the case of Zion's Camp required tremendous faith, perhaps even "Abrahamic" faith and a willingness to sacrifice lives.[34] The Lord allowed Joseph and the members of Zion's Camp to pass through a trying and seemingly unsuccessful mission to redeem Zion by physical force. After the Zion's Camp sacrifice was made, and in the midst of the resulting uncertainty and trial of faith, the Lord was more specific, stating, "The power to redeem Zion would come not from a confrontation in Missouri but from an endowment in the house of the Lord back in Kirtland."[35]

The Lord's redemption of Zion by power flowing from covenants and endowments in the temple is the consistent thread running through revelations of Zion and all policies given in all times. Nephi saw this redemption of Zion in the latter days as "the power of the Lamb of God . . . descended . . . upon the covenant people of the Lord who were scattered upon all the face of the earth: and they were armed with righteousness and with the power of God in great glory."[36] The language used in the dedicatory prayer of the Kirtland Temple echoes this prophecy as Joseph pled, "We ask thee, Holy Father, that thy servants may go forth from this house armed with thy power."[37] The necessity of temples and temple covenants and the power that would flow through them is intricately linked with the cause of Zion at a very early stage of the Restoration. The relationship of the power to redeem and establish Zion with temple covenants and the strengthening of stakes resonates in Moroni's final plea to his latter-day readers: "Put on thy beautiful garments, O daughter of Zion: and strengthen thy stakes and enlarge thy borders."[38] Joseph Smith taught, "The object of gathering . . . the people of God in any age" is to "build unto the Lord a house to prepare them for the ordinances" of the temple.[39]

Joseph's project of building Zion extended to include the enlarged borders of new cities appointed as gathering places for the Saints who came increasingly from outside the United States. When the Saints left Missouri and settled in Nauvoo, Joseph's conception of Zion enlarged, and he is recorded as declaring "that Zion referred to all of North and South America and anywhere Saints gathered."[40] One example of Joseph's enlarged conception of Zion is a March 1841 revelation giving "the will of the Lord concerning the saints in the Territory of Iowa." They were told to "gather themselves together unto the places which I shall appoint unto them by my servant Joseph, and build up cities." Furthermore, the Lord spoke to "all those that come from the east, and the west and the north and the south" were to "take up their inheritance" in an appointed city "and in all the stakes which" the Lord had appointed.[41]

Zion in the West

Brigham Young biographer John Turner suggests that in 1844, Joseph's "final" conception of Zion as all of North and South America and his counsel to elders that churches should be built where converts received the gospel was Joseph hinting to "an end to the doctrine of gathering."[42] Turner sees Brigham Young as turning this vision another direction and seeing Joseph Smith's words as "a prediction of a glorious and expansive future for the church."[43] Joseph may have been foreseeing the end of the gathering as it had been administered during the early years of the Restoration but certainly not the end of the doctrine of gathering. Brigham Young's vision of gathering and establishing Zion was specific to his period of the ongoing Restoration. Changes in conceptions, articulations, and administration do not equal changes in foundational doctrines.

Turner suggests, "Whereas Smith built cities of Zion, Young more literally established God's kingdom upon the earth. He spoke of the construction of many temples and encouraged the planned dispersal of Mormon emigrants throughout the region." Turner also argues that Brigham Young established "a new model of gathering" in the Great Basin.[44] It enriches our understanding of LDS history to envision Brigham Young's "new model of gathering." However, we can be mindful of the ways Brigham Young's administration of the "gathering"—and any Latter-day prophet for that matter—resonates with foundational doctrines of Zion built by Joseph Smith. As another scholar explains, "From its earliest day, Mormonism's message of restoration of Primitive Christianity went hand-in-glove with a policy of gathering its converts to central locations: initially Ohio, then Missouri, then Illinois, and finally the Great Basin."[45] Although the central geographical gathering location has varied, the principles have remained unchanged. A revelation given through Brigham Young at Winter Quarters proclaimed "the Word and Will of the Lord concerning the Camp of Israel in their journeying to the West." The revelation encouraged Saints to use all their "influence and property to remove this people to the place where the Lord shall locate a stake of Zion."[46] The revelation also echoed a familiar theme promising that "Zion shall be redeemed in mine own due time."[47] Brigham Young continued to appoint other places "for the work of the gathering" as the early revelation had specified.[48] He continued to build temples and stakes, and his success in settling a major portion of the western United States attests to his project of enlarging the borders of Zion.

In 1881, John Taylor spoke of how he was "endeavoring to build up the Zion of our God" by traveling around "all through the Territory, visiting almost all the settlements." He stressed that Zion was "not confined to our prominent cities, but includes all the cities of the Saints."[49] During the presidency of John Taylor, Orson Pratt spoke on how the Lord would "stretch forth the curtains of Zion; He will lengthen her cords and strengthen her Stakes and will multiply them not only throughout this mountain Territory, but throughout the united States."[50] Then, in an attempt to reconcile the place of the "City of Zion when it is built in Jackson County," Pratt clarified that the city of Zion will not be called a stake since "the Lord never called it a Stake in any revelation." Rather, "It is to be the headquarters, it is to be the place where the Son of Man will come and dwell . . . it will be the great central city, and the outward branches will be called Stakes wherever they shall be organized as such."[51]

Historical events have played a role in changing conceptions of Zion. An important example of this occurred in 1887, when the anti-polygamy-driven Edmunds-Tucker Act was passed which, among other detrimental financial implications for the Church, dissolved the Perpetual Emigrating Fund. This reality occurred in tandem with the closing of the frontier era, since "by the end of the nineteenth century virtually all habitable locations within the Mormon domain that were suitable for agriculture had been occupied."[52] Thus, during the concluding years of the nineteenth century, Church leaders saw the need to reenvision the policies surrounding the building of Zion and began to de-emphasize gathering to the Great Basin. In 1911, an official letter from the First Presidency "urged converts to stay where they were and live according to the ideals of Zion in their own homelands." Scholars have interpreted this to have caused a transformation of "Zion in the hearts and minds of the Latter-day Saints from a literal place to an ideal."[53] Harold B. Lee articulated the way in which this 1911 policy reflected the doctrine of gathering outlined in D&C 101:20–21. As mentioned previously, President Lee emphasized that gathering places were to be appointed by the Lord. He also emphasized that when the Lord "directed that these gathering places should not be changed" the Lord "gave one qualification: 'Until the day cometh when there is found no more room for them; and then I have other places which I will appoint unto them, and they shall be called stakes, for the curtains or the strength of Zion.'"[54] This qualification was thus present in the foundations of the Restoration and not solely a modification growing out of modernization.

Modern Conceptions of Zion

Gathering to an appointed place "ended in the early 1950s, when President David O. McKay issued a call for Saints to 'gather' together in their home-lands and backed this call up through the creation of stakes, meeting-houses, and temples worldwide."[55] According to biographers, David O. McKay brought the "rise of Modern Mormonism."[56] An illustrative anec-dote from President McKay's biography tells of an interview by *New York Times* reporter Alden Whitman who asked McKay, "What do you regard as the most outstanding accomplishment of your ministry as President of the Church?" to which McKay replied, "The making of the Church a world-wide organization."[57] One of the ways he did this was through his expan-sion of Zion to include international temples and stakes. Scholars argue that McKay's focus on international temple and stake building was in part an effort to "stem the tide of foreign immigration to Utah."[58] While this may be one aspect of the policy, the vision of enlarging the borders of Zion was undoubtedly a central motivation. The temples built during the McKay administration in Europe and New Zealand proved crucial to expanding the reach of Zion. It was unique to build temples prior to the firm establish-ment of stakes in these countries, but it was a "calculated risk" that proved to "anchor church members in their native countries, thus curtailing emi-gration to the United States and allowing the creation of overseas stakes."[59] Scholars have argued that McKay abandoned the doctrine of gathering[60] and that "coincident with the decision to urge people to stay in their native lands was a redefinition of the concept of Zion."[61] Furthermore, policy changes and expansion of international temples and stakes are often cast as a drastic change in the doctrines surrounding Zion, that although Zion "had earlier referred to a geographical location, now it was recast as a state of being."[62] To conflate policy changes to changing of doctrine is problematic and overlooks the ways Zion has always been both a state of being in the foundational scriptural literature as well as a geographical place. As this chapter has shown, from the foundations of the Restoration, Zion was conceptualized to include the building of units that are called stakes, which simultaneously support the "tent of Zion," and function as new center places of gathering. The doctrine of gathering is constant, but the conceptions of *how* to gather logistically change and even expand.

A helpful metaphor to understand the internationalization of Latter-day Zion suggests that religions are like tents with fluid boundaries and thus "yield themselves to be discreetly and deliberately dismantled, relocated and reassembled. Religions are not finished products; they constantly hand themselves over to their adherents."[63] I find this especially helpful building on Isaiah's use of the metaphorical tent of Zion with curtains, cords, and borders and the way the structure of the modern Church has evolved to allow for a metaphorical one-tent structure to stretch over vast distances, oceans, and borders. While never letting go of the ideal of the "one heart and one mind" single tent of Zion, the institutional Church clearly saw the need for simplified tents (missions, districts, and branches) that can be dismantled and transported and reassembled anywhere in the world as stakes anchoring the larger tent are established. When a stake of Zion is organized, it is "handed over to its adherents," in that the local leadership becomes responsible and independent in administering the programs of the Church and a new center of Zion is created.

The process of building from small groups of members, which grow into branches that eventually become part of districts, which work persistently to become a stake, is an arduous task. Leaders of the Church prior to the global expansion that took place in the last half of the twentieth century understood that the "cause of Zion" as it had evolved in the Great Basin was not easily transportable internationally. Priesthood correlation can be seen as part of the process of dismantling that the LDS Church has undertaken in order to make the Church organization transportable. Matthew

Bowman charts this correlation effort, noting its initial growth from 1945 to 1978. By the mid-twentieth century, auxiliary programs of the Church were almost completely autonomous: writing their own curriculum, publishing journals independently, and overseeing their own finances. This resulted in "fragmentation, overlap and dysfunction" according to Bowman.[64] Thus, during the McKay administration, a correlation committee was organized to "correlate the courses of study given by the Quorums and auxiliaries of the Church," which eventually extended their reach to correlate and centralize authority over budgets, periodicals, and other programs and bring them under the control of committees headed by members of the Quorum of the Twelve.[65] Harold B. Lee, who spoke often of enlarging the borders of Zion through strengthening her stakes, was the chairman of the Correlation Committee.[66] Critics of correlation view it as a complication or added scaffolding, but as Bowman explains, "correlation made it possible for Mormonism to become a global religion," as it simplified and stream-lined what was a before a "patchwork quilt of curriculum" allowing it to be exportable overseas.[67]

One example of the dismantling of provincial difficult-to-transport elements of Mormonism was the revelation in 1978 granting priesthood authority to every worthy male member of the Church. The Gospel Topics essay "Race and the Priesthood" explains, "As the Church grew worldwide, its overarching mission to 'go ye therefore and teach all nations' seemed increasingly incompatible with the priesthood and temple restrictions."[68] The wording of the revelation, now canonized as Official Declaration 2 ("The Lord has now made known his will for the blessing of all his children throughout the earth"[69]), indicates not only the extension of priesthood authority but the fact that "the Church's scope and ambitions were broadening," and "the goal of becoming a truly global church suddenly seemed within reach."[70] Helping students to understand the global implications of the 1978 revelation can aid in understanding the process of growth in the cause of Zion. During General Conference in October of 1978, President Kimball put an emphasis on the word "must" as he quoted, "The Lord declared: 'For Zion *must* increase in beauty, and in holiness; her borders *must* be enlarged; her stakes *must* be strengthened; yea, verily I say unto you Zion *must* arise and put on her beautiful garments.'"[71] Then President Kimball reiterated the revised gathering policy by saying, "We are building up the strength of

Zion—her cords or stakes—throughout the world. Therefore we counsel our people to remain in their native lands and gather out the elect of God and teach them the ways of the Lord."[72]

The establishment of international stakes accompanied changes in the conception of the gathering and building of Zion. Rather than gathering to a centralized Zion, members were told to remain in their native lands where stakes of Zion would be driven into foreign soil, thus strengthening Saints in "distant" locations. Church leader Elder Bruce R. McConkie explained the change in policy to a congregation of members in 1977 in Lima, Peru. His talk, which was reprinted in the Church's official periodical the *Ensign* at the request of then Church president Spencer W. Kimball, divides the "gathering of Israel and the establishment of Zion in the latter days" into three phases or periods.

Phase one began with the establishment of the Church in 1830. It included Joseph Smith's First Vision and the appearance of Moses to the Kirtland Temple in 1836 to restore the keys of the gathering of Israel. That phase ends, according to McConkie, with the "secure establishment of the Church in the United States and Canada, a period of about 125 years." Phase two began with "the creation of stakes of Zion in overseas areas beginning in the 1950s" and will end when Christ returns. Phase three spans the Millennium, "from our Lord's second coming until the kingdom is perfected and the knowledge of God covers the earth" to the end of that thousand year period.[73]

In order to explain the change in conceptions of gathering and establishing Zion, McConkie argued that gathering facilitates the community building needed to strengthen the covenant people and the receipt of temple blessings. During phase one it was necessary to gather to "the tops of the mountains of North America" where there were "congregations strong enough for the Saints to strengthen each other" and where there were temples "where the fullness of the ordinances of exaltation are performed."[74] McConkie proclaimed, "We are living in a new day. The Church of Jesus Christ of Latter-day Saints is fast becoming a worldwide church," and the evidence of this "new day" is the building of temples and stakes "at the ends of the earth." He emphasized that "the gathering place for Peruvians is in the stakes of Zion in Peru, or in the places which soon will become stakes. The gathering place for Chileans is in Chile; for Bolivians it is in Bolivia; for

Koreans it is in Korea; and so it goes through all the length and breadth of the earth."[75]

Elder McConkie's message is indicative of the manner in which general Church leaders have continued to further envision the establishment of Zion. Neal A. Maxwell effectively taught about the duality of building Zion. Elder D. Todd Christofferson reiterated Elder Maxwell's quotable phrase about the need for Latter-day Saints to "establish our residence in Zion and give up the summer cottage in Babylon" in a conference address entitled, "Come to Zion."[76] Elder Christofferson reminded members of the first attempt to establish Zion in Missouri and the reasons the Lord gave for their not obtaining it.[77] Then he cautioned, "Rather than judge these early Saints too harshly, however, we should look to ourselves to see if we are doing any better."[78] Elder Christofferson declared, "Zion is Zion because of the character, attributes, and faithfulness of her citizens."[79] Then he added, "If we would establish Zion in our homes, branches, wards and stakes, we must rise to this standard."[80] Elder Christofferson listed three things required for building Zion. He enumerated, "It will be necessary (1) to become unified in one heart and one mind; (2) to become, individually and collectively, a holy people; and (3) to care for the poor and needy with such effectiveness that we eliminate poverty among us. We cannot wait until Zion comes for these things to happen—Zion will come only as they happen."[81] When Church leaders in the twenty-first century teach about establishing Zion, they are not solely referring to an ideal but are speaking to members in the entire world who are carrying on the work of building actual stakes of Zion. President Gordon B. Hinckley spoke about the establishment of Zion, yet even more importantly expanded its global existence through the instigation of building smaller temples in more of the world and beginning programs like the Perpetual Education Fund.

The Church of Jesus Christ of Latter-day Saints is expanding into a global church and beginning to fully realize the Lord's prophetic admonition, "For Zion must increase in beauty, and in holiness; her borders must be enlarged; her stakes must be strengthened."[82] Efforts to enlarge the borders of Zion and strengthen her stakes bring beauty, which comes from the diversity of members, and holiness, as the blessings of the temple and the power to redeem Zion flow into the lives of more of the Lord's children all over the earth. Latter-day Saints in the "borders" of Zion have a strong love and devotion to the Savior and his restored gospel. International members relish opportunities to participate in Church education programs and have the need to envision themselves in the ongoing Restoration of the gospel. Furthermore, students studying the foundations of the Restoration need to envision their role in the work of establishing Zion. A discussion of the establishment of Zion in Missouri or any other point in LDS history should ultimately lead to a discussion of how the revelations and foundations laid by Joseph Smith prophesy of the eventual internationalization of Zion. Such a discussion can assist students in envisioning expanded borders of Zion and their role in the work of bringing its establishment.

Notes

1. See quote by Dieter F. Uchtdorf, "Are You Sleeping through the Restoration?," *Ensign*, May 2014, 59.

2. D&C 82:13–14.

3. Joel 2: 28–32; italics added; Joseph Smith—History 1:40.

4. 1 Nephi 13:37.

5. 1 Nephi 22:14; see also 2 Nephi 26:30–31; 2 Nephi 27:3; 2 Nephi 28:21.

6. 2 Nephi 10:13; see also 2 Nephi 6:13.

7. Mosiah 15:29.

8. 3 Nephi 16:18; 3 Nephi 21:1.

9. 4 Nephi.

10. Moroni 10:31.

11. Ether 13:2–12

12. 3 Nephi 20:10–21:29.

13. See Heading by John Whitmer to Revelation, September 1830-A in Revelation Book 1. See also *Joseph Smith Papers*, "Historical Introduction" for Revelation, September 1830-A [D&C 29], http://josephsmithpapers.org/paperSummary/revelation-september-1830-a-dc-29?p=.

14. D&C 29:7–12.

15. D&C 6:6; 11:6; 12:6; 14:6; 21:7.

16. Richard Bushman, *Joseph Smith: Rough Stone Rolling* (New York: Alfred A. Knopf, 2005), 138.

17. Moses 7:18.

18. D&C 29:7–8.

19. D&C 28:8–9. See also "Covenant of Oliver Cowdery and others, 17 October 1830," http://josephsmithpapers.org/paperSummary/covenant-of-oliver-cowdery-and-others-17-october-1830?p=1. According to the "Historical Introduction" to the document, "The signed covenant indicates that Cowdery, Whitmer, Pratt, and Peterson were to not only preach the gospel among the Lamanites but also 'rear up a pillar as a witness where the Temple of God shall be built' in the New Jerusalem."

20. See "Letter to the Church in Colesville, 2 December 1830," http://josephsmithpapers.org/paperSummary/letter-to-the-church-in-colesville-2-december-1830?p=2#!/paperSummary/letter-to-the-church-in-colesville-2-december-1830&p=2.

21. D&C 45:64–66; 48:3–6.

22. D&C 57:1–2.

23. D&C 57:3.

24. D&C 133:8–9.

25. D&C 82:13.

26. D&C 82:14.

27. D&C 109:59.

28. Terryl Givens and Fiona Givens, *The Crucible of Doubt: Reflections on the Quest for Faith* (Salt Lake City: Deseret Book, 2014), 124.

29. D&C 100:13.

30. Joseph Smith, Kirtland, Ohio, to Edward Partridge, William W. Phelps, John Whitmer, Algernon Sidney Gilbert, John Corrill, Isaac Morley, and all Saints, Independence, Missouri, 10 December 1833, Joseph Smith Letterbook 1, in handwriting of Frederick G. Williams, http://josephsmithpapers.org/paperSummary/letterbook-1?p=22#!/paperSummary/letterbook-1&p=83.

31. D&C 101:17–20.

32. Harold B. Lee, "Strengthen the Stakes of Zion," *Ensign*, July 1973, 4.

33. Steve Harper, *Making Sense of the Doctrine and Covenants: A Guided Tour through Modern Revelations* (Salt Lake City: Deseret Book, 2008), 381; D&C 103:15.

34. D&C 101:4.

35. Harper, *Making Sense of the Doctrine and Covenants*, 381; D&C 105:11, 18, 33.

36. 1 Nephi 14:14.

37. D&C 109:22.

38. Moroni 10:31.

39. *Joseph Smith Papers*, History 1838–1856, volume D-1, June 11, 1843; see also David A. Bednar, "Honorably Hold a Name and Standing," *Ensign*, April 2009.

40. See http://josephsmithpapers.org/place/zion-place. See also Martha Jane Knowlton, Notebook, 19 July 1840, ca. 1850, Church History Library; Joseph Smith, "Church History," *Times and Seasons,* 1 March 1842, 710; Andrew F. Ehat and Lyndon W. Cook Jr., eds., *The Words of Joseph Smith: The Contemporary Accounts of the Nauvoo Discourses of the Prophet Joseph Smith* (Provo, UT: Religious Studies Center, Brigham Young University, 1980), 362–85; Wilford Woodruff Journal, 8 April 1844, http://josephsmithpapers.org/place/zion-place?p=1&highlight=zion%20place.

41. D&C 125:1–4.

42. John G. Turner, *Brigham Young: Pioneer Prophet* (Cambridge, MA: Harvard University Press, 2012), 106.

43. Turner, *Brigham Young*, 106.

44. Turner, *Brigham Young*, 181.

45. Gregory A. Prince and Wm. Robert Wright, *David O. McKay and the Rise of Modern Mormonism* (Salt Lake City: University of Utah Press, 2005), 363.

46. D&C 136:1, 10.

47. D&C 136:18.

48. D&C 101:20.

49. John Taylor, "The Building Up of Zion," discourse delivered at Box Elder County, 19 October 1881. See *Journal of Discourses* 22:312.

50. Orson Pratt, "The Divine Authority of the Holy Priesthood, Etc.," 10 October 1880, in *Journal of Discourses*, 22:27.

51. Pratt, "The Divine Authority of the Holy Priesthood, Etc.," 22:27.

52. Prince and Wright, *David O. McKay*, 363.

53. Seth L. Bryant, Henri Gooren, Rich Phillips, and David G. Stewart Jr., "Conversion and Retention in Mormonism," *The Oxford Handbook of Religious Conversion*, ed. Lewis R. Rambo and Charles E. Farhadian (New York: Oxford University Press, 2014), 763.

54. Lee, "Strengthen the Stakes of Zion," 4. See also D&C 101:20–21.

55. Fred E. Woods, "Gathering to Zion 1840–1890," in *Mapping Mormonism: An Atlas of Latter-day Saint History*, ed. Brandon Plewe, S. Kent Brown, Donald Q. Cannon, and Richard H. Jackson (Provo, UT: BYU Press, 2012), 104.

56. See Prince and Wright, *David O. McKay*.

57. Prince and Wright, *David O. McKay*, 358.

58. Prince and Wright, *David O. McKay*, 256.

59. Prince and Wright, *David O. McKay*, 261.

60. Prince and Wright, *David O. McKay*, 372.

61. Prince and Wright, *David O. McKay*, 366.

62. Prince and Wright, *David O. McKay*, 366.

63. Sathianathan Clarke, "Section Three: Transformations of Caste and Tribe," in *Religious Conversion in India: Modes, Motivations, and Meanings*, ed. Rowena Robinson and Sathianathan Clarke (New Delhi: Oxford University Press, 2003), 217.

64. Matthew Bowman, *The Mormon People: The Making of an American Faith* (New York: Random House, 2012), 194.

65. Bowman, *Mormon People*, 194.

66. See Lee, "Strengthen the Stakes of Zion," 4; Harold B. Lee, "Make Our Lord and Master Your Friend," in Conference Report, October 1968, 59; Harold B. Lee, "The Work in Great Britain," in Conference Report, April 1960, 106. All of these conference addresses focus on the question of "Where is Zion?" and how the "Lord has placed the responsibility of directing the work of gathering in the hands of his divinely appointed leaders" and the importance of stakes of Zion all over the world.

67. Bowman, *Mormon People*, 191.

68. https://www.lds.org/topics/race-and-the-priesthood?lang=eng.

69. See Official Declaration 2.

70. Bowman, *Mormon People*, 215.

71. Spencer W. Kimball, "The Fruit of Our Welfare Services Labors," *Ensign*, November 1978, 76.

72. Kimball, "The Fruit of Our Welfare Services Labors," 76.

73. Bruce R. McConkie, "Come: Let Israel Build Zion," *Ensign*, May 1977, 115.

74. McConkie, "Come: Let Israel Build Zion," 117.

75. McConkie, "Come: Let Israel Build Zion," 117–18.

76. See Neal A. Maxwell, *A Wonderful Flood of Light* (Salt Lake City: Bookcraft, 1990), 47; quoted in D. *Todd Christofferson, "Come to Zion," Ensign*, November 2008, 39.

77. See D&C 101:6 and 105:3–4.

78. D. Todd Christofferson, "Come to Zion," *Ensign*, November 2008, 38.

79. Christofferson, "Come to Zion," 38.

80. Christofferson, "Come to Zion," 38.

81. Christofferson, "Come to Zion," 38.

82. D&C 82:13–14.

9

The History and Doctrine of the Adam-ondi-Ahman Revelation (D&C 116)

Alexander L. Baugh

Alexander L. Baugh is a professor of Church history
and doctrine at Brigham Young University.

Latter-day Saints have some rather unique beliefs and views regarding
Adam and Eve that are not held by other Christian faiths and traditions. Most of these are associated with differences in doctrinal interpretations and explanations, but members of other faiths (and perhaps some
members of the Church as well) might be surprised to learn that LDS tradition holds that the Garden of Eden was located in the vicinity of Jackson
County, Missouri. This understanding does not come from Joseph Smith's
recorded revelations, but rather is based on statements made by him and reported by contemporaries who heard and recorded what the Prophet was
reported to have said. For example, in a conversation between Brigham
Young and Orson Hyde, Young said, "I have never been in Jackson County.
Now it is a pleasant thing to think of and to know where the Garden of
Eden was. Did you ever think of it? I do not think many do, for in Jackson
County was the Garden of Eden. Joseph has declared this, and I am as much
bound to believe that as to believe that Joseph was a prophet of God."[1]
Heber C. Kimball no doubt also learned about Eden's location from his

close association with Smith. In a talk given in 1863, Kimball said, "The spot chosen for the Garden of Eden was Jackson County, in the state of Missouri, where Independence now stands."[2]

Another rather peculiar view held by the Latter-day Saints regarding Adam and Eve is the understanding regarding the location where they lived following their expulsion from the Garden of Eden—Adam-ondi-Ahman. And although no mention is made in Joseph Smith's revelations which indicate that the original paradisiacal Garden of Eden was in Jackson County, one of the Prophet's canonized revelations, Doctrine and Covenants section 116, does state where Adam-ondi-Ahman was located—namely, in Daviess County, Missouri.[3]

Developmental Understanding of Adam-ondi-Ahman

Much of what Joseph Smith taught and understood came developmentally, "line upon line, precept upon precept, here a little and there a little" (2 Nephi 28:30), and his understanding about Adam-ondi-Ahman is just one example. The Prophet's precursory understanding about Adam-ondi-Ahman may have come as early as June 1830 and February 1831, when he received the "visions of Moses," which marked the beginning of his inspired revision of the Bible, and which was later canonized in 1880 as the Book of Moses in the Pearl of Great Price. Chapters 5 and 6 describe the beginnings of Adam and Eve's mortal sojourn following their expulsion from the Garden of Eden, which events likely occurred at Adam-ondi-Ahman.

An interesting inclusion in the "Book of Commandments and Revelations" (also identified as Revelations Book 1) is a March 1832 entry titled "A Sample of pure Language given by Joseph the Seer" (fig. 1). Given in a question-answer format, a portion of the text reads as follows:

Question	What is the name of God in pure Language
Answer	Awman.
Q	The meaning of the pure word Awman.
A	It is the being which made all things in all its parts.
Q	What is the name of the Son of God.
A	The Son Awman.[4]

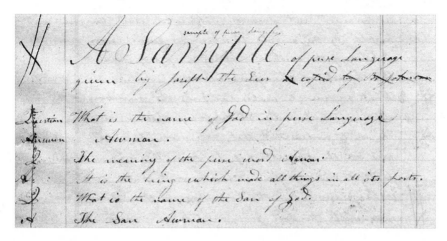

Figure 1. "A Sample of pure Language given by Joseph the Seer," circa March 1832, "Book of Commandments and Revelations," 144, Joseph Smith Papers, Church History Library, Salt Lake City, Utah; reproduced in Robin Scott Jensen, Robert J. Woodford, and Steven C. Harper, eds., Revelations and Translation Volume 1: Manuscript Revelations Books, *vol. 1 of the Revelations and Translation series of* The Joseph Smith Papers, *ed. Dean C. Jessee, Ronald K. Esplin, and Richard Lyman Bushman (Salt Lake City: Church Historian's Press, 2011), 205.*

Although the text addresses only the meaning of the word "Awman" and does not specifically mention the larger term "Adam-ondi-Ahman," it nonetheless suggests that Joseph Smith received revelatory knowledge about the meaning or origin of the word "Awman" as being the proper noun or name of God the Father.

Additional events in the mid-1830s likely expanded Joseph Smith's understanding of Adam's role in mortality as well as his understanding of Adam-ondi-Ahman. Beginning in November 1834 and continuing through March 1835, during the second session of the School of the Elders (previously the School of the Prophets), seven theological lectures on faith were presented in the school. Significantly, "Lecture Second," the longest lecture in the series, totaling nearly twenty-four pages (including the catechism), discusses Adam and Eve and their Fall, their expulsion from Eden, and the patriarchal lineage of their posterity.[5]

Revelatory Understanding of Adam-ondi-Ahman

Concurrent with the information presented about Adam and Eve in the 1834–35 session of the School of the Elders, between 1 March and 4 May 1835,

Joseph Smith and Oliver Cowdery produced a revelatory document containing information regarding the authority associated with both the Aaronic and Melchizedek Priesthoods as well as instructions relative to the duties and responsibilities of the various priesthood offices and quorums. The revelation (currently D&C 107) also included an account of the conferral of the holy priesthood by Adam upon the ancient patriarchs Seth, Enos, Cainan, Mahalaleel, Jared, Enoch, and Methuselah (eight generations total), followed by Lamech, who was ordained by Seth, followed by Noah, who was ordained by Methuselah (ten generations total). At this point, the revelation included the following information about the significance of the area known as Adam-ondi-Ahman anciently:

> Three years previous to the death of Adam, he called Seth, Enos, Cainan, Mahalaleel, Jared, Enoch, and Methuselah, who were all high priests, with the residue of his posterity who were righteous, into the valley of Adam-ondi-Ahman, and there bestowed upon them his last blessing. And the Lord appeared unto them, and they rose up and blessed Adam, and called him Michael, the prince, the archangel. And the Lord administered comfort unto Adam, and said unto him: I have set thee to be at the head; a multitude of nations shall come of thee, and thou art a prince over them forever. And Adam stood up in the midst of the congregation; and, notwithstanding he was bowed down with age, being full of the Holy Ghost, predicted whatsoever should befall his posterity unto the latest generation. These things were all written in the book of Enoch, and are to be testified of in due time.[6]

This passage marks the first time the full title "Adam-ondi-Ahman" is mentioned in its entirety in any of the Prophet's historical or revelatory documents.

William W. Phelps and the Poetic Verse "Adam-ondi-Ahman"

A key figure in the developmental understanding of the historical and doctrinal significance of Adam-ondi-Ahman was William W. Phelps (fig. 2). In

May 1835, he and John Whitmer, both members of the Missouri presidency, arrived in Kirtland to assist in the printing operations of the Church. Their responsibilities included reprinting *The Evening and the Morning Star* (first published in Independence, Missouri) and printing the *Latter Day Saints' Messenger and Advocate* and *Northern Times* (periodicals), the first edition of the Doctrine and Covenants, and the Church's first hymnal. Immediately upon his and Whitmer's arrival, Phelps immersed himself in the printing operations, which included editing, arranging, typesetting, and printing each of the

Figure 2. William Wines (W. W.) Phelps, daguerreotype collection, circa 1850–60, Church History Library, Salt Lake City.

manuscripts for the various publications. Although Frederick G. Williams (owner and proprietor), Oliver Cowdery (office and business manager), and John Whitmer (editor of the *Messenger and Advocate*) oversaw the day-to-day printing operations, Phelps, as an ad hoc editor, played a major role in all of the editorial decisions.

Phelps's appointment to work in the printing office in Kirtland provided him with opportunities to publish his own articles and prose in the *Messenger and Advocate* (something he had done regularly as the previous editor and printer of *The Evening and the Morning Star*), and he took full advantage of his situation. Not surprising, in the June 1835 issue of the *Messenger and Advocate*, two poems by Phelps, published a month after he first began his work in the printing office, appeared in the periodical, one of which was titled "Adam-ondi-Ahman" (see fig. 3):

> This world was once a garden place,
> With all her glories common;
> And men did live a holy race
> And worship Jesus face to face,
> In Adam-ondi-Ahman.

We read that Enoch walk'd with God,
Above the power of Mammon:
While Zion spread herself abroad,
And saints and angels sung aloud
In Adam-ondi-Ahman.

Her land was good and greatly blest,
Beyond old Israel's Canaan;
Her fame was known from east to west;
Her peace was great, and pure the rest—
Of Adam-ondi-Ahman.

Hosanna to such days to come—
The Savior's second comin'—
When all the earth in glorious bloom,
Affords the saints a holy home
Like Adam-ondi-Ahman.[7]

In the first verse of the poem one might erroneously conclude that Phelps describes the conditions that existed in the garden of Eden, but this is not the case. He clearly refers to the conditions of the earth after the Fall—when Adam and Eve had procreated and begun the human race—and suggests that the entire earth was in a garden-like state, but certainly not equal to that of the conditions in the garden of Eden. Perhaps it was because of this garden-like condition that the antediluvian patriarchs and their posterity lived for hundreds of years. And although the ages of the patriarchs from Adam to Noah are given in the Bible in Genesis chapter 5, "Lecture Second" (for which Phelps probably set the printed type) also discusses the ages of the patriarchs in great detail.[8] In writing about the longer lifespans enjoyed by Adam and his posterity, the ancient Jewish historian Flavius Josephus wrote that one reason why they lived so long was because "their food was then fitter for the prolongation of life."[9] Was the extended life span of the patriarchs due to the earth's garden-like state, which Phelps writes about in his poem? Possibly.

In the fourth and fifth lines of the first verse, Phelps also writes that Jesus was worshipped "face to face" at Adam-ondi-Ahman. Again, Phelps refers not to the time when Adam and Eve were in the Garden of Eden,

144   MESSENGER AND ADVOCATE.

lately attended, and I am' inclined to think, that the good results will long be experienced by many hundreds. I am satisfied, that the church received additional strength, (though they were by no means weak in the faith before,) and many others received a degree of testimony of the great work of the Lord in the last days, that will be as good seed sown upon good ground. May it be even so, till the knowledge of the glory of our Redeemer shall fill the earth, and all his chosen ones, shout hosannah! Amen.   C.

John's definition of God is the nearest to perfection of any that we know of. It is like the "pearl of great price, or the diamond of all worth." By beginning at the letter G, in the middle of the table below, the reader may read till he is satisfied, up, down, and each side, and continually learn that *God is love.*

<pre>
            E
           EVE
          EVOVE
         EVOLOVE
        EVOLSLOVE
       EVOLSISLOVE
      EVOLSIDISLOVE
     EVOLSIDODISLOVE
    EVOLSIDOGODISLOVE
     EVOLSIDODISLOVE
      EVOLSIDISLOVE
       EVOLSISLOVE
        EVOLSLOVE
         EVOLOVE
          EVOVE
           EVE
            E   P.
</pre>

Adam-ondi-Ahman.

BY W. W. PHELPS.

This world was once a garden place,
    With all her glories common;
And men did live a holy race,
    And worship Jesus face to face,
        In Adam-ondi-Ahman.

We read that Enoch walk'd with God,
    Above the power of Mammon;
While Zion spread herself abroad,
    And saints and angels sung aloud
        In Adam-ondi-Ahman.

Her land was good and greatly blest,
    Beyond old Israel's Canaan;
Her fame was known from east to west;
    Her peace was great, and pure the rest—
        Of Adam-ondi-Ahman.

Hosanna to such days to come—
    The Savior's second comin'—
When all the world in glorious bloom,
    Affords the saints a holy home
        Like Adam-ondi-Ahman.

Sabbath Hymn.

BY THE SAME.

Gently raise the sacred strain,
For the Sabbath's come again.
        That man may rest,
    And return his thanks to God,
    For his blessings to the blest.

Blessed day, devoid of strife,
For to seek eternal life,
        That great reward,
    And partake the sacrament,
    In remembrance of the Lord.

Sweetly swell the solemn sound,
While we bring our gifts around,
        Of broken hearts,
    As a willing sacrifice,
    Showing what his grace imparts.

Happy type of things to come,
When the saints are gather'd home,
        To praise the Lord,
    In eternity of bliss,
    All as one, with one accord.

Holy, holy is the Lord;
Precious, precious is his word,
        Repent and live;
    Though your sins are crimson red,
    O repent and he'll forgive.

Softly sing the joyful lay
For the saints to fast and pray,
        As God ordains,
    For his goodness and his love
    While the Sabbath day remains.

DIED—In Clay county, Missouri, May 1, ADALAIDE, daughter of John E. and Betsey Page, aged two years, eight months and twenty days.

——— In Grove, Allegany county, N. Y. April 3, Mrs. CYNTHIA ALVORD, wife of Elias Alvord, aged.———

THE LATTER DAY SAINTS'
Messenger and Advocate,
IS EDITED BY
JOHN WHITMER.
And published every month at Kirtland, Geauga Co. Ohio, by
F. G. WILLIAMS & Co.

At $1, per an. in advance. Every person procuring ten new subscribers, and forwarding $10, current money, shall be entitled to a paper one year, gratis. All letters to the Editor, or Publishers, must be
☞ POST PAID. ☜

No subscription will be received for a less term than one year, and no paper discontinued till all arrearages are paid, except at the option of the publishers.

Figure 3. W. W. Phelps, "Adam-ondi-Ahman," Latter Day Saints' Messenger and Advocate 1, no. 9 (June 1835): 144.

where they were in the presence of Jehovah from time to time and where they would have worshipped him in person ("face to face"). True, after they were cast out of Eden they were indeed shut out of God's presence, but eventually Adam was permitted to enjoy heavenly communication with deity once again, which would have taken place at Adam-ondi-Ahman (for example, see Moses 6:51–68).[10] Phelps may also be referring to the great council meeting held three years previous to the death of Adam when all of Adam and Eve's righteous posterity did indeed worship Jesus "face to face" at Adam-ondi-Ahman.

In the second and third verses, Phelps highlights the ministry of Enoch and the eventual establishment of the city of Zion. "We read that Enoch walk'd with God," he writes, and indeed Enoch did. Speaking of the ancient patriarch, a verse in Joseph Smith's March 1835 revelation on priesthood reads, "And he [Enoch] saw the Lord, and he walked with him, and was before his face continually; and he walked with God three hundred and sixty-five years."[11] Did Phelps become acquainted with this passage while setting the type for the Doctrine and Covenants? One can only guess. Phelps also notes the notoriety that Enoch's city of Zion achieved because of the city's righteousness; hence the line, "Her fame was known from east to west."

Phelps concludes his lyrical canto with a climactic futuristic expression: "Hosanna to such days to come—The Savior's second comin'." And what will the earth be like after that glorious event takes place? "Like Adam-ondi-Ahman."

Phelps could not have learned about the significance of Adam-ondi-Ahman until after his arrival in Kirtland in May 1835. After all, he was living in Missouri during the time the second session of the School of the Elders was being held, which meant that he could not have been privy to the teachings and doctrines which were discussed in the school related to Adam and Eve's expulsion from Eden and their sojourn in mortality, and which may have included conversations about Adam-ondi-Ahman. Furthermore, he could not have learned about the information in the revelatory document on priesthood which contained the information regarding the great council meeting held at Adam-ondi-Ahman until after his arrival in Kirtland. So how did he gain the information about the significance of Adam-ondi-Ahman being Adam and Eve's homeland in order to write a poem about it?

He more likely learned it from Joseph Smith himself. When Phelps came to Kirtland, he lived in Joseph Smith's home, where they no doubt enjoyed many gospel conversations, which could have included discussions about Adam, the patriarchs, and Adam-ondi-Ahman. As noted, Phelps could also have easily picked up the information about Adam-ondi-Ahman while preparing the manuscript containing the instructions on priesthood for publication in the Doctrine and Covenants, or while setting the type. Regardless, the fact that Phelps chose to publish his poetic composition about the beginnings of the human race clearly indicates he was intrigued, if not inspired, by his newfound understanding regarding earth's early families.

Preparing and Publishing the 1835 Edition of the Doctrine and Covenants

The publication committee completed the work of printing the first edition of the Doctrine and Covenants in August 1835, and in September the first bound copies were made available for purchase.[12] The revelatory document containing the instructions on priesthood was published as "Section III. On Priesthood." The text about the gathering of Adam and Eve's righteous posterity at Adam-ondi-Ahman three years previous to Adam's death appears in verses 28 and 29 (fig. 4).[13]

In preparing the manuscript revelations in Revelation Book 1 for inclusion in the 1835 Doctrine and Covenants, Phelps also took the liberty to make a number of additions and editorial changes to the revelations, including a 1 March 1832 revelation by Joseph Smith. In the published version of the revelation, Phelps inserted a rather lengthy phrase (49 words) about the establishment of Adam-ondi-Ahman and the authority of Michael, or Adam. The insertion appears in the latter part of verse three of section 75 of the 1835 edition and reads as follows: "who hath appointed Michael, your prince, and established his feet, and set him upon high; and given unto him the keys of salvation under the counsel and direction of the Holy One, who is without beginning of days or end of life."[14] While Joseph Smith may have authored these words and directed that they be inserted as part of the printed text, Phelps may have written and inserted them and the Prophet given his approval.

One additional editorial revision to the 1 March 1832 revelation is worth mentioning. The manuscript of the revelation appears immediately following the document titled "A Sample of pure Language given by Joseph the Seer" in Revelation Book 1. As noted earlier, the "Sample" clarifies that the name of Jesus Christ in the "pure language" was "Son Awman," so it is not surprising that, in keeping with that designation, Phelps replaced "Jesus Christ" with "Son Ahman" in the revelation,[15] which change also appeared in the published version of the revelation in the 1835 edition of the Doctrine and Covenants.[16]

Joseph Smith Sr.'s Patriarchal Blessing

On 18 December 1833, during a special blessing meeting held in Kirtland, Joseph Smith pronounced spiritual blessings upon Oliver Cowdery and several members of the Smith family, including his father, Joseph Smith Sr.; but only a portion of the blessings was recorded on that occasion.[17] However, sometime during the latter part of September 1835, following the publication of the Doctrine and Covenants, Cowdery copied into Patriarchal Blessing Book 1 additional background information on the December 1833 blessing meeting, including the fact that it was on this occasion that Joseph Smith Sr. was ordained to the office of patriarch to the Church.[18] In addition, Cowdery expanded Joseph Sr.'s blessing to include the same text found in D&C 3:28 of the 1835 edition of the Doctrine and Covenants (D&C 107:53–55), which contained the information about the council meeting held at Adam-ondi-Ahman three years previous to Adam's death. Following this inclusion, the blessing then reads: "So shall it be with my father; he shall be called a prince over his posterity, holding the keys of the patriarchal priesthood over the Kingdom of God on earth, even the Church of the Latter Day Saints: And he shall sit in the general assembly of patriarchs, even in council with the Ancient of days when he shall sit and all the patriarchs with him—and enjoy his right and authority under the direction of the Ancient of days" (fig. 5).[19] It is not known who authored the expanded text—Oliver Cowdery or Joseph Smith. Perhaps the Prophet directed that it be written by Cowdery, or he authorized or approved what Cowdery wrote. Regardless, the added text provided additional pertinent information on the significance of Adam-ondi-Ahman. For example, mention is made that Joseph

25 Methuselah was 100 years old when he was ordained un
der the hand of Adam.

26 Lamech was 32 years old when he was ordained under
the hand of Seth.

27 Noah was 10 years old when he was ordained under the
hand of Methuselah.

28 Three years previous to the death of Adam, he called
Seth, Enos, Cainan, Mahalaleel, Jared, Enoch and Methuselah, who were all high priests, with the residue of his posterity, who were righteous, into the valley of Adam-ondi-ahman,
and there bestowed upon them his last blessing. And the
Lord appeared unto them, and they rose up and blessed Adam,
and called him Michael, the Prince, the Archangel. And
the Lord administered comfort unto Adam, and said unto him,
I have set thee to be at the head: a multitude of nations shall
come of thee; and thou art a prince over them for ever.

29 And Adam stood up in the midst of the congregation, and
notwithstanding he was bowed down with age, being full of
the Holy Ghost, predicted whatsoever should befall his posterity unto the latest generation. These things were all written in the book of Enoch, and are to be testified of in due
time.

30 It is the duty of the twelve, also, to ordain and set in order all the other officers of the church, agreeably to the revelation which says:

31 To the church of Christ in the land of Zion, in addition
to the church laws, respecting church business: Verily, I say
unto you, says the Lord of hosts, There must needs be presiding elders, to preside over those who are of the office of an
elder; and also priests, to preside over those who are of the
office of a priest; and also teachers to preside over those who
are of the office of a teacher, in like manner; and also the
deacons: wherefore, from deacon to teacher, and from teacher
to priest, and from priest to elder, severally as they are appointed, according to the covenants and commandments of the
church; then comes the high priesthood, which is the greatest of all. Wherefore, it must needs be that one be appointed,
of the high priesthood, to preside over the priesthood; and he
shall be called president of the high priesthood of the church,
or, in other words, the presiding high priest over the high
priesthood of the church. From the same comes the administering of ordinances and blessings upon the church, by the
laying on of the hands.

32 Wherefore the office of a bishop is not equal unto it; for
the office of a bishop is in administering all temporal things:
nevertheless, a bishop must be chosen from the high priest-

*Figure 4. D&C 3:28–29 (1835 edition) [D&C 107:53–57] containing the text associated with
Adam-ondi-Ahman.*

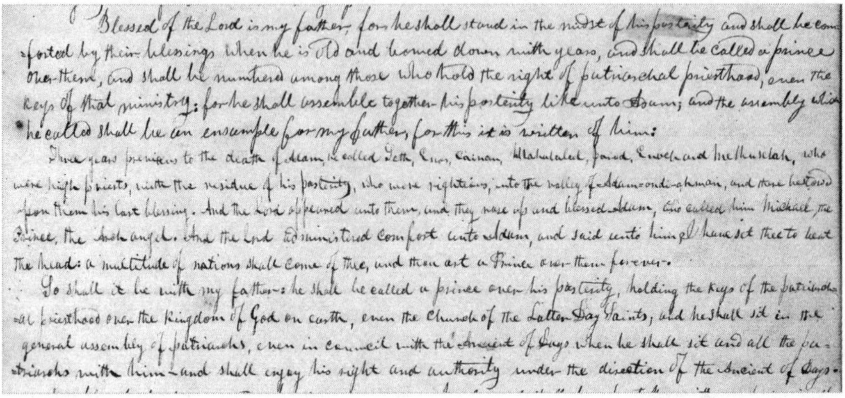

Figure 5. Joseph Smith Sr. revised patriarchal blessing, Patriarchal Blessing Book 1, p. 9, CHL. The second paragraph in the blessing includes the added material about the council meeting held three years previous to Adam's death at Adam-ondi-Ahman which appeared in the 1835 edition of the Doctrine and Covenants (D&C 3:28–29 [D&C 107:53–57]). The third paragraph contains the additional text, which promised Joseph Smith Sr. that he would be present at the future grand council with Adam, who is also identified as "Ancient of days."

Smith Sr. held the keys of the "patriarchal priesthood," an obvious reference to Father Smith's ordination to the office of patriarch to the Church. In his capacity as the presiding patriarch, he was also promised he would sit in council with a "general assembly of patriarchs." It is important to recognize that the expanded blessing speaks in *future* tense regarding a council meeting *yet to come*, whereas previous statements about Adam-ondi-Ahman refer only to the council meeting held anciently. Finally, and perhaps the most significant insertion, is the reference made to the "Ancient of days" also being present in the future council. The title or designation "Ancient of days" is given three times in the Bible, each of which appears in Daniel 7 (vv. 9, 13, and 22), where Daniel sees a vision of the last days and the earthly kingdoms that prevailed prior to the end of the world:

> I beheld till the thrones were cast down, and the Ancient of days did sit, whose garment was white as snow, and the hair of his head like the pure wool: his throne was like the fiery flame, and his wheels as burning fire.
>
> A fiery stream issued and came forth from before him: thousand thousands ministered unto him, and ten thousand times ten thousand stood before him: the judgment was set, and the books were opened. . . .

> I saw in the night visions, and, behold, one like the Son of man came with the clouds of heaven, and came to the Ancient of days, and they brought him near before him.
>
> And there was given him dominion, and glory, and a kingdom, that all people, nations, and languages, should serve him: his dominion is an everlasting dominion, which shall not pass away, and his kingdom that which shall not be destroyed. (Daniel 7:9–10, 13–14)

Then in the verses that follow, the Saints are told that the kingdoms of the earth would reign and prevail:

> Until the Ancient of days came, and judgment was given to the saints of the most High; and the time came that the saints possessed the kingdom. (v. 22)

The general view held by Christian scholars and clergy regarding the identity of the personage referred to as the "Ancient of days" in Daniel 7 is none other than God. Notably, the designation appears twice in the expanded text of Joseph Smith Sr.'s 1835 blessing, but there is no indication regarding the personage's identity. It would not be until 1838 that Joseph Smith would specifically identify him. In summary, the text from the expanded blessing of the Prophet's father alludes to a future council at Adam-ondi-Ahman over which the "Ancient of days" would preside.

"Adam-ondi-Ahman" Included in the First LDS Hymnal (1835)

At the completion of the publication of the 1835 Doctrine and Covenants in September 1835, W. W. Phelps turned his attention to revising the collection of hymns Emma Smith had selected for publication by April 1832—a task long overdue.[20] It is not known how much say Emma had in the publication process at this point, and although Phelps likely consulted with her, he also may have taken some personal liberty in the project when, independent of Emma, he included "Adam-ondi-Ahman" and possibly other selections of his writings as part of the ninety hymns that made up the compilation. Phelps made a couple of minor changes in the wording, one of which was part of the first sentence. In the version of the poem that appeared in the

SACRED HYMNS.   29 30   SACRED HYMNS.

Like Enoch too, I will proclaim,
A loud Hosanna to his name.

3 Hosanna, let the echo fly
From pole to pole, from sky to sky,
And saints and angels, join to sing,
Till all eternity shall ring.

4 Hosanna, let the voice extend,
Till time shall cease, and have an end;
Till all the throngs of heav'n above,
Shall join the saints in songs of love.

5 Hosanna, let the trump of God,
Proclaim his wonders far abroad,
And earth, and air, and skies, and seas,
Conspire to sound aloud his praise.

HYMN 23. P. M.

1 This earth was once a garden place,
With all her glories common;
And men did live a holy race,
And worship Jesus face to face,
In Adam-ondi-Ahman.

2 We read that Enoch walk'd with God,
Above the pow'r of Mammon:
While Zion spread herself abroad,

And saints and angels sung aloud
In Adam-ondi-Ahman.

3 Her land was good and greatly blest,
Beyond old Israel's Canaan:
Her fame was known from east to west;
Her peace was great, and pure the rest
Of Adam-ondi-Ahman.

4 Hosanna to such days to come—
The Savior's second comin'—
When all the earth in glorious bloom,
Affords the saints a holy home
Like Adam-ondi-Ahman.

HYMN 24. P. M.

1 Gently raise the sacred strain,
For the Sabbath 's come again,
That man may rest,
And return his thanks to God,
For his blessings to the blest.

2 Holy day, devoid of strife,
For to seek eternal life,
That great reward,
And partake the sacrament,
In remembrance of the Lord.

Figure 6. "This earth was once a garden place," hymn no. 23, in Emma Smith, comp., A Collection of Sacred Hymns for the Church of the Latter Day Saints *(Kirtland, OH: F. G. Williams and Co. 1835), 29–30.*

Messenger and Advocate, the first line reads: "*This world* was once a garden place." The hymn version reads: "*This earth* was once a garden place." Why Phelps made the change is not known. It doesn't alter the meaning in any way, but the latter version is easier to say. The hymn appears as hymn number twenty-three. None of the hymns are titled, but are designated in the index at the back of the book under the title of the first line. So in the case of "Adam-ondi-Ahman," it is indexed as "This earth was once a garden place," reflecting the change Phelps made to the original text (see fig. 6).[21]

The 1835 hymnal actually came off the press in February or March 1836, just in time for the dedication of the Kirtland House of the Lord.[22] During the dedication services held on 27 March, six hymns were sung or performed, three of which were authored by Phelps: "Now Let Us Rejoice," "The Spirit of God," and "Adam-ondi-Ahman."[23] The melody to which "Adam-ondi-Ahman" was sung was likely to the tune "Prospect of Heaven,"

Figure 7. "Prospect of Heaven," in William Walker, comp., The Southern Harmony, and Musical Companion (Philadelphia: E. W. Miller, 1854), 24. Although this version of "Prospect of Heaven" appeared in a later edition by Walker, it would have been the same as that published in the 1835 edition. The middle tune line bears a similar melody to the tune that "Adam-ondi-Ahman" is sung to today and was likely the one that was sung by the Latter-day Saints in the late 1830s.

found in *The Southern Harmony, and Musical Companion*, a popular tune book first published in 1835 (fig. 7).[24] "Adam-ondi-Ahman" quickly became a popular favorite of the Latter-day Saints, particularly during the next two years (1836–38). Following the expulsion of the Saints from Missouri in 1839, however, it was not sung as often, but by then it had become part of the Mormon consciousness, and it appeared in Mormon hymnals thereafter.[25]

The Location of Adam-ondi-Ahman

In late 1837, the Church in Kirtland was in turmoil. At the core of the problem was the failure of the Kirtland Safety Society, established by Church leaders in late 1836. Most of the two hundred individuals who invested in the Safety Society were Church members, some of who blamed Joseph Smith for their losses, thereafter questioning his authority and ability to receive divine direction. Lacking confidence in the First Presidency's leadership, several dissidents sought to take control of the Church, threatened the leaders with civil and criminal lawsuits, and made threats against their lives. Such actions led the Prophet and those faithful to him and his leadership to abandon Kirtland and relocate with the Saints living in Caldwell County, Missouri. Joseph Smith and his family made a hasty departure on 12 January 1838. Following an arduous two-month journey in the dead of winter, they arrived in Far West, Missouri, on 14 March.

With the expectation that a large number of Latter-day Saints in the East would relocate to northern Missouri later that spring and summer, and

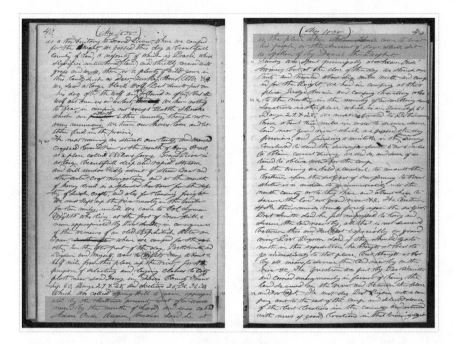

Figure 8. George W. Robinson's entry in Joseph Smith's March–September 1838 Journal (sometimes called the Scriptory Book) containing the entry about Spring Hill as the location for Adam-ondi-Ahman.

in accordance with a revelation received by Joseph Smith on 26 April 1838, which indicated that other places besides Far West "should be appointed for stakes in the regions round about" (see D&C 115:17–18), the Prophet made plans to explore the region of Daviess County, situated north of Caldwell, for future Mormon settlement sites. Significantly, at that time the federal government had not surveyed the county, so no actual land sales had taken place. Instead, federal laws permitted individuals to file preemption land claims, which allowed them to claim, occupy, and improve up to 160 acres of land without making any payment. Later, when the government brought the land up for sale, the individual claiming the preemption had the first right to purchase the property at $1.25 per acre. This arrangement was ideal for the Mormons, especially those coming from the East who had little or no money. These immigrants could simply file a preemption claim for property and legally settle on the land without having to pay for it upfront.[26]

On 18 May, Joseph Smith and a small company of men set out from Far West on an exploratory mission to Daviess County to locate other areas for

Figure 9. Location of Tower Hill, 2002. Photograph by Alexander L. Baugh.

possible future Mormon settlement. The following day, 19 May, the company arrived at the homesite of Lyman Wight, who lived near the base of a gentle sloping hill, called "Spring Hill" by the Latter-day Saints who had settled in the region.[27] On this occasion, George W. Robinson, Smith's clerk, recorded a significant entry in the Prophet's journal regarding the area: "Spring Hill a name appropriated by the bretheren [*sic*] present, But afterwards named by the mouth of [the] Lord and was called Adam Ondi Awmen [Adam-ondi-Ahman], because said he it is the place where Adam shall come to visit his people, or the Ancient of days shall sit as spoken of by Daniel the Prophet" (fig. 8).[28] The entry is significant for two reasons. First, it marks the first time that Joseph Smith identified the location where Adam-ondi-Ahman was actually located; and second, it specified that the "Ancient of days" spoken of by Daniel was none other than Father Adam, who, at a future day, would appear at Adam-ondi-Ahman to a gathering of faithful Saints in fulfill-ment of Daniel's prophecy (see Daniel 7:9–10, 13–14). After identifying the region, the Prophet spent a few more days surveying the area, then returned to Far West, where he arrived on 24 May.[29]

On this same occasion, Joseph Smith also stated that his company discovered the remains of "an old Nephitish Alter [sic] an[d] Tower." It is important to note that the account given in the Prophet's published history has been altered and incorrectly identifies that what they discovered on this occasion was "an old *Nephite* altar or tower"—the word *Nephite* replacing *Nephitish*, suggesting that the remains originated with the Nephite civilization in the Book of Mormon.[30] To add to the confusion, later accounts given by some of the Prophet's contemporaries incorrectly identified the structure as being an altar constructed by Adam. But Joseph Smith's record does not describe it as being Nephite or Adamic. The entry made by Robinson simply states that the company discovered the remains of an ancient ("old") Native American Indian ("Nephitish") structure of some kind (fig. 9).[31]

Adam-ondi-Ahman Settlement Development

In preparation for the anticipated Mormon influx into the region, Joseph Smith spent the better part of the month of June 1838 in the vicinity of Adam-ondi-Ahman, surveying the area, laying out the community, and assisting in the establishment of homes and farms. William Swartzell, a recent Mormon convert from Ohio who arrived in Missouri in late May, wrote that while he was working alongside the Prophet digging a well, he suggested the new community should have a name. "Brother Joseph placed his back against a small shade tree," Swartzell reported, and then looking toward heaven said, "It does not take me long to get a revelation from heaven, and this stake, or city, shall be called Adam-on-Diammon" [sic].[32] About this same time, John Corrill remembered that Joseph Smith provided an interpretation regarding the meaning of Adam-ondi-Ahman: "Smith gave it the name, . . . which he said was formerly given to a certain valley, where Adam, previous to his death, called his children together and blessed them. The interpretation in English is 'The valley of God, in which Adam blessed his children.'"[33]

The new settlement emerged almost overnight, and within a matter of a few weeks, Adam-ondi-Ahman, which also began to be called "Diahman" for short, became the center of activity for Mormons living in the area and

Figure 10. Aerial view of Adam-ondi-Ahman locations: Lyman Wight cabin and ferry site, Adam-ondi-Ahman settlement and probable temple block location, and Tower Hill. Courtesy of Alexander L. Baugh.

the largest village community in Daviess County.[34] "Many of the Church became elated with the idea of settling in and round about the new town," wrote John Corrill, "especially those who had come from Kirtland, as it was designed more particularly for them" (fig. 10).[35]

On 28 June, Joseph Smith presided at a council meeting held in a grove near the home of Lyman Wight. Here, the Adam-ondi-Ahman stake was organized, with John Smith as president, and Reynolds Cahoon and Lyman Wight as counselors. A high council was also chosen, and Vinson Knight was called as to serve on a temporary basis as bishop. Not surprising, the meeting closed with the singing of "Adam-ondi-Ahman."[36] The creation of the stake at Adam-ondi-Ahman marked the third stake organized in the Church (fig. 11).[37]

In anticipation of additional ecclesiastical leadership needed for the Missouri and Adam-ondi-Ahman stakes, in a revelation dictated by Joseph Smith on 8 July 1838, William Marks, president of the Kirtland stake, and Newel K. Whitney, the bishop in Kirtland, were instructed to vacate Kirtland and relocate with the main body of Saints in northern Missouri. "Let them settle up their business speedily and journey from the land of Kirtland," the revelation read. "Therefore if they tarry, it shall not be well with them." Believing that the two men might suppose their responsibilities

Figure 11. On 28 June 1838, John Smith (left), Reynolds Cahoon (center), and Lyman Wight (right) were appointed as the presidency of the Adam-ondi-Ahman stake.

in Ohio outweighed the need for them to move to Missouri, the revelation issued a mild reproof. "Is there not room enough on the mountains of Adam-ondi-Ahman, and on the plains of Olaha Shinehah, or the land where Adam dwelt, that you should covet that which is the drop, and neglect the more weighty matters?" The revelation called for the appointment of Marks to preside as the president of the Missouri stake at Far West, while Whitney was called to serve as a bishop at Adam-ondi-Ahman.[38] Both Marks and Whitney never filled these appointments, because they never joined the Saints in northern Missouri. En route from Ohio, when they learned of Governor Boggs's removal order, they remained in Illinois—Marks in Quincy and Whitney in Carrollton. Later, in October 1839, Marks was appointed to be the first president of the Commerce (later Nauvoo) stake, while Whitney served as a bishop.

In planning the settlement, community leaders reserved land for a temple. William Swartzell noted in his journal that the initial settlement of Adam-ondi-Ahman was platted to be a two-mile square, laid out in one-acre lots, with the temple located on a four-acre lot in the square's center.[39] The four-acre lot Swartzell referred to was probably the public square. The fact that the temple lot in Far West was also situated on the public square supports that conclusion. Significantly, the lot for the temple at Adam-ondi-Ahman was also dedicated. According to Heber C. Kimball, shortly after the Mormons raided Gallatin on 18 October 1838, he and a number of other Church leaders came from Far West to Adam-ondi-Ahman where they met

Joseph Smith, Sidney Rigdon, Hyrum Smith, and several hundred Mormon men who were preparing to defend the Saints living in the region. On this occasion, Kimball noted that stakes were put in the ground to designate "the four corners of a temple block," after which the site was dedicated by Brigham Young. It is important to note that Kimball's report indicates that Young dedicated the *block*, or the square, where the temple would be built, not the actual site for the temple itself.⁴⁰

Adam-ondi-Ahman had a short existence—less than six months (June through mid-November 1838). The events associated with the 1838 Missouri-Mormon war led to the state-authorized evacuation of the Mormons from northern Missouri, which forced the Mormons to give up their property, abandon their settlements, and dissolve the Missouri and Adam-ondi-Ahman stakes.⁴¹

Joseph Smith's Doctrinal Teachings Concerning Adam-ondi-Ahman (1839)

Joseph Smith is also known to have provided what should be considered inspired doctrinal commentary regarding some of the future events associated with Adam-ondi-Ahman. In remarks he gave (probably to the Twelve in preparation for their collected mission to Great Britain later that summer) sometime between 26 June and 4 August 1839, in Montrose, Lee County, Iowa, or Commerce (later Nauvoo), Hancock County, Illinois, he is recorded as having said the following statements regarding the past and future council meeting at Adam-ondi-Ahman:

> Daniel vii speaks of the Ancient of days he means the old-est man, our father Adam, Michael, he will call his children together and hold a Council with them, to prepare them for the coming of the Son of Man. He (Adam) is the father of the human family and presides over the Spirits of all men, and all that have had the Keys must stand before him in this grand Council this may take place before some of us leave this stage of action. The Son of Man stands before him and there is given him glory and Dominion: Adam delivers up his stewardship to Christ that which was delivered to him as holding the Keys

of the Universe, but retains his standing as head of the human family.

*   *   *   *   *   *

I saw Adam in the valley of Ah-dam ondi ahman he called together his children and blessed them with a Patriarchal Blessing the Lord appeared in their midst and he (Adam) blessed them all and foretold what should befall them to the latest generation.

*   *   *   *   *   *

We ought to have the building up of Zion as our greatest object—When wars come we shall have to flee to Zion—The cry is to make haste,—The last revelation says "Ye shall not have time to have gone over the Earth until these things come. It will come as did the Cholera, War, and Fires burning, Earthquakes one pestilence after another &c until the Ancient of Days come then judgment will be given to the saints."[42]

Canonization

The 1844 edition of the Doctrine and Covenants published in Nauvoo, and the 1845–69 editions printed in Liverpool, England, contained the same scriptural texts about Adam-ondi-Ahman that were included in the 1835 Kirtland edition, so a general understanding about the concepts related to Adam-ondi-Ahman would have been somewhat familiar to many first and second generations of Latter-day Saints. However, in the early issues of the *Deseret News* printed in Salt Lake City, the editors, in collaboration with the historians in the Church Historian's Office, published passages from Joseph Smith's personal journals and histories, which information was likely not known to the general membership of the Church. On 2 April 1853, the paper included a lengthy extract for the date of 19 May 1838, from Joseph Smith's March–September 1838 journal, which contained the text on the occasion when the Prophet identified the location of Adam-ondi-Ahman in Daviess County, Missouri. A few slight changes were made to the published version of the text, although none of the alterations changed the meaning

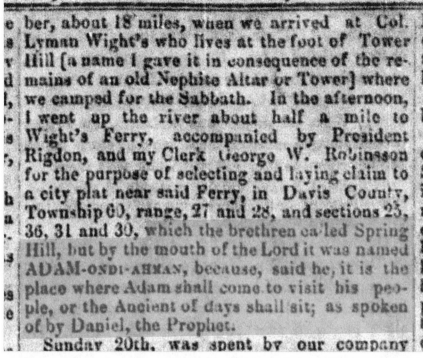

e ber, about 18 miles, when we arrived at Col.
s Lyman Wight's who lives at the foot of Tower
r Hill [a name I gave it in consequence of the re-
d mains of an old Nephite Altar or Tower] where
l, we camped for the Sabbath. In the afternoon,
- I went up the river about half a mile to
s Wight's Ferry, accompanied by President
-, Rigdon, and my Clerk George W. Robinson
for the purpose of selecting and laying claim to
b a city plat near said Ferry, in Davis County,
a Township 60, range, 27 and 28, and sections 25,
- 36, 31 and 30, which the brethren called Spring
s Hill, but by the mouth of the Lord it was named
ADAM-ONDI-AHMAN, because, said he, it is the
s place where Adam shall come to visit his peo-
e ple, or the Ancient of days shall sit; as spoken
of by Daniel, the Prophet.
Sunday 20th, was spent by our company

Figure 12. Excerpt from "History of Joseph Smith," in Deseret News *3, no. 10 (2 April 1853), 1. The published entry is taken from Joseph Smith's March–September 1838 Journal, 43–44, also in JSP, J1:271. The inclusion of this account would have been the first time that the general membership of the Church learned how Joseph Smith came to identify the location of Adam-ondi-Ahman.*

of the original entry (fig. 12).[43] The inclusion of this account would have been the first time that the general membership of the Church learned how Joseph Smith came to identify the location of Adam-ondi-Ahman..

Beginning in 1874, Orson Pratt was called as the new Church Historian and Recorder, and under the direction of Brigham Young he began to prepare a new edition of the Book of Mormon and Doctrine and Covenants. In editing and revising the revelations for publication in what became the 1876–80 editions, Pratt added twenty-six sections, including the portion of the text from Joseph Smith's 1838 journal about the discovery of the location of Adam-ondi-Ahman, something he, as a close associate of the Prophet, would have been very familiar with. Pratt also composed an introduction, or heading, to the revelation, which reads: "Revelation to Joseph, the Seer, given near Wight's Ferry, at a place called Spring Hill,

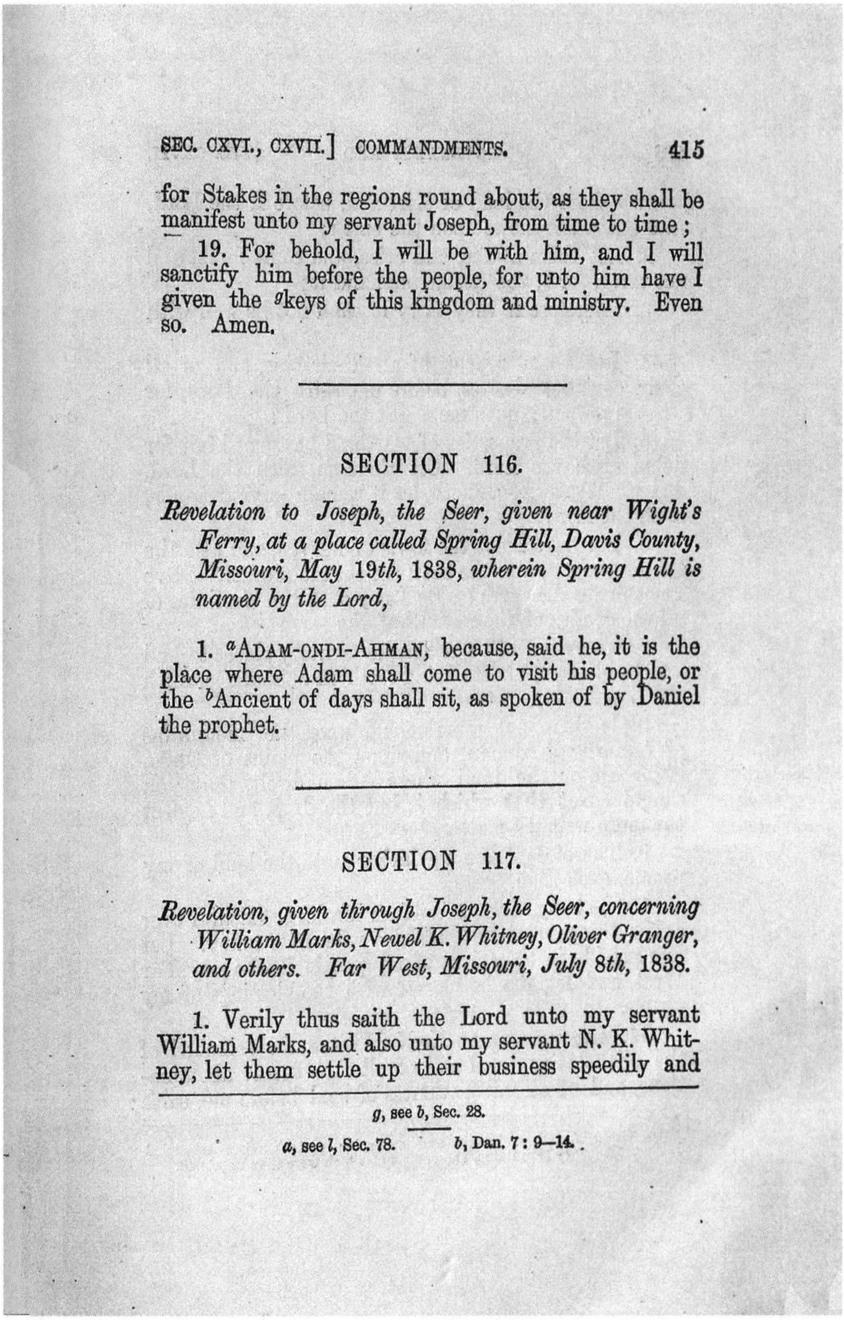

SEC. CXVI., CXVII.]   COMMANDMENTS.   **415**

for Stakes in the regions round about, as they shall be
manifest unto my servant Joseph, from time to time;
19. For behold, I will be with him, and I will
sanctify him before the people, for unto him have I
given the *g*keys of this kingdom and ministry. Even
so. Amen.

SECTION 116.

Revelation to Joseph, the Seer, given near Wight's
Ferry, at a place called Spring Hill, Davis County,
Missouri, May 19th, 1838, wherein Spring Hill is
named by the Lord,

1. *a*ADAM-ONDI-AHMAN, because, said he, it is the
place where Adam shall come to visit his people, or
the *b*Ancient of days shall sit, as spoken of by Daniel
the prophet.

SECTION 117.

Revelation, given through Joseph, the Seer, concerning
William Marks, Newel K. Whitney, Oliver Granger,
and others.   Far West, Missouri, July 8th, 1838.

1. Verily thus saith the Lord unto my servant
William Marks, and also unto my servant N. K. Whitney, let them settle up their business speedily and

---

g, see *b*, Sec. 28.

a, see *l*, Sec. 78.   *b*, Dan. 7: 9—14.

Figure 13. D&C 116 as it appeared in the 1876–80 edition of the Doctrine and Covenants.

Davis [Daviess] County, Missouri, May 19th, 1838, wherein Spring Hill is named by the Lord." He then included as the text of the revelation: "Adam-ondi-Ahman, because, said he, it is the place where Adam shall come to visit his people, or the Ancient of days shall sit, as spoken of by Daniel the prophet." A comparison of Pratt's text with the original from Joseph Smith's journal shows the wording to be precisely the same, though minor changes were made in spelling, punctuation, and capitalization. The new revelation became section 116 in the 1876 edition and all subsequent editions (fig. 13).[44] In 1921, in revising the revelations and headings for yet another edition, the Scripture Committee added a portion of Pratt's heading to the revelation, "Spring Hill is named by the Lord," to the original manuscript text. The 2013 section heading reads precisely the same as the 1921 version, with the exception that the *History of the Church* reference ("HC 3:35") has been deleted.

Conclusion

The Latter-day Saints have a unique and exclusive understanding of Adam and Eve's sojourn following their expulsion from the Garden of Eden which differs from other religious traditions. This knowledge came about incrementally through Joseph Smith's revision of the Bible, in discussions about Adam and Eve and their posterity given during the School of the Elders, and by direct revelation. In at least three instances, the Prophet received revelatory explanations or information regarding Adam-ondi-Ahman. The first of these occurred in early 1835, when he learned about the great council meeting held at Adam-ondi-Ahman three years previous to Adam's death in which the premortal Jehovah appeared to Adam and his righteous posterity (see D&C 107: 53–57). The second instance occurred in September 1835, when Oliver Cowdery was copying into the Patriarchal Blessing Book the patriarchal blessing given to Joseph Smith Sr. in 1833. At that time the Prophet authorized the inclusion of a passage into his father's blessing which indicated Adam was the "Ancient of days" spoken of in the book of Daniel in the Old Testament who would appear unto his posterity in the last days, along with Jesus Christ. The third revelatory occasion took place on 19 May 1838, when it was revealed to Joseph Smith that the area known as Spring

Hill in Daviess County, Missouri, was the ancient location of Adam-ondi-Ahman and the place where Daniel's prophecy would take place (D&C 116).

A discussion of Adam-ondi-Ahman would not be complete without mention of the contributions made by William W. Phelps and Orson Pratt. In his role as editor of the 1835 edition of the Doctrine and Covenants, Phelps revised earlier revelatory texts to reflect the added understanding Joseph Smith had received by 1835 about Adam-ondi-Ahman and standardized the spelling (D&C 78:15–16, 20). In addition, Phelps's poetic rendition "Adam-ondi-Ahman" became a favorite hymn sung by the early Saints and has remained a favorite among LDS congregations to the present day. The singing of this hymn has helped to impress upon the minds and hearts of the Latter-day Saints, both past and present, the significance of Adam's homeland. In addition, Orson Pratt's inspired decision to include the relatively short but significant entry from Joseph Smith's March–September 1838 journal about the discovery of the location of Adam-ondi-Ahman as a separate section in the 1876 edition of the Doctrine and Covenants elevated the passage to scripture. This addition provided a greater sense of spiritual meaning to the location and the prophetic events Latter-day Saints believe will transpire there before the Second Coming of Christ.

Notes

1. Wilford Woodruff, *Wilford Woodruff's Journal, 1833–1898*, 9 vols. typescript, ed. Scott G. Kenny (Midvale, UT: Signature Books, 1983–1984), 5:33. See also Journal History of the Church, 15 March 1857, 1, Church History Library, Salt Lake City, Utah, hereafter cited as CHL.

2. Heber C. Kimball, in *Journal of Discourses*, 26 vols. (Liverpool: F. D. Richards, 1855–86), 10:235, 27 June 1863.

3. In 1839, Reed Peck provided an early statement regarding Joseph Smith's teachings about the location of the Garden of Eden and Adam-ondi-Ahman. He wrote, "Adam-ondi-Ahman . . . was the place to which Adam fled when driven from the garden of Eden in Jackson County." See Reed Peck to "Dear Friends," 18 September 1839, 19–20, Henry E. Huntington Library, San Marino, California.

4. "A Sample of pure Language given by Joseph the Seer," circa March 1832, in Robin Scott Jensen, Robert J. Woodford, and Steven C. Harper, eds., *Revelations and Translations, Volume 1: Manuscript Revelations Books*, vol. 1 of the Revelations and Translation series of *The Joseph Smith Papers*, ed. Dean C. Jessee, Ronald K. Esplin, and Richard Lyman Bushman (Salt Lake City: Church Historian's Press, 2011), 204–6, hereafter cited as *JSP*, R1. The original spelling of Awman was A-w-m-e-n, with an "e." However an unidentified scribe changed each "e" to an "a." The "Q" and "A" formatting

was also later cancelled. In an 1855 address given by Orson Pratt, he discussed the meaning of the word Ahman: "There is one revelation that this people are not generally acquainted with. I think it has never been published, but probably it will be in the Church History. It is given in questions and answers. The first question is, 'What is the name of God in the pure language?' The answer says, 'Ahman.' 'What is the name of the Son of God?' Answer, 'Son Ahman—the greatest of all the parts of God excepting Ahman.'" Orson Pratt, in *Journal of Discourses*, 2:342, 18 February 1855. It's clear that Pratt was referencing the entry found in Revelation Book 1 when he stated that there was a "revelation" which had not been published, which gave the name of God.

5.   See "Lecture Second," in Doctrine and Covenants of the Church of the Latter Day Saints (Kirtland, OH: F. G. Williams & Co., 1835), 12–35, hereafter cited as D&C (1835). The lecture appears on pages 12–25, the catechism on pages 25–35. See also Robin Scott Jensen, Richard E. Turley Jr., and Riley M. Lorimer, eds., *Revelations and Translations, Volume 2: Published Revelations*, vol. 2 of the Revelations and Translations series of *The Joseph Smith Papers*, ed. Dean C. Jessee, Ronald K. Esplin, and Richard Lyman Bushman (Salt Lake City: Church Historian's Press, 2011), 322–45, hereafter cited as *JSP*, R2. It is important to note that a significant portion of the text in "Lecture Second" draws heavily from the information given in the JST found in Moses chapter 6.

6.   See D&C 3:28–29 (1835) [D&C 107:53–57]; also in *JSP*, R2:396. No handwritten manuscript of the document is known to exist. See also "Instruction on Priesthood, between ca. 1 Mar. and ca. 4 May 1835," in Matthew C. Godfrey, Brenden W. Rensink, Alex D. Smith, Max H Parkin, and Alexander L. Baugh, eds., *Documents Volume 4: April 1834–September 1835*, vol. 4 of the Documents series of *The Joseph Smith Papers*, ed. by Dean C. Jessee, Ronald K. Esplin, and Richard Lyman Bushman (Salt Lake City: Church Historian's Press, 2016), 308–21.

7.   W. W. Phelps, "Adam-ondi Ahman," *Latter Day Saints' Messenger and Advocate* 1, no. 9 (June 1835): 144. Phelps included a second poem in the same issue titled "Sabbath Hymn," now more commonly titled "Gently Raise the Sacred Strain," which hymn is the opening theme song for the weekly radio and television broadcast of the Mormon Tabernacle Choir.

8.   See "Lecture Second," Doctrine and Covenants (1835), 20–21, vv. 37–43; see also *JSP*, R2:330–31. Following the flood, the lives of the prophets from Shem to Abraham were shortened, although they continued to live for hundreds of years. See Genesis chapter 11, and "Lecture Second," 22–24, vv. 45–52; see also *JSP*, R2: 332–34. In the Book of Mormon, Lehi indicates that the lives of earth's early families "were prolonged, according to the will of God, . . . and their time was lengthened" (2 Nephi 2:21). A passage in the Doctrine and Covenants also implies a longer lifespan of the ancients. See D&C 3:18–27 (1835) [D&C 107:41–52]; see also *JSP*, R2:395.

9.   Flavius Josephus, *The Works of Flavius Josephus*, trans. William Whiston (Grand Rapids, MI: Kregel Publications, 1960), 29.

10.   Moses 6:51 states that the Lord "called upon our father Adam by his own voice." This may have only been an audible communication, but Jehovah may have also been seen on this occasion.

11.   D&C 3:24 (1835) [D&C 107:49]; see also *JSP*, R2:395.

12.   See Peter Crawley, *A Descriptive Bibliography of the Mormon Church: Volume 1, 1830–1847* (Provo, UT: Religious Studies Center, 1997), 56.

13.   See note 6.

14.   D&C 75:3 (1835) [D&C 78:15–16]; also in *JSP*, R2:515.

15.   See *JSP*, R1:209 [D&C 78:20]. In making this particular change, Phelps replaced the "w" in "Awman" with an "h" ("Awman" to "Ahman"). He also used the "Ahman" spelling in the poem "Adam-ondi-Ahman."

16.   D&C 75:5 (1835) [D&C 78:20]; also in *JSP*, R2:515. From a letter written by W. W. Phelps to his wife Sally on 26 May 1835, it appears that it was while he was review-ing and editing the revelations contained in Revelation Book 1, that he came across the document titled "A Sample of pure Language given by Joseph the Seer," which, as noted, appears immediately after the 1 March 1832 revelation. On page three of the letter to Sally, Phelps provided her with "A specimen of some of the 'pure language,'" containing some of the same phrases used in the "Sample," with a few additions. See W. W. Phelps to Sally Phelps, 26 May 1835, copy of the original in the W. W. Phelps Papers, MS 810, box 2, folder 1, L. Tom Perry Special Collections, Harold B. Lee Library, Brigham Young University, Provo, Utah.

17.   For the abbreviated account of Joseph Smith Sr.'s blessing, see Dean C. Jessee, Mark Ashurst-McGee, and Richard L. Jensen, eds., *Journals Volume 1: 1832–1839*, vol. 1 of the Journal series of *The Joseph Smith Papers*, ed. by Dean C. Jessee, Ronald K. Esplin, and Richard Lyman Bushman (Salt Lake City: Church Historian's Press, 2008), 23.

18.   See Joseph Smith Sr. blessing, Patriarchal Blessing Book 1, pp. 8–9, CHL. In addition to being set apart as the patriarch of the Church, Joseph Sr. was also ordained as an assistant president in the First Presidency.

19.   Ibid., 9.

20.   In a letter to his wife, Sally, dated 11 September 1835, Phelps wrote that he was "revising hymns for a hymn Book." See Bruce A. Van Orden, "Writing to Zion: The William W. Phelps Kirtland Letters (1835–1836)," *BYU Studies* 33, no. 3 (1993): 563. However, Phelps had received the commission to do this over three years earlier. At a meeting of the Literary Firm on 30 April 1832, it was "Ordered by the Council that the Hymns selected by sister Emma be corrected by Br. William W. Phelps." See Donald Q. Cannon and Lyndon W. Cook, eds., *Far West Record: Minutes of The Church of Jesus Christ of Latter-day Saints, 1830–1844* (Salt Lake City: Deseret Book, 1983), 46. The revelation instructing Emma Smith to compile a selection of hymns was given in July 1830. See Michael Hubbard MacKay, Gerrit J. Dirkmaat, Grant Underwood, Robert J. Woodford, and William G. Hartley, eds., *Documents Volume 1: July 1828–June 1831*, vol. 1 of the Document series of *The Joseph Smith Papers*, ed. by Dean C. Jessee, Ronald K. Esplin, and Richard Lyman Bushman (Salt Lake City: Church Historian's Press, 2013), 164; also *JSP*, R1:33 [D&C 25:11–12].

21.   Emma Smith, comp., *A Collection of Sacred Hymns for the Church of the Latter Day Saints* (Kirtland, OH: Printed by F. G. Williams and Co., 1835), 29–30. Of the ninety hymns, twenty-six are authored by Phelps. Although the hymnal bears an 1835 publication date, it was not completed until sometime in February or March 1836. See Crawley, *A Descriptive Bibliography of the Mormon Church*, 1:59.

22. Crawley, *A Descriptive Bibliography of the Mormon Church*, 59.

23. See Manuscript History of the Church, 27 March 1836, Vol. B–1, 716, 722, CHL; *Latter Day Saints' Messenger and Advocate* 2, no. 6 (March 1836): 276–77, 280–81.

24. Michael Hicks, *Mormonism and Music: A History* (Urbana and Chicago: University of Illinois Press, 1989), 23, 33 note 16. Given the irregularities of the meter, Hicks has concluded that the tune would have been something similar to what is sung in the Church today. Michael Hicks to Alexander L. Baugh, 11 January 2016.

25. See Michael Hicks, "What Hymns Early Mormons Sang and Why They Sang Them," *BYU Studies* 47, no. 1 (2008): 98–102. In a survey of early church records Hicks notes that between 1830–1838, "Adam-ondi-Ahman" was sung more than any other hymn. The hymn currently appears in *Hymns of The Church of Jesus Christ of Latter-day Saints* (Salt Lake City: The Church of Jesus Christ of Latter-day Saints, 1985), no. 49.

26. See Jeffrey N. Walker, "Mormon Land Rights in Caldwell and Daviess Counties and the Mormon Conflict of 1838: New Findings and New Understandings," *BYU Studies* 47, no. 1 (2008): 5–55; also Leland H. Gentry, "The Land Question at Adam-ondi-Ahman," *BYU Studies* 26, no. 2 (Spring 1986): 45–56.

27. Lyman Wight moved to the Grand River region in Daviess County in February 1838. Lyman Wight to Wilford Woodruff, 24 August 1857, CR 100 93, CHL.

28. Joseph Smith Jr., Journal, March–September 1838, 43–44, Joseph Smith Papers, CHL, also in *JSP*, J1:271. This journal is sometimes referred to as the Scriptory Book. It is important to note that the entry was made by George W. Robinson, Joseph Smith's clerk, but it is not known when Robinson made the entry. He may have made it at the time Smith identified the site, but since they were "exploring," this seems unlikely. It is more reasonable to conclude that Robinson took notes, then made the entry from his notes at a more convenient time, perhaps later that day or a day or two later, or he may have waited until he and Joseph Smith returned to Far West, which was not until 1 June. See *JSP*, J1:274.

29. Smith, Journal, 45; *JSP*, J1:275. On 26 May, two days after he returned to Far West, Joseph Smith went on another short expedition to Daviess County, but returned on 1 June in anticipation of the birth of his son Alexander Hale Smith, who was born the following day, 2 June 1838. See Smith, Journal, 45; *JSP* J1:276.

30. *JSP*, J1:271.

31. Robinson's description of what Joseph Smith's company discovered on this occasion aligns with the findings from an archaeological excavation conducted at the site in 1979 and 1980 by Ray T. Matheny, a former professor of anthropology at Brigham Young University. Matheny and his team concluded that what Joseph Smith and his company discovered on this occasion were the remains of some structure that was part of an ancient Native American burial ground dating to the early part of the Late Woodland period (AD 500–1000). See Ray T. Matheny and D. Robert Carter, "Adam-ondi-Ahman Field Analysis, 1980–1982," 31–39, L. Tom Perry Special Collections, Harold B. Lee Library, Brigham Young University, Provo, Utah, copy in possession of the author. Based on Matheny's findings, it can be concluded that additional ruins and remains seen and discovered by Mormons in the vicinity of Adam-ondi-Ahman in

1838 also originated from Native Americans of the same period. For a brief synopsis of this argument see Alexander L. Baugh, "Joseph Smith in Northern Missouri, 1838," in *Joseph Smith: The Prophet & Seer*, ed. Richard Neitzel Holzapfel and Kent P. Jackson (Provo, UT: Religious Studies Center; Salt Lake City: Deseret Book, 2010), 305–7.

32.   William Swartzell, *Mormonism Exposed, Being a Journal of a Residence in Missouri from the 28th of May, to the 20th of August* (Pekin, OH: By the author, 1840), 11–12. Swartzell's entry is under the date of 11 June 1838.

33.   John Corrill, *A Brief History of the Church of Christ of Latter Day Saints* (St. Louis: by the author, 1839), 28; also in Karen Lynn Davidson, Richard L. Jensen, and David J. Whittaker, eds., *Histories Volume 2: Assigned Histories, 1831–1847*, vol. 2 of the Histories series of *The Joseph Smith Papers*, ed. by Dean C. Jessee, Ronald K. Esplin, and Richard Lyman Bushman (Salt Lake City: Church Historian's Press, 2012), 163. See also Joseph Smith to Stephen Post, 17 September 1838, 1, Stephen Post Papers, CHL. Orson Pratt provided this explanation regarding the meaning of Adam-ondi-Ahman: "Perhaps you may be anxious to know what 'Ondi–Ahman' means. It means the place where Adam dwelt. 'Ahman' signifies God. The whole term means Valley of God, where Adam dwelt. It is in the original language spoken by Adam, as revealed to the Prophet Joseph." Orson Pratt, in *Journal of Discourses*, 18:343, 17 February 1877.

34.   During the summer and fall of 1838, several hundred Mormon families settled in Daviess County, mostly at Adam-ondi-Ahman. In November, when the Mormons agreed to leave the state, an estimated 1,200 to 1,500 Mormons resided in the county. See Alexander L. Baugh, "Settling Northern Missouri," in *Mapping Mormonism: An Atlas of Latter-day Saint History*, ed. Brandon S. Plewe (Provo, UT: BYU Press, 2012), 48–49.

35.   Corrill, *A Brief History*, 163; also *JSP*, H2:163.

36.   "Conference Minutes," *Elders' Journal* 1, no. 4 (August 1838): 60–61. See also Swartzell, *Mormonism Exposed*, 14–15.

37.   The first two stakes were the Kirtland stake, organized 17 February 1834, and the Missouri stake, organized 3 and 7 July 1834.

38.   *JSP*, J1:289–90 [D&C 117:1, 3, 10–11]. William Marks's call to preside over the Missouri stake was precipitated by another revelation also received on 8 July 1838, which called for all the members of the Quorum of the Twelve to prepare to serve a collective mission to Great Britain the following spring (1839). See *JSP*, J1:285 [D&C 118]. At the time, Thomas B. Marsh, David W. Patten, and Brigham Young—the three senior members of the Twelve—also served as the Missouri presidency. Thus, the call for all the members of the Twelve to serve in Great Britain meant that the entire presidency of the Missouri stake would need to be replaced. In response to that need, Marks was called to replace Marsh, although no other names were put forward to replace Patten and Young as counselors in the presidency. As noted in the text, Vinson Knight's appointment to serve as the bishop at Adam-ondi-Ahman was only temporary, suggesting that Whitney would fill that position when he arrived in Missouri.

39.   Swartzell, *Mormonism Exposed*, 24. Swartzell's entry about the temple being located on a four-acre lot in the center of the community was dated 22 July 1838.

40.   Orson F. Whitney, *Life of Heber C. Kimball, An Apostle* (Salt Lake City: Juvenile Instructor, 1888), 222–23; also in Whitney, *Life of Heber C. Kimball*, 2nd ed.

(Salt Lake City: Bookcraft, 1945), 208–09. See also Leland H. Gentry, "Was a temple site ever dedicated at Adam-ondi-Ahman?" *Ensign* 4, no. 4 (April 1974): 16.

41. See Robert J. Matthews, "Adam-ondi-Ahman," *BYU Studies* 13, no. 1 (Autumn 1972): 27–35. For a more complete survey of the Adam-ondi-Ahman community, see Leland H. Gentry, "Adam-ondi-Ahman: A Brief Historical Survey," *BYU Studies* 13, no. 4 (Summer 1973): 553–76. Gentry's article makes a number of important contributions regarding the historical development of the Adam-ondi-Ahman settlement. However, in the section titled "The Altar-Tower Question," 564–76, he accepts as face value a number of questionable eyewitness accounts, secondhand accounts, and late reminiscences and reports regarding the ancient remains discovered at Adam-ondi-Ahman. In so doing, he overanalyzes the subject and comes to a number of confusing and questionable conclusions (e.g., a Nephite and an Adamic altar, one altar verses two altars, where each were located, a stone wall being one of the altars). Alvin R. Dyer perpetuated some of these same conclusions. See Alvin R. Dyer, *The Refiner's Fire: The Significance of Events Transpiring in Missouri* (Salt Lake City: Deseret Book, 1976), 176.

42. Manuscript History of the Church, Vol. C–1, addenda, 11, 13.

43. "History of Joseph Smith," *Deseret News* 3, no. 10 (2 April 1853): 1.

44. D&C 116:1 (1876–80).

10

Hyrum Smith's Liberty Jail Letters

Kenneth L. Alford and Craig K. Manscill

Kenneth L. Alford is a professor of Church history and
doctrine at Brigham Young University.

Craig K. Manscill is an associate professor of
Church history and doctrine at Brigham Young University.

The story of Liberty Jail has frequently been told from the perspective of Joseph Smith, but the experience of Hyrum Smith has largely been ignored. Hyrum wrote and received several letters while in Liberty Jail, and his letters provide valuable information about conditions and events during the imprisonment, give context to events in the Church at large, and add insights into the struggles his family endured during the Missouri persecutions and as refugees in Illinois. A close study of Hyrum's letters provides insights into the development, writing, and doctrines espoused in Doctrine and Covenants 121, 122, and 123.

Prelude to Liberty Jail

Joseph Smith, Sidney Rigdon, Parley P. Pratt, and other leaders were betrayed at Far West into the hands of Major General Samuel D. Lucas and the Missouri militia on 31 October 1838.[1] Hyrum Smith and Amasa

Lyman were captured later that day while attempting to flee to Iowa.² In
Richmond, Missouri, on 29 November 1838, Austin A. King, a fifth judicial
circuit judge, signed the court order charging six prisoners with "treason
against the state of Missouri."³ The six men were Joseph Smith, who would
turn thirty-four years old in three weeks; Sidney Rigdon, forty-five; Hyrum
Smith, thirty-eight; Alexander McRae, thirty-one, the youngest member of
the group; Lyman Wight, forty-two; and Caleb Baldwin, forty-seven, who
was the oldest.

Hyrum later testified that he heard the judge say "that there was no law
for us, nor for the Mormons, in the state of Missouri; that he had sworn to
see them exterminated, and to see the Governor's order executed to the very
letter, and that he would do so."⁴ The detainees were bound over to Sheriff
Samuel Hadley for transport to Liberty Jail. Prior to being taken to jail, they
were handcuffed and chained together. During the course of his work, the
blacksmith informed the prisoners that "the judge [had] stated his intention to keep us in jail until all the Mormons were driven out of the state."⁵
With the exception of Sidney Rigdon, who was freed on 5 February 1839,
the detainees would be incarcerated the entire winter—from 1 December
1838 until 6 April 1839—in the unheated jail.⁶

Isolated from Church headquarters, the jailed Church leadership was
rendered unable to lead the Church out of Missouri. Communication with
the outside world was limited to letters and visitors. As Liberty is forty miles
from Far West, it was possible for family, friends, and Church leaders to call
on the prisoners. All of the men except Hyrum received visits from their
wives during December.⁷ They were visited in January over twenty times,
with all of the wives visiting at least once. During one of those visits, Hyrum
blessed his newborn son, Joseph Fielding Smith.⁸ Jail visitors decreased during February and March as an increasing number of Church and family
members fled Missouri for the safety of Illinois.

Hyrum later commented, "We endeavored to find out for what cause
[we were to be thrust into jail], but all that we could learn was [that it was]
because we were Mormons."⁹ Life in the jail was difficult; Hyrum further
reported that "poison was administered to us three or four times, the effect
it had upon our systems was, that it vomitted us almost to death, and then
we would lay in a torpid stupid state, not even caring or wishing for life."
He also said, "We were also subjected to the necessity of eating human flesh

for the space of 5 days or go without food, except a little coffee or a little corn bread—the latter I chose in preference to the former. We none of us partook of the flesh except Lyman Wight."[10]

Bishop Partridge's 5 March Letter

On 5 March, Bishop Edward Partridge wrote a letter from Quincy, Illinois, to the "Beloved Brethren" in Liberty Jail, providing details of the Church in Illinois. Partridge explained that he wrote because of "an opportunity to send direct to you by br[other] Rogers."[11] In addition to Partridge's letter, David Rogers also carried a 6 March letter from Don Carlos and William Smith, two of Joseph and Hyrum's brothers, and a 7 March letter from Emma, Joseph's wife.[12] Rogers left Quincy on 10 March 1839 and delivered the letters on 19 March.[13]

Liberty Jail Correspondence

In the difficult conditions of Liberty Jail, the prisoners faced several challenges when it came to writing and receiving letters. The first problem, as Hyrum mentioned in his 19 March letter to his wife Mary, was that they were often in need of paper and ink. The second was difficulty receiving letters. And third was the challenge of finding trustworthy people to deliver their letters. As an increasing number of Church members fled Missouri, letters became the only viable means of communication with family members and Church leaders now in Illinois.

We are currently aware of eight letters Hyrum Smith wrote from Liberty Jail (see tables 1 and 2). Seven of them are dated and were penned during March and April 1839. At least four of the letters, and possibly five, were written prior to Joseph's 20 March letter of instruction, portions of which would be canonized as Doctrine and Covenants 121–123. Hyrum's first two letters, both dated 16 March, were written to Hannah Grinnals and his wife, Mary Fielding Smith. Hannah was a longtime, trusted friend, who lived with Hyrum and Mary for almost twenty years. She first appears in the historical record in 1837 giving aid to Hyrum's family when his daughter Sarah was born and his first wife, Jerusha, died while he was away on Church business. Hannah likewise assisted Mary with Joseph F. Smith's birth on

13 November 1838, almost two weeks after Hyrum had been arrested.[14] When Hyrum wrote to Hannah from Liberty Jail, he thanked her for "friends[h]ip you have manifested towards my family I feel grateful to you for your Kindness." He included words of encouragement and counsel to his daughter Lovina and to Clarinda, who was likely Hannah's daughter, as well as general counsel to his other children "little John little Hiram little Jerusha & little Sarah" that they "must be good little children till farther [sic] comes home." He also confided to Hannah, "I want you should stay with the family and nev[e]r leave them My home shall be your home for I shall have a home though I have none now . . . my house shall be your home."[15]

Hyrum's six remaining letters were written to Mary. While we can date five of those letters (19 March, 20 March, 23 March, 3 April, and 5 April), the sixth remains undated because the first page is missing.[17] Hyrum

Table 1. Hyrum Smith's Liberty Jail Letters

Hyrum's Liberty Jail Letters	Date
To Hannah Grinnals (family friend) (words of encouragement and friendship)	16 March 1839
To Mary Fielding Smith (wife) (shared details of an attempted jail break)	16 March 1839
To Mary Fielding Smith (discussed what it was like to be imprisoned)	19 March 1839
To Mary Fielding Smith (gently chided Mary for not writing to him more often)	20 March 1839
To Mary Fielding Smith (primarily paraphrased a Robert Burns poem)	23 March 1839
To Mary Fielding Smith (primarily a discussion of family matters)	3 April 1839
To Mary Fielding Smith (a discussion of family matters and a fellow prisoner)	5 April 1839 (based on a Liberty, Missouri postmark; the letter itself is undated)
To Mary Fielding Smith (compared his situation in jail to Joseph in Egypt)	Undated

Table 2. Joseph Smith's Liberty Jail Letters

Joseph's Liberty Jail Letters[16]	Date
To Emma Hale Smith (wife) (informed his wife that they had arrived at the jail)	1 December 1838
To the Saints in Caldwell County (guidance and instructions)	16 December 1838
To Presendia Huntington Buell (friend) (thanked her for friendship and interest in their welfare)	15 March 1839
To the Church at Quincy, Illinois (includes the text of D&C 121–123)	20 March 1839
To Emma Hale Smith (responded to a letter from her)	21 March 1839
To Isaac Galland (businessman) (expressed a desire to purchase land from him)	22 March 1839
To Emma Hale Smith (expressed his love and gave her advice and encouragement)	4 April 1839

addressed the undated letter to Mary at Quincy, Illinois, which provides some clue as to the approximate date it was written. Joseph and Hyrum's families left Far West on 7 February. We are uncertain when they reached Illinois, but we know that they settled in Quincy, Illinois, prior to 5 March 1839. In his 5 March letter to the Liberty Jail inmates, Bishop Edward Partridge informed Joseph and Hyrum that "Brother Joseph's wife lives at Judge [John] Cleveland[']s, I have not seen her but I sent her word of this opportunity to send to you. Br[other] Hyrum's wife lives not far from me." Bishop Partridge added, "I have been to see her a number of times, her health was very poor," implying that Mary Fielding Smith had arrived in Quincy well before 5 March.[18]

In a 6 March letter to Hyrum and Joseph written from Quincy, their younger brother Don Carlos explained, "Father's family have all arrived in this state except you two. . . . Emma and Children are well, they live three miles from here, and have a tolerable good place. Hyrum's children and mother Grinolds[19] are living at present with father; they are all well, Mary

[Fielding Smith] has not got her health yet, but I think it increases slowly. She lives in the house with old Father Dixon, likewise Br[other] [Robert B.] Thompson and family; they are probably a half mile from Father's."[20] Based on the short time Joseph and Hyrum remained incarcerated after Joseph's 20 March letter (they left the jail, never to return, on 6 April), there is a greater possibility that the undated letter from Hyrum to Mary was written prior to Joseph's 20 March letter of counsel and instruction rather than on some later date.

Joseph's 20 March 1839 Letter

In a long letter dated 20 March, Joseph wrote "to the church of the Latterday saints at Quincy Illinois and scattered abroad and to Bishop [Edward] Partridge in particular." The letter consists of two lengthy parts. Both parts have been assigned a 20 March 1839 date by historians.[21] The first seventeen pages, labeled by the Joseph Smith Papers project as 20 March 1839–A, include text that would eventually be canonized as Doctrine and Covenants 121:1–33. The 20 March[22] letter is signed by the five men who remained in Liberty Jail—Joseph Smith, Hyrum Smith, Lyman Wight, Caleb Baldwin, and Alexander McRae.[23] The letter was recorded "by Alexander McRae and Caleb Baldwin, who acted as scribes for Joseph Smith."[24] Historian Stephen C. Harper concluded that "frequent misplaced and misspelled words show the rush in which the dictation was scribbled down."[25] Inspection of the original pages shows that Joseph made a few corrections to the text.

The second part of that letter, identified in the Joseph Smith Papers as 20 March 1839–B, is an additional nine handwritten pages. Those pages begin with the heading "Continued to the church of Latter-day-saints" and are signed by the same five detainees. One of the purposes of the additional pages was "to offer further reflections to Bishop [Edward] Partridge and to the church of Jesus Christ of Latter day saints whom we love with a fervent love."[26] It is certainly possible that both parts of the letter had been composed in a single sitting or on a single day, but it seems somewhat irregular that the authors would sign their names twice to the same letter. It is from the second part that Doctrine and Covenants 121:34–46, 122, and 123 were later excerpted and added to the Doctrine and Covenants.

Joseph addressed a cover letter, written on 21 March 1839 to his "Affectionate Wife" Emma. Joseph explained that he sent "an Epistle to the church directed to you because I wanted you to have the first reading of it and then I want Father and Mother to have a coppy of it keep the original yourself as I dectated the matter myself." At the end of his three-page cover letter, Joseph touchingly asked his wife, "My Dear Emma do you think that my being cast into prison by the mob renders me less worthy of your friendship," and then he provided the answer he hoped to receive: "No I do not think so."[27]

Lyman Wight's journal states that "Brother Ripley [almost certainly Alanson Ripley, a participant in Zion's Camp who served on a committee to remove poor members of the Church from Missouri] came in and took our package of letters for Quincy" on 22 March—possibly providing sufficient time and opportunity for the second part of Joseph's letter to have been dictated and signed on 21 March along with Joseph's cover letter to Emma.[28]

Hyrum's Relationship with Joseph's 20 March Letter

The letter dictated by Joseph Smith on 20 March (and possibly 21 March) contains "some of the most sublime revelations ever received by any prophet in any dispensation."[29] It is reasonable to consider that many of the thoughts, feelings, doctrines, counsel, and teachings found throughout the letter—in both the canonized and noncanonized sections—had been germinating for many weeks prior to being recorded. With so little to occupy their time in jail, Joseph and his fellow prisoners had many days to reflect upon the content expressed in that letter. That would be especially true for conversations Joseph had with his beloved brother Hyrum. The overlapping content in Joseph's and Hyrum's letters demonstrate that they included some of that conversation in their letters. Hyrum's letters demonstrate that some of the ideas in Doctrine and Covenants 121–123 took shape orally before they were committed to paper.

Excerpts from Hyrum's letters are included in tables 3–7. Text in the left-hand columns is from Hyrum's Liberty Jail diary and letters. The right-hand columns list similarly themed excerpts from Doctrine and Covenants 121, 122, and 123. We will leave it to the reader to draw conclusions as to

Table 3. Excerpts from Hyrum Smith's Diary, March 1839

Hyrum's Diary	Canonized Portions of Joseph's Letter
"I was with several others Committed to Jail for my religion" (15 March 1839)	"And if thou shouldst be cast into the pit" (D&C 122:7)
"the same acqisations was had a gainst the son of god" (15 March 1839)	"The Son of Man hath descended below them all" (D&C 122:8)
"Kept in close Confine ment and our familees we're Driven out of the state they also were Robed of all theyr [*smudged*] goods and substance for theyr suport all most maked [naked] and Destitute as they were when they were born in to the world all this by a hellish mob let loose by the athoreties of the state to prac-tise their wicked Designs upon an inosent people and for no other cause than to put Down their <our> Religion" (18 March 1839)	"It is an imperative duty that we owe to God, to angels, with whom we shall be brought to stand, and also to ourselves, to our wives and children, who have been made to bow down with grief, sor-row, and care, under the most damning hand of murder, tyranny, and oppres-sion, supported and urged on and upheld by the influence of that spirit which hath so strongly riveted the creeds of the fathers, who have inherited lies, upon the hearts of the children, and filled the world with confusion, and has been growing stronger and stronger, and is now the very mainspring of all corrup-tion, and the whole earth groans under the weight of its iniquity" (D&C 123:7)

whether or not the presumed interchange of ideas between brothers can be seen within Hyrum's letters and diary entries.

Diary entries: Hyrum Smith kept a contemporary diary while incarcer-ated in Liberty Jail. The three excerpts in Table 3 are entries from Hyrum's diary dated 15 March and 18 March, which share similar sentiments to verses found in Doctrine and Covenants 122 and 123.

Hyrum's 16 March letter to Mary Fielding Smith. In this letter, addressed to "Mary, my dear Companion," Hyrum shared details regarding an attempted jail break. As he explained:

> Some friend put some auguers [augers] in to the window &
> an iron bar we made a hole in through the logs in the lower
> room & through the stone wall all but the out side stone which

was suffitiently large to pass out when it was pushed out but we were hind[e]red for want of handles to the auguers the logs were so hard that the handles would split & we had to make new ones with our fire wood we had to bore the hole for the shank with my penknife which delayed time in Spite of <all> we could do the day of Examination came on before in the after noon. that Evening we was ready to make our Essape [escape] & we were discovered & prevented of making our Essape there apeared to be no hard feelings on the part of the Sheriff & Jailor but the old Baptists & prisbiterians & Me[t]hodests were very mutch Excited they turned out in tens as volenteers to gard the Jail till the Jail was mended.[30]

Hyrum closed this letter with the following plea: "O god in the name of thy son preserve the life & health of my bosom companeon & may she be prsious [precious] in thy sight & all the little children & that is pertaining to my family & hasten the time when we shall meet in Each others Embrass [Embrace]." The following statements in this letter sound similar to text included in Doctrine and Covenants 121–123.

Hyrum's 19 March letter to Mary Fielding Smith. From this letter we learn that Hyrum was ill—"q[u]ite out of hea[l]th to day have Kept my bed all day"—the day before Joseph dictated his 20 March letter. He expressed his disappointment "that I did not hear from you & the family by your own pen" and let her know that "brother Pa[r]tr[i]dge says he imformed you

Table 4. Excerpts from Hyrum Smith's 16 March 1839 Letter to Mary Fielding Smith

Hyrum's Correspondence	Canonized Portions of Joseph's Letter
"O god how long shall we suffer these things will not though [thou] deliver us & make us free Still thy will be done O lord."	"O God, where art thou? . . . How long shall thy hand be stayed . . . Yea, O Lord, how long shall they suffer these wrongs and unlawful oppressions" (D&C 121:1–3)
"O lord god wilt though [thou] hear the pra[y]er of your servant"	"let thine ear be inclined" (D&C 121:4)
"May the lord bless you & give you stren[g]th to Endure all these things"	"And then, if thou endure it well, God shall exalt thee on high . . ." (D&C 121:8)

of the oppertunity of sending [a letter] by brother Rodgers." He conceded that "I do not Know but your was sick so that you could not write." Hyrum shared that he was "verry anxious to hear from you," and he worried about his family. "I have been informed," he wrote, "that you are sepperated from the family . . . on this side of the river & you on the other . . . my feelings & anxiety is sutch that my sleep has departed from me." And then Hyrum confided that his jail experience was wearing on him: "My faith understanding & Judgement is not suffitient to over come these feelings of sorrow a word from you might possibly be sattisfactory or in degree relieve my feelings of anxiety that sleep may return." He also provided a glimpse into the physical toll life in jail exacted. "Excuse my poor writing my nerves are some what affected & <my hands> are this Evening q[u]ite swolen & fingers are stiff & painfull with the rheum[a]tism."[31] Two statements from this letter sound similar to the canonized portions of Joseph's 20 March letter.

Hyrum's 20 March letter to Mary Fielding Smith. Hyrum informed Mary that David Rogers visited that morning and that Alanson Ripley was also there and "is a going to start back to [*faded*] this after noon." Ripley did not depart on 20 March, though, because Joseph's cover letter to Emma, which he carried to Illinois, is dated on the following day. Toward the end of this letter, Hyrum again gently chided Mary for not writing: "I thought if you could not write you could send a friendly word, . . . I do not wish to harrow up your feelings if they are inocent but I thought it strange that you did not send one word to me when I thought you Knew I was so anxious to hear from you. . . . If you have no feelings for me as a husband you could sent or

Table 5. Excerpts from Hyrum Smith's 19 March 1839 Letter to Mary Fielding Smith

Hyrum's Correspondence	Canonized Portions of Joseph's Letter
"God has said that he would deliver us from the power of our Enemeis in his own due time we try to be as patient as possible"	"My son, peace be unto thy soul; thine adversity and thine afflictions shall be but a small moment; And then, if thou endure it well, God shall exalt thee on high; thou shalt triumph over all thy foes" (D&C 121:7–8)
"the bonds of true friendship & love"	"Thy friends do stand by thee, and they shall hail thee again with warm hearts and friendly hands" (D&C 121:9)

Table 6. Excerpts from Hyrum Smith's 20 March 1839 Letter to Mary Fielding Smith

Hyrum's Correspondence	Canonized Portions of Joseph's Letter
"if you have not forsaken me"	"O God, where art thou? And where is the pavilion that covereth thy hiding place?" (D&C 121:1)
"our Enemies must be left without Excuse those that seek our hurt will see their folly sooner or later"	"Let thine anger be kindled against our enemies; and, in the fury of thine heart, with thy sword avenge us of our wrongs" (D&C 121:5)
"our sufferings will only cal[l] to mind the sufferings of the aintients [ancients]"	"Remember thy suffering saints, O our God . . . Thou art not yet as Job" (D&C 121:6–10)
"we must be patient in tribulation"	"If thou art called to pass through tribulation" (D&C 122:5)

caused to be sent some information concerning the little babe or those little children that lies near my hart." Unlike the other letters to Mary, this letter has no signature or address.[32] As this letter is dated the same day as Joseph's letter, it is no surprise that several concepts from the latter found their way into the former.

Hyrum's undated (presumably before 20 March) letter to Mary Fielding Smith. This letter is addressed (on the final page) to "Mrs Mary Smith, Q[u]incy Adams Co Ilinois." In the extant pages, Hyrum compares the prisoner's situation to Joseph in Egypt who "was sold by his bretheren notwithstanding he was cast in to prison for many years yet the power of wisdom was there all though men thought to disgrace him but they fail'd." He shared his opinion with Mary that "bonds and imprisenments and persecutions are no dis grace to the Saints it is that is common in all ages of the world since the days of adam for he was persecuted by his own posterity in the days of Seth with sutch violence the he had to flee out of his own count[r]y to an other land." He closed this letter by asking Mary to "pray for me my companion I will pray for <you> unceasingly as mutch as I can." After signing his name, he asked Mary to "Excuse all imperfections."[33]

Table 7. Excerpts from an Undated Letter from Hyrum Smith to Mary Fielding Smith

Hyrum's Correspondence	Canonized Portions of Joseph's Letter
"that the wicked ungodly oppresser shall come to a speedy distruction and have no Excuse in the Day of Judgement"	"Let thine anger be kindled against our enemies; and, in the fury of thine heart, with thy sword avenge us of our wrongs" (D&C 121:5)
"he was patient in tribulation and harkened to that redeeming power that saves" "wisdom shows us that these things are for our salvation spiritualy and temporaly" "all these things are to make us wise and inteligent that we may be the happy recippient of the hi[gh]est glory"	"And then, if thou endure it well, God shall exalt thee on high; thou shalt triumph over all thy foes." (D&C 121:8)
"bonds and imprisenments and persecutions are no dis grace to the Saints"	"And those who swear falsely against my servants, that they might bring them into bondage and death" (D&C 121:18)
"that what we do not learn by precept we may learn by Experince"	"We have learned by sad experience that it is the nature and disposition of almost all men, as soon as they get a little authority, as they suppose, they will immediately begin to exercise unrighteous dominion" (D&C 121:39)
"the scepter of the kingdom shall be in their hands"	"thy scepter an unchanging scepter of righteousness and truth" (D&C 121:46)
"if they are cast in to the pit it shall b[*faded*] be with them and deliver them all though th[e]y are left in bonds"	"And if thou shouldst be cast into the pit" (D&C 122:7)

As these letter excerpts demonstrate, Hyrum Smith appears to have been involved in discussions regarding the doctrines and concepts included in Joseph's 20 March letter. For a brief time, that letter of instruction served almost as a de facto Church presidency while the Church was deprived of

Joseph and Hyrum's presence. It should not come as a surprise that Joseph and Hyrum discussed much of the contents of Joseph's 20 March letter; they were experiencing the same trying conditions, emotions, and family difficulties. Plus, there was a strong and lifelong bond between them.

There are additional similarities to Joseph's 20 March letter in Hyrum's subsequent letters and diary entries, but they do not necessarily reflect discussions that could have occurred between Joseph and Hyrum prior to Joseph dictating the 20 March letter.

Release from Liberty Jail

The five prisoners left Liberty Jail on 6 April and were taken to Daviess County to appear before Judge Birch. For ten days a ribald and irreverent grand jury boasted of abuses they had perpetrated on the Mormons. Hyrum reported that after ten days of the grand jury's drunken antics, "we were indicted for treason, murder, arson, larceny, theft, and stealing."[34] The prisoners requested a change of venue to Marion County, but were granted instead a change to Boone County. "They fitted us out with a two horse wagon, and horses, and four men, besides the sheriff, to be our guard," according to Hyrum. "There were five of us [prisoners]. We started from Gallatin the sun about two hours high, P.M., and went as far as Diahman that evening and staid till morning. There we bought two horses of the guard, and paid for one of them in our clothing, which we had with us; and for the other we gave our note." Upon reaching Boone County, "we bought a jug of whiskey; with which we treated the company." The sheriff informed the prisoners that Judge Birch had instructed him "never to carry us to Boon[e] county . . . and said he, I shall take a good drink of grog and go to bed, and you may do as you have a mind to. Three others of the guard drank pretty freely of whiskey, sweetened with honey; they also went to bed, and were soon asleep, and the other guard went along with us, and helped to saddle the horses."[35]

Joseph and Hyrum mounted the horses, and Caleb Baldwin, Lyman Wight, and Alexander McRae started walking to Quincy, Illinois. Joseph and Hyrum reached Quincy on 22 April 1839, where they found their families "in a state of poverty, although in good health."[36] Their extended ordeal had reached an end.

Aftermath

Joseph's 20 March letter was considered a historical document and was not canonized during Joseph and Hyrum's lifetime. Both parts of the 20 March 1839 letter were published several times prior to Doctrine and Covenants 121–123 being canonized, including excerpts printed in the *Times and Seasons*, the *Deseret News*, and the British *Millennial Star*.[37] Sometime prior to 15 January 1875, Elder Orson Pratt received an assignment from Brigham Young to work on a new edition of the Doctrine and Covenants, "arranging the order in which the revelations are to be inserted." Elder Pratt "divided the various revelations into verses, and arranged them for printing, according to the order of date in which they were revealed."[38] Responsibility regarding which excerpts from the 20 March letter would be canonized was also apparently left to Elder Pratt. The seven excerpts (five which were stitched together to become Doctrine and Covenants 121 with one contiguous excerpt providing the text for sections 122 and 123) were included in the 1876 edition of the Doctrine and Covenants. The Pearl of Great Price was sustained as one of the four standard works of the Church during the October 1880 general conference; Doctrine and Covenants 121, 122, and 123 were canonized at the same time.[39]

Notes

1. It is insightful to note that both Lilburn W. Boggs and Samuel D. Lucas were residents of Jackson County, Missouri, and had figured prominently in the 1833 expulsion of the Saints. In 1833, Boggs was Missouri's lieutenant governor and Lucas was a county court justice and colonel of local militia. See Leland H. Gentry and Todd M. Compton, *Fire and Sword: A History of the Latter-day Saints in Northern Missouri, 1836–39* (Salt Lake City: Greg Kofford Books, 2011), 15.

2. Church Educational System, *Church History in the Fulness of Times Student Manual: Religion 341 through 343* (Salt Lake City: The Church of Jesus Christ of Latter-day Saints, 2003), 205.

3. Judge King had determined the outcome before the hearing. "If a Cohort of angels were to come down and declare we were clear Donaphan said it would all be the same for he King had determined from the begining to Cast us into prison." Sidney Rigdon, Joseph Smith, et al., Petition Draft ("To the Publick"), circa 1838–1839, 45b, http://josephsmithpapers.org/paperSummary /sidney-rigdon-js-et-al-petition-draft-to-the-publick-circa-1838-1839.

4. Statement of Hyrum Smith, 1 July 1843, History, 1838–1856, volume D-1 [1 August 1842–1 July 1843], 1615, http://josephsmithpapers.org/paperSummary /history-1838-1856-volume-d-1-1-august-1842-1-july-1843?p=260.

5. History, 1838–1856, volume D-1 [1 August 1842–1 July 1843], 1615, http://joseph smithpapers.org/paperSummary/history-1838-1856-volume-d-1-1-august-1842-1 -july-1843.

6. Clark V. Johnson, ed., *Mormon Redress Petitions: Documents of the 1833–1838 Missouri Conflict* (Provo, UT: Religious Studies Center, 1992), 680–81. On 1 July 1843, Sidney Rigdon testified before the Municipal Court of Nauvoo that in January 1839, "I was ordered to be discharged from prison, and the rest remanded back. . . . It was some ten days after this before I dared leave the jail. . . . Just at dark, the sheriff and jailer came to the jail with our supper. . . . I whispered to the jailer to blow out all the candles but one, and step away from the door with that one. All this was done. The sheriff then took me by the arm, and an apparent scuffle ensued. . . . We reached the door, which was quickly opened, and we both reached the street. He took me by the hand and bade me farewell, telling me to make my escape, which I did with all possible speed." See also History, 1838–1856, volume E-1 [1 July 1843–30 April 1844], http://josephsmithpapers .org/paperSummary/history-1838-1856-volume-e-1-1-july-1843-30-april-1844?p=21.

7. Joseph Smith III and Heman C. Smith, *The History of the Reorganized Church of Jesus Christ of Latter Day Saints, 1836–1844* (Lamoni, IA: Herald Publishing House, 1896), 2:309. Mary Fielding Smith had recently given birth to a son, Joseph F. Smith on 13 November 1838, and her health remained poor for many weeks.

8. Joseph Smith III and Heman C. Smith, *History of the Reorganized Church*, 2:315.

9. "Statement of Hyrum Smith, July 1, 1843," History, 1838–1856, volume D-1 [1 August 1842–1 July 1843], 1615, http://josephsmithpapers.org/paperSummary /history-1838-1856-volume-d-1-1-august-1842-1-july-1843?p=260.

10. Hyrum Smith, quoted in Lucy Mack Smith, *History*, 1845, 273, http:// josephsmithpapers.org/paperSummary/lucy-mack-smith-history-1845?p=281.

11. Edward Partridge to Beloved Brethren, 5 March 1839, http://josephsmith papers.org/paperSummaryletter-from-edward-partridge-5-march-1839?p=1.

12. Letter from Don Carlos Smith and William Smith, 6 March 1839. Emma Smith to Joseph Smith, 7 March 1839, http://josephsmithpapers.org/paperSummary/letter -from-emma-smith-7-march-1839.

13. Elder David White Rogers, Journal History, 17 March 1839, Church History Library, Salt Lake City, 2–4. The typewritten copy of Rogers's statement that appears in the Journal History is dated 1 February 1839 at Quincy, Illinois. The date is somewhat problematic because the majority of the statement outlines events that occurred well after 1 February 1839. It seems likely that Rogers began his statement, which details his efforts with S. Bent and Israel Barlow to find a suitable location for the Saints to settle in Illinois, on 1 February and simply did not redate the completed statement. Rogers recorded: "We left Far West on the 20th. I have visited the brethren in Richmond Jail in the meantime. And on the morrow [21 March] we visited the Prophet Joseph Smith in Liberty Jail." There appears to be a dating error in Rogers's account, though,

because both Hyrum and Joseph wrote that they received Bishop Partridge's letter on 19 March—not 21 March as Rogers remembered. In a letter to his wife, Mary, dated 19 March, Hyrum wrote that "we receaved a letter this evening from brother [Edward] Pa[r]tridge by the hand of brother Rodgers it was q[u]ite late when it came to us & we was out of paper except this scrap & the mesinger said he should start very Erley in the morning." Hyrum Smith to Mary Fielding Smith, 19 March 1839, holograph MS 2779, Church History Library, Salt Lake City. In his 20 March letter (a few lines prior to the location where the text for D&C 121:7–25 would later be extracted), Joseph stated that "we received some letters last evening one from Emma one from Don C. Smith and one from Bishop Partridge all breathing a kind and consoling spirit"— showing that Rogers arrived at the jail on 19 March. Jospeh Smith to the Church and Edward Partridge, 20 March 1839–A, Church History Library, Salt Lake City, http://josephsmithpapers.org/paperSummary/letter-to-the-church-and-edward-partridge-20-march-1839-a.

14. Lucy Mack Smith referred to Hannah as "Mrs. Grenolds." The spelling "Grinnals" is from the Nauvoo Temple Endowment Register, which records her endowment on 31 December 1845 and gives her date of birth as 3 November 1783. The Hannah Grennell (born 3 November 1796, Killingsworth, Connecticut) found in the Church's patriarchal blessing index may be the same person despite the discrepancy in the year of birth. The blessing, given in Nauvoo on 4 July 1845, records her parents as William Woodstock and Elizabeth with no last name given. The patriarchal blessing indicates that Hannah would receive her companion and children in the resurrection of the just, suggesting that she may have been a widowed mother of more than one child. The 1850 federal census lists a sixty-six-year-old Hannah Grennells, born in Connecticut, as a member of Mary Smith's home. This is consistent with the 1840 federal census (from Hancock County, Illinois), which lists a woman between fifty and sixty years of age living in Hyrum's home. If the girl listed with Hannah in the 1840 census is her daughter Clarinda, then she and Hyrum's daughter Lovina were near the same age. According to historian Don C. Corbett, Hannah "died two years after Mary Smith, who passed away on 21 September 1852 at the age of fifty-eight." If Hannah died in 1854, however, she would have been seventy according to the 1850 federal census. Mary Fielding Smith's obituary appeared in the 11 December 1852, *Deseret News*; if Hannah had a published obituary, it is yet to be located. Considering Hannah's long-term relationship and significant contributions to Hyrum's family, there is an amazing paucity of information about her. See Don Cecil Corbett, *Mary Fielding Smith: Daughter of Britain* (Salt Lake City: Deseret Book, 1970); Pearson H. Corbett, *Hyrum Smith, Patriarch* (Salt Lake City: Deseret Book, 1976); and Orson F. Whitney, *Life of Heber C. Kimball* (Salt Lake City: Bookcraft, 1978).

15. Hyrum Smith to Sister Grinnals, 16 March 1839, Special Collections, Harold B. Lee Library, Brigham Young University, VMSS 774, series 2, box 1, folder 18–20. All transcriptions of Hyrum's Liberty Jail letters and diaries are from the Hyrum Smith Papers Project directed by Craig K. Manscill.

16. H. Dean Garrett, "Seven Letters from Liberty," in *Regional Studies in Latter-day Saint Church History: Missouri*, ed. Arnold K. Garr and Clark V. Johnson (Provo, UT: Department of Church History and Doctrine, Brigham Young University, 1994), 189–90.

17. The 1839 Hyrum Smith to Mary Fielding Smith letters are located at the Church History Library, Salt Lake City, MS 2779.

18. Edward Partridge to Beloved Brethren, 5 March 1839, http://joseph smithpapers.org/paperSummary/letter-from-edward-partridge-5-march-1839. Bishop Partridge also kindly included what he knew about the status and location of Lyman Wight's, Caleb Baldwin's, and Alexander McRae's wives and families.

19. One of the many alternate spellings of Grinnals.

20. Letter from Don Carlos Smith and William Smith, 6 March 1839, http://josephsmithpapers.org/paperSummary/letter-from-don-carlos-smith -and-william-smith-6-march-1839.

21. The Joseph Smith Papers project has assigned a 20 March 1839 date to both parts of the "D&C 121–123 letter." http://josephsmithpapers.org/paperSummary /letter-to-the-church-and-edward-partridge-20-march-1839-a?p=1&highlight=To%20 the%20church%20of%20the%20Latterday%20saints%20at%20Quincy%20 Illinois%20and%20scattered%20abroad%20and%20to%20Bishop.

22. The LDS *History of the Church* incorrectly lists the date of this important letter as 25 March 1839. A note in that volume states that it "was written between the 20th and 25th of March." See B. H. Roberts, *History of the Church of Jesus Christ of Latter-day Saints* (Salt Lake City: Deseret Book, 1978), 3:289.

23. Joseph Smith to the Church and Edward Partridge, 20 March 1839–A, http:// josephsmithpapers.org/paperSummary/letter-to-the-church-and-edward-partridge -20-march-1839-a. When the six prisoners were remanded to Liberty Jail by Judge Austin A. King for the "said charge of treason," Sidney Rigdon was "to answer in the county of Caldwell." The other five prisoners were "to answer in the county of Daviess." Partially as a result, Sidney Rigdon was released from Liberty Jail on 5 February, well before the 20 March letter was written. See Joseph Smith III and Heman C. Smith, *The History of the Reorganized Church,* 2:294.

24. Dean C. Jessee and John W. Welch, "Revelations in Context: Joseph Smith's Letter from Liberty Jail, 20 March 1839," *BYU Studies* 39, no. 3 (2000): 125.

25. Steven C. Harper, *Making Sense of the Doctrine and Covenants* (Salt Lake City: Deseret Book, 2008), 448.

26. Joseph Smith to the Church and Edward Partridge, 20 March 1839–B, http:// josephsmithpapers.org/paperSummary/letter-to-the-church-and-edward-partridge -20-march-1839-b.

27. Joseph Smith to Emma Smith, 21 March 1939, http://josephsmithpapers.org /paperSummary/letter-to-emma-smith-21-march-1839?p=3.

28. Ripley had made previous visits to the jail. See Joseph Smith III and Heman C. Smith, *History of the Reorganized Church,* 2:315–23, and Hyrum Smith to Mary Fielding Smith, 16 March 1839, holograph MS 2779, Church History Library, Salt Lake City.

29. Neal A. Maxwell, "A Choice Seer," *Ensign,* August 1986, https://www.lds .org/ensign/1986/08/a-choice-seer?lang=eng.

30. Hyrum Smith to Mary Fielding Smith, 16 March 1839, holograph.

31. Hyrum Smith to Mary Fielding Smith, 19 March 1839, holograph.

32. Hyrum Smith to Mary Fielding Smith, 20 March 1839, holograph.

33. Hyrum Smith to Mary Fielding Smith, undated, holograph (written from Liberty Jail).

34. "Statement of Hyrum Smith, July 1, 1843," History, 1838–1856, volume D-1 [1 August 1842–1 July 1843], 1617, http://josephsmithpapers.org/paperSummary /history-1838-1856-volume-d-1-1-august-1842-1-july-1843?p=262.

35. "Statement of Hyrum Smith, July 1, 1843," History, 1838–1856, volume D-1 [1 August 1842–1 July 1843], 1618.

36. "Statement of Hyrum Smith, July 1, 1843," 1618.

37. As noted by Jessee and Welch (page 131), the 20 March letter was published in the *Times and Seasons*, May and July 1840; the *Deseret News*, 26 January and 2 February 1854; and the *Millennial Star*, December 1840, October 1844, also 27 January and 10 February 1855.

38. Church Historian's Office, Journal (CR 100 1), 1844–1879, 15 January 1875, Church History Library, Salt Lake City. See also Journal History, 15 January 1875 and "New and Revised Edition of the Book of Doctrine and Covenants," Historian Office Journal, 15 January 1875, 70.

39. Richard E. Turley Jr. and William W. Slaughter, *How We Got the Doctrine and Covenants* (Salt Lake City: Deseret Book, 2012), 98–99.

11

William W. Phelps:
His Contributions to
Understanding the Restoration

Bruce A. Van Orden

Bruce A. Van Orden is a professor emeritus of Church
history and doctrine, Brigham Young University.

Members of The Church of Jesus Christ of Latter-day Saints have long held a fascination for William W. Phelps (1792–1872) for primarily two reasons: his magnificent hymns of the Restoration and, after his apostasy, for being warmly received back into fellowship through the magnanimity of the Prophet Joseph Smith. Less well known are his calling as "printer unto the church" (D&C 57:11–13), his multiple leadership experiences in the infant Church, and his seemingly unending list of theological and historical writings that affected the onward glide of the Restoration of the gospel and the Church.[1] This paper will explore Phelps's writings as they pertain to the Restoration.

W. W. Phelps's Entry into the Kingdom of God

William Wines Phelps was born 17 February 1792, in Dover, Hanover Township, Morris County, New Jersey, as the first child of Enon Phelps and Mehitable Goldsmith. His first name and curious middle name came from a close friend of his parents, William Winds (earlier Wines), a famous general in the Revolution. Phelps spent the first eight years of his life in rural northern New Jersey and the rest of his youth in rural Cortland County in central New York. As an adult, Phelps displayed a vast array of knowledge of printing, surveying, languages, history, geography, topography, meteorology, climatology, rhetoric, and theology. He taught himself mostly through his many books, but he also was mentored by learned individuals and completed a printing office apprenticeship. Phelps always referred to himself as W. W. Phelps, although the Prophet often called him William.

At the end of the War of 1812, in which he participated, William married Sally Waterman, who also hailed from central New York. In 1815, Phelps started his printing and newspaper career in his native Cortland County. In 1820 he became an editor of a politically partisan newspaper in the city of Cortland. He verbally attacked his foes and they him. In 1827, Phelps helped found a religious/social/political movement called Anti-Masonry, a populist movement that accused Freemasons of secretly dominating elected and appointed political offices and of ruthlessly using elitism and favoritism. Anti-Masonry was determined to oust these members of Freemasonry from local and national political offices. W. W. Phelps became an Anti-Masonic editor of two newspapers in New York State (where Anti-Masonry was the strongest): the *Lake Light* in Trumansburg and later the *Ontario Phoenix* in Canandaigua. Phelps took some credit for electing many Anti-Masons to the New York legislature in 1828 and 1830. His name was held for good or ill in New York political and journalism circles.

By his own account, Phelps was a deeply religious person who studied the Bible devotedly, but who did not join any particular denomination. His curiosity led him to purchase several copies of the Book of Mormon (some of them to sell in his own printing office) on 9 April 1830. He and Sally read the book from start to finish within a few days and became converted to its truth. While investigating Mormonism, Phelps became acquainted personally with several key figures in the birth of the Latter-day Saint faith: Joseph Smith Jr., Joseph Smith Sr., Samuel H. Smith, Sidney Rigdon, and Thomas B. Marsh. Because of his increasing interest in the Latter-day Saints, Phelps was mocked by other newspaper editors and was jailed for about ten days in Lyons, New York (on charges of not paying his debts to Anti-Masonic businessmen who underwrote the *Phoenix*). When he was finally released in

June 1831, Phelps resigned his editorship and took his family to join with the Mormons in Kirtland, Ohio. Phelps went to the doorstep of Joseph Smith and requested that the Prophet seek a revelation as to God's will for Phelps. The result was Doctrine and Covenants 55, which charged Phelps to be baptized and ordained an elder, to "preach repentance and remission of sins," to go with Joseph to locate the land of Zion in the west, to eventually plant his family in that land, to print Church literature, and to take a lead in educating children in the Church.

Summary of Phelps's Service in the Church

The purpose of this chapter is *not* to provide a biography of W. W. Phelps. However, we do need a general grasp of his many contributions to the Church and to the Restoration generally. Further, we can neither understand nor appreciate the significance of his many published writings that also aided in the Restoration without a sketch of his work in the Church. The following is a brief recitation of his versatile contributions during each stage of the early Church's development.[2]

1. He aided Joseph Smith, Sidney Rigdon, Edward Partridge, and several other elders to identify the Land of Zion in Jackson County, Missouri, and the temple lot in Independence, and to dedicate these sites to the Lord.

2. He was called to be "printer unto the Church." In this capacity he directed the Church-owned "W. W. Phelps & Co." printing establishment in Independence. He edited Mormonism's first periodical, *The Evening and the Morning Star*, from June 1832 to July 1833, at which time the printing press was destroyed by an anti-Mormon mob. Along with Oliver Cowdery and John Whitmer, Phelps prepared the type and printed off numerous sheets for the Book of Commandments, a compilation of sixty-five of the early revelations to the Prophet Joseph Smith. Phelps, Cowdery, and Whitmer were in the process of preparing thirteen additional revelations for inclusion in the Book of Commandments when the press was destroyed.

3. Along with six other high priests, Phelps presided over the Saints in Jackson County, and when they were forced out, in Clay County.

4. When Zion's Camp under Joseph Smith arrived in Missouri in 1834, Phelps was called as an "assistant president" in a new Missouri Church presidency. David Whitmer was the president and John Whitmer an additional

"assistant president." Phelps was called with fifteen other Missouri elders to go to Kirtland, where the "House of the Lord," or temple, was being constructed, to receive his endowment of "power from on high" (D&C 95:8).

5. As a member of the Missouri presidency, and because the president, David Whitmer, was absent most of the time, Phelps assumed the leading role of directing ecclesiastically the Church in Clay County from 1834 to 1836 and then in Caldwell County in 1837.

6. Phelps spent eleven months in Kirtland, from May 1835 to April 1836. His assignments were multiple and important: assist in the initial publication of the Doctrine and Covenants, coedit the *Latter Day Saints' Messenger and Advocate*; sit in on many leadership council meetings with the other Church presidents from both Ohio and Missouri (the others were Joseph Smith Jr., Oliver Cowdery, Sidney Rigdon, Frederick G. Williams, Hyrum Smith, Joseph Smith Sr., David Whitmer, and John Whitmer); prepare the Church's first hymnbook, *A Collection of Sacred Hymns*, for publication in 1836 (although it bears the date 1835), for which he wrote at least thirty-five of the ninety hymns; serve on the Kirtland Temple dedication committee; and participate in all the Kirtland endowment ceremonies that included solemn assemblies, sacred washings and anointings, and a mighty outpouring of God's Holy Spirit as on the Day of Pentecost at the dedication services.

7. Back in Missouri, Phelps, along with John Whitmer, Edward Partridge, and John Corrill, identified a new and isolated location for an all-Mormon community: Far West, Caldwell County. He and these other leaders directed the gathering of the Saints to this new portion of Zion and guided Far West to become a thriving city. There Phelps identified a spot for a new "House of the Lord." (Unfortunately, Phelps and most of the other original Missouri Church leaders left the Church in 1838 over disagreements over how to deal with complex leadership issues and jealousies.)

8. When he returned to the Church in Nauvoo in late 1841, Phelps became an indefatigable aide to Joseph Smith. With Willard Richards, Phelps helped compile the official *History of the Church*. He served on the city council and as clerk of the mayor's court. Phelps became Joseph Smith's chief political clerk and, as such, was the ghostwriter for Joseph's principal political documents, including the platform for his presidential campaign. Most significantly, even though he was not the nominal editor, Phelps was the chief day-to-day administrator of the Nauvoo printing office in writing

editorials, presidential campaign pieces, and many doctrinal articles in the name of Joseph Smith.[3] Phelps was also among the Church leaders involved with the Prophet in receiving and administrating the endowment of the holy priesthood prior to completing the temple. He also was selected as a key member of the Council of Fifty.

9. Phelps was intimately involved with the *Nauvoo Expositor* affair, the destruction of a press that published an issue critical of Mormon leaders. This destruction spiraled downward to the Prophet's jailing and assassination in Carthage.

10. With Willard Richards, Phelps helped hold the Nauvoo Saints together in peace following the martyrdom until all the Apostles could return from their mission in the East. Phelps also gave Joseph Smith's eulogy. In the aftermath of the martyrdom, he used his considerable influence in August and September 1844 to sustain the Twelve Apostles as leaders during the succession crisis. He assisted the Twelve in directing Nauvoo when enemies sought to drive the Saints out of Illinois; specifically, he helped Brigham Young and the Twelve conduct over five thousand Saints through their endowment ceremonies in the temple. Phelps also stayed behind in Nauvoo to perform necessary business after the main body of the Saints began their trek to the West.

11. In Deseret, Phelps continued his influence in the Church, but primarily as a senior statesman. He went to Boston to obtain a newfangled press, which the *Deseret News* ended up using for over forty years. Phelps was a founding member of the board of trustees for the University of Deseret, served as Speaker of the House in the Utah Territorial legislature, helped develop the Deseret Alphabet, served as Utah's chief weatherman, published the Church's official almanac, and wrote many articles and poems for the *Deseret News*.

Publisher of Early Doctrines of the Restoration

W. W. Phelps promulgated all of the basic doctrines of the early Restoration through his printing and publishing work with *The Evening and the Morning Star*, the *Latter Day Saints' Messenger and Advocate*, the *Times and Seasons*, the *Wasp*, the *Nauvoo Neighbor*, and the *Deseret News*. He also contributed significantly to the publishing of God's holy word: printing numerous chapters from the Book of Mormon and of Joseph Smith's revelations in *The Evening and the Morning Star* (at a time when copies of the Book of Mormon were scarce and there were not yet any printed copies of the latter-day revelations); the Book of Commandments; two editions of the Doctrine and Covenants; the "Prophecy of Enoch" (Moses 5–7 in the Pearl of Great Price); the first hymnal *Sacred Hymns*; and the Book of Abraham. And in all of his writings, he worked hard to put forward the doctrines of the Restoration: he became one of the early Church's hymn writers, and he wrote extensive essays. His essays span across a myriad of gospel topics: on the importance of the Book of Mormon and all forms of scripture, the significance of revelations to Joseph Smith, the "gathering" of Israel, the building up of Zion, the signs of the times, preparing for Christ's Second Coming, living the gospel in purity, the importance of eternal marriage, the plan of salvation, the priesthood, the government of God, and all the gospel ordinances, including the ordinances in the "House of the Lord." This chapter will now highlight some of his published teachings, although time and space constrict a full appreciation of Phelps's multiple writings on Restoration themes.

The Book of Mormon Is God's Holy Word

Throughout his lengthy publishing career, Phelps repeatedly emphasized how important the Book of Mormon is to the Restoration. He taught the Saints that the fullness of the gospel was contained therein. Writing to Oliver Cowdery, Phelps left his testimony of the book:

> Whenever I have meditated upon the book of Mormon, and looked ahead at the glory which will be brought to pass by that, and the servants of God, I have been filled with hope; filled with light; filled with joy, and filled with satisfaction. What a wonderful volume! what a glorious treasure! By that book I learned the right way to God; by that book I received the fulness of the everlasting gospel; by that book I found the new covenant; by that book I learned when the Lord would gather scattered Israel; by that book I saw that the Lord had set his hand the second time to gather his people, and place them in

their own land; by that book I learned that the poor Indians of America were some of the remnants of Israel; by that book I learned that the new Jerusalem, even Zion was to be built up on this continent; by that book I found a key to the holy prophets; and by that book began to unfold the mysteries of God, and I was made glad.[4]

Gathering of Israel

Establishing Zion was of prime importance in Phelps's voluminous writings, especially in *The Evening and the Morning Star*. In July 1833, Phelps exclaimed, "No one that believes in the revelations of the Lord can or will deny the gathering of the saints to holy places, in the last days."[5] In order to establish Zion, he emphasized four forms of "gathering." First, Phelps referred to the gathering of righteous Saints to the land of Zion in western Missouri where they would live harmoniously together while striving to keep all the commandments of God. Second was the gathering of Lamanite remnants from the "tribe of Joseph," whom he basically identified as the Indians of North America, but who also would include all native tribes in the western hemisphere. The Indians would come to be near Zion and then would help build the New Jerusalem. Third was the return of the lost ten tribes from the lands of the North to their inheritance. Fourth was the gathering or the return of the Jews to the land of their inheritance in the Holy Land, or Palestine. This would be their Jerusalem, their Zion, and would correspond to the New Jerusalem and the latter-day Zion headquartered in Jackson County.

In his writings, W. W. Phelps identified the gathering spot for the latter-day Zion to be in what he and others called "the far west," that area in western Missouri that included Jackson County and was also in the center of the North American continent. He enthusiastically exclaimed:

When we consider that the land of Missouri is the land where the saints of the living God are to be gathered together and sanctified for the second coming of the Lord Jesus, we cannot help exclaiming with the prophet, O land be glad! and O earth, earth, earth, hear the word of the Lord: For Zion's sake will

I not hold my peace, and for Jerusalem's sake I will not rest, until the righteousness thereof go forth as brightness, and the salvation thereof as a lamp that burneth. And the Gentiles shall see thy righteousness, and all kings thy glory: and thou shalt be called by a new name, which the mouth of the Lord shall name. Thou shalt also be a crown of glory in the hand of the Lord, and a royal diadem in the hand of thy God.[6]

Repeatedly, Phelps urged "the disciples in Zion" to be pure in heart, to keep all the commandments of God, and to give an example to the world by doing so.[7] Thus they would prove worthy to be part of the heavenly Zion.

W. W. Phelps frequently brought forward his ideas regarding the gathering of the seed of Joseph as represented by the American Indians. He believed that the gathering of Indians was under the supervision of God himself. The gathering was simultaneous to the arrival of the Saints in western Missouri. Strikingly, Phelps insisted that the Indian Removal Act of 1830 promoted by United States president Andrew Jackson was the means of doing God's will.[8] All Indian tribes were at that very moment being moved to lands owned by the United States but west of any of the then-existing states of Missouri and Arkansas. These places were in present-day Kansas and Oklahoma. That these locations were so near the land of Zion in Missouri, he believed, was according to God's providence. Phelps gladly stated:

It is not only gratifying, but almost marvelous, to witness the gathering of the Indians. The work has been going on for some time, and these remnants of Joseph gather by hundreds and settle west of the Missouri, and Arkansas. And is not this scripture fulfilling: Give ear, O Shepherd of Israel, thou that leadest Joseph like a flock, through the instrumentality of the government of the United States? For it is written, Behold I will lift up my hand to the Gentiles, and set up my standard to the people: and they shall bring thy sons in their arms, and thy daughters shall be carried upon their shoulders.[9]

Regularly, Phelps informed his readers of the latest removal of specific Indian tribes to nearby locations. Phelps also knew that many Indian tribes were beyond the Rocky Mountains and believed that they, in God's good time, would also be gathered in. The same would be true, he surmised, for all native peoples in the western hemisphere, all of whom in his estimation were descended from Book of Mormon peoples.

The next gathering of note to connect with the Second Coming was that of the ten tribes. Phelps figured that since they were the first to be scattered, they could the last to be gathered. He utilized multiple passages to make his case from Deuteronomy, 1 Kings, 2 Kings, Isaiah, Jeremiah, Ezekiel, and Ezra in the Old Testament and from present-day Jacob 5 and 3 Nephi 15 and 16 in the Book of Mormon. Phelps conceded that he didn't know where the ten tribes were lost, but he hypothesized that it might have been somewhere near the North Pole, because that region had not yet been explored by man. After all, the lost tribes went northward and would be called from the north to go back to their lands of inheritance. Phelps even went as far as to say that they would come back with great rejoicing when the voice of the Lord called them.[10]

The final gathering would be that of the Jews. "The assembling of the Jews at Jerusalem," wrote Phelps in January 1833, is one of "the signs of the times" taking place right at that moment.[11] Often Phelps inserted news reports that he had received through the mail that showed an increasing interest from many European Jews to move to Jerusalem. He knew that the Book of Mormon prescribed the return of the Jews to the Holy Land as a necessary prelude to the Second Coming of Christ and his millennial reign. He excitedly wrote of the hearts of the Jews turning to the true God.[12]

More on the Indians and Becoming "White and Delightsome"

After the W. W. Phelps & Co. press in Independence was destroyed in July 1833, Phelps's doctrinal writings would have to wait until the *Latter Day Saints' Messenger and Advocate* began its run in October 1834 in Kirtland. He pursued the same general themes that he had emphasized in *The Evening and the Morning Star*, and his enthusiasm and pedantry were similar to his previous writings. He especially expanded upon the future role of the Indians.

Before he left Missouri for Kirtland, in the fall of 1834, Phelps visited Fort Leavenworth, located west of the Missouri River in present-day Kansas.

The garrison was established both to protect arriving Indian tribes and to guard against a possible Indian uprising. It also protected the lucrative fur trade with Rocky Mountain Indians. William was definitely emotionally moved: "I saw a noble looking, portly Indian, dressed and harnessed in fine style for hunting, and for the life of me, I could not help composing the following lines" that he entitled "The Red Man." The poem later became a hymn.

> O stop and tell me, Red Man,
> Who are ye? why you roam?
> And how you get your living?
> Have you no God;—no home?
> With stature straight and portly,
> And decked in native pride,
> With feathers, paints, and broaches,
> He willingly replied:—
> "I once was *pleasant Ephraim,*
> When Jacob for me pray'd;
> But oh! how blessings vanish,
> When man from God has stray'd;
> Before your nation knew us,
> Some thousand moons ago,
> Our fathers fell in darkness,
> And wander'd to and fro.
> And long they've liv'd by hunting,
> Instead of work and arts,
> And so our race has dwindled
> To idle Indian hearts.
> Yet hope within us lingers,
> As if the Spirit spoke:—
> He'll come for your redemption,
> And break your Gentile yoke:
> And all your captive brothers,
> From every clime shall come,
> And quit their savage customs,
> To live with God at home.

Then joy will fill our bosoms,
And blessings crown our days,
To live in pure religion,
And sing our Maker's praise."[13]

Phelps was certain that the Indian races would be redeemed and likely in short order. Months after he had arrived in Kirtland, in October 1835, William declared emphatically, "The Indians are the people of the Lord; they are of the tribes of Israel; the blood of Joseph, with a small mixture of the royal blood of Judah, and the hour is nigh when they will come flocking into the kingdom of God, like doves to their windows; yea, as the book of Mormon foretells—they will soon become a white and delightsome people."[14] This latter point, that Lamanites would become "white and delightsome" once converted to the true gospel, would persist as perceived Mormon doctrine for at least another century and a half.

Indeed, Phelps interpreted a darker skin color to be a curse:

God causes the saints, or people that fall away from his church to be cursed in time, with a black skin? Was or was not Cain, being marked, obliged to inherit the curse, he and his children, forever? And if so, as Ham, like other sons of God, might break the rule of God, by marrying out of the church, did or did he not, have a Canaanite wife, whereby some of the black seed was preserved through the flood, and his son, Canaan, after he laughed at his grand father's nakedness, heired three curses: one from Cain for killing Abel; one from Ham for marrying a black wife, and one from Noah for ridiculing what God had respect for? Are or are not the Indians a sample of marking with blackness for rebellion against God's holy word and holy order? And can or can we not observe in the countenances of almost all nations, except the Gentile, a dark, sallow hue, which tells the sons of God, without a line of history, that they have fallen or changed from the original beauty and grace of father Adam?[15]

Obviously, Phelps helped define a doctrine about a curse of black or dark skin that continued for many years in many parts of Mormonism.

The Second Coming of the Savior Is Nigh

All the while that W. W. Phelps referred to the various aspects of the "gathering," he boldly posited that the Second Coming of the Lord Jesus Christ was quickly approaching. He laid out extensively from the biblical record what he considered to be the current "age of the world," that is, from the creation of Adam and Eve to that particular moment in August 1832. Based on his mathematical calculations, Phelps concluded:

> Set it down so, at 1832 [the year he wrote this piece], and, with the old and new eras, we have Five thousand nine hundred and ninety one years; leaving the world NINE years from the beginning of the seven thousandth year, or sabbath of creation: But as all have the privilege of ascertaining such facts for themselves, we ask no man to take our word for the age of the world; the word of the Lord is enough, and whether it be 160, or only 9 years to the morning of the Great Day, is not so much matter, as the solemn reality—Are we ready?[16]

Clearly, Phelps felt that great exertions needed to be made by the missionaries and the Saints to prepare quickly for what was to come, maybe even as early as 1841!

In every issue *of The Evening and the Morning Star,* editor Phelps laid out prospects for the Second Coming and referred to "signs of the times" that were part of the current age. He pointed out that these signs were in fulfillment of ancient prophecies from both the Bible and the Book of Mormon. To amplify his point, Phelps quoted numerous articles from other newspapers to demonstrate how these signs in his estimation were being fulfilled. His exuberance for the subject is obvious from the following:

> We live in a great time; one of the most eventful periods that has ever been: it is not only the time when the captivity of Jacob's tents will return, but it is the time when the wicked and their works shall be destroyed; when the earth shall be restored to its former beauty and goodness, and shall yield its increase; when plagues shall be sent to humble the haughty, and bring them, if they will, to a knowledge of God: yea, it is a time when the wicked can not expect to see the next generation; yea, it is that

great time, when none shall live in the second generation unless they are pure in heart.[17]

Phelps strived to keep his readers informed that many calamities had already started to affect the earth. In this, he particularly emphasized the rapid spread of "the cholera." Month after month, editor Phelps included stories of how the plague was spreading from city to city, from country to country. In September 1832, he vigorously commented:

> Not since the flood, if we think right, has the Lord sent the same pestilence, or destruction, over the whole earth at once: But the Cholera, which has swept its thousands in Asia, Africa, Europe and America, gives a solemn token to a wondering world, that it will do so. Let the reader remember that all flesh is grass, but, that amidst all the judgments of the Lord, the righteous have never been forsaken. The spread of the Cholera, may be likened unto the ripple or wave, formed by casting a stone into a pond of water: ring follows ring till they meet the shore: It is said to be in nearly all the eastern cities. Well has Isaiah said, When the overflowing scourge shall pass through, then ye shall be trodden down by it.—From the time that it goeth forth it shall take you: for morning by morning shall it pass over, by day and by night.[18]

In January 1833 he published many articles from around the nation and the world that demonstrated that "plague, pestilence, famine and the sword" were bringing grief upon the world's inhabitants.[19] In June 1833 Phelps again published multiple examples of grievous events in many locations, but observed, "All must come to pass, but the end is not yet."[20]

Phelps also spread the fervor about the Second Coming in his hymns. For instance, the Christmas carol "Joy to the World," by Isaac Watts, appeared in the Church's original hymnbook. What is not normally realized is that Phelps altered the language of this song in the book to give it a distinct Second Coming flavor. He entitled it "The Second Coming of our Savior." His changes or additions in the wording are noted in italics:

> JOY to the world! the Lord *will* come!
> *And* earth receive her King;

Let ev'ry heart prepare him room,
And *saints* and angels sing.
Rejoice! rejoice! *when Jesus* reigns,
And saints their songs employ:
While fields and floods, rocks, hills and plains,
Repeat the sounding joy.
No more *will* sin and sorrow grow,
Nor thorns infest the ground;
He'*ll* come *and* make the blessing flow
Far as the curse was found.
Rejoice! Rejoice! in the Most High,
While Israel spreads abroad,
Like stars that glitter in the sky,
And ever worships God.[21]

Rear Children in Righteousness

William W. Phelps urged his readers in *The Evening and the Morning Star* to bring up their children in the nurture and admonition of the Lord. Repeatedly he gave tips to accomplish this. In an article entitled "Children," he indicated that it was praiseworthy to teach children "science and learning." However, he insisted, "How much more necessary is it, that the disciples of Jesus Christ should teach their children, not only in common learning to transact business among men, but in the knowledge of God, which points out their way to eternal life?" He urged the Saints to keep their children free from all forms of "vice and folly." This would best be achieved, he thought, by keeping the Sabbath day holy and by the family as a whole uniting in petitioning God for his blessings. He wrote, "Here [in Sabbath services] they may grow up in righteousness, and be prepared to meet their Lord in peace, when he comes in his glory."[22]

Interpreter of Nauvoo Doctrine in Nauvoo and Salt Lake City

When W. W. Phelps returned to the fold of Christ in 1841, he spent several hours virtually every day at Joseph Smith's side. He learned firsthand of the exciting and new doctrines that had been revealed to the Prophet in Liberty Jail and in Nauvoo. Phelps would then go to the Nauvoo printing office to promote these doctrines. These came in the form of editorials, some of them even ghostwritten in the name of Joseph Smith. Others were simply commentary on the signs of the times and of new discoveries in the Americas that appeared to validate the Book of Mormon. After Joseph's martyrdom, Phelps continued to advocate the Prophet's teachings, both in prose and in poetry, on the nature of God, the Saints' quest for eternal life and exaltation, and the glory of eternity in the celestial realm. This was also true in Salt Lake City as Phelps continued to write multiple pieces of poetry for the *Deseret News* and the Church's annual almanac. The most famous and doctrinally rich of these was "There Is No End," later called "If You Could Hie to Kolob," which he wrote for Brigham Young in 1856.

> If you could hie to Kolob in the twinkling of an eye,
> And then continue onward with that same speed to fly,
> Do you think that you could ever, through all eternity,
> Find out the generation where Gods began to be?
> Or see the grand beginning, where space did not extend?
> Or view the last creation, where Gods and matter end?
> Methinks the Spirit whispers, "No man has found 'pure
>   space,'
> Nor seen the outside curtains, where nothing has a place."
> The works of God continue, and worlds and lives abound;
> Improvement and progression have one eternal round.
> There is no end to matter; there is no end to space;
> There is no end to spirit; there is no end to race.
> There is no end to virtue; there is no end to might;
> There is no end to wisdom; there is no end to light;
> There is no end to union; there is no end to youth;
> There is no end to priesthood; there is no end to truth.
> There is no end to glory; there is no end to love;
> There is no end to being; there is no death above.
> There is no end to glory; there is no end to love;
> There is no end to being; there is no death above.[23]

Summary

In my research for my biography of Phelps, I have concluded that this un-usual man contributed more to the understanding of Latter-day Saint doc-trines of the Restoration in Joseph Smith's lifetime than nearly any other preacher of righteousness other than the Prophet himself. His contributions came primarily from his writings in early Latter-day Saint periodicals at a time when most Mormons learned their doctrine from these publications. I hasten to add that Phelps's devoted love of the Restoration was founded entirely on the fact that God had called anew a prophet for the last days even as he had in previous dispensations and had granted this prophet rev-elations that brought together all the revelations of the past into one great understanding of eternity. While it is true that others like Sidney Rigdon and Oliver Cowdery contributed mightily to doctrinal understanding, they did not do so until the 1830s. It is also true that individuals from the apostle-ship like Brigham Young, Parley P. Pratt, Orson Pratt, Heber C. Kimball, John Taylor, and Wilford Woodruff carried on the mantle of explaining the Restoration's foundations through Joseph Smith, but their doctrinal impact did not begin until the 1840s.

Most of W. W. Phelps's teachings have survived the test of time, albeit with modifications. One only needs to review the beauty and richness of the wording in his hymns to appreciate his influence. Ponder carefully the word-ing of his hymns the next time you sing each of them in Church and realize how much participants in the Kingdom of God in these last days have been affected by them. These include "The Spirit of God (like a Fire Is Burning)," "Redeemer of Israel," "Now Let Us Rejoice (in the Day of Salvation)," "Praise to the Man (Who Communed with Jehovah)," "O God, the Eternal Father," "Gently Raise the Sacred Strain," "Adam-ondi-Ahman," and "If You Could Hie to Kolob."

It's true that Phelps's enthusiasm for the Second Coming of the Savior in his lifetime was somewhat misguided from what we know now. So, too, were his predictions that the Indians would be redeemed rather quickly. However, nearly every disciple in the 1830s and early 1840s believed the same things, even Joseph Smith most of the time. In addition, Phelps's interpretation of the curse of a dark skin has been repudiated by revelation in recent decades, but he was not alone in this thinking at the time. For writings like this, we know that Phelps was a product of his historical moment—and it does not diminish our appreciation for his fervor and dedication to the early Church.

We, like W. W. Phelps, can sing in appreciation for the Prophet of the Restoration, Joseph Smith Jr. In Phelps's words:

> Now we'll sing with one accord, for a prophet of the Lord,
> Bringing forth his precious word, cheers the Saints as anciently.
> When the world in darkness lay, Lo! He sought the better way,
> And he heard the Savior say, "Go and prune my vineyard, son!"
> And an angel surely then, for a blessing unto men,
> Brought the priesthood back again in its ancient purity.
> Even Joseph he inspired; yea, his heart he truly fired
> With the light that he desired for the work of righteousness.
> And the Book of Mormon true, with its cov'nant ever new,
> For the Gentile and the Jew, he translated sacredly.
> God's commandments to mankind, for believing Saints designed,
> And to bless the seeking mind, came to him from Jesus Christ.
> Precious are the years to come, while the righteous gather home
> For the great millennium, when they'll rest in blessedness.
> Prudent in this world of woes, they will triumph o'er their foes,
> While the realm of Zion grows purer for eternity.[24]

Notes

1.   I am presently completing a biography of W. W. Phelps. See also a recent biographical essay I published: "'We'll Sing and We'll Shout': Who Is the Real William W. Phelps?," *Mormon Historical Studies* 16, no. 1 (Spring 2015): 1–77.

2.   For readers interested in more details of W. W. Phelps's various contributions to the Church, please contact me.

3.   My conclusions about Phelps's Nauvoo contributions are not yet widely known. The following peer-reviewed articles refer to his ghostwriting: Bruce A. Van

Orden, "William W. Phelps's Service in Nauvoo as Joseph Smith's Political Clerk," *BYU Studies* 32, nos. 1–2 (Winter/Spring 1992): 81–94; Michael Hicks, "Joseph Smith, W. W. Phelps, and the Poetic Paraphrase of 'The Vision,'" *Journal of Mormon History* 20, no. 2 (1994): 63–84; and Samuel Brown, "The Translator and the Ghostwriter: Joseph Smith and W. W. Phelps," *Journal of Mormon History* 34, no. 2 (Winter 2008): 26–62. According to my careful analysis, I have added even more to the list of ghost-written articles by Phelps in chapter 23 of my forthcoming biography.

4.   "Letter No. 10," *Latter Day Saints' Messenger and Advocate* 1 (September 1835): 177–78.

5.   "The Gathering, &c," *The Evening and the Morning Star* 2 (July 1833): 2 [106]; punctuation standardized. In the original printing, this newspaper did not have page numbers until the June 1833 issue. I have given the page number according to each monthly issue for this and subsequent footnotes.

6.   "The Far West," *The Evening and the Morning Star* 1 (October 1832): 5

7.   An example of such an admonition is also found in "The Far West," *The Evening and the Morning Star* 1 (October 1832): 5. Other prime examples are found in "Zion," *The Evening and the Morning Star* 1 (December 1832): 6, and "Let Every Man Learn His Duty," *The Evening and the Morning Star* 1 (January 1833): 5.

8.   See, for example, "The New-Year," *The Evening and the Morning Star* 1 (January 1833): 7.

9.   "The Indians," *The Evening and the Morning Star* 1 (December 1832): 6.

10.   Phelps waxed eloquent in "Ten Tribes," *The Evening and the Morning Star* 1 (October 1832): 1–2.

11.   "Signs of the Times," *The Evening and the Morning Star* 1 (January 1833): 6.

12.   For examples of articles on the Jews, see "Restoration of the Jews," *The Evening and the Morning Star* 1 (August 1832): 5; "The Book of Mormon," *The Evening and the Morning Star* 1 (January 1833): 3; "The Book of Mormon," *The Evening and the Morning Star* 1 (February 1833): 3.

13.   "The Red Man," *Latter Day Saints' Messenger and Advocate* 1 (December 1834): 34, emphasis added. See also *Sacred Hymns*, 83–84.

14.   "Letter No. 11," *Latter Day Saints Messenger and Advocate* 2 (October 1835): 194.

15.   "Letter No. V," *Latter Day Saints' Messenger and Advocate* 1 (March 1835): 82.

16.   "Present Age of the World," *The Evening and the Morning Star* 1 (August 1832): 6. The capitalization of the word *nine* is in the original.

17.   "The Last Days," *The Evening and the Morning Star* 1 (February 1833): 1.

18.   "The Cholera," *The Evening and the Morning Star* 1 (September 1832): 1.

19.   "In These Last Days!," *The Evening and the Morning Star* 1 (January 1833): 8.

20.   *The Evening and the Morning Star* 2 (June 1833): 7–8.

21.   "The Second Coming of the Savior," *The Evening and the Morning Star* 1 (December 1832): 8, emphasis added.

22.   "Children," *The Evening and the Morning Star* 1 (May 1833): 5–6.

23.   "If You Could Hie to Kolob," *Hymns of The Church of Jesus Christ of Latter-day Saints* (Salt Lake City: The Church of Jesus Christ of Latter-day Saints, 1985), no. 284.

24.   "Now We'll Sing with One Accord," *Hymns*, no. 25.

12

Framing the Restoration and Gathering

ORSON HYDE AND EARLY MORMON UNDERSTANDINGS OF ISRAEL, JEWS, AND THE SECOND COMING

Andrew C. Reed

Andrew C. Reed is an assistant professor of
Church history and doctrine at Brigham Young University.

One of the main themes of the Book of Mormon is the role that Jews have historically played in God's work and the central place they will assume in the latter days. Within the opening chapters of the Book of Mormon, Nephi makes clear the need for his family to understand and acknowledge God's interaction with their ancestors through the "record of the Jews and also a genealogy of [their] forefathers" (1 Nephi 3:3). The stated purpose for Nephi and his brothers' return to Jerusalem was to procure the record so that they might "preserve unto [their] children the language of [their] fathers" as well as the "words which have been spoken by the mouth of all the holy prophets" (1 Nephi 3:19–20). From the beginning of Nephi's narrative, it is clear that he and his family need to understand and also identify with biblical Israel. Despite the theological import of these statements, this scriptural narrative does not fully account for early Mormon interest in contemporary Jews and Judaism.[1] There was a far more immediate concern in early Mormonism regarding Jews than simply the idea that the Book of Mormon was an ancient Jewish record.[2]

225

There are many possible origins for Mormon interest in Judaism. The most familiar source for members of the Church is the Book of Mormon. The authors of the Book of Mormon were remarkably aware of their own internal purposes and the larger divine narrative of the text they produced. Nephi, one of the first prophetic figures encountered in the book, argued, "I, Nephi, received a commandment that the ministry and the prophecies, the more plain and precious parts of them, should be written upon these plates, and that the things, which were written should be kept for the instruction of my people, who should possess the land, and also for other wise purposes, which purposes are known unto the Lord" (1 Nephi 19:3). Nephi drew this larger narrative of "wise purposes" into a lengthy discussion of covenants made between God and the biblical fathers (see 1 Nephi 17:26; 22:7–10) and an eventual moment when the covenant people (Israel) will be gathered along with "every nation, kindred, tongue and people (see 1 Nephi 19: 15–17). The Book of Mormon framed the long narrative of God acting in the world and infused early Mormonism with a sense of responsibility and longing for the Millennium when God would commence a full gathering of Israel (see 2 Nephi 30:1–9).

The title page of the Book of Mormon notes that it was "written to the Lamanites, who are a remnant of the house of Israel; and also to the Jew and Gentile" and is "to show unto the remnant of the House of Israel the great things the Lord hath done for their fathers; and that they may know the covenants of the Lord, that they are not cast off forever."[3] Thus, not only did Lehi and his family need the brass plates for their immediate spiritual welfare, they were also forever tied to the community that created the record for them (see D&C 3:16).[4] Early members of the Church firmly held the belief that Jews would eventually regather to Palestine. As premillennialists, they also viewed the process as one where they would work alongside God to accomplish this essential step in ushering in the Second Coming.

In order to better understand why Mormons were so preoccupied with the history and beliefs of Jews and Judaism, we need to know the religious climate surrounding that interest. Using the historian's lens allows us to locate possible extant sources available to Joseph Smith and the early Saints to explain in real terms the gathering process spoken of in the Book of Mormon. Further, by examining the life of Orson Hyde and his interest in Judaism as a living religion in his own day, Hyde's trip to Palestine in

1841 becomes part of the process of revelation—questions or ideas being raised and then instruction divinely received. Seeing Hyde's trip at the intersection of personal interest, prophetic revelation, and growing social concern clarifies the LDS doctrine of gathering for the modern reader. Hyde was in Britain between 1837 and 1838 and joined his fellow missionaries in London, Liverpool, Preston, and other major cities. It was also in these cities where Britain's Jews were present in the largest numbers.[5] It was this experience that likely sparked an interest among these early missionaries for Jews and Judaism as living communities and made the idea of "gathering" more tangible to them.

After Joseph Smith's translation of the Book of Mormon and the subsequent establishment of The Church of Jesus Christ of Latter-day Saints (March–April 1830), the most significant moment of development and implementation of this gathering was Orson Hyde's journey from the United States through Europe and Palestine. Hyde was an early Mormon Apostle who expressed strong interest in all things Judaic. Further, the subject of Judaism and Jews collectively was one that occupied the attention of many of the early Apostles, particularly as they undertook missionary efforts in the British Isles.[6]

With the charge to begin thinking about a millennial reign of Christ, early Mormon Apostles followed the prophetic call to undertake evangelizing missions to Great Britain in 1838. On 8 July 1838, the Prophet Joseph Smith received a revelation in which God called members of the Quorum of the Twelve Apostles to depart the following spring "to go over the great waters, and there promulgate [his] gospel" (see D&C 118:4–5).[7] This prophetic call of the Twelve would eventually open up "an effectual door" (D&C 112:19) for the expansion of missionary efforts that brought about a strong cohort of future Church leaders and provided essential converts en masse. An added benefit of this journey to Great Britain was that it placed Mormon Apostles in a hotbed of Jewish discussions about gathering to Palestine and creating a space where Jews could live peaceably among themselves without abandoning their religious identity through conversion or assimilation.[8] To wit, in January 1839, the social reformer Anthony Ashley-Cooper, known as Lord Ashley (1801–55), published a tract in the *Quarterly Review* in London that encouraged a social perspective married with evangelical impetus bent on regathering Jews to their biblical homeland. In addition to comments about the nature of the political strife in Egypt in the mid-nineteenth century, he argued for a greater sense of Christian appreciation for Jews as "the remnant of a people which produced poets like Isaiah and Joel; kings like David and Josiah; and ministers like Joseph, Daniel, and Nehemiah; but above all, as that chosen race of men, of whom, the Saviour of the world came according to the flesh."[9] This type of rhetoric was common in Britain, and the early missionaries and Apostles likely encountered many of these ideas as they mingled in British society.

As Latter-day Saints gradually pieced together an identity based in an adoptive relationship to ancient Israel, they necessarily drew parallels to God's covenanted relationship to Jews. Latter-day Saints understood their role in similar fashion for the modern, American context. Mormon theology maintains that the spiritual blessings made to Abraham and his posterity continue even up to this day and will be essential to an eventual gathering of God's children (D&C 27:10). In its theology—if not fully within its practice and rhetoric—early Mormonism rejected traditional Christian supersessionism (the notion that the gospel of Christ completely outmoded and supplanted the Old Testament, the law of Moses, and the religion of the Israelites), opting instead for a view that emphasized the centrality of covenant and universality of its application.[10] In so doing, they joined a powerful wave of American Christian thought that emphasized the continued covenant with Israel, mediated through a profound sense of American exceptionalism.[11] Added to this was the premillennialist notion that if Christ is to reign upon the earth (Articles of Faith 1:10) then there must be a necessary gathering of Israel before the Second Coming.[12] Joseph Smith obtained much of his theological understanding through Protestant theologians and drew upon themes and ideas common to his era.[13] The Book of Mormon's stated mission is "to the convincing of the Jew and Gentile that Jesus is the Christ, the Eternal God."[14] For Joseph Smith, as well as many of the earliest Saints, the belief that their message contained in sacred scripture needed to reach all people led to strong rhetoric that reeked of philosemitic overtones.[15] For early Latter-day Saints, it made perfect sense that Jews were God's chosen people and that they were, by God's continued grace, still integrally connected and relevant to the story of gathering. They, like many European Christians, esteemed Jews as necessary partners. However, they also exhibited at times sentiments that were overtly negative toward Jews, drawn from their reading and interpretation of scripture.

From its beginnings in the first half of the nineteenth century, Mormonism drew heavily upon biblical motifs to help solidify the community of believers as an American Israel. One who looks at the history of the emergence of Mormonism out of American revivalism need not look too far before noticing terms such as "Israel," "Zion," or "Jerusalem" applied systematically to the community. In fact, Brigham Young (1801–77), the second President of the Church, was often referred to as an "American Moses."[16] Early comparisons of Brigham Young to Moses and the Mormon trek west as an Exodus experience further infused biblical motifs into Mormon self-perceptions. In the formative years of Mormonism in America, its first President, Joseph Smith Jr. (1805–44), learned Hebrew along with other leading men in the Church. In his role as a modern-day prophet, Smith claimed authority to receive revelation for members of the Church as well as the world and the ability to translate ancient records; the most notable translation was the Book of Mormon. In connection with his desire to study the Bible and eventually to retranslate it, Smith decided upon the necessity of knowing Hebrew for his work. To fulfill this desire, Smith hired Joshua Seixas, a prominent Jewish scholar from New York to instruct Church leaders in Hebrew during a seven-week course that cost 320 dollars.[17] Their willingness to pay such fees suggests that their interest was sincere and that at least some of them felt an immediacy in their efforts to better understand the Bible. Further, when these early Mormons read the biblical text, they read it in such a way as to link ancient Israel to a new Israel through a process of spiritual adoption.[18] Even within Mormonism's own narrative of ancient peoples, the connections with ancient Israel are central to their understanding of where their records originated and how they became heirs to the blessings promised to Abraham in the book of Genesis.

Orson Hyde's journey to Europe and Jerusalem is the subject of numerous accounts of early Mormon missionary efforts and travels abroad.[19] For Hyde and John E. Page (his appointed companion for his mission to Palestine), there can be little doubt that the impetus for any enthusiasm must have largely rested with Hyde.[20] Before embarking toward England in 1840, Hyde wrote to Joseph Smith and suggested that the work of the missionaries ought to be "spread . . . among all people, Languages and tongues so far as possible; and gather up all jewels among the Jews besides."[21] In a letter dated 14 May 1840, Joseph Smith responded to Hyde and Page:

> If there is anything calculated to interest the mind of the saints, to awaken in them the finest sensibilities, . . . surely it is the great and precious promises, made by our heavenly father to the children of Abraham . . . Bretheren [sic] you are in the path way to Eternal Fame! and immortal Glory; and inasmuch as you feel interested for the covenant people of the Lord, the God of their Father shall bless you. Do not be discouraged on account of the greatness of the work . . . He who scattered Israel has promised to gather them; therefore, inasmuch as you are to be instrumental in this great work, he will endow you with power, wisdom, might, and intelligence, and every qualification necessary.[22]

The echoing of Book of Mormon and Doctrine and Covenants claims about the children of Abraham, combined with the prophetic call to gather scattered Israel, made Orson Hyde long to see the cities he once saw in vision and fulfill his mission to the people God had long prepared.

The idea that Christianity functioned allegorically to fulfill all Old Testament prophecies about Israel was firmly fixed in nineteenth-century Christian parlance.[23] This rhetoric, coupled with the Book of Mormon text, led Hyde and other early Mormons to consider the possibility that there might be a literal gathering of Israel (or Jews) back to Palestine in preparation for the Second Coming. Wilford Woodruff, one of the Twelve Apostles in Britain, wrote in his journal: "I addressed in the fore part of the day. Had the Chills & fever in the Afternoon but met with the saints in the evening & broke bread unto them. My mind is much interested these days in the gathering of the Jews for they are now fast fulfilling the scriptures by returning to Jerusalem."[24] Further, Woodruff noted on 2 November 1840 that there were efforts by Moses Montefiore, a brother-in-law to the Rothchild patriarch and highly influential Jewish communal leader in London, to establish banks as a precursor to a Jewish return to their Palestinian homeland.[25] Thus, as will be shown later with Hyde, early Mormon interests in Judaism depended upon a steep learning curve for many of the Apostles during their 1840 mission in Britain. While there, they learned through newspapers and meetings with local Jewish leaders about the plight of Europe's Jews in the 1840s which gave context to and formed the Mormon response that ultimately pushed Hyde toward Palestine. Therefore, Hyde's writings from his Palestinian mission reflect a concerted effort to see Jews as a historical nation with contemporary relevance.

Mormons were certainly not the only American religious groups to foster such an interest. We might look no further than Alexander Campbell's *Christian System* to get a sense of the growing interest in Jews and Judaism among nineteenth-century ministers. In his lengthy sermon detailing the "Jewish Institution"—that is, the law of Moses and the process of transition from Jewish communal life focused on patriarchal family to nation—Campbell argued for typological understanding of pre-Rabbinic Judaism. He suggested that "the Jewish institution is not to be regarded only in its political, moral, and religious aspects, but especially in its figurative and prospective character. God so wisely and benevolently contrived it from its origin to its close, that its whole history . . . should exactly and impressively shadow forth the new institution with the fates and fortunes of the subjects of this new and more glorious order of things."[26]

From this perspective, Judaism and its historical antecedents ought to be seen as part of God's grand plan and as one step along the way for God's justice and eventual mercy to work their way through the human family. Such a view, indeed a supersessionist one at heart, should not surprise us given the millenarian view of many nineteenth-century Christian movements. Reverend Charles Buck's 1821 *Theological Dictionary* argued that Judaism is "but a temporary dispensation, and was to give way, at least the ceremonial part of it, at the coming of the Messiah."[27] Campbell suggested, however, that it was imperative for the nineteenth-century Christian who sought divine knowledge about God to know something of "Adam, Abel, Noah, Melchizedek, Isaac, Jacob, Joseph, Moses, Aaron, Joshua, Samson, David, Jonah, . . . and of *ordinances*, the passover, the scape-goat, the red heifer, the year of jubilee, the law of the leper, the kinsman redeemer, the cities of refuge; together with all the sacrifices, washings, anointings, and consecrations of the *holy* nation."[28] Further, the Christian mind ought to know of "the furnishing of a new alphabet and language, (the elements of heavenly science,) without which it would appear to have been almost, if not altogether, impossible to learn the spiritual things or to make any proficiency in the knowledge of those relations which Christianity unfolds. The language of the new institution is therefore explained by that of the old. No one can understand the dialect of the kingdom of heaven who has not studied the dialect of the antecedent administrations of heaven over the patriarchs and Jews."[29] The world that Joseph Smith, Orson Hyde, and others operated within was well accustomed to discussions about the theological import of Jews within Christian worldviews. Because of the pervasiveness of the Jews' figurative position within the Christian mind, the end result was often a general negation of living, contemporary Jews. That is to say, among nineteenth-century Christians the image of biblical Israel was somehow disconnected from Jews that they met on the street. They often invoked the claim that modern Jews continued to survive if only to serve as a valuable reminder that this "fallen race," as Hyde once called them, was to endure godly punishment for their rejection of Jesus.[30]

While Mormonism had all the requisite theological dictates to find historical Judaism as an attractive object of study and inquiry, Orson Hyde's writings reflect a different concern with Judaism than the strictly theological arguments of Campbell and others. Hyde reflected a growing awareness of the immediate plight of Jews in Europe, Russia, and Palestine during the nineteenth century. As it turns out, this was also a characteristic of Woodruff's tone and content. Woodruff noted that after Hyde made his way to Manchester to meet with other members of the Twelve in April 1841, he "appealed powerfully to the meeting & covenanted with the saints present in a bond of mutual prayer. During his mission to Jerrusalem and the east which was sustained on the part of the hearers with a harty Amen."[31] The following day, Woodruff continued:

> Before we left the Twelve lade hands upon the head of Elder {Kimball} Orson Hyde & Blessed him in the name of the Lord, as he had ben set apart by the first Presidency to take a mission to the Holy land, the City of Jerrusalem whare Jesus Dwelt, for the purpose of laying the foundation of a great work in that land. This is the first mission that any man has taken to the land of Asia belonging to the church of Christ of Latter Day Saints. Much of the Spirit of God rested upon us when we blessed him, Elder Kimball was mouth & Elder Taylor scribe.[32]

As was his habit of doing, Hyde sought introduction while in London through a network of contacts with "some of the principal Jews in the place."[33] One of these Jews was the aged chief rabbi of England (referred to in Hyde's letters as "the President Rabbi of the Hebrews in England"), Solomon Hirschell (1762–1842).[34] Hirschell was born in London but trained according to Polish (most likely Lithuanian) Jewish tradition, following in the footsteps of the Gaon of Vilna (Elijah ben Schlomo Zalman), and was a lifelong enemy of the growing reform movement in the nineteenth century. As the chief rabbi, his responsibility was to the British Empire and it was through him that all queries regarding Jewish life and practice in Britain were adjudicated.[35] As evidenced in his later writing to Joseph and others, Hyde's efforts to meet with Hirschell proved to be profoundly influential to his view of Judaism in the nineteenth-century European context. In his 1842 letter to Parley P. Pratt in Liverpool, Hyde argued:

> There is an increasing anxiety in Europe for the restoration of that people; and this anxiety is not confined to the pale of any religious community, but it has found its way to the courts of kings. Special ambassadors have been sent, and consuls and consular-agents have been appointed. The rigorous policy which has hitherto characterised the course of other nations towards them, now begins to be softened by the oil of friendship, and modified by the balm of humanity.[36]

In order to see the context behind this letter, we ought to be aware of Hirschell's own interests in the final year of the aged rabbi's life. Perhaps the most crucial and contentious year in the first half of the nineteenth century for European and Middle Eastern Jews was 1840. This year and the years immediately following were long foretold by Jews as the advent of the messianic age. Moses Hess (1812–75),[37] the German-Jewish writer, acknowledged the year 5600 as the messianic year. Hess went so far as to include as a sign that this was under way during the events in Damascus in 1840. Jacob Katz argued that "in all the lands of eastern Europe, the opinion was widespread that the approaching year 5600 was the year of the redemption."[38] This belief seems to have originated with Talmudic and Zohar passages that made reference to the messianic age. Given the traditionally accepted six-thousand-year life span of the world, Talmudic tractate Sanhedrin (99a) contains the following statement:

> "Rejoice greatly, O daughter of Zion, shout, O daughter of Jerusalem, behold your king comes to you; he is just and has salvation; lowly and riding upon an ass and upon a colt the foal of an ass" (Zech. 9:9). . . . R. Eliezer says, "The days of the Messiah will be forty years. . . . R. Dosa says "Four hundred years. Here it is written, 'And they shall serve them and they shall afflict them four hundred years.' (Gen. 15:13) and elsewhere Make us glad according to the days wherein you have afflicted us" (Ps. 90:15).[39]

Arie Morgenstern uses this passage as a way of showing the Talmudic foundations of the dating to then draw the argument toward an examination of just how pervasive this sense of messianic hope was throughout the whole of nineteenth-century Europe and the Mediterranean world.[40] Many Jews held that if Rabbi Dosa's prediction proved accurate, the messianic year ought to occur in or near 1840 (5600) to allow time for the four hundred year period of cleansing and torment to occur before the 6000th year.[41] The *Zohar*, a thirteenth-century mystical text likely composed by Moses de Leon of Guadalajara (d. 1305), also makes reference to the flood in the time of Noah and then predicts that a "flood" of knowledge and wisdom would come forth, based on the same dating schema, around the year 1840.[42] This line of thinking fit well into the Christian understanding that the events leading Jews and Christians to think about a future home for Jews in Palestine was connected to the divine narrative that both groups saw unfolding, albeit with noticeable differences.

When Hyde arrived in London for the first time, and particularly on his Palestine trip, he surely encountered "principal Jews" who helped him see their social and messianic worldview and their hope for a brighter future for Jews both in Europe and in their traditional homeland. Later nineteenth-century Jewish expectations of a return to Jerusalem accelerated *aliyot* (singular *aliyah*), or mass waves of migration toward Jerusalem, to begin the long process of resettling *Eretz Yisrael*. It was against great struggle that even earlier Jewish settlers attempted to establish an Ashkenazic Jewish presence in Palestine with very little natural or economic resources.[43] By the time

Hyde encountered Jerusalem, he was seeing a world enmeshed in dramatic chaos and transition with a very uncertain future.[44]

Just before his arrival in Jerusalem, Hyde ported in Beirut, a central destination of European Jewish migration in the 1830s. Hyde commented on the Christian clergy that he encountered in the various cities that echoed his own desire to see *Eretz Yisrael* flourish once again. However, he was quite cynical of their approach. He noted:

> The course which the popular clergy pursue at this time in relation to the Divine economy, looks to me as though they would say; "O Lord! We will worship thee with all our hearts, serve thee with all our souls and be very pious and holy. We will even gather Israel, convert the heathen, and bring in the millennium, if you will only let us alone that we may do it in our own way, and according to our own will. But if you speak from heaven to interfere with our plans, or cause any to see visions or dream dreams or prophecy whereby we are disturbed or interrupted in our worship, we will exert all our strength and skill to deny what you say, and charge it home upon the devil or some wild fantastic spirit, as being its author."[45]

Hyde ventured then to show how the gathering of Israel might be better facilitated by Christians, and Mormons in particular. In his letter to the Twelve, dated 1 January 1842, Hyde argued, "It was by political power and influence that the Jewish nation was broken down, and her subjects dispersed abroad; and I will here hazard the opinion, that by political power and influence, they will be gathered and built up; and further, that England is destined, in the wisdom and economy of heaven, to stretch forth the arm of political power, and advance in the front ranks of this glorious enterprise. . . . This opinion I submit, however, to your superior wisdom to correct, if you shall find it wrong."[46]

There were good reasons for Hyde to think that England would be the country to lead this effort to redeem Israel in 1841 and 1842—reasons that were entirely political and related to the philanthropic endeavors of wealthy British Jews in Britain. One example who was well known to Rabbi Hirschell was Moses Montefiore, one of Britain's wealthiest and most internationally recognized philanthropists and a Jewish advocate, who approached the Viceroy of Egypt, Mehemet Ali (1769–1849) with a proposal for Jewish recolonization in the region.[47]

Jews across the globe focused on Beirut's neighboring city of Damascus in 1840 for political reasons. In February of that year, an Italian monk named Father Thomas, along with his servant, disappeared in Damascus. The charge of ritual murder was levied against the city's Jewish population and they were convicted. Ritual murder consists of a charge against Jews that historically drew upon "secrets" found in the Talmud and other texts that supposedly prescribed the use of Christian blood for ritual purposes, most often the mixing of blood with flour for the Matza dough. This case grew into a *cause célèbre* that drew the attention and consternation of European Jews broadly. Presiding Jews from Britain and France came to the aid of Damascus Jews. The likes of Moses Montefiore and Adolf Cremieux made numerous trips to the region seeking to learn more of the case and force the hand of local officials to release the Jews, overturn the conviction, and assert control over the region again. The whole of European Jewish attention was focused on the region to which Hyde would travel because of the Damascus affair. Those leading Jews with whom he met in 1840 and 1841 in Germany and England were among those community leaders who were petitioning Damascus officials, the Catholic Church, Ottoman officials, and world leaders to put a stop to the accusations.

Further, the Damascus affair also contributed to the first publications in 1841 of the *Jewish Chronicle* that served for the rest of the nineteenth century as the journal of world Jewry.[48] In nearly every edition, one can find news from around the world concerning Jewish developments, interfaith strife, celebrations, and other notable occurrences. Funded by wealthy Jews in Britain, the *Jewish Chronicle* served in the 1840s as the clarion call for assistance and support of impoverished Jewish communities of the *aliyot*, Russia, and the United States. Hyde's claims that the way to further the gathering of Jews to Palestine was through humanitarian efforts echoes similar claims from Hirschell, Montefiore, Cremieux, and other Jews who worked tirelessly on behalf of worldwide Jewry.[49] One of the major news stories that developed on the pages of the *Jewish Chronicle* was the changing tide of Russian treatment of Jews and Count Pavel Kiselev's efforts to incorporate Jewish schools and institutions within the vast Russian Empire.

For Hyde, the events in Russia and England suggested that the moment was indeed upon them; regardless of whether 1840 was truly a messianic year, it was a critical moment in the unfolding of God's work in the world. He tied together at least two of the sources for his optimism when he wrote: "But on the land of Joseph, far in the west, where the spread eagle of America floats in the breeze and shadows the land . . . shall Zion rear her stately temples and stretch forth the curtains of her habitation. The record of Mormon chimes in so beautifully with the scriptures to establish this position, that an honest and faithful examination of the subject is all that is required to expel every doubt from the heart."[50] It was clear even in 1840, as Woodruff noted in his journal, that Mormon Apostles found themselves fully engaged in this work of finding avenues for facilitating a modern, yet no less prophetic, gathering of Israel. Woodruff argued:

> But in the midst of this mighty struggle, there is a small portion of the Community among the Nations of the Earth, who are looking upon other signs of this present generation as indicating a day big with events, even the restoration of primitive Christianity, the proclamation of the fulness of the Everlasting gospel among all nations both Gentile & Jew, the restoration of the Jews to their own land, the rebuilding of Jerrusalem, great changes, Judgments, wars, & revolutions of the gentile nations, the Second Advent of the Mesiah in the Clouds of heaven, & the great Millennium or rest of the Saints of one thousand years all of which events have been predicted by the Holy Prophets who have Spoken since the world began.[51]

Thus, the magnitude of the prophetic call of the Twelve to gather in Britain in 1840 weighed heavily upon those who took the charge and viewed, as part of their mission, the responsibility to begin a period of concerted effort to figure out how Israel might be gathered again.

At the conclusion of his mission, when the Twelve were again gathered on the American side of the Atlantic, Woodruff reported that "Elder Orson Hyde delivered an interesting discourse at President Joseph Smiths giving an account of his travels at Jerusalem & home again which was interesting. He saw the medeteranean [sic] & dead sea at the same time from mount Olivet. Saw smoke or fog continually arising from the dead sea. Spoke of the sepulcher & many things that put him in mind of the days of Christ. He published our principles in the German language & circulated them among the various nations."⁵² Without seeing the prophetic nature of the mission of the Twelve to Britain and the necessity of their being in Britain in 1840 and 1841 when the world was focused upon the "Jewish Question" in Europe, Hyde's journey to Palestine appears void of any real significance for the broader Church. Seeing 1840 Britain as necessary for the fulfillment of the revelation in Doctrine and Covenants 118 helps to situate the work for the eventual gathering of Jews to Palestine as part of the early Latter-day Saint work of preparing the world for the anticipated millennial reign of the Savior, Jesus Christ.

Notes

1.   This interest was evidently not limited to a scriptural fascination as seen in the account in Joseph Smith's journal of the visit of Robert Matthews (who claimed the title "Prophet Matthias"). Joseph Smith indicated that "Curiosity to see a man that was reputed to be a jew [*sic*] caused many to call during the day and more particularly at evening suspicions were entertained that said Joshua was the noted Mathias of New York, spoken so much of in the public prints on account of the trials he underwent in that place before a court of justice, for murder manslaughter comtempt of court whiping his Daughter &c for the two last crimes he was imprisoned, and came out about 4, months since, after some, equivocating he confessed that he was realy Mathias." Joseph Smith, Journal, 1835–1836, in Dean C. Jessee, Mark Ashurst-McGee, and Richard L. Jensen, eds., *Journals, Volume 1: 1832–1839*, vol. 1 of the Journals series of *The Joseph Smith Papers*, ed. Dean C. Jessee, Ronald K. Esplin, and Richard Lyman Bushman (Salt Lake City: Church Historian's Press, 2008), 93–95. Based on this account it is difficult to say what caused more people to show up at Joseph Smith's home when word got out, but at least a few were seemingly interested in the claim of Matthias as a Jewish prophet rather than his notoriety as criminal.

2.   A short survey of relevant titles on the subject of early Mormon understandings of Israel, Jews, and Judaism include the following: Shalom Goldman, *God's Sacred Tongue: Hebrew & the American Imagination* (Chapel Hill: University of North Carolina Press, 2004), 176–98; Victor L. Ludlow, "Jews," in *Book of Mormon Reference Companion*, ed. Dennis L. Largey (Salt Lake City: Deseret Book, 2003), 463–64; Robert L. Millet, "Gathering of Israel," in Robert L. Millet and others, *LDS Beliefs: A Doctrinal Reference* (Salt Lake City: Deseret Book, 2011), 247–49.

3.   Title page, the Book of Mormon.

4.   A careful reading of the Doctrine and Covenants and the Book of Mormon reveals a constant interplay between biblical motif, modern parallels, and a grand narrative of events that will occur as the events of the Second Coming unfold. The

Latter-day Saint understanding of this process builds this relationship between the Book of Mormon families and the biblical peoples by locating common stories and parallels. Alma 46:23–24 builds upon the narrative of Joseph in Egypt and the Lord's preservation of peoples for divine purposes. Similarly, Nephi attempted to instruct his brothers by showing them the remarkable parallel of their own story with that of Moses and the Israelites, as well as Abraham, Isaac, and Jacob (1 Nephi 17:26–40).

5.   David Cesarani, *The Jewish Chronicle and Anglo-Jewry, 1841–1991* (Cambridge: Cambridge University Press, 1994), 5. Cesarani argues that there were 30,000 to 40,000 Jews in England in the 1840s.

6.   Examples of this include the following: Scott G. Kenney, ed., *Wilford Woodruff's Journal, 1833–1898* Typescript (Midvale, UT: Signature Books, 1983), 2:364; and Hyde, *A Voice from Jerusalem: A Sketch of the Travels and Ministry of Elder Orson Hyde,* (Liverpool: P. P. Pratt, 1842), iii.

7.   Richard L. Evans, *A Century of "Mormonism" in Great Britain: A Brief Summary of the Activities of the Church of Jesus Christ of Latter-day Saints in the United Kingdom, with Emphasis on its Introduction One Hundred Years Ago* (Salt Lake City: Deseret News Press, 1937), 85–94.

8.   Abigail Green, "The British Empire and the Jews: An Imperialism of Human Rights?" *Past & Present,* no. 199 (May 2008), 175–205. The prevalence of this idea in the United States was richly documented in the journal of the Society for the Meliorating of the Condition of the Jews, *Israel's Advocate* (1823–27). The serial essay, "The Restoration of the Jews Contemplated and Urged," *Israel's Advocate* 1, no. 1 (January 1823) detailed how American Christians and government officials might aid in the relief of European Jews. Abigail Green, *Moses Montefiore: Jewish Liberator, Imperial Hero* (Cambridge: Harvard University Press, 2010), 127. Green argues that most British Evangelicals "regarded this development [diplomatic discussions about a Jewish presence in the Middle East] as a world-historical event that would pave the way for the coming of the messiah."

9.   Anthony Ashley-Cooper (Lord Ashley, Earl of Shaftesbury), review of "Letters on Egypt, Edom, and the Holy Land," *Quarterly Review* 63 (January and March 1839): 192. The *Quarterly Review,* founded in 1809, was intended as a Tory highbrow journal that would record "the advance of knowledge in every field of human enterprise." See Joanne Shattock, *Politics and Reviewers: The Edinburgh and the Quarterly* (London: Leicester University Press, 1989), 3–4. According to one historian, *Quarterly Review* sold 8,500 copies in 1841 and was read by many of Britain's elites. See Richard D. Altick, *Punch: The Lively Youth of a British Institution 1841–1851* (Columbus: Ohio State University Press, 1997), 35.

10.   Supersessionism describes the Christian belief that Jews, as a result of their "blindness" and rejection of Jesus Christ have been temporarily displaced as the covenanted people and have ceded that position to Christians. Christian supersessionism does not necessarily demand that Jews will never hold a position within the kingdom of God, but it certainly delays or places restrictions upon it. Supersessionism depends upon a typological reading of scriptural passages that allows for Christians to identify moments where Israel lost its favored position. For example, some have read Matthew

21:28–41 as an indication that God has revoked his covenant with Israel because they killed Jesus Christ, whom they took for the heir. See Christopher M. Leighton, "Christian Theology After the Shoah," in *Christianity in Jewish Terms*, ed. Tikva Frymer-Kensky and others (Boulder, CO: Westview, 2000), 36–48.

11.   Doctrine and Covenants 10:49–50 connects the Book of Mormon translation process in 1828–29 to the coming forth of the gospel message and the preparation of "this land" and the blessing pronounced upon it by those who compiled it for that express purpose. Robert K. Whalen, "'Christians Love the Jews!' The Development of American Philo-Semitism, 1790–1860," *Religion and American Culture: A Journal of Interpretation* 6, no. 2 (Summer 1996), 225–59.

12.   Shalom Goldman, *Zeal for Zion: Christians, Jews, and the Idea of the Promised Land* (Chapel Hill: North Carolina University Press, 2009), 12–13.

13.   J. Spencer Fluhman, *"A Peculiar People": Anti-Mormonism and the Making of Religion in Nineteenth-Century America* (Chapel Hill: University of North Carolina Press, 2012), 28, 83–84; Goldman, *God's Sacred Tongue*, 190; Kent P. Jackson, "Joseph Smith's Biblical Antiquity," in *Approaching Antiquity: Joseph Smith and the Ancient World*, ed. Lincoln H. Blumell, Matthew J. Grey, and Andrew H. Hedges (Provo, UT: Religious Studies Center; Salt Lake City: Deseret Book, 2015), 166.

14.   Title Page, the Book of Mormon. Emphasis in original. For more on the significance and interpretation of this in Latter-day Saint teaching and doctrine today, see the following two essays: Shon D. Hopkin, "To the Convincing of the Jew and Gentile that Jesus Is the Christ," in *The Coming Forth of the Book of Mormon: A Marvelous Work and a Wonder*, 44th Annual Brigham Young University Sidney B. Sperry Symposium, ed. Dennis L. Largey and others (Provo, UT: Religious Studies Center; Salt Lake City: Deseret Book, 2015), 281–99; and Jared W. Ludlow, "'They Are Not Cast Off Forever': Fulfillment of the Covenant Purposes," in *The Coming Forth of the Book of Mormon*, 266–79.

15.   Jonathan Karp and Adam Sutcliffe, "A Brief History of Philosemitism," in *Philosemitism in History*, ed. Jonathan Karp and Adam Sutcliffe (Cambridge: Cambridge University Press, 2011), 6. Philo-Semitism is "the idealization of Jews and Judaism by non-Jews." There is no single definition that the majority of scholars who study relations between Jews and Christians readily agree upon. This disagreement is the result of various strands of Philo-Semitism that combine adoration and criticism in their discussions that might appear, at least on the surface to be very pro-Jewish in tone. However, within many of these critiques, there is the underlying belief among Christians that all Jews will eventually need to adopt Christianity and accept Jesus Christ as Savior.

16.   Brigham Young was referred to as "the Moses of the Latter days" by Edward W. Tullidge in 1876. He wrote in his biography of the prophet, "Here we have him at once in the character of the modern Moses. It is no fanciful conceit of the author to thus style him to-day, after he and his people have built up a State fabric, with three hundred cities and settlements, networked with railroads and the electric telegraph; for at that very period his name rang throughout America, and reverberated in Europe, as the Moses of the 'latter days,' and the Mormons were likened to the children of Israel in the wilderness." Tullidge, *Life of Brigham Young; or Utah and Her Founders*

(New York: n.p., 1876), 6. Others commented further on the character of Young as Moses including John T. Caine, a territorial delegate in Washington. When asked by Frank G. Carpenter of the *New York World* to comment on Young, Caine replied: "He was a great man. . . . The work of Moses leading the children of Israel through the wilderness was nothing to his taking that band of Mormons over the untrodden wilderness of the great American desert and of settling them in the heart of it. Moses only traveled a few hundred miles. Brigham's band traversed thousands. It took Brigham Young less than a year to find his land of Canaan, while Moses wandered around for fully forty." See Frank G. Carpenter, "Talk with the Utah Delegate," *Deseret Weekly News*, 25 October 1890, 584. In 1854, the Scottish writer and social commentator, Thomas Carlyle suggested in a brief essay on Mormons that "No Czar of Russia is so absolute as Joseph Smith's successor." See Clyde de L. Ryals, "Thomas Carlyle on the Mormons: An Unpublished Essay" *Carlyle Studies Annual* 15 (1995), 51. Leonard J. Arrington, *Brigham Young: American Moses* (Urbana: University of Illinois Press, 1986). Arrington adopted this appellation as a fitting title for his landmark biography on Brigham Young.

17.   Joseph Smith, History, 6 January 1836, in Karen Lynn Davidson, et al., eds., *Histories, Volume 1: 1832–1844*, vol. 1 of the Histories series of *The Joseph Smith Papers*, ed. Dean C. Jessee, Ronald K. Esplin, and Richard Lyman Bushman (Salt Lake City: Church Historian's Press, 2012), 168. For more on Seixas and his connection to Joseph Smith, see Goldman, *God's Sacred Tongue* 176–98. One of the most successful students in Seixas's lectures was Orson Hyde, who wrote a personal letter to his teacher on 31 March 1836. Hyde wrote: "The time has arrived when your valuable course of Heb. Instruction with us has come to a close; and I am unwilling for you to leave without expressing on my parts the deep sense I have of your indefatigable labours, and the intense interests you have manifested by employing all, and the most efficient means in your power to advance us in the knowledge of the Heb. Scriptures. It is but justice to say that our expectations under your very valuable course of instruction, have been more than realized. The extra privileges which I have enjoyed with you in consequences of local circumstances, call for my grateful acknowledgement and inspire my head to call upon Heaven for blessings to rest upon you, and upon your beloved family. Should any institution, class, or people wish to acquire a knowledge of the Hebrew Language (did they know your superior qualifications,) I am confident they would not ask, What are the terms of tuition? But can we obtain him?" Hyde Family Papers, University of Utah J. Willard Marriott Special Collections, MS 193, box 1, folder 1.

18.   See the concise article on the subject of Mormonism and its use of ancient Israel in W. D. Davies, "Israel, the Mormons and the Land" in *Reflections on Mormonism: Judaeo-Christian Parallels*, ed. Truman G. Madsen (Provo, UT: Religious Studies Center, 1978), 79–96.

19.   Among the many secondary sources that relay Orson Hyde's story, see for example, "Orson Hyde's Trip to the Holy Land 1841 A.D.," extracts from the writings of Marvin S. Hill and Joseph S. Hyde, compiled by Glenn E. Nielson, February 1963, L. Tom Perry Special Collections, Harold B. Lee Library, Provo, UT; Myrtle Hyde, *Orson Hyde: The Olive Branch of Israel* (Salt Lake City: Agreka, 2000), 111–30; Grant Underwood, *The Millenarian World of Early Mormonism* (Urbana: University of

Illinois, 1999), 63–6; Howard H. Barron, *Orson Hyde: Missionary, Apostle, Colonizer* (Bountiful, UT: Horizon, 1978), 113–41; Marvin S. Hill, "An Historical Study of the Life of Orson Hyde, Early Mormon Missionary and Apostle from 1805–1852" (master's thesis, Brigham Young University, 1955), 43–65, 110–18.

20.   Myrtle Stevens Hyde, *Orson Hyde: The Olive Branch of Israel* (Salt Lake City: Agreka, 2000), 112–14. In early March 1840, Hyde saw in vision the cities he was to visit including Constantinople, Amsterdam, and Jerusalem. According to Myrtle Hyde, the vision lasted six hours. Hyde indicated that it lasted "for a number of hours." On 4 March 1840, Hyde related the events to Joseph Smith who reacted with equal enthusiasm. See Hyde, *A Voice from Jerusalem*, iii.

21.   Orson Hyde and John E. Page, Letter, 1 May 1840, Columbus, OH, to Joseph Smith, Nauvoo, IL; in Joseph Smith, Letterbook 2, 144–45, handwriting of Howard Coray, Church History Library, Salt Lake City, http://josephsmithpapers .org/paperSummary/letter-from-orson-hyde-and-john-e-page-1-may-1840?p=1 &highlight=orson%20hyde#!/paperSummaryletter-from-orson-hyde-and-john-e -page-1-may-1840.

22.   Joseph Smith, Letter, 14 May 1840, Nauvoo, IL, to Orson Hyde and John E. Page, Cincinnati, OH, in Joseph Smith, Letterbook 2, 146–47, handwriting of Howard Coray, Church History Library, http://josephsmithpapers.org/paperSummary/letter -to-orson-hyde-and-john-e-page-14-may-1840.

23.   From among many possible early nineteenth-century American sources, one might look at William Cogswell, *The Harbinger of the Millennium* (Boston: Pierce and Parker, 1833); John Jacob Bergmann, "The Restoration of the Jews Contemplated and Urged," *Israel's Advocate* 1, no. 1–7 (January 1823–July 1823); or for Britain, see for example, Ashley-Cooper, review of "Letters on Egypt, Edom, and the Holy Land," 166–92.

24.   *Wilford Woodruff's Journal*, 1:364.

25.   *Wilford Woodruff's Journal*, 1:367.

26.   Alexander Campbell, *The Christian System, in Reference of Primitive Christianity as Plead in the Current Reformation*, 4th ed. (Cincinnati: H. S. Bosworth, 1866), 140.

27.   Rev. Charles Buck, *A Theological Dictionary* (Philadelphia: W. W. Woodward, 1821), 278.

28.   Campbell, *Christian System*, 141; emphasis in original.

29.   Campbell, *Christian System*, 141.

30.   Orson Hyde, *A Voice from Jerusalem*, 9. Hyde, in giving a description of his mission, wrote: "But against this heavenly message, streaming from the bosom of the compassionate God, with the purest love and good-will to a fallen race, and beaming in the face of men with a celestial radiance, is arranged the cold-hearted prejudices of an unbelieving world. Well did the Savior ask this question,—'When the son of man cometh, shall he find faith on the earth?'"

31.   *Wilford Woodruff's Journal*, 2:85.

32.   *Wilford Woodruff's Journal*, 2:86.

33.   Orson Hyde, *A Voice from Jerusalem*, 10.

34. Hirschell was the Chief Rabbi from 1802 to 1842. Orson Hyde's letter to Hirschell was published in *Times and Seasons*, 1 Oct. 1841, 2:551–55. In the article, Hyde mentioned that Hirschell broke his femur, an injury that had him laid up for some time, and later, in 1842, he fell again and broke his collar bone, after which he died. Orson Hyde, Letter, Ratisbon, Bavaria, to Joseph Smith, Nauvoo, IL, 17 July 1841, in *Times and Seasons*, 15 October 1841, 2:570–73.

35. Hirschell was often referred to in the press as "the high priest" of British Jewry. Hillary L. Rubinstein, "Hirschell (Hirschel, Herschell), Solomon (1762–1842)," in *Oxford Dictionary of National Biography*, ed. H. C. G. Matthew and Brian Harrison (Oxford: Oxford University Press, 2004), 27: 311–312.

36. Hyde, *A Voice from Jerusalem*, 14–15.

37. Hess, a *maskil*, or "enlightened scholar," found a new sense of Jewish identity through a growing Jewish nationalism that helped him navigate the difficult issue of whether Jews might ever find a home in Europe or whether they need look elsewhere. *The Revival of Israel: Rome and Jerusalem*, trans. Meyer Waxman (Lincoln: University of Nebraska Press, 1995), 43. See also Michael Brenner, *Zionism: A Brief History* (Princeton: Markus Weiner, 2003), 11–13; Howard M. Sachar, *A History of Israel: From the Rise of Zionism to Our Time*, 3rd ed. (New York: Alfred A. Knopf, 2007), 11–12; Robert M. Seltzer, *Jewish People, Jewish Thought: The Jewish Experience in History* (Upper Saddle, NJ: Prentice Hall, 1980), 686–89. For more on Moses Hess, see Ken Koltun-Fromm, *Moses Hess and Modern Jewish Identity* (Bloomington: Indiana University Press, 2001).

38. Jacob Katz, "On the Year 5600 as a Messianic Year and its Influence on the Efforts of *Perushim* to Hasten the Redemption" (Hebrew), *Cathedra* 24 (1982), 73, quoted in Arie Morgenstern, *Hastening Redemption: Messianism and the Resettlement of the Land of Israel* (Oxford: Oxford University Press, 2006), 23–49. For more on the *Perushim* movement, see Green, *Moses Montefiore*, 116–17. See also Israel Bartal, "Messianism and Nationalism: Liberal Optimism vs. Orthodox Anxiety," *Jewish History* 20, no. 1 (2006), 5–17; and Chaim I. Waxman, "Messianism, Zionism, and the State of Israel," *Modern Judaism* 7, no. 2 (May 1987), 175–92.

39. Jacob Neusner, *Talmud, Sanhedrin* 99a, vol. 16 (Peabody, MA: Hendrickson, 2011), 529.

40. Morgenstern, *Hastening Redemption*, 23–24.

41. The work of Arie Morgenstern has shown the broad acceptance of the 1840 date as the dawn of the messianic age as critical for the work of the Jews in the world. See Morgenstern, *Hastening Redemption*, 23–49.

42. *Zohar* 1.117a, Pritzker Edition, trans. Daniel C. Matt (Stanford: Stanford University Press, 2004), II: 180. The passage 1:117a reads: "Every sixty years of that sixth millennium, *he* is invigorated, scaling its rungs. In the six hundredth year of the sixth, springs of wisdom will open above, springs of wisdom below, and the world will preare to enter the seventh, just like a person preparing on the sixth day, as the sun is about to set, to enter Sabbath. Your mnemonic: *In the six hundredth year of Noah's life . . . all the springs of the great abyss burst and the sluices of heaven were opened* (Genesis 7:11)." The sixth millennium is traditionally symbolized by the Hebrew letter ו (vav),

hence the "mystery of the ו" is the beginning line of *Zohar* 1.117a;. The symbolic numerical representation of ו is six, hence the beginning of the sixth millennium was 1240/41 C.E., making 1840 (six hundred years later) the designated year for this flood of wisdom. The messianic millennium, according to Jewish tradition, will commence 2240/41 C.E.

43.   Green, *Moses Montefiore*, 112–19; Morgenstern, *Hastening Redemption*, 72–73.

44.   Hyde, *A Voice from Jerusalem*, 34–35. Hyde's sense of urgency and potential for danger seems to have been a statement about both the general state of affairs, but also out of fear for his own life. At the conclusion of his last letter, dated 20 October 1841, Hyde noted, "I have many particulars that I would like to write, but time will not allow at this time. You will hear from me again by the first opportunity, if the Arabs don't kill me."

45.   Hyde, *Voice from Jerusalem*, 12–13.

46.   Hyde, *Voice from Jerusalem*, 14.

47.   Simon Sebag Montefiore, *Jerusalem: The Biography* (New York: Vintage, 2011), 343–46.

48.   Cesarani, *Jewish Chronicle*, 9.

49.   Hyde, *A Voice from Jerusalem*, 14–15. Hyde is careful here to make the connection between a softened political and social outlook that benefits Jews and their imminent return to the scriptural basis mentioned above that ties Jews and Mormons to the "god of Abraham, Isaac, and Jacob."

50.   Hyde, *A Voice from Jerusalem*, 18.

51.   *Wilford Woodruff's Journal*, 2:1 (1 January 1841).

52.   *Wilford Woodruff's Journal*, 2:194 (11 December 1842).

13

The Doctrines of Eternal Marriage and Eternal Families

Daniel K Judd and Jacob D. Judd

Daniel K Judd is a professor of ancient scripture
at Brigham Young University.

Jacob D. Judd is the director of the LDS Institute
of Religion in Chicago, Illinois.

The doctrines of eternal marriage and the eternal family are teachings unique to The Church of Jesus Christ of Latter-day Saints. While the structure and practice of marriage and family have been and continue to be redefined in many countries and religious traditions throughout the world, these doctrines of the restored gospel remain uncompromised but not unchallenged. In the United States for example, fundamental changes to the definition of marriage have recently taken place.[1] These changes have led to both civil and uncivil debate arising from different interpretations of history, doctrine, scripture, and of the Prophet Joseph Smith's foundational revelations regarding eternal marriage and the eternal family.

In addition to reviewing the historical contexts in which the doctrines of eternal marriage and the eternal family were restored, this chapter will demonstrate how marriage and family relationships are vital parts in the process of sanctification that leads to the exaltation of the individual and of the family. This discussion will also affirm the significance of the unique contributions the doctrines of eternal marriage and eternal family bring to the present debate concerning homosexual and heterosexual family and marital relationships.

Historical Overview

The first indication of the eternal nature of family relationships in this dispensation was alluded to in Joseph Smith's earliest revelations. The Book of Mormon prophet Moroni included the following words from the writings of the prophet Malachi during his visit with Joseph Smith on 21 September 1823:

> Behold, I will reveal unto you the Priesthood, by the hand of Elijah the prophet, before the coming of the great and dreadful day of the Lord.
>
> And he shall plant in the hearts of the children the promises made to the fathers, and the hearts of the children shall turn to their fathers.
>
> If it were not so, the whole earth would be utterly wasted at his coming. (D&C 2:1–3, see also Malachi 4:5–6)

While the implications of this prophecy may not have been fully understood by the young Prophet when Moroni first appeared (Joseph was seventeen years old), his understanding would mature as additional heavenly messengers were sent by the Lord to instruct him. After the completion and dedication of the Kirtland Temple on 27 March 1836, the Prophet Joseph began to understand the doctrine of the eternal family with greater clarity. Section 110 of the Doctrine and Covenants includes the fulfillment of Malachi's prophecy concerning the coming of Elijah as well as includes the visitation of other heavenly beings.

After being visited by the Lord, the prophet Moses appeared and "committed unto [them] the keys of the gathering of Israel" (D&C 110:11). The Prophet Joseph then recorded: "After this, Elias appeared, and committed the dispensation of the gospel of Abraham, saying that in us and our seed all generations after us should be blessed" (D&C 110:12). While the identity of the "Elias" in this text has not been identified, he apparently lived during the time of Abraham and held keys relative to eternal marriage and family.

Elder Bruce R. McConkie explained the purpose for the coming of Elias as follows:

> Elias appeared, and committed the dispensation of the gospel of Abraham," meaning the great commission given to Abraham that he and his seed had a right to the priesthood, the gospel, and eternal life. Accordingly, Elias promised those upon whom these ancient promises were then renewed that in them and in their seed all generations should be blessed. (D&C 110:12–16.) Thus, through the joint ministry of Elijah, who brought the sealing power, and Elias, who restored the marriage discipline of Abraham, the way was prepared for the planting in the hearts of the children of the promises made to the fathers.[2]

Following Elias came the long-awaited and much-anticipated coming of Elijah, the prophet who bestowed the priesthood keys upon Joseph Smith and Oliver Cowdery. These keys enabled couples and families to be sealed for eternity.

> Behold, the time has fully come, which was spoken of by the mouth of Malachi—testifying that he [Elijah] should be sent, before the great and dreadful day of the Lord come—
>
> To turn the hearts of the fathers to the children, and the children to the fathers, lest the whole earth be smitten with a curse—
>
> Therefore, the keys of this dispensation are committed into your hands; and by this ye may know that the great and dreadful day of the Lord is near, even at the doors. (D&C 110:14–16)

While Joseph now possessed the keys necessary to organize eternal marriages and eternal families, it does not appear that he did so for at least four years. After moving to Nauvoo, Illinois, in 1839, Joseph formally introduced various doctrines and practices that would fully realize Malachi's promise to "turn the hearts of the fathers to the children, and the children to the fathers." On 15 August 1840, during the funeral of Seymour Brunson, a member of the high council and bodyguard to Joseph Smith, the Prophet himself first began to discuss sacred ordinances being performed for the dead. After reading extensively from 1 Corinthians 15, Joseph informed the Saints that they "could now act for their friends who had departed this life, and that the plan of salvation was calculated to save all who were willing to obey the requirements of the law of God."[3] Reportedly, Jane Neymon (also Neyman, Nyman), a woman who attended the funeral, was so inspired by the concept of vicarious baptism for the dead that she immediately asked Harvey Olmstead to baptize her in behalf of her deceased son, Cyrus. Her request was granted and, with Vienna Jaques as witness, the first proxy baptism for the dead in the dispensation of the fullness of times was performed.[4]

Although Joseph's language regarding baptism for the dead is reported to have instructed the Saints that they could "act for their friends," when put into practice the proxy work almost always followed familial ties. According to Susan Easton Black's research into proxy work done during the Nauvoo period, only 203 of the 6,818 proxy baptisms performed were for "friends." All others were performed for uncles, aunts, parents, siblings, in-laws, spouses, children, and so forth. Joseph's first major revelation during the Nauvoo period laid the pragmatic framework for later revelations regarding the eternal family.[5]

Between 1841 and 1844, Joseph Smith would both privately and publicly introduce the doctrines of eternal marriage and eternal families. Joseph would also be asked to follow the example of some of the Lord's servants in biblical times and practice plural marriage (see Genesis 16; Jacob 2:30). Beginning with Louisa Beaman in April 1841, Joseph entered into a number of polygamous relationships. Some scholars offer a possible reason for these relationships: "These sealings may have provided a way to create an eternal bond or link between Joseph's family and other families within the Church. These ties extended both vertically, from parent to child, and horizontally, from one family to another."[6] The reality of God-sanctioned polygamous unions is evidence for some fluidity in the definition of marriage and family. While the number of participants varied as instructed by the Lord, the necessity of those relationships being between man and woman has not. There is no scriptural precedent for authorized homosexual unions.

One of the Prophet Joseph Smith's first public sermons on eternal relationships came during a sermon to the Saints in Ramus, Illinois. Joseph taught, "And that same sociality which exits among us here [in mortality] will exist among us there [in the world to come]" (D&C 130:2).

Contextually, the "sociality" most prevalent during the 1800s was that of the family specifically and not merely general human interaction. Of that time, the *Encyclopedia of American Social History* reports, "Most families, regardless of class or ethnic background, were nuclear in structure; between 1 and 3 percent of households contained a solitary resident, and between 9 and 12 percent of households contained extended families."[7] Furthermore, it is clear from the revelations and other writings of Joseph Smith and other leaders that have followed that the meaning of the word "sociality" includes marriage and family relationships.[8]

In a later discussion, parts of which became canonized as scripture, the Prophet Joseph explained the following to Benjamin F. Johnson and his wife Melissa LeBaron Johnson concerning the eternal nature of marriage and family relationships:

> In the celestial glory there are three heavens or degrees;
>
> And in order to obtain the highest, a man must enter into this order of the priesthood [meaning the new and everlasting covenant of marriage];
>
> And if he does not, he cannot obtain it.
>
> He may enter into the other, but that is the end of his kingdom; he cannot have an increase. (D&C 131:1–4)

The bracketed phrase "meaning the new and everlasting covenant of marriage" included in this scriptural text first appears in the 1876 edition of the Doctrine and Covenants and clarifies that the Prophet Joseph was teaching Brother and Sister Johnson that eternal marriage was necessary in order to attain exaltation. The following entry (Tuesday, 16 May 1843) from the journal of William Clayton confirms that Joseph Smith was indeed teaching the doctrine of eternal marriage and not simply about the necessity of receiving the priesthood. Brother Clayton recorded Joseph Smith's words as follows:

> Except a man and his wife enter into an everlasting covenant and be married for eternity, while in this probation; by the power and authority of the Holy priesthood; they will cease to increase when they die, that is, they will not have any children after the resurrection; but those who are married by the power

and authority of the Priesthood in this life, and continue without committing the sin against the Holy Ghost, will continue to increase and have children in the celestial glory."[9]

A journal entry from Joseph Smith dated 24 November 1835 suggests that the doctrine of eternal marriage was being discussed prior to the 1843 revelations. After requesting the couple being married, Lydia Goldthwaite and Newel Knight, to "join hands," the Prophet Joseph introduced the ordinance by teaching that "marriage was an institution of heaven, instituted in the garden of Eden."[10]

The phrase "institution of heaven" is significant in light of the historical and cultural context in which it was delivered. The early American culture, of which the Latter-day Saints were a part, was heavily influenced by the Puritans who immigrated to America in the early 1600s. The Puritans had left England in large part because they rejected the Church of England's assertion that marriage was a religious covenant and not a civil contract. Joseph Smith's teachings were much more in line with the pre-Reformation beliefs and practices that viewed marriage as a sacrament than with the teachings and practices of the churches in the nineteenth century. Describing marriage as having a heavenly connection was incongruous with the prevailing religious and civil perspectives of the time.[11]

Furthermore, the 1835 Doctrine and Covenants includes the following direction concerning the wording of the wedding ceremony specific to that time:

> You both mutually agree to be each other's companion, husband and wife, observing the legal rights belonging to this condition; that is, keeping yourselves wholly for each other, and from all others, during your lives. And when they have answered "Yes," he shall pronounce them "husband and wife" in the name of the Lord Jesus Christ, and by virtue of the laws of the country and authority vested in him: "may God add his blessings and keep you to fulfill your covenants from *henceforth and forever.* Amen."[12]

The phrase "henceforth and forever" is an important contrast with the phrases "till death us do part" and "so long as ye both shall live," which are included in *The Book of Common Prayer*, the handbook used by the Protestant clergy of the day and which were the norm for marital vows in the 1830s.[13]

The following statement from Elder Parley P. Pratt recorded sometime in 1839 or 1840 clearly and eloquently illustrates that the doctrines of eternal families and eternal marriage were being taught prior to the time the formal revelations were given in 1843:

> [The Prophet Joseph Smith] taught me many great and glorious principles concerning God and the heavenly order of eternity. It was at this time that I received from him the first idea of eternal family organization, and the eternal union of the sexes in those inexpressibly endearing relationships which none but the highly intellectual, the refined and pure in heart, know how to prize, and which are at the very foundation of everything worthy to be called happiness.
>
> Till then I had learned to esteem kindred affections and sympathies as appertaining solely to this transitory state, as something from which the heart must be entirely weaned, in order to be fitted for its heavenly state.
>
> It was Joseph Smith who taught me how to prize the endearing relationships of father and mother, husband and wife; of brother and sister, son and daughter.
>
> It was from him that I learned that the wife of my bosom might be secured to me for time and all eternity; and that the refined sympathies and affections which endeared us to each other emanated from the fountain of divine eternal love. It was from him that I learned that we might cultivate these affections, and grow and increase in the same to all eternity; while the result of our endless union would be an offspring as numerous as the stars of heaven, or the sands of the sea shore.
>
> It was from him that I learned the true dignity and destiny of a son of God, clothed with an eternal priesthood, as the patriarch and sovereign of his countless offspring. It was from him that I learned that the highest dignity of womanhood was, to stand as a queen and priestess to her husband, and to reign

for ever and ever as the queen mother of her numerous and still increasing offspring.

I had loved before, but I knew not why. But now I loved—with a pureness—an intensity of elevated, exalted feeling, which would lift my soul from the transitory things of this grovelling sphere and expand it as the ocean. I felt that God was my heavenly Father indeed; that Jesus was my brother, and that the wife of my bosom was an immortal, eternal companion; a kind ministering angel, given to me as a comfort, and a crown of glory for ever and ever. In short, I could now love with the spirit and with the understanding also.[14]

Elder Pratt articulates the theological and practical benefits that were inspired from Joseph Smith's teachings regarding eternal marriage and the eternal family. In Joseph's theology, families are more than a social construct for the perpetuation of humanity in mortality, but were to continue beyond this mortal sphere. When family relationships are understood in this light, the importance of Elijah's return and the consequences of not heeding Malachi's warning begin to be more clearly understood. President Joseph Fielding Smith taught:

Through the power [and keys] of this priesthood which Elijah bestowed, husband and wife may be sealed, or married for eternity; children may be sealed to their parents for eternity; thus the family is made eternal, and death does not separate the members. *This is the great principle that will save the world from utter destruction.*[15]

President Smith's warning about "utter destruction" provides commentary on the concluding verse of the Lord's words in Malachi that if the hearts of parents and children are not turned one to another the earth will be smitten with a curse (see Malachi 4:5–6). The First Presidency and the Quorum of the Twelve Apostles refer to this and other prophetic warnings in "The Family: A Proclamation to the World":

We warn that individuals who violate covenants of chastity, who abuse spouse or offspring, or who fail to fulfill family responsibilities will one day stand accountable before God. Further, we warn that the disintegration of the family will bring upon individuals, communities, and nations the calamities foretold by ancient and modern prophets.[16]

Having provided historical context for many of the earliest doctrinal statements concerning the introduction of eternal marriage and eternal families in the early part of the nineteenth century, this chapter will address the following questions:

- Why is there not more scriptural evidence that the doctrines of eternal marriage and eternal families were taught and practiced anciently?
- Why are eternal marriage and the eternal family such important parts of God's purposes?
- Why is marriage and family necessary in the world to come?
- Why must marriage be restricted to relationships between a man and a woman?

Why Is There Not More Scriptural Evidence?

The absence of well-defined biblical and historical evidence for the doctrinal teachings of eternal marriage and eternal families does not necessarily provide evidence of their absence from the lives of the people who lived at the times these texts and records were being recorded. For most of human history, marriage and family have been the cultural subtext upon which societies were formed. The ubiquity of such institutions oftentimes caused them to be left out of recorded history. An example of the scriptural evidence that does exist on the enduring nature of the marital relationship includes the Savior's teachings on marriage in the Gospel of Mark:

> But from the beginning of the creation God made them male and female. For this cause shall a man leave his father and mother, and cleave to his wife; And they twain shall be one flesh: so then they are no more twain, but one flesh. What therefore God hath joined together, let not man put asunder. (Mark 10:6–9, see also Matt. 16:18–19, 1 Cor. 11:11, and Eph. 3:15)

The scriptural texts most often cited as evidence for marriage ending at death are found in the synoptic accounts of the Sadducees asking the Savior, "Whose wife of them is she?" (Luke 20:33; see Matthew 22:23–30, Mark 12:19–25; Luke 20:27–36), after presenting a scenario of seven brothers who were married, at different times, to the same woman. Luke's account of the Savior's response to his inquisitors is representative of each of the synoptic descriptions:

> And Jesus answering said unto them, The children of this world marry, and are given in marriage: But they which shall be accounted worthy to obtain that world, and the resurrection from the dead, neither marry, nor are given in marriage. (Luke 20:34–35)

Commenting on this verse, New Testament scholar and Anglican cleric R. T. France explained:

> In response to this concern Jesus offers . . . a view of eternal life in which marriage is apparently irrelevant. For those whom marriage is the basis of the deepest joy and love on earth, this is a hard saying. It may be mitigated by the fact that what Jesus excludes from the afterlife is the *process* of 'marrying and being given in marriage' rather than the resultant *state* of being married.[17]

Professor France's explanation is consistent with Latter-day Saint theology that teaches that "not only the ordinance of baptism, but also the sealing of families together [including husbands and wives] as an eternal unit *must be done on the earth*."[18] Indeed, there will be no marrying and giving in marriage in the world to come, therefore these ordinances must be performed in mortality on behalf of someone else who has died and gone on to the spirit world.

The Lord, speaking through the Prophet Joseph Smith, taught that the reason some will not be allowed to experience marriage in heaven is that the marriage has not been authorized by the proper authority and that they "did not abide by my [the Savior's] Law." The Lord's words are as follows:

Therefore, if a man marry him a wife in the world, and he marry her not by me nor by my word, and he covenant with her so long as he is in the world and she with him, their covenant and marriage are not of force when they are dead, and when they are out of the world; therefore, they are not bound by any law when they are out of the world.

Therefore, when they are out of the world they neither marry nor are given in marriage; but are appointed angels in heaven, which angels are ministering servants, to minister for those who are worthy of a far more, and an exceeding, and an eternal weight of glory.

For these angels did not abide my law; therefore, they cannot be enlarged, but remain separately and singly, without exaltation, in their saved condition, to all eternity; and from henceforth are not gods, but are angels of God forever and ever. (D&C 132:15–17)

Elder McConkie provided the following explanation pertaining to the assertion that there is no marriage in heaven:

He [Jesus Christ] is not denying but limiting the prevailing concept that there will be marrying and giving in marriage in heaven. He is saying that as far as "they" (the Sadducees) are concerned, that as far as "they" ("the children of this world") are concerned, the family unit does not and will not continue in the resurrection.[19]

President Brigham Young taught that the doctrines and ordinances embraced and practiced in the restored Church today were taught and practiced anciently:

The plan of salvation and the revelations of the will of God to man are unchanged, although mankind have not for many ages been favored therewith, in consequence of apostasy and wickedness. There is no evidence to be found in the Bible that the Gospel should be one thing in the days of the Israelites, another

in the days of Christ and his Apostles, and another in the 19th
Century, but, on the contrary, we are instructed that God is
the same in every age, and that his plan of saving his children
is the same. . . . He has not changed his laws, ordinances and
covenants pertaining to Himself and the salvation of mankind.
The plan of salvation is one, from the beginning of the world to
the end thereof.[20]

The fullness of the doctrines of eternal marriage and family relationships is unique to The Church of Jesus Christ of Latter-day Saints, but there
is some evidence of other faith traditions who have embraced (at least in part)
similar teachings. John Meyendorff, a scholar and cleric in the (Eastern)
Orthodox Church, described the Orthodox belief in eternal marriage as
follows: "Christian marriage consists in transforming and transfiguring a
natural human affection between a man and a woman into an eternal bond
of love, which cannot be broken even by death."[21] Reverend Meyendorff
and those of the Orthodox tradition believe that their church is a continuation of the church established by Jesus Christ and that the doctrine of
eternal marriage can be traced to the earliest Christian teachings. Emanuel
Swedenborg, an eighteenth-century scientist and mystic, taught that "it follows that there are marriages in the heavens just as there are on the earth."[22]

While there are other churches and traditions that teach the doctrines
of eternal marriage and eternal families to a limited degree, it appears that
for the most part these doctrines were among the "plain and precious" (1
Nephi 13:28) doctrinal principles and covenants that were lost to humankind in the centuries following the mortal ministry of Jesus Christ.

The Book of Mormon prophet Nephi describes this doctrinal absence
as follows: "They have taken away from the gospel of the Lamb many things
which are plain and most precious; and also many covenants of the Lord
have they taken away" (1 Nephi 13:26). The prophet Isaiah described the loss
of such covenants when he prophesied, "They have transgressed the laws,
changed the ordinance, broken the everlasting covenant" (Isaiah 24:5).

The Prophet Joseph Smith taught, "From sundry revelations which had
been received, it was apparent that many important points, touching the
Salvation of man, had been taken from the Bible, or lost before it was compiled."[23] Many other scholars and Church leaders from throughout history

have made similar statements. Writing as early as the third century AD, Origen, the noted Christian theologian, recorded:

> The differences among the [biblical] manuscripts have become great, either through the negligence of some copyists or through the perverse audacity of others; they either neglect to check over what they have transcribed, or, in the process of checking, they lengthen or shorten as they please.[24]

While it is beyond the scope of this chapter to discuss the *negligence* of some copyists, a brief discussion of the changes to the text that were *intentional* is relevant to explaining why the doctrines of eternal marriage and the eternal family are not more apparent in the scriptural text of the Bible. New Testament scholar Bart Ehrman has written:

> Whatever else we may say about the Christian scribes—whether of the early centuries or of the Middle ages—we have to admit that in addition to copying scripture, they were changing scripture. Sometimes they didn't mean to—they were simply tired, or inattentive, or, on occasion, inept. At other times, though, they did mean to make the changes, as when they wanted the text to emphasize precisely what they themselves believed.[25]

One of the personal beliefs that has influenced the translation, transmission, and interpretation of biblical text has been identified by Professor Bruce M. Metzger, a respected New Testament scholar, as an "increasing emphasis on asceticism in the early Church."[26] Just as some copyists and scholars allowed their belief in the doctrine of the Trinity to motivate their addition of forty-one words to the fifth chapter of 1st John (see 1 John 5:7–8) to validate their doctrinal belief that the Father and the Son are different manifestations of the same being, others allowed their belief in the practice of asceticism to validate their distortion of scriptural texts to minimize the importance of marriage and family relationships.[27] *The Oxford Dictionary of the Christian Church* includes the following description of asceticism:

> In the early Christian centuries many ascetic practices seem to have become fairly widespread, the chief of them being renunciation of marriage, home, and property; some ascetics

practised extreme forms of fasting and self-deprivation. In the popular mind there seems to have been an association between the abandonment of human comforts and the acquisition of miraculous powers.[28]

While some biblical texts that challenge allegiance to marriage and family can be understood in terms of not allowing our love of family to take precedence over our love of God (doing so would be a form of idolatry), other scriptural passages encourage the idea that to truly worship God we must be hostile towards our family, or at least acknowledge that devotion to family is a weaker form of discipleship. The contrast between Matthew 10:37 and Luke 14:26 illustrates the difference between loving God and disparaging family:

He that loveth father or mother more than me is not worthy of me: and he that loveth son or daughter more than me is not worthy of me. (Matthew 10:37)

If any man come to me, and hate not his father, and mother, and wife, and children, and brethren, and sisters, yea, and his own life also, he cannot be my disciple. (Luke 14:26)

The qualifications of discipleship do not include the idea that we must "hate" members of our family, but they do include putting the Savior before anything or anyone else in our lives (see Matthew 10:37). It is apparent from the textual changes in the Joseph Smith Translation of Luke 14:26 that Joseph Smith was not comfortable with the traditional text found in the King James Version. In addition to adding the word "husband" to the list of those whom the disciples of Christ should not allow to come before God in their lives, the JST also clarifies the text by adding, "*or in other words, is afraid to lay down his life for my sake,* cannot be my disciple" (Joseph Smith Translation, Luke 14:26; hereafter cited as JST).

Another example of the influence of asceticism on the early Christian church includes the practice of celibacy. Celibacy was understood by many in the early Christian church as a "higher choice" than marriage.[29] While marriage and family were seen as being a necessary condition to perpetuate humankind, those living the celibate life were understood to be living a higher law "in advance [of] the nuptial realities of heaven."[30] The philosophy of asceticism and the practice of celibacy are additional explanations for the text discussed earlier, that in "the resurrection from the dead" they "neither marry, nor are given in marriage" (Luke 20:35). Marriage was seen as a temporal necessity, but it would have no meaning in the world to come.

The Apostle Paul's writings include the words of a letter written to him which stated, "It is good for a man not to touch a woman" (1 Corinthians 7:1). Paul's words have been interpreted by some to justify the philosophy of asceticism. The writings of Paul, while acknowledging that he was speaking by "permission, and not of commandment" (1 Corinthians 7:6), record Paul as saying, "I would that all men were even as I myself" (1 Corinthians 7:7), which appears to be saying that he was single for a specific purpose, not that he believed the relationship between men and women to be inferior to those who were celibate. While the Joseph Smith Translation clarifies that the text of 1 Corinthians 7 was written to those "who are called unto the ministry" (JST, 1 Corinthians 7:29) to remain unmarried for a time, other translations of this text have been interpreted by some to justify lifelong celibacy.[31]

In a revelation given through the Prophet Joseph Smith concerning the practice of celibacy among the early sect known as the Shakers, the Lord taught, "Whoso forbiddeth to marry is not ordained of God, for marriage is ordained of God unto man" (D&C 49:15). President Joseph Fielding Smith explained, "This statement in relation to marriage was given to correct the false doctrine of the Shakers that marriage was impure and that a true follower of Jesus Christ must remain in the condition of celibacy to be free from sin and in full fellowship with Christ."[32]

Why Are Eternal Family Relationships So Important in God's Purposes?

For Latter-day Saints, the family (including marriage) and the Church offer two primary kinds of "sociality" (D&C 130:2), which are a part of the Lord's "work and glory—to bring to pass the immortality and eternal life of man" (Moses 1:39). The Church, however, is second to the family in God's plan for the salvation of his children. Elder M. Russell Ballard taught, "The Church ... is the scaffolding that helps support and strengthen the family."[33] President Boyd K. Packer explained further:

Every law and principle and power, every belief, every ordinance and ordination, every covenant, every sermon and every sacrament, every counsel and correction, the sealings, the calls, the releases, the service—all these have as their ultimate purpose the perfection of the individual and the family.[34]

The only influence more central to the justification, sanctification, and the exaltation of humankind than the family is the Lord Jesus Christ and his atoning sacrifice. Families, as imperfect at they are, have great power to bless. President Packer taught, "Even a rickety marriage will serve good purpose as long as two people struggle to keep it from falling down around them."[35] The Apostle Paul counseled, "The unbelieving husband is sanctified by the wife, and the unbelieving wife is sanctified by the husband," and through them the children are made holy (1 Corinthians 7:14). Philosopher Michael Novak described the sanctifying power of marriage and family relationships as follows:

Marriage is an assault upon the lonely, atomic ego. Marriage is a threat to the solitary individual. Marriage does impose grueling, bumbling, baffling, and frustrating responsibilities. Yet if one supposes that precisely such things are the preconditions for all true liberation, marriage is not the enemy of moral development in adults. Quite the opposite. . . . Being married and having children has impressed on my mind certain lessons, for whose learning I cannot help being grateful. Most are lessons of difficulty and duress. Most of what I am forced to learn about myself is not pleasant. . . . Seeing myself through the unblinking eyes of an intimate, intelligent other, an honest spouse, is humiliating beyond anticipation. Maintaining a familial steadiness whatever the state of my own emotions is a standard by which I stand daily condemned. A rational man, acting as I act? . . . My dignity as a human being depends more on what sort of husband and parent I am, than on any professional work I am called upon to do. My bonds to them hold me back (and my wife even more) from many sorts of opportunities. And yet these do not feel like bonds. They are, I know, my liberation.

They force me to be a different sort of human being, in a way in which I want and need to be forced.[36]

While stable marriage and family relationships are vital to the temporal progress of humankind, the doctrines of *eternal* marriage and *eternal* family include an additional principle that is unique to the restored gospel. Not only can marital and familial relationships continue beyond the grave, but also couples, as resurrected beings, can "have an increase" (D&C 131:4), or, as the Lord described to the Prophet Joseph Smith, husbands and wives may have "a continuation of the seeds" in the world to come:

> And again, verily I say unto you, if a man marry a wife by my word, which is my law, and by the new and everlasting covenant, and it is sealed unto them by the Holy Spirit of promise, by him who is anointed, unto whom I have appointed this power and the keys of this priesthood; and it shall be said unto them—Ye shall come forth in the first resurrection; and if it be after the first resurrection, in the next resurrection; and shall inherit thrones, kingdoms, principalities, and powers, dominions, all heights and depths—then shall it be written in the Lamb's Book of Life. . . . And they shall pass by the angels, and the gods, which are set there, to their exaltation and glory in all things, as hath been sealed upon their heads, which glory shall be a fulness and a continuation of the seeds forever and ever. (D&C 132:19)

Elder Melvin J. Ballard taught the principle of eternal increase in this way:

> What do we mean by endless or eternal increase? We mean that through the righteousness and faithfulness of men and women who keep the commandments of God they will come forth with celestial bodies, fitted and prepared to enter into their great, high and eternal glory in the celestial kingdom of God; and unto them, through their preparation, there will come spirit children.[37]

The doctrines of eternal marriage and eternal families provide a unique perspective on the same-sex marriage debate. Just as procreation through heterosexual union is one of the major purposes of marriage between a man and woman in mortality, the same is true in the life to come. The following statement from "The Family: A Proclamation to the World" has eternal as well as temporal implications: "Marriage between man and woman is essential to His eternal plan."[38]

Why Must Marriage Be between a Man and a Woman?

The first principle taught in "The Family: A Proclamation to the World" is that "marriage between a man and a woman is ordained of God."[39] This statement is consistent with the words of the Apostle Paul when he concluded, "Nevertheless neither is the man without the woman, neither the woman without the man, in the Lord" (1 Corinthians 11:11). This applies not only to mortals but also to the Divine. Although the doctrine is not fully understood, it is a part of Latter-day Saint theology to affirm the existence of a Divine Feminine, a Mother in Heaven.[40] Elder Erastus Snow taught:

> "What," says one, "do you mean we should understand that Deity consists of man and woman?" Most certainly I do. If I believe anything that God has ever said about himself . . . I must believe that deity consists of man and woman. . . . There can be no God except he is composed of the man and woman united, and there is not in all the eternities that exist, or ever will be, a God in any other way.[41]

More recently, Elder Dallin H. Oaks of the Quorum of the Twelve Apostles taught, "Our theology begins with heavenly parents. Our highest aspiration is to be like them."[42]

While arguments for and against gender stereotypes are common (i.e., *Men Are from Mars* and *Women Are from Venus*),[43] the doctrinal reality is that "the nature of male and female spirits is such that they complete each other."[44] While it is also true that "our claims for the role of marriage and family," and the specific roles of men and women, "rest not on social science but on the truth that they are God's creation,"[45] a sampling of research studies that address these issues is worth noting.

It is beyond the purpose of this chapter to provide a comprehensive discussion of the findings from social science research concerning the importance of marriage and family relationships, but there are many research findings that are consistent with the teachings of prophets both ancient and modern. The following statements are a representative sample of conclusions supported by respected research in the field of marriage and family:

- Marriage increases the likelihood that fathers and mothers have good relationships with their children. . . .
- Children are most likely to experience family stability when they are born into a married family. . . .
- Growing up outside an intact marriage increases the likelihood that children will themselves divorce or become unwed parents. . . .
- Children who live with their own two married parents enjoy better physical health, on average, than do children in other family forms. . . .
- Marriage is associated with better health and lower rates of injury, illness, and disability for both men and women. . . .
- Children whose parents divorce have higher rates of psychological distress and mental illness. . . .
- Cohabitation is associated with higher levels of psychological problems among children. . . .
- Family breakdown appears significantly to increase the risk of suicide. . . .
- Married mothers have lower rates of depression than do single or cohabiting mothers.[46]

These conclusions are supported by the research of many scholars, including professors W. Bradford Wilcox, William Doherty, John Gottman, David Popenoe, Linda Waite, and Judith Wallerstein.

This research, however, is not without its critics. For the studies that conclude that divorce is detrimental to children, there are others that argue the opposite. When the conclusions of one study state that children raised by homosexual parents are disadvantaged, the conclusions of other studies are contradictory and call those findings into question.[47] The reality that there

264 Daniel K Judd and Jacob D. Judd

is so much controversy in the social sciences regarding these topics underscores the need for an epistemology that includes revelatory and prophetic guidance. President Hugh B. Brown made the following comment concerning the place of academic research in relationship to prophetic revelation:

> The Church of Jesus Christ of Latter-day Saints accepts newly revealed truth, whether it comes through direct revelation or from study and research. We deny the common conception of reality that distinguishes radically between the natural and the supernatural, between the temporal and the eternal, between the sacred and the secular.[48]

Elder Packer taught that there is, however, a prioritization between the sacred and the secular:

> It is an easy thing for a man with extensive academic training to measure the Church using the principles he has been taught in his professional training as his standard. In my mind it ought to be the other way around. A member of the Church ought always, particularly if he is pursuing extensive academic studies, to judge the professions of man against the revealed word of the Lord.[49]

While heterosexual marriage is the standard the Lord and his servants have established for procreating and nurturing children, they have also taught that animosity towards those who embrace or practice homosexuality, or any other lifestyle that is not in harmony with the Savior and his servants' teachings has no place in the restored gospel. After receiving a petition from the Human Rights Campaign to change its stance on same-sex attraction, leaders of the Church issued the following statement:

> As a church, our doctrinal position is clear: any sexual activity outside of marriage is wrong, and we define marriage as between a man and a woman. However, that should never, ever be used as justification for unkindness. Jesus Christ, whom we follow, was clear in His condemnation of sexual immorality, but never cruel. His interest was always to lift the individual, never to tear down.[50]

"The Family: A Proclamation to the World" warns that those who "abuse spouse or offspring, or who fail to fulfill family responsibilities will one day stand accountable before God."[51] To abuse someone physically or emotionally because of their sexual orientation or other alternative lifestyle is immoral and is not in harmony with the teachings of Jesus Christ.

The scriptures teach that Zion can only be reached as its inhabitants are "of one heart and one mind, and [dwell] in righteousness; and there [are] no poor among them" (Moses 7:18). While often thought of in terms of monetary resources, "no poor among them" could also be understood in terms of family. There are those in the Church who are "family rich" and those that are "family poor." In other words, there are families who fit the definitions described in the Family Proclamation and families who do not. Those who are blessed to participate in a family where "husband and wife . . . love and care for each other and for their children"[52] have a responsibility to reach out and share with those who do not. As members of the Church strive to become "of one heart and one mind," divisions created by socioeconomic or familial inequalities can be identified and resolved. While scientific research and vigorous debate can certainly assist in such resolutions, following the revealed will of God, as provided by his ordained servants, is what will ultimately create a Zion people and culture.

Conclusion

Marriage between a man and a woman and the family they procreate has been the Lord's standard of marital and familial structure from the beginning. In Genesis we read: "Therefore shall a man leave his father and his mother, and shall cleave unto his wife: and they shall be one flesh" (Genesis 2:24). The same standard was repeated by the Lord to Joseph Smith in 1831: "Wherefore, it is lawful that he should have one wife, and they twain shall be one flesh, and all this that the earth might answer the end of its creation" (D&C 49:16). The practice of marriage was formally modified for a season with the introduction of plural marriage in 1841 (see D&C 132), but marriage then, as it is now, was a means to an end—the immortality and eternal life of Heavenly Father's children (see Moses 1:39). Unlike the arguments of those who contend for relationships contrary to the Lord's plan for the destiny of his children, marriage as defined by God is for much more than meeting the personal pleasures and needs of those involved. Instead, as Elder Robert D. Hales of the Quorum of the Twelve Apostles has taught, "dating and marriage aren't final destinations. They are the gateway to where you ultimately want to go."[53] As outlined by the Lord's servants, the ultimate destination for individuals and families is eternal life with God and the opportunity to become like him. Such is the purpose of marriage and family, and any aberration from that purpose brings with it the warnings outlined by prophets both ancient and modern. The unique doctrines of eternal marriage and eternal families clearly articulate that marriage has a temporal and an eternal purpose.

Notes

1.   The Supreme Court of the United States of America ruled in favor of same-sex marriage on 26 June 2015.

2.   Bruce R. McConkie, *A New Witness for the Articles of Faith* (Salt Lake City: Deseret Book, 1985), 322.

3.   Simon Baker, as cited in *The Words of Joseph Smith,* ed. Andrew F. Ehat and Lyndon W. Cook (Provo, UT: Religious Studies Center, 1980), 49.

4.   Alexander L. Baugh, "'For This Ordinance Belongeth to My House': The Practice of Baptism for the Dead Outside the Nauvoo Temple," *Mormon Historical Studies,* no. 1 (Spring 2002): 48. In the early days of the Church, people were baptized for individuals regardless of gender, but now females act as proxies for females, and males only for males. See *Journal of Discourses* (London: Latter-day Saints' Book Depot, 1854–86), 5:85.

5.   Susan Easton Black, "'A Voice of Gladness for the Living and the Dead' (D&C 128:19)," *Religious Educator* 3, no. 2 (2002): 143–44.

6.   "Plural Marriage in Kirtland and Nauvoo." LDS.org essay, https://www.lds .org/topics/plural-marriage-in-kirtland-and-nauvoo?lang=eng.

7.   "Family Structures," in *Encyclopedia of American Social History,* ed. Mary K. Cayton, Elliott J. Gorn, and Peter W. Williams (New York: Charles Scribner's Sons, 1993), 3:1935.

8.   See Henry B. Eyring, "Families Can Be Together Forever," *Ensign,* June 2015, 4.

9.   Michael Hubbard MacKay, Gerrit J. Dirkmaat, Grant Underwood, Robert J. Woodford, and William G. Hartley, eds., *Documents, Volume 1: July 1828–June 1831,* vol. 1 of the Documents series of *The Joseph Smith Papers,* ed. Dean C. Jessee, Ronald K. Esplin, Richard Lyman Bushman, and Matthew J. Grow (Salt Lake City: Church Historian's Press, 2013), 16.

10.   Karen Lynn Davidson, David J. Whittaker, Mark Ashurst-McGee, and Richard L. Jensen, eds., *Histories, Volume 1: Joseph Smith Histories, 1832–1844,* vol. 1 of the Histories series of *The Joseph Smith Papers,* ed. Dean C. Jessee, Ronald K. Esplin, and Richard Lyman Bushman (Salt Lake City: Church Historian's Press, 2012), 656.

11. Lawrence Foster, *Religion and Sexuality: The Shakers, the Mormons, and the Oneida Community* (Urbana and Chicago: University of Illinois Press, 1984), 136.

12. Doctrine and Covenants, 1835 edition, Section CI (101), verse 2; emphasis added, http://josephsmithpapers.org/paperSummary/doctrine-and-covenants-1835.

13. *The Book of Common Prayer, and Administration of the Sacraments, and Other Rites and Ceremonies of the Church, According to the Use of the United Church of England and Ireland,* (London: George Eyre and Andrew Strahan, 1820). 353.

14. *Autobiography of Parley P. Pratt,* ed. Parley P. Pratt Jr. (Salt Lake City: Deseret Book, 1938/1985), 259–60.

15. Joseph Fielding Smith, *Doctrines of Salvation,* comp. Bruce R. McConkie (Salt Lake City: Bookcraft, 1976), 2:118, emphasis in original.

16. "The Family: A Proclamation to the World," *Ensign,* November 2010, 129.

17. R. T. France, *The Gospel of Mark: A Commentary on the Greek Text* (Grand Rapids, MI: Erdmans, 2002), 472; emphasis in original.

18. Eldred G. Smith, "Do Not Procrastinate," *Ensign,* November 1974, 25–26, emphasis added.

19. Bruce R. McConkie, *Doctrinal New Testament Commentary* (Salt Lake City: Deseret Book, 1975), 1:606.

20. Brigham Young, in *Journal of Discourses* (London: Latter-day Saints' Book Depot, 1865), 10:324.

21. John Meyendorff, *Marriage: An Orthodox Perspective* (St. Vladimir's Crestwood, NY: St. Vladimir's Seminary Press, 1975), 69.

22. Emmanuel Swedenborg, *Heaven and Hell,* trans. G. F. Dole (New York: Swedenborg Foundation, 1990), 285.

23. Joseph Smith, History, 1838–1856, vol. A-1, created 11 June 1839–24 Aug. 1843, http://josephsmithpapers.org/paperSummary/history-1838-1856-volume-a-1-23-december-1805-30-august-1834.

24. Origen, *Commentary on Matthew 15:14,* in Bruce Metzger and Bart D. Ehrman, *The Text of the New Testament: Its Transmission, Corruption, and Restoration,* 4th ed. (New York: Oxford University Press, 2005), 200.

25. Bart D. Ehrman, *Misquoting Jesus: The Story Behind Who Changed the Bible and Why* (New York: Harper Collins, 2005), 210.

26. Bruce M. Metzger and Bart D. Ehrman, *The Text of the New Testament: Its Transmission, Corruption, and Restoration,* 4th ed. (New York: Oxford University Press, 2005), 268.

27. See Ehrman, *Misquoting Jesus: The Story Behind Who Changed the Bible and Why,* 81–82.

28. F. L. Cross and E. A. Livingstone, eds., *The Oxford Dictionary of the Christian Church,* 3rd ed. rev. (Oxford: Oxford University Press, 2005), 114.

29. Elizabeth A. Clark, *Reading Renunciation: Asceticism and Scripture in Early Christianity* (Princeton: Princeton University Press, 1999), 144.

30. Patricia Snow, "Dismantling the Cross," *First Things,* April 2015, 34.

31. Will Deming, *Paul on Marriage & Celibacy: The Hellenistic Background of 1 Corinthians 7,* 2nd ed. (Grand Rapids, MI: Wm. B. Eerdmans, 2004), 107–27.

32. Joseph Fielding Smith, *Church History and Modern Revelation* (Salt Lake City: Deseret Book, 1953), 1:209.

33. M. Russell Ballard, "Feasting at the Lord's Table," *Ensign*, May 1996, 81.

34. Boyd K. Packer, "The Power of the Priesthood," *Ensign*, May 2010, 9.

35. Boyd K. Packer, "Marriage," *Ensign*, May 1981, 14.

36. Michael Novak, "The Family Out of Favor," *Harper's Magazine*, April 1976, 39, 41.

37. *Melvin J. Ballard—Crusader for Righteousness*, ed. M. Russell Ballard (Salt Lake City: Bookcraft, 1966), 211.

38. "The Family: A Proclamation to the World," 129.

39. "The Family: A Proclamation to the World," 129.

40. David L. Paulsen and Martin Pulido, "'A Mother There': A Survey of Historical Teachings about Mother in Heaven," *BYU Studies* 50, no. 1 (2011): 70–97.

41. Erastus Snow, in *Journal of Discourses* (London: Latter-day Saints' Book Depot, 1865), 19:269–70.

42. Dallin H. Oaks, "Apostasy and Restoration," in Conference Report, April 1–2, 1995.

43. Julia T. Wood, "A Critical Response to John Gray's Mars and Venus Portrayals of Men and Women," *Southern Communication Journal* 67, no. 2 (2002): 201–10.

44. The Church of Jesus Christ of Latter-day Saints, *Handbook 2: Administering the Church* (2010), 1.3.1.

45. D. Todd Christofferson, "Why Marriage, Why Family," *Ensign*, May 2015, 50–53.

46. W. Bradford Wilcox, *Why Marriage Matters, Third Edition: Thirty Conclusions from the Social Sciences* (New York: Institute for American Values, 2011), 14–15, 28, 31, 33, 35–36.

47. Loren Marks, "Same-Sex Parenting and Children's Outcomes: A Closer Examination of the American Psychological Association's Brief on Lesbian and Gay Parenting," *Social Science Research* 41, no. 4 (2012): 735–51.

48. Hugh B. Brown, "They Call for New Light," in Conference Report, April 1964, 81–82.

49. Boyd K. Packer, "The Mantle is Far, Far Greater Than the Intellect," Fifth Annual CES Symposium on the Doctrine and Covenants and Church History, August 22, 1981, 1.

50. "Church Responds to HRC Petition: Statement on Same-Sex Attraction," 12 October 2010, http://www.mormonnewsroom.org/article/church -mormon-responds-to-human-rights-campaign-petition-same-sex-attraction.

51. "The Family: A Proclamation to the World," 129.

52. "The Family: A Proclamation to the World," 129.

14

What Is a Temple?

FULFILLMENT OF THE COVENANT PURPOSES

Richard O. Cowan

Richard O. Cowan is a professor emeritus of
Church history and doctrine, Brigham Young University.

The Latter-day Saints have become known as a temple-building people. Their understanding of the nature and unique mission of these sacred structures unfolded over the years. Hence, if they were asked at different times what a temple was, their answers would have likely been different. Elder James E. Talmage pointed out that "while the general purpose of temples is the same in all times," there is still "a definite sequence of development in the dealings of God with man." Therefore, "we may affirm that direct revelation of temple plans is required for each distinctive period of the Priesthood's administration." Consequently, Elder Talmage concluded that the temple buildings themselves are a tangible record of God's unfolding revelations to his people concerning temple work.[1] This chapter will show how revelation guided the designing of latter-day temples, what the facilities of individual temples were designed to accommodate, how they were used, and how all these changes reflected the Saints' unfolding understanding of the nature of temples.

In former dispensations, temples served two distinct functions. First, the Lord promised to reveal himself to his people in the portable tabernacle (see Exodus 25:8, 22). Second, ancient temples were also where the people performed sacred priesthood ceremonies or ordinances such as sacrificial offerings (see D&C 124:38).

Both of these functions needed to be restored as part of the latter-day "restitution of all things" (Acts 3:21), but this restoration did not come all at once. The Lord had declared that he would "give unto the children of men line upon line, and precept upon precept, here a little and there a little" (2 Nephi 28:30; Isaiah 28:10). This principle was clearly reflected in the unfolding revelation of temple service in the present dispensation and the consequent design of early Latter-day Saint temples.

Restoration of Temple Worship Beginning at Kirtland

The first specific information about building a latter-day temple came in July of 1831 when the Prophet Joseph Smith learned that one was to be located at Independence, Missouri (see D&C 57:1–3). He placed a cornerstone there early the next month, but the next step in temple building would come a year and a half later in Ohio rather than in Missouri.[2]

The Saints received their first real glimpse into the nature of temple service in connection with instructions concerning the School of the Prophets. Near the end of 1832, the Lord directed the brethren at Kirtland to build a "house" for this school (D&C 88:119). Only the worthy were to attend. "He that is found unworthy," the Lord instructed, "shall not have place among you; for ye shall not suffer that mine house shall be polluted by him" (D&C 88:134; compare 97:15–17). Later, those who participated in the school were required to observe the Word of Wisdom and agreed not to divulge the sacred matters discussed there.[3] These requirements clearly anticipated practices that would later be associated with temple worship.

Further insights came by revelation the following June, when the Lord admonished the Kirtland Saints to move forward with the building of his house in which, he declared, "I design to endow those whom I have chosen with power from on high" (D&C 95:8). Historian David J. Howlett observed that receiving such a spiritual manifestation represented one Mormon response to the yearning of millennial or perfectionist evangelicals, who after

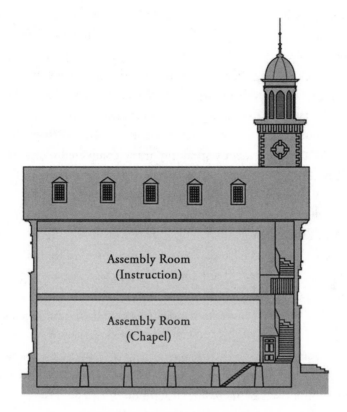

Kirtland Temple (1836)

their conversion wondered "if there were not more of God's powerful grace yet to be experienced."[4] The revelation instructed that the house should not be built "after the manner of the world," but according to a pattern which would be made known to three brethren whom the Saints would appoint. Specifically, the temple's "inner court" (main interior space) would have two levels. The main floor would be a chapel where the Saints might fast, pray, and partake of the sacrament. The second floor was to have another large room to serve as a school for those called into the Lord's service (see D&C 95:8, 13–17). Hence, the main spaces in the Kirtland Temple were intended for activities which were about the same as what was typically taking place in most church buildings of the time.

A conference of high priests met two days later to consider building the temple. In accordance with the Lord's instructions, they appointed three men, the recently formed First Presidency, "to create a draft or construction" of the temple. Truman O. Angell, later one of the supervisors of temple construction, explained how the Lord impressively fulfilled his promise to show the building's design. On an occasion when the presidency knelt in prayer, the building appeared before them in vision. "After we had taken a good look at the exterior," Frederick G. Williams (the second counselor) testified, "The building seemed to come right over us." This let them also view its interior. While subsequently speaking in the completed temple, President Williams affirmed that the hall in which they were convened coincided in every detail with the vision given to the Prophet.[5]

"Joseph not only received revelation and commandment to build a Temple," President Brigham Young later affirmed, "but he received a *pattern* also, as did Moses for the Tabernacle, and Solomon for his Temple; for without a pattern, he could not know what was wanting, having never seen [a temple], and not having experienced its use."[6] Elder Orson Pratt similarly testified, "When the Lord commanded this people to build a house in the land of Kirtland, in the early rise of this church, he gave them the pattern by vision from heaven, and commanded them to build that house according to that pattern and order; to have the architecture, not in accordance with architecture devised by men, but to have every thing constructed in that house according to the heavenly pattern that he by his voice had inspired to his servants."[7]

In the light of this revealed "pattern" concerning Kirtland, the brethren promptly began developing plans for a similar but larger building for Independence, Missouri. They prepared a series of sketches as planning progressed. Even though the initial drawings were superseded, they were not thrown away because paper was scarce. (Over a century later, some of these preliminary sketches would be rediscovered as backing to which papyrus fragments had been glued for preservation.) Even these early drawings for the temple in Zion depicted features that would characterize the Kirtland Temple: the unique series of pulpits at each end of the main halls and box pews with reversible seating.

On 25 June 1833, Joseph Smith sent his plat for the city of Zion together with plans for the "House of the Lord for the Presidency" to the brethren in Missouri. This plan set forth the pattern of wide streets crossing at right angles, which would in later decades become a familiar and welcome characteristic of Mormon settlements. There were to be twenty-four "temples" at the center of the city assigned to the various priesthood quorums. The Prophet anticipated that these twenty-four buildings would be needed to serve a variety of functions such as meetinghouses, places of worship, and schools. Because all inhabitants of the city would be expected to live on a celestial level (see D&C 105:5), all these buildings would fit the first function of temples—places of communication between heaven and earth.

A revelation received in August 1833 spoke of a similar but smaller complex of sacred buildings in the heart of Kirtland. It included the Lord's house, another building "for the work of the presidency, in obtaining revelations," and a third for printing the scriptures. These structures were to be of uniform size and, like the temple, were to be kept "holy" and "undefiled" (see D&C 94:1–12).[8]

Even though the Kirtland Temple's exterior may have looked something like the New England meetinghouses of the time, it was the revealed design of the interior that made the building truly unique. Typically, the two rows of windows on a church illuminated the main floor and balcony of a single large hall. In Kirtland, however, these windows were for the two main rooms, one above the other. Four levels of pulpits at both ends of these auditoriums were the unique feature of the Kirtland Temple. Block wooden initials on these pulpits helped Church members to understand the relative authority of various priesthood leaders, with Melchizedek at the west and Aaronic at the east.[9] Seating in the main part of the hall was reversible so the congregation could face either set of pulpits. Painted canvas partitions, or "veils," could be rolled down from the ceiling to divide the room into four quarters, enabling a separate meeting to be conducted in each area.

When the temple was completed, sacrament and other worship meetings convened in the large hall on the ground floor. The School of the Prophets and other instructional meetings were held on the second floor. Priesthood groups and leaders often met in the five small rooms on the attic floor which also served as classrooms. Thus, because the temple was the only church building in Kirtland, it was essentially a meetinghouse accommodating a variety of other functions, but there were no facilities particularly designed for ordinances. Specifically, Brigham Young later pointed out that the Kirtland Temple "had no basement in it, nor a font, nor preparations to give endowments for the living or the dead."[10]

Still, remarkable spiritual experiences during early 1836 confirmed that the Lord accepted the temple. On 21 January, Joseph Smith received the vision of the celestial kingdom in which he learned that "all who have died without a knowledge of this gospel, who would have received it if they had been permitted to tarry, shall be heirs of the celestial kingdom of God" (D&C 137:7). Even though sacred ordinances for the dead were not specifically mentioned on this occasion, this revelation did lay the doctrinal foundation for the work to which temples ultimately would be devoted.

These pentecostal experiences climaxed with the dedication of the temple on 27 March 1836. The dedicatory prayer, which had been given to the Prophet by revelation, petitioned that the Lord would accept the temple which had been built "through great tribulation . . . that the Son of Man might have a place to manifest himself to his people" (D&C 109:5). Specifically, the Prophet prayed that God's "holy presence [might] be continually in this house," and that all who enter might "feel [his] power, and feel constrained to acknowledge that [he] has sanctified it, and that it is [his] house, a place of [his] holiness" (D&C 109:12–13). The prayer then acknowledged that the Lord's servants would go forth from the temple armed with power and testimony (see D&C 109:22–23). One week later, on 3 April, the Savior appeared to accept the temple, and the ancient prophets Moses, Elias, and Elijah restored keys of authority (see D&C 110).

Hence, the Lord's house in Kirtland fulfilled the first main function of temples: To be a place of revelation from God to man. "The prime purpose in having such a temple," Elder Harold B. Lee explained, "seems to have been that there could be restored the keys, the effective keys necessary for the carrying on of the Lord's work." He concluded that the events of 3 April 1836 were "sufficient justification for the building of [this] temple."[11]

Not long after such glorious experiences had lifted the Saints, however, the forces of apostasy and persecution increased. In less than two years, the faithful were compelled to flee from their homes and temple in Ohio. Most settled at Far West in northern Missouri. Here, the Lord once again commanded the Church to "build a house unto me, for the gathering together of my saints, that they may worship me." Ordinances were not mentioned; they were still yet to be revealed. As at Kirtland, the temple was to be built according to a "pattern" which the Lord would show (see D&C 115:8–10, 14).

As had been the case at Independence (about eighty miles further south), persecution would also prevent construction of this temple.

Sacred Ordinances and the Nauvoo Temple

Fleeing from their persecutors in Missouri, the Latter-day Saints settled in western Illinois at a place they named Nauvoo, a Hebrew word meaning "beautiful." Within two years, they began construction on yet another temple. Before this edifice was completed, sacred ceremonies or ordinances were restored which would be reflected in the temple's ultimate design.

Joseph Smith first taught the practice of vicarious baptisms for the dead on 15 August 1840.[12] Almost immediately, Church members began receiving this ordinance in the Mississippi River in behalf of deceased loved ones.

Another ordinance taught at Nauvoo was the endowment. Some practices in the Kirtland Temple had anticipated portions of the endowment, but the more complete form of this ordinance was first given to a group of selected brethren on 4 May 1842 in the assembly room on the second floor of Joseph Smith's red brick store in Nauvoo. Under the Prophet's direction, this room was partitioned into areas representing stages in man's progress back into the presence of God. Participants moved from one area to the next as the endowment instructions unfolded. Some historians note that several Latter-day Saints had become involved with Freemasonry and that this may have helped them appreciate the idea of a building designed for special teachings and rituals.[13]

Among the other blessings revealed during these years was marriage for eternity. In May 1843, the Prophet instructed the Saints that in order to attain the highest degree of the celestial kingdom, one must enter into this "new and everlasting covenant of marriage" (see D&C 131:1–4). Two months later, he recorded a revelation outlining the great blessings promised to faithful recipients of this ordinance (see D&C 132:7–19).

The Nauvoo Temple followed the basic concept of the Lord's house in Kirtland, having two large auditoriums for general meetings. Still, reflecting the Saints' growing knowledge about sacred priesthood ordinances, the temple would also include spaces for administering them. Early in August 1840, the First Presidency declared, "The time has now come, when it is

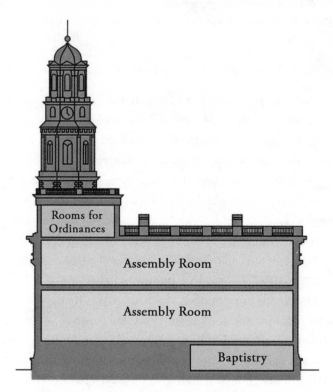

Rooms for
Ordinances

Assembly Room

Assembly Room

Baptistry

Nauvoo Temple (1845)

necessary to erect a house of prayer, a house of order, a house for the worship of our God, where *the ordinances can be attended to agreeably to His divine will.*"[14] A revelation received on 19 January 1841, directed Latter-day Saints to gather precious materials from afar and build a house "for the Most High to dwell therein. For there is not a place found on earth that he may come to and restore again that which was lost unto you, or which he hath taken away, even the fullness of the priesthood." The revelation also insisted that ordinances such as baptisms for the dead belong in the temple, so Joseph directed the Saints to provide a font there (see D&C 124:25–30). Hence, the Nauvoo sanctuary was to serve both functions of temples—being a place of contact between God and man and also a place where sacred priesthood ordinances could be performed.

As had been the case in Kirtland, Joseph Smith insisted that the basic plan of the Nauvoo Temple was a result of revelation. When architect William Weeks questioned the appropriateness of placing round windows on the side of the building, for example, Joseph explained that the small rooms in the temple could be illuminated with one light at the center of each of these windows and that "when the whole building was thus illuminated, the effect would be remarkably grand. "I wish you to carry out *my* designs. I have seen in vision the splendid appearance of that building illuminated, and will have it built according to the pattern shown me."[15] The temple's two large meeting halls had high, arched ceilings, leaving space for a row of small rooms between the arch and the outside walls, each room having one of the round windows. The temple also would include a baptismal font in the basement and facilities for the other sacred ordinances on the attic level.

In November 1841, only seven months after temple cornerstones had been laid, a font in the basement was covered by a temporary enclosure, and the members commenced performing baptisms for the dead there. In coming months, the Prophet and Apostles frequently officiated personally in the font. As the lower assembly hall was completed, conferences and other meetings were held there. A visitor to the Nauvoo Temple just after the Saints had left referred to this auditorium as the "grand hall for the assemblage and worship of the people."[16] As had been the case in Kirtland, there were pulpits at each end of the room representing various offices in the priesthood. Reversible seating again enabled the congregation to face either end of the hall.

The Nauvoo Temple's exterior had some unique features. These included thirty pilasters containing symbolic ornamental stones. The base of each pilaster was a large stone depicting the crescent moon. Each capital featured the sun's face. In the cornice above each pilaster was a five-pointed star. Among other things, these stones may have reminded the Saints that there are three degrees of glory and that faithfully receiving the ordinances of the temple is essential to attaining the highest exaltation in heaven.

As Joseph entered the final months of his life, he exhibited an increasing urgency to make temple blessings available to the Saints. His martyrdom on 27 June 1844 caused only a temporary lull in temple construction. The Saints knew they would soon be forced to leave Nauvoo and lose access to the temple; yet amid preparations for their exodus, the Saints were willing to expend approximately one million dollars to fulfill their Prophet's plans of erecting the "House of the Lord," where they could receive its sacred blessings.

Specific areas in the temple were completed and dedicated piecemeal so that ordinance work could begin as soon as possible. On 30 November 1845, Brigham Young and twenty others who had received their endowment from Joseph Smith in 1842 gathered to dedicate the attic story for ordinance work. As they had done in the red brick store, they divided the central hall with temporary partitions into separate areas representing distinct stages in man's eternal progress. The east end had a large Gothic window and was furnished with fine carpets and wall hangings. This most beautiful area represented the celestial kingdom. When Joseph Fielding entered this part of the temple for the first time, he felt as though he had truly "gotten out of the World."[17] Flanking each side of the central hall were six rooms, about fourteen feet square, which served as private offices for Church leaders, as places where priesthood quorums could gather for prayer, or for the initiatory ordinances connected with the endowment. Some of these side rooms contained altars at which sacred sealing ordinances were received.

Endowments were given beginning on 10 December. The number of Saints entering the temple increased as their exodus from Nauvoo drew closer. On 12 January, Brigham Young recorded, "Such has been the anxiety manifested by the saints to receive the ordinances [of the Temple], and such the anxiety on our part to administer to them, that I have given myself up entirely to the work of the Lord in the Temple night and day, not taking more than four hours sleep, upon an average, per day, and going home but once a week." Others of the Twelve were "in constant attendance," but had to leave the temple from time to time "to rest and recruit their health."[18] During the eight weeks prior to the exodus, approximately 5,500 were endowed, fulfilling Joseph Smith's compelling desire to make these blessings available to the Saints in Nauvoo.

Thus, in contrast to the Kirtland Temple, which was a building intended primarily for meetings of the Saints, the Nauvoo Temple was also a place for sacred ordinances, with spaces in the attic and basement devoted to that purpose. This understanding of the two buildings' different functions may have been reflected in how the Saints normally referred to them. Typically,

they called the structure in Kirtland "the Lord's House," and the building in Nauvoo a "temple." All forty references to Kirtland in the Doctrine
and Covenants used the word *house*, while 88 percent of the references to
Nauvoo used the word *temple*. In the *History of the Church*, 75 percent of the
references to Kirtland used the word *house*, and 93 percent of the references
to Nauvoo used the word *temple*. Even though a dictionary from that time
defined temple as "a public edifice erected in honor of some deity" or as "an
edifice erected among Christians as a place of public worship,"[19] the Latter-
day Saints in Nauvoo appear to have used it in a more specific sense.

Even though the Nauvoo Saints had learned that sacred ordinances were
a major purpose of the temple, the concept of it being a multifunction structure lingered. During the hectic time just before and following the exodus,
some of the Saints slept, ate, or tended babies in the unused small rooms on
the mezzanines above the two main halls. Some people even used the unfin-
ished second-floor auditorium for "dancing and recreation."[20] Concerned
about such irregularities, Elder Heber C. Kimball insisted that only persons
with official invitations be admitted to the temple. In this way he was able to
restore proper order. This foreshadowed the issuing of recommends to those
judged by local Church leaders to be worthy of temple attendance.

Temples in the Tops of the Mountains

After their historic exodus to the Rocky Mountains, the Latter-day Saints
continued to build temples. Within days of President Brigham Young's arrival
in the Salt Lake Valley in July 1847, he designated the site for the future temple, and Wilford Woodruff placed a stake in the ground to mark the spot.[21]

On 23 December 1847, an official circular letter from the Twelve invited
the Saints to gather and bring precious metals and other materials "for the
exaltation . . . of the living and the dead," for the time had come to build the
Lord's house "upon the tops of the mountains."[22] This reflected an expanded
understanding of temple function. Soon afterward, President Young named
Truman O. Angell Sr. as temple architect, a post he would hold until his
death in 1887.

Cornerstones for the Salt Lake Temple were laid on 6 April 1853. On
this occasion, President Young declared:

I scarcely ever say much about revelations, or visions, but suffice it to say, five years ago last July [1847] I was here, and saw in the Spirit the Temple not ten feet from where we have laid the Chief Corner Stone. I have not inquired what kind of a Temple we should build. Why? Because it was represented before me. I have never looked upon that ground, but the vision of it was there. I see it as plainly as if it was in reality before me. Wait until it is done. I will say, however, that it will have six towers, to begin with, instead of one. Now do not any of you apostatize because it will have six towers, and Joseph only built one. It is easier for us to build sixteen, than it was for him to build one. The time will come when there will be one in the centre of Temples we shall build, and on the top, groves and fish ponds. But we shall not see them here, at present.[23]

William Ward, Truman Angell's assistant, later recalled how the prophet Brigham shared his vision: "Brigham Young drew upon a slate in the architect's office a sketch, and said to Truman O. Angell: 'There will be three towers on the east, representing the President and his two counselors; also three similar towers on the west representing the Presiding Bishop and his two counselors; the towers on the east the Melchisedek priesthood, those on the west the Aaronic priesthood.'"[24]

Even though the Saints had learned that performing ordinances was an important temple function, the majority of the space in buildings designed during the pioneer period was still for general meetings. Angell's original plan called for the Salt Lake Temple's interior to follow the Kirtland and Nauvoo pattern, having two large halls for general meetings. A font as well as rooms for the endowment and sealings would all be confined to the basement.

Meanwhile, during the pioneers' early years in the Salt Lake Valley, temple blessings had already been given in various places outside of temples, including the top of Ensign Peak and Brigham Young's office. By 1852, endowments were being given in the Council House, located on the southwest corner of what are now South Temple and Main Streets. This facility also accommodated a variety of other ecclesiastical and civic functions, so a separate place was needed where the sacred temple ordinances could be given in a more secluded setting. The Endowment House, a two-story adobe structure dedicated in 1855 to serve as a temporary facility while the Salt Lake Temple was being completed, was located in the northwest corner of Temple Square. It was the first building to be designed exclusively for sacred ordinances and to have separate permanent rooms with murals painted on the walls to represent the different stages of man's progression back to God as discussed in the temple endowment.

As had been the case with Joseph Smith, Brigham Young demonstrated during the final years of his life a heightened drive to reemphasize temple service. In the St. George Temple, dedicated just a few months before President Young's death in 1877, members performed the first vicarious ordinations, endowments, and sealings of children to parents for the dead. Thus, Elder Bruce C. Hafen has suggested that the restoration of temple service was completed in three stages: Kirtland, Nauvoo, and St. George.[25]

Although temple functions were changing, Brigham Young and the architects were reluctant to deviate from the design established by Joseph Smith. Therefore, the St. George Temple, built during the 1870s, still followed closely the pattern of the Nauvoo Temple with two large meetings halls. When it opened, the plan was to conduct all ordinances except sealings in the basement. Thus, this arrangement did not follow the pattern of the Endowment House but was similar to that proposed a quarter of a century earlier for the Salt Lake Temple. Areas for the endowment were partitioned by temporary painted dividers called screens. Within a few weeks, however, temple leaders realized that the "ordinance rooms in the basement were not of sufficient size to accommodate the crowds that continued flocking to the temple." After "much discussion," they "determined to make greater use of the lower main assembly room [immediately] above the basement." At first, this entire hall represented the terrestrial kingdom, and the tower room behind the Melchizedek Priesthood pulpits represented the celestial. Soon afterwards, however, portions of the large hall were set off by screens to form the terrestrial and celestial rooms, rooms in the tower being used for sealings.

As endowments for the dead quickly became the activity occupying the most time in the temple, Church leaders felt the need to have facilities that would more adequately accommodate this function. That there would be variations in temple design had been made known to President Brigham

Salt Lake Temple

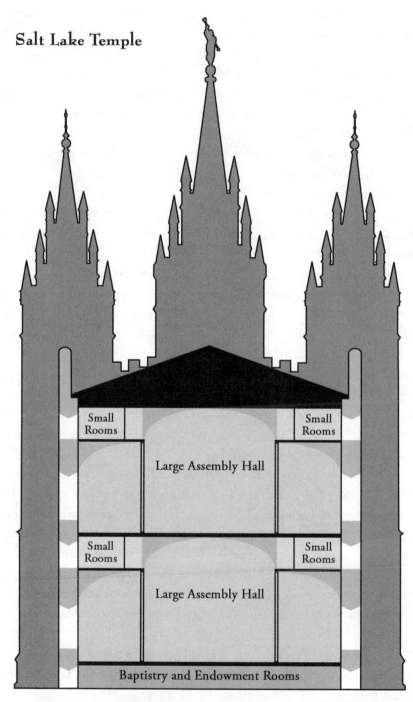

Small Rooms

Small Rooms

Large Assembly Hall

Small Rooms

Small Rooms

Large Assembly Hall

Baptistry and Endowment Rooms

Proposed Original Cross-Section

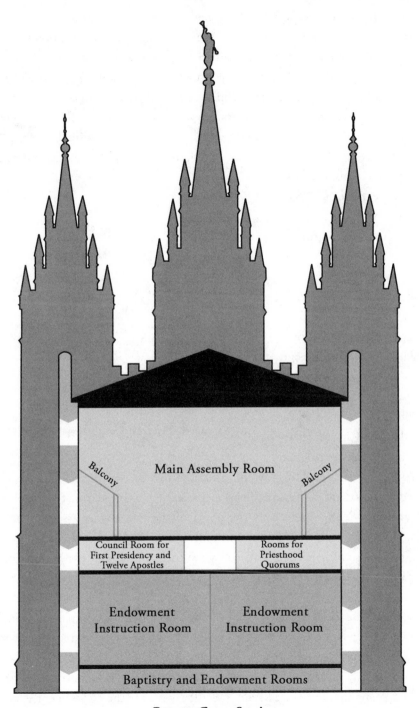

Balcony

Main Assembly Room

Balcony

Council Room for
First Presidency and
Twelve Apostles

Rooms for
Priesthood
Quorums

Endowment
Instruction Room

Endowment
Instruction Room

Baptistry and Endowment Rooms

Present Cross-Section

Young in St. George. "Oh Lord," he had prayed, "show unto thy servants if we shall build all temples after the same pattern." "Men do not build their homes the same when their families are large as when they are small," came the inspired response. "So shall the growth of the knowledge of the principles of the gospel among my people cause diversity in the pattern of temples."[28] Years earlier, at the time ground was broken for the Salt Lake Temple, President Young had taught that the order of priesthood ordinances is made known by revelation, and therefore we should know what facilities must be included in our temples.[27]

The pattern of separate ordinance rooms for the endowment, first seen in the Endowment House, would be reflected more fully in the Manti and Logan Temples. Architectural historian Paul Anderson believed that the basic designs for these two temples was "probably worked out in Salt Lake City under the supervision of Brigham Young."[28]

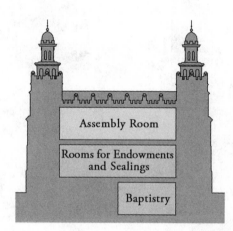

Logan and Manti Temples (1880s)

Both buildings would have two towers. The lower half of each temple was divided into specific rooms designed for presenting temple ordinances more effectively; only the upper of the two former assembly halls remained a space for general meetings. Hence these buildings represented a shift in designing temples to better serve their unique ordinance function, expanding this area from just the basement to the entire lower half of the structure.

The Salt Lake Temple's exterior walls were nearing completion in the mid-1880s when Church leaders considered changing the interior plan to match the concept adopted for Manti and Logan. Truman O. Angell Jr., who was assisting his elderly father in completing drawings for the Salt Lake Temple, pointed out that having specific rooms for the endowment would accommodate three hundred persons in a session—more than twice the number that could be served in the basement under the original arrange-ment. These changes were consistent with President Young's 1860 instruc-tions that the temple would not be designed for general meetings, but rather it would "be for the endowments—for the organization and instruction of the Priesthood."²⁹

While the focus has shifted from general meetings to performing ordi-nances, temples still fulfilled their first traditional function—being a place of revelation between God and man. An outstanding example was the Savior's appearance to President Lorenzo Snow in the large corridor just outside the celestial room of the Salt Lake Temple. President Snow later described what happened: "It was right here that the Lord Jesus Christ appeared to me at the time of the death of President Woodruff. He instructed me to go right ahead and reorganize the First Presidency of the Church at once and not wait as had been done after the death of the previous presidents, and that I was to succeed President Woodruff. . . . He stood right here, about three feet above the floor. It looked as though He stood on a plate of solid gold."³⁰

Because of its location near Church headquarters, the Salt Lake Temple also plays a unique and significant role in Church governance. An inter-mediate floor was added to this temple's design, with special rooms for the use of the General Authorities. Key decisions are made following prayerful consideration by the Council of the First Presidency and Quorum of the Twelve Apostles, who meet weekly in their council room on this floor. These decisions include such matters as ordaining and setting apart new Presidents of the Church, appointing other General Authorities, creating new mis-sions and stakes, and approving Church programs. Notable examples have included the 1952 decision to build temples overseas, the determination in 1976 to add sections 137 and 138 to the Doctrine and Covenants, and the 1978 revelation extending the priesthood to all worthy males (D&C: Official Declaration 2).

More Recent Temples

In the early twentieth century, the remaining plans for a large upper meet-ing hall were also omitted, beginning with the Hawaii Temple dedicated in 1919. Hence, temples had completed the transition from a multipur-pose structure designed primarily for general meetings, as at Kirtland, to

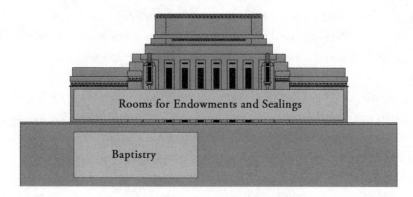

Hawaii Temple (1919)

buildings designed exclusively for sacred ordinances. Since that time, only the Los Angeles and Washington D.C. Temples, the second and third largest in the Church, would include the large upper solemn assembly hall.

Since the midpoint of the twentieth century, Church leaders have approved changes which have enabled temples to perform their ordinance function more efficiently. Beginning with the Swiss Temple, dedicated in 1955, films have facilitated the presentation of the endowment in diverse languages and in a smaller space. Increasing the number of presentation rooms to six at the Ogden and Provo Temples, dedicated in 1972, enabled endowment sessions to begin every twenty minutes. In 1997, at the Mormon colonies in northern Mexico, President Gordon B. Hinckley was inspired to formulate a plan for accommodating all temple functions in much smaller structures, making temple blessings increasingly available even to Saints in remote areas of the world.

Thus, the design of more than 150 temples stands as a tangible reminder of how temple service was restored line upon line. Because the recent spread of temples worldwide has made their sacred blessings accessible to an ever-growing number of Church members, the challenge for Latter-day Saints is to show their appreciation by entering these sacred houses, enriching their own lives, and making temple ordinances available to their kindred dead.

Notes

1. James E. Talmage, *The House of the Lord* (Salt Lake City: Bookcraft, 1962), 110–11.

2. Joseph Smith History, vol. A-1, 330, Church History Library.

3. Orlen C. Peterson, "A History of the Schools and Educational Programs of the Church . . . in Ohio and Missouri, 1831–1839" (master's thesis, BYU, 1972), 23–24.

4. David J. Howlett, *Kirtland Temple: The Biography of a Shared Mormon Sacred Space* (Urbana: University of Illinois Press, 2014), 17.

5. Marvin E. Smith, "The Builder," *Improvement Era*, October 1942, 630.

6. Brigham Young, in *Journal of Discourses* (Liverpool: Franklin D Richards, 855), 2:31, 6 April 1853; emphasis in original.

7. Orson Pratt, in *Journal of Discourses*, 14:273, 9 April 1871.

8. In the light of new information discovered in connection with the Joseph Smith Papers Project, the date of this revelation has been changed to 2 August 1833, beginning with the 2013 edition of the Doctrine and Covenants.

9. For a more complete discussion of the Kirtland Temple's pulpits and their relationship to the twenty-four temples in Zion, see Richard O. Cowan, "The House of the Lord in Kirtland: A Preliminary Temple," in *Regional Studies in Latter-day Saint Church History: Ohio* (Provo, UT: Department of Church History and Doctrine, Brigham Young University, 1990), 112–18.

10. Brigham Young, in *Journal of Discourses*, 1 January 1877, 18:303.

11. Harold B. Lee, "Correlation and Priesthood Genealogy," address at Priesthood Genealogical Research Seminar, 1968 (Provo, UT: BYU Press, 1969), 60, quoted in Cowan, *Temples to Dot the Earth* (Salt Lake City: Bookcraft, 1989), 33.

12. Obituary for Seymour Brunson, *Times and Seasons*, September 1840, 1:176.

13. For a discussion of this topic, see Michael W. Homer, *Joseph's Temples: The Dynamic Relationship between Free Masonry and Mormonism* (Salt Lake City: University of Utah Press, 2014).

14. Joseph Smith, History, 1838–1856, vol. C-1, Church History Library.

15. Joseph Smith, History, 1838–1856, vol. E-1, Church History Library; emphasis in original.

16. Quoted in E. Cecil McGavin, *The Nauvoo Temple* (Salt Lake City: Deseret Book, 1962), 92.

17. Andrew F. Ehat, ed., "'They Might Have Known That He Was Not a Fallen Prophet'—The Nauvoo Journal of Joseph Fielding," *BYU Studies* 19, no. 2 (Winter 1979): 158–59.

18. Smith, *History of the Church*, 7:567.

19. *Noah Webster's First Edition of an American Dictionary of the English Language*, facsimile edition (San Francisco: Foundation for American Christian Education, 1967), s. v. "temple."

20. Stanley B. Kimball, *Heber C. Kimball: Mormon Patriarch and Pioneer* (Chicago: University of Illinois Press, 1986), 117.

21.   Matthias F. Cowley, *Wilford Woodruff: History of His Life and Labors* (Salt Lake City: Bookcraft, 1964), 619–20; *History of the Church*, 3:279–80. After reviewing various diary entries, Randall Dixon believes that this event took place on 26 July 1847 (statement to the author, 6 May 2010).

22.   James R. Clark, comp., *Messages of the First Presidency* (Salt Lake City: Bookcraft, 1965), 1:333.

23.   Brigham Young, in *Journal of Discourses*, 1:133.

24.   "Who Designed the Temple?" *Deseret Weekly*, 15 April 1892, 578.

25.   See Bruce C. Hafen, Book Review of Blaine M. Yorgason, Richard A. Schmutz, and Douglas D. Alder, "All That Was Promised: The St. George Temple and the Unfolding of the Restoration," *BYU Studies* 54, no. 3 (2015): 193.

26.   Erastus Snow, 20 November 1881, St. George Stake Historical Record, Church History Library.

27.   Brigham Young, 14 February 1853, in *Journal of Discourses*, 1:277–78.

28.   Paul L. Anderson, "William Harrison Folsom: Pioneer Architect," *Utah Historical Quarterly* 43 (Summer 1975): 253.

29.   Brigham Young, in *Journal of Discourses*, 8:203.

30.   LeRoi C. Snow, "An Experience of My Father's," *Improvement Era*, September 1933, 677, 679.

15

The Restoration of the Perpetual Covenant to Hallow the Sabbath Day

Mary Jane Woodger

Mary Jane Woodger is a professor of Church history
and doctrine at Brigham Young University.

The commandment to keep the Sabbath day holy is as ancient as the earth itself, dating back to the Creation of the world, when after six days of labor the Lord rested from his work (see Genesis 2:2–3). God then commanded Moses on Mount Sinai, "Remember the Sabbath day, to keep it holy" (Exodus 20:8). Then in 2015 for the first time, a Churchwide "local and regional leadership training" was conducted where leaders received "instruction on the topic of strengthening faith in God by observing the Sabbath day with greater purpose."[1] This emphasis on keeping the Sabbath day holy was initiated in a general conference address given by Elder Russell M. Nelson (who is now President of the Quorum of the Twelve) in April of that same year. Elder Nelson explained, "The Sabbath was given as a perpetual covenant, a constant reminder that the Lord may sanctify His people." With the restoration of all things, this covenant was made between the Lord and his people once again. As Elder Nelson said, "It has been renewed in these latter days as part of a new covenant with a promise" (see D&C 59:9–16).[2]

Part of the New and Everlasting Covenant Restored by Joseph Smith

President Brigham Young made the following observation that the Sabbath day was indeed part of the new covenant:

> As to keeping the Sabbath according to the Mosaic Law, indeed, I do not; for it would be almost beyond my power. Still, under the new covenant, we should remember to preserve holy one day in the week as a day of rest—as a memorial of the rest of the Lord and the rest of the Saints; also for our temporal advantage, for it is instituted for the express purpose of benefiting man.[3]

Brigham Young saw the commandment to hallow the Sabbath day as a part of the new and everlasting covenant revealed by our Father in Heaven in this dispensation, and other apostles and prophets agreed. For instance, Elder John W. Taylor of the Quorum of the Twelve declared that Sabbath-day observance was "part and parcel of the new covenant God has made with his people in the latter day."[4]

Prominence of the Sabbath Day in General Conference Addresses

The repetition of this commandment has become commonplace among Latter-day Saints since 7 August 1831 when section 59 of the Doctrine and Covenants was revealed. The word *Sabbath* has been used 2,715 times in general conferences from 1850 to October 2015. As shown in the graph below there have been times when there has been an increase in counsel about Sabbath-day observance. Though General Authorities seldom give justification for emphasizing the Sabbath day in their general conference addresses, some reasons may be deduced for a heavier emphasis of this topic at one time more than another. One explanation is that cultural trends often preclude General Authority inclusion. For instance, stressing Sabbath-day observance between 1880 and 1900 coincided with a move away from agrarian life to urban living. With this shift came more opportunity for Latter-day Saints to be gainfully employed on Sundays, and, therefore, this new way to break the commandment was addressed. Another increase in General Authority attention to this subject took place from 1920 to 1940. This intensification is parallel to the advancement of Latter-day Saint participation in more Sunday sports and movies. It can also be observed that during World War II and the Great Depression, the topic of keeping the Sabbath day holy was advanced often but never linked to these events in leaders' talks.

Some General Authorities have included this subject in their addresses more than others. More than any other Apostle, Joseph Fielding Smith spoke about keeping the Sabbath day holy. During his inclusion in the Quorum of the Twelve Apostles, the amount of times the Sabbath day was mentioned in general conference was frequent, especially when compared with the decades immediately before and after his apostleship. Elder Joseph Fielding Smith explained his reasons for constantly speaking on this topic:

> We have, been taught to observe the Sabbath day from the beginning, and to keep it holy. And many other commandments, which we hear reiterated from the stand, . . . God has given unto us, that we might grow nearer unto him and be built up in the faith and strengthened. No commandment, at any time, has He given us, that was not for our comfort and blessing. They are not given merely to please the Lord, but to make us better men and women, and worthy of salvation and exaltation in His kingdom. We know our duty; we know what is required of us, and that the Lord will not hold him guiltless who, understanding these things, will go contrary to that which he has been commanded.[5]

The recent emphasis on the Sabbath day, however, is incomparable to any other era. With just being halfway through the 2010s decade, there are already 143 uses of the term "Sabbath day" in general conference. If this trend continues, the current decade will have more said about the Sabbath day in general conference than any previous decade. With the current emphasis of Sabbath-day observance, one is hard pressed to find a cultural parallel for this constant inclusion or a prominence of any particular leader speaking on the subject. Elder M. Russell Ballard gave this brief explanation for the current importance given to keeping the Sabbath day holy: "We felt that it was urgent that we strengthen the faith of our people. The world seems to be getting a little . . . more difficult. . . . We're hoping that home activities will be more centered on learning and knowing more about the life and ministry of the Savior and the great plan of happiness that our Heavenly Father has given us to live by."[6]

From Rules and Regulation to a Sign of Devotion

Though an underlining message in all general conference addresses about keeping the Sabbath day holy is consistent—to love God and act in a way that shows our love, respect, and honor for him—the interpretation, counsel, and instruction concerning the Sabbath day has not been constant throughout the history of the Church. A pattern can be observed with the various counsels about Sabbath-day observance that replicates ancient patterns of counsel that went from providing specific regulations and rules to inviting the inward adoption of gospel principles. Though each generation can be seen as having unique circumstances that make counsel vary by some degree throughout the years, the pattern still exists. From the beginning of the Church to present day, the theme of "Keeping the Sabbath Day Holy" has evolved in its role, prevalence, and usage by prophets.

This evolution of the Sabbath day principle in the latter days closely follows the progress that took place from the institution of Mosaic law to Christian practice. President James E. Faust of the First Presidency said, "The Mosaic injunctions of Sabbath day observance contained many detailed dos and don'ts. This may have been necessary to teach obedience to those who had been in captivity and had long been denied individual freedom of choice. Thereafter, these Mosaic instructions were carried to many unwarranted extremes which the Savior condemned." Elder Faust reiterated that in our generation, "God has recognized our intelligence by not requiring endless

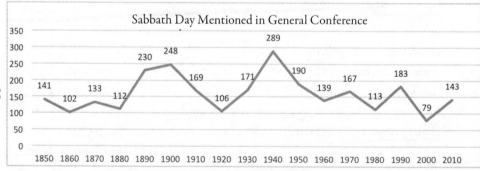

restrictions. Perhaps this was done with a hope that we would catch more of the spirit of Sabbath worship rather than the letter thereof."[7]

Just as the Savior tried to turn people's hearts to the Sabbath instead of restricting them to Mosaic rules, so too can this change be seen in the history of The Church of Jesus Christ of Latter-day Saints. Counsel given in general conference has progressed from detailed specific dos and don'ts to a broader view of the covenant of keeping the Sabbath day holy as a sign of our devotion written upon our hearts.

Scriptural Foundation

General Authorities consistently used two Sabbath-day scriptural passages to link Mosaic law to the new and everlasting covenant. Most often, they would first cite the Sabbath-day passage from the Ten Commandments given to Moses on Mount Sinai:

> Remember the sabbath day, to keep it holy. Six days shalt thou labor, and do all thy work:
>
> But the seventh day is the sabbath of the Lord thy God: in it thou shalt not do any work, thou, nor thy son, nor thy daughter, thy manservant, nor thy maidservant, nor thy cattle, nor thy stranger that is within thy gates:
>
> For in six days the Lord made heaven and earth, the sea, and all that in them is, and rested the seventh day: wherefore the Lord blessed the sabbath day, and hallowed it. (Exodus 20:9–11)

General Authorities reiterated that this fourth commandment was a perpetual covenant that had never been rescinded. Most especially the first three prophets of the twentieth century, Joseph F. Smith, Heber J. Grant, and George Albert Smith, repeated the commandment given on Mount Sinai. George Albert Smith was adamant that the commandment was still binding on latter-day Israel. He also declared, "If the people of the world had observed the Ten Commandments from that time until now, we would be a much different world. There would be millions of people who would live longer than they have lived and be happier."[8] The proceeding generation of General Authorities also spoke authoritatively about the fourth commandment. For instance, then Apostle Joseph Fielding Smith was very clear that the Saints should not believe that the commandment to keep the Sabbath day was part of the law of Moses that had been done away with in Christ. He informed, "The Decalogue was older than Moses, it continued after Moses passed away. The Lord has reiterated these commandments, he has renewed them and commanded us in our day to observe them and keep them sacredly and holy."[9] Mid- and latter-twentieth-century General Authorities, including Sylvester Q. Cannon, Spencer W. Kimball, N. Eldon Tanner, L. Tom Perry, James E. Faust, and Russell M. Nelson, also referred to the Decalogue.[10] Moreover, Elder James E. Faust observed, "The divine law of the Sabbath has been emphasized repeatedly over the centuries more than any other commandment."[11] Elder L. Tom Perry said that our treatment of the Sabbath day could be compared to those of former generations. He suggested, "One way to measure ourselves and compare us to previous generations is by one of the oldest standards known to man—the Ten Commandments."[12]

In 1949, President J. Reuben Clark Jr. explained that the reason this Mosaic law became so rule- and regulation-oriented was because it was one of the hardest commandments for the children of Israel to keep. He explained:

> Ancient Israel found that one of its most difficult command-ments to observe was that of remembering the Sabbath day. After they were led into captivity, they were among a people who knew not the Sabbath which they knew, and very soon they began to partake, as we are partaking (and let me say it is amazing how we follow round the clock of earlier peoples in our wanderings, or beginning of wanderings from the early tenets as they were taught to us) of the sins of those among whom they lived. It came to be, as it is with us, that not alone was the mat-ter one of laboring on the Sabbath, but it was also one of recre-ation on the Sabbath. So rather trivial regulations (as they seem to us) were made by captive Israel in order to prevent ancient Israel from breaking the Sabbath.[13]

President Clark's observation also explains why in the early days of the modern Church there was much more specificity in the counsel given on hallowing the Sabbath day.

The other scriptural passage that General Authorities most often use in counsel to keep the Sabbath day holy comes from section 59 of the Doctrine of Covenants. In almost every case, when a modern Apostle has spoken of the Sabbath day, passages or at least wording from this scripture block was included in his address:

> For verily this is a day appointed unto you to rest from your labors, and to pay thy devotions unto the Most High;
>
> Nevertheless, thy vows shall be offered up in righteousness on all days and at all times;
>
> But remember that on this, the Lord's day, thou shalt offer thine oblations and thy sacraments unto the Most High, confessing thy sins unto thy brethren, and before the Lord.
>
> And on this day thou shalt do none other thing, only let thy food be prepared with singleness of heart that thy fasting may be perfect, or, in other words, that thy joy may be full (D&C 59: 9–13).

This passage of scripture became the basis of counsel given over the history of the Church. Section 59 has been referred to in general conference addresses regarding the Sabbath day more in the twentieth century than even in the nineteenth century when it was first received.

Working on the Sabbath

It is noteworthy that the Sabbath day is one of the first things that President Brigham Young spoke of upon entering the valley. This incident has been brought up by Joseph Fielding Smith, LeGrand Richards, George Albert Smith, and Gordon B. Hinckley in general conference.[14] President Hinckley described what happened:

> On July 24, 1847, the pioneer company of our people came into this valley. . . . The next day, Sabbath services were held both in the morning and in the afternoon. There was no hall of any kind in which to meet. I suppose that in the blistering heat of that July Sunday they sat on the tongues of their wagons and leaned against the wheels while the Brethren spoke. The season

was late, and they were faced with a gargantuan and immediate task if they were to grow seed for the next season. But, President Young pleaded with them not to violate the Sabbath then or in the future.[15]

On that first Sabbath in the Salt Lake Valley, President Brigham Young told the brethren that they must not work on Sunday and that they would lose five times as much as they would gain by it.[16] He was adamant from the very outset that the Latter-day Saints of his generation keep the covenant of hallowing the Sabbath day.

Pioneers did not have to worry about specific counsel regarding shopping, attending sports, or going to the theater on Sunday, but they did have a lot of work to do in order to survive in a new land, especially with planting crops. Brigham Young, in trying to teach the Saints about keeping the Sabbath day holy, encouraged them not to work on the hallowed day. At one point, he even criticized one Latter-day Saint "because he planted some potatoes on the Sabbath day before he came to church."[17] Not working on the Sabbath has been constantly addressed throughout all generations of The Church of Jesus Christ of Latter-day Saints. President Wilford Woodruff also warned about farming on the Sabbath: "I do not believe that any man, who has ever belonged to this Church and kingdom, since its organization, has made anything by attending to his farm on the Sabbath. . . . The Spirit of God does not like it, it withdraws itself from us, and we make no money by it."[18]

The idea that working on the Sabbath would not prove to be beneficial was mentioned repeatedly over the years. For instance, President George Albert Smith said, "I want to say that you lose every time you violate the Sabbath day, you lose more than you can gain, no matter what you may think you are going to gain."[19] Likewise, President David O. McKay declared, "The farmer who makes his boys go out and haul hay, even when a storm is coming, is doing his boys an injustice. It would be much better to let that hay be destroyed than to deprive those boys of a sense of coming nearer to the Eternal Spirit, and partake of the sacrament."[20]

As Latter-day Saints progressed from an agrarian society to an urban one, counsel changed in relationship to working on the Sabbath day. In 1978, President Spencer W. Kimball was pleased to report that in his extensive travels he found "many thankful people who forgo the Sabbath day profits." Then in a new turn of counsel, he cautioned Latter-day Saints to not make others work either. He taught, "Businesses will not be open on the Sabbath if they are not patronized on that holy day. The same is true of resorts, sporting events, and recreation areas of all kinds. Pursuit of the almighty dollar is winning, it seems, over the Lord's commandment, 'Keep my Sabbaths, and reverence my sanctuary' (Lev. 19:30)." President Kimball continued, clarifying that keeping the Sabbath requires more than sacrificing worldly pleasures. He said, "It is not enough to refrain from movie-going, hunting, fishing, sports, and unnecessary labor on the Sabbath." [21]   Elder Mark E. Petersen of the Quorum of the Twelve taught, "If we are to do none other thing on Sunday but to devote the day to holy purposes, what is our situation if we willfully choose to operate our businesses on the Sabbath, or if we patronize such Sunday businesses, or if we go to places of recreation on Sunday?" [22]

Inappropriate Activities on the Sabbath

The quote above brings up another repeated Sabbath-day counsel: many recreational activities are not Sabbath-day worthy. The concern for young people and their activities on the Sabbath day was a constant in the addresses of the Brethren. For example, President Joseph F. Smith spoke of "gangs about the streets, using obscene language, throwing rocks at and scuffling with each other, going riding, walking, fishing, hunting, &c., on the Sabbath day." [23]   He warned, "One of these evils is a growing tendency, especially on the part of our youth, to pay but little attention to, if not to ignore, the observance of the Sabbath day. The Sabbath is a day of rest and of worship, designated and set apart by special commandment of the Lord to the Church of Jesus Christ of Latter-day Saints, and we should honor and keep it holy. We should also teach our children this principle." [24]

Some Latter-day Saints began to think that if they attended their religious meetings on Sunday, then they could do anything else they wanted to do and still be honoring the Sabbath. The Brethren became very clear that this was not the case, and they would pay a price for such actions. President George Albert Smith cautioned that with such behavior, "the Spirit of our Heavenly Father will withdraw from them." [25]   As sports and media entered the lives of Latter-day Saints, General Authorities also spoke of these aspects of life being incongruent with Sabbath-day worship. In the 1970s, shopping on Sunday became a topic of concern. President Spencer W. Kimball said, "We call attention also to the habit in which many buy their commodities on the Sabbath. Many employed people would be released for rest and worship on the Sabbath if we did not shop on that day. Numerous excuses and rationalizations are presented to justify the Sunday buying. We call upon all of you to keep the Sabbath holy and make no Sunday purchases."[26]

Regulation- and Rule-Bound Counsel

In going from Mosaic regulation to heartfelt devotion, there were many steps along the way in the counsel from General Authorities. One sees in early Church history the listing of many dos and don'ts of what Latter-day Saints could or could not do on the Sabbath day. One interesting incident from Elder George A. Smith shows the extreme strictness that was going on in Sabbath observance. One time when he was visiting a stake, he found local leaders debating about whether or not Latter-day Saints could even discuss the subject of temporal welfare on the Sabbath. Local leaders were telling their congregations that they should not speak of such things as "donations, emigration, teams, building meeting-houses, or of Tithing," on the Sabbath. After learning of this particular stake's eccentric restrictions, Elders George A. Smith and Ezra T. Benson occupied the whole Sabbath day "in telling how to make bread, build cities, make farms, fences, and in fact we told them how to do every useful thing that we could think of." They "asserted that a certain amount of temporal preparation was necessary in order that a man might enjoy his religion."[27]

Specific rules such as the one discussed above were often given late into the nineteenth and early twentieth centuries. For instance, President Joseph F. Smith censured listening to secular music on the Sabbath.[28] Latter-day Saints were encouraged instead to "[sing] the songs of Zion." In 1900, Elder Francis M. Lyman gave a list of appropriate Sunday activities, saying, "The Sabbath day should be occupied in our home temples, in home study, in home reading, in home prayer." He also suggested that "the fathers and mothers will, perhaps, find themselves pretty well 'stumped' at times to know just exactly how to handle the little ones; but they must not be wearied."[29]

Elder John Henry Smith of the Quorum of the Twelve Apostles was very decisive in his list of dos and don'ts. He counseled that the Sabbath day "should not be spent in visiting neighbors, in mingling with one another upon the streets, or in going to pleasure resorts." Instead, the Saints "should seek to study the Scriptures at home, and equip ourselves by communion with the Spirit."[30] Even as late as 1 September 1928, the First Presidency published an editorial in the *Deseret News*, which commanded specifically that "Latter-day Saints may not go on Sunday to movies, to baseball, football, or basketball games, or to any other kind of commercial entertainments, or engage in avoidable commercial activities, or go hunting, fishing, golfing, or skiing on this day."[31]

In 1949, the subject of Sunday music was broached once again, but the regulation was tempered when President J. Reuben Clark Jr. of the First Presidency suggested that Latter-day Saints could "listen to good music in the home," but they were not to "go joy riding, nor to beach parties, nor on picnics!"[32] On the subject of watching movies, he instructed, "There is a great difference between looking at a good movie in your home and going to a movie house, a very great difference. But the home movies we look at should be of a kind that teach things specified in the revelations as in order in the house of prayer."[33]

Twenty years later in 1969, then Elder Spencer W. Kimball published *The Miracle of Forgiveness*. Within this volume, he gave lists of what to do on the Sabbath, unlike his predecessors who had listed what not to do. He wrote:

> Abstinence from work and recreation is important but insufficient. The Sabbath calls for constructive thoughts and acts, and if one merely lounges about doing nothing on the Sabbath, he is breaking it. To observe it, one will be on his knees in prayer, preparing lessons, studying the gospel, meditating, visiting the ill and distressed, sleeping, reading wholesome material, and attending all the meetings of that day to which he is expected. To fail to do these proper things is a transgression on the omission side.[34]

As the prophet, President Spencer W. Kimball was still giving lists to the Saints. In 1978, President Kimball's list of appropriate Sabbath activities also included "studying the scriptures, attending church meetings to learn and to worship, writing letters to absent loved ones, comforting the sorrowing, visiting the sick, and, in general, doing what the Lord would have us do on this, his holy day."[35] President Kimball's administration instituted the consolidated meeting schedule. As the prophet, he made it clear that the extra hours on the Sabbath day that were now available from a reduction in meetings should be spent with families: "Therefore, take time to be together as families to converse with one another, to study the scriptures, to visit friends, relatives, and the sick and lonely. This is also an excellent time to work on your journals and genealogy. Do not neglect those among us who do not now have the blessings of living in traditional families. These are special souls who often have special needs. Do not let them become isolated from you or the activities of your ward or your branch."[36]

Counsel to Attend Church Meetings

One thing that was absolute that did not change over the span of generations was that Latter-day Saints were instructed to attend Church meetings on the Sabbath. Especially in the first two decades of the twentieth century, this counsel was renewed repeatedly. Elder Hyrum Smith of the Quorum of the Twelve Apostles in October 1906 reported that some "sacrament meetings and Sabbath meetings [were] not as well attended as they should be."[37] Elder George Albert Smith also spoke in general conference about low attendance and cautioned, "Men and women who go from year to year without partaking of the Lord's Supper, gradually lose the Spirit of our Heavenly Father; they forfeit its companionship where they have had opportunity to participate in that blessing, but have failed to take advantage of it. The Sacrament is of great importance. The Lord Himself ordained that we partake of these emblems."[38]

In 1907, President Anthon H. Lund of the First Presidency talked about the great expense the Church was incurring in erecting meetinghouses and tied it to the importance of Sabbath worship: "We hope that the people who are so willing to build meeting houses will also be willing to use them . . . on the Sabbath day." He then warned, "Unless the Saints attend their meetings it will be hard for them to keep alive in the Gospel."[39] Nine years later, he talked of ways to make the meetings more attractive through music and defined that it was "[the Saints'] duty in attending their meetings" and to listen to what is said.[40]

Often quoting section 59, General Authorities told Latter-day Saints to go to the "house of prayer" and renew their covenants so they could keep "unspotted from the sins of the world."[41] In October 1916, Elder Rudger J. Clawson also encouraged Saints to go to church. He warned that it was not enough to "remain at home upon the Sabbath day, even to read, or to read good books, or to read the scriptures, when they ought to be in the house of prayer, in the house of worship, in the house of the Lord, where they are commanded to go."[42]

In 1936, Elder Richard R. Lyman of the Quorum of the Twelve Apostles outlined the purpose of Sunday meetings as follows:

> We do not go to our places of worship for the purpose of acquiring scholarship; we do not go there to learn history or mathematics or science. The purpose of our going to our sacrament meetings is to worship. We cannot get faith by logic any more than we can get learning by simply longing for it. Partaking worthily of the Sacrament of the Lord's Supper is an important and fundamental part of that worship, and it is this intense and genuine worship, this prayerful spirit that will bring . . . light and inspiration.[43]

Attending Church meetings was the most important thing to do on the Sabbath, and, according to President Kimball, resting did not mean "indolent lounging about the home all day or puttering around in the garden, but a consistent attendance at meetings for the worship of the Lord." Agreeing with what Elder Lyman said above, President Kimball told the Saints they should not expect to go to Sabbath meetings to be entertained or amused, but should go to worship. He was clear that worshipping during the sacrament meeting was the responsibility of the individual member: "If the Sacrament meeting is a failure to you, you are the one that has failed. No one can worship for you; you must do your own serving of the Lord."[44]

In the April general conference of 1946, Elder Marion G. Romney said that it was of overwhelming importance to have regular attendance of sacrament meetings and also gave a promise to the Saints if they would go to church. He promised, "If we will increase our attendance from about twenty percent to forty percent, we shall double our spiritual power for righteousness in the world."[45]

Individual Internalization

As time went on, counsel from General Authorities in relationship to Sabbath-day observance became more internal, less rigid, and inexplicit. This type of instruction appeared sporadically and then with more and more frequency. In April 1915, President Joseph F. Smith began to give this type of counsel: "God made or designated the Sabbath day for a day of rest, day of worship, a day for goodly deeds, and for humility and penitence, and the worship of the Almighty in spirit and in truth."[46] Here, specific rules were not mentioned. Latter-day Saints were not told exactly what goodly deeds to do, only to do them. President Francis M. Lyman of the Quorum of the Twelve also gave some very general counsel when he instructed that on the Sabbath, Latter-day Saints should "refrain from all labor, from all secular and improper pleasures, and spend the day in the service and worship of the Lord."[47] Again, the Saints were told to spend the day in service and worship but not told what that entailed. Listeners in general conference had to internalize what such instruction meant for each one of them in their individual lives.

A few years later in 1923, Elder James E. Talmage simply told the Saints that they were not obeying the law if they were idle, and he instructed, "We should be active and in service, but Sabbath-day work should be directly the service of God and not the secular and wage-earning service of man."[48] This vague counsel left it up to the individual to decide what "service of God" entailed. Presiding Bishop Sylvester Cannon was aware that many Latter-day Saints did not want this new type of counsel; instead, they wanted a list so that they could justify doing something if it was not included as being unacceptable by the Brethren. In general conference of 1926, Bishop Cannon gave a broad definition of what was appropriate without defining specific activities that would break the Sabbath:

Many people question at times how we should observe it, or what it is that might be considered as breaking the Sabbath. Surely anything that interferes with the spirit of peace conformable to the Sabbath is breaking the Sabbath. There should be nothing that interferes with our worship or that causes our minds to be diverted, nor any act of ours that causes our minds to de detracted from the spirit of that day; but in all of our acts upon that day we should exercise and devote our minds and thoughts to those things that shall help us to grow in faith, in righteousness and in good works.[49]

Except for these sparse examples cited above, most other counsel for Sabbath-day observance was very explicit. It was not until the 1980s that most of the General Authorities gave counsel that was broad and self-determined. For instance, in 1991 Elder Marvin J. Ashton of the Quorum of the Twelve Apostles gave direction about each Latter-day Saint's personal involvement with the Sabbath. He instructed, "Sometimes the freedoms and blessings of the Sabbath can be lost by attitudes that allow selfishness and lack of personal involvement in tried-and-true patterns. Sabbath days can be lost an hour at a time. Sabbath days can be lost an outing at a time.[50]

Sacrament Spirituality

Though the counsel of the last two decades of the twentieth century took on a more general, less detailed tone, one constant was always present in teachings about hallowing the Sabbath: the sacrament was to be the preeminent activity for Latter-day Saints on Sunday. Whereas earlier attending Church meetings had been of great importance, what was done during the sacrament became the focus in the twenty-first century. The sacrament service even became more internalized as the years went by. By way of illustration, Elder L. Tom Perry of the Quorum of the Twelve Apostles mentioned in 2006 that he remembered that when he was a little child, beautiful music was played during the passing of the sacrament. He then explained that this practice was stopped because the Brethren wanted the minds of the Latter-day Saints to focus on the atoning sacrifice of the Lord and Savior, Jesus

Christ. Elder Ashton then gave some individually prescribed counsel suggesting that during the administration of the sacrament, Latter-day Saints set aside the world. As he put it, the sacrament should be a "period of spiritual renewal as we recognize the deep spiritual significance of the ordinance offered to each of us personally. If we were to become casual in partaking of the sacrament, we would lose the opportunity for spiritual growth."[51]

Elder L. Tom Perry gave entire talks on the importance of the sacrament in 1984 and 2006. In 1984 he explained, "Partaking of the sacrament [is] basic for our observance of the Lord's day."[52] He spoke of the power of the sacrament on each individual by telling the story of a poor woman who faithfully went to church every week. Her husband, however, did not. Week after week, she urged him, but he wouldn't go. "Finally, tiring of her pestering, he said, 'Give me one good reason why I should go to church.' Her reply was, 'I can't explain to you why I go. All I can tell you is that I go in empty and come out full.'"[53] As illustrated in this story, counsel about the sacrament was now about thoughts, feelings, and attitudes, rather than behavior and actions.

This type of counsel was very pronounced in the general conference held directly after the Sabbath-day leadership training. In October 2015, three General Authorities all gave the same kind of counsel that concentrated on emotions and spirituality. Elder Claudio R. M. Costa of the First Quorum of the Seventy disclosed:

> While pondering on the Sabbath day I felt a deep gratitude for the blessing and privilege of being able to partake of the sacrament. For me that is a very solemn, sacred, and spiritual moment. . . . The sacrament is . . . a time for Heavenly Father to teach us about the Atonement of His Beloved Son—Our Savior, Jesus Christ—and for us to receive revelation about it. . . . It is a time for us to reverently ask God for this knowledge. And if we do, I have no doubt that we will receive this knowledge, which will bless our lives beyond measure. I love the Sabbath, the sacrament, and what they mean.[54]

Elder D. Todd Christofferson concurred when he pointed out, "The wards and branches of the Church offer a weekly gathering of respite and renewal, a time and place to leave the world behind—the Sabbath. It is a day to 'delight thyself in the Lord,' to experience the spiritual healing that comes with the sacrament, and to receive the renewed promise of His Spirit to be with us."[55] In addition, President Henry B. Eyring said, "You know from the words of the sacrament prayer how that promise is fulfilled ... 'that they may always have his Spirit to be with them.' ... For that reason alone, it is easy to see why the Lord's servants have tried to increase our desire to worship God in our sacrament meetings. If we partake of the sacrament in faith, the Holy Ghost will then be able to protect us and those we love from the temptations that come with increasing intensity and frequency."[56]

Devotion and Personal Application

In 1991, Elder James E. Faust made a very clear demarcation that Sabbath day doings were no longer going to be defined by the Brethren. That responsibility now was clearly the auspices of each Latter-day Saint. He acknowledged:

> Where is the line as to what is acceptable and unacceptable on the Sabbath? Within the guidelines, each of us must answer this question for ourselves. While these guidelines are contained in the scriptures and in the words of the modern prophets, they must also be written in our hearts and governed by our conscience.... It is quite unlikely that there will be any serious violation of Sabbath worship if we come humbly before the Lord and offer him all our heart, our soul, and our mind. (See Matt. 22:37.) ... What is worthy or unworthy on the Sabbath day will have to be judged by each of us by trying to be honest with the Lord. On the Sabbath day we should do what we have to do and what we ought to do in an attitude of worshipfulness and then limit our other activities.[57]

Here Elder Faust clearly placed keeping the covenant of hallowing the Sabbath Day in the realm of personal accountability. Though some Latter-day Saints were clamoring for another list of "acceptable" and "unacceptable" activities, Elder Faust placed Sabbath-day decisions squarely on the shoulders of each individual.

In 1999, Elder Dallin H. Oaks of the Quorum of the Twelve Apostles made it clear that specific rules about the Sabbath were a thing of the past.

He stated, "Teachers who are commanded to teach 'the principles of [the] gospel' and 'the doctrine of the kingdom' (D&C 88:77) should generally forgo teaching specific rules or applications. For example, . . . they would not provide a list of dos and don'ts for keeping the Sabbath day holy." Elder Oaks was clear that once teachers have "taught the doctrine and the associated principles from the scriptures and the living prophets, such specific applications or rules are generally the responsibility of individuals and families."[58] Sabbath-day instruction had covered the same path that the children of Israel had trod. They had gone from rules and regulations to devotion and personal application.

Elder Quentin L. Cook described the result of this new form of Sabbath counsel in October 2015 general conference: "For members of The Church of Jesus Christ of Latter-day Saints, honoring the Sabbath is a form of righteousness that will bless and strengthen families, connect us with our Creator, and increase happiness. The Sabbath can help separate us from that which is frivolous, inappropriate or immoral. It allows us to be in the world but not of the world."[59]

Conversely, in 2015, then Elder Russell M. Nelson used his own life experience as a pattern for what had happened Churchwide in Sabbath-day counsel. He disclosed that as a youth he had participated in the Mosaic approach to the Sabbath where he had studied others who had a compiled list of things to do and things not to do. He then explained how the Sabbath day later became internalized in his life:

> It wasn't until later that I learned from the scriptures that my conduct and my attitude on the Sabbath constituted a sign between me and my Heavenly Father. With that understanding, I no longer needed lists of dos and don'ts. When I had to make a decision whether or not an activity was appropriate for the Sabbath, I simply asked myself, "What sign do I want to give to God?" That question made my choices about the Sabbath day crystal clear. Though the doctrine pertaining to the Sabbath day is of ancient origin, it has been renewed in these latter days as part of a new covenant with a promise.[60]

The Sabbath as a Delight and Sign of Our Devotion

With the current emphasis of Sabbath-day observance by the First Presidency and Quorum of the Twelve, a new way of looking at our part of the covenant of hallowing the Sabbath has taken place. Recent apostles have talked about how living the commandment to keep the Sabbath day holy is an individual commitment that signifies our love for the Lord. Detailed dos and don'ts of keeping the Sabbath day holy are no longer taught. Moreover, Elder Nelson challenged Latter-day Saints to write this perpetual covenant in their hearts.[61]

As General Authority counsel has evolved from Mosaic rules to inner strength, Elder Nelson described the difference that following such counsel has made in the lives of Latter-day Saints: "A sacred Sabbath truly is a delight."[62] Likewise, Elder Quentin L. Cook also pronounced the improvement that had come about with the direction members had been given about hallowing the Sabbath day. In the October 2015 general conference he disclosed:

> In the last six months, a most remarkable change has occurred in the Church. This has been in response of the members to renewed emphasis on the Sabbath day by the First Presidency and Quorum of the Twelve and to President Russell M. Nelson's challenge to make the Sabbath a delight. Many members understand that truly keeping the Sabbath day holy is a refuge from the storms of this life. It is also a sign of our devotion to our Father in Heaven and an increased understanding of the sacredness of sacrament meeting. Still, we have a long way to go, but we have a wonderful beginning. I challenge all of us to continue to embrace this counsel and improve our Sabbath worship.[63]

The reason that General Authority counsel has changed from a list of dos and don'ts to suggestions in recent trainings is unclear. Many reasons can be postulated for this transformation. Recently it was pointed out that General Authorities did not want to prescribe what to do and not to do on the Sabbath.[64] One reason might be that Latter-day Saints are now living in a time when they use agency more wisely to make decisions on their own. Another cause for this lack of specifics might be that Latter-day Saints will qualify for even more blessings as they individually receive their own revelation about appropriate Sabbath-day activities. One thing, however, is clear as we study the evolution of counsel on this subject: unlike the previous generations, the responsibility has now shifted from leaders to individual members to find out what the Lord would have them do.

Promises and blessings have expanded as this new responsibility has been given. As Elder L. Whitney Clayton of the Presidency of the Seventy described, "The day would become sweeter for them individually, sweeter for them as families, sweeter for all the members of the Church. Their faith would be deepened, their ability to move ahead in life with confidence and optimism and happiness at home and at church and in every situation would be amplified by their having turned to the Lord more fully on the Sabbath Day."[65] As Latter-day Saints embrace Sabbath-day counsel that emphasizes inner strength, spirituality, and devotion rather than temporal rules, Sabbath worship will become a delight and a sign of each Latter-day Saint's devotion.

Notes

1. The Church of Jesus Christ of Latter-day Saints, "Church Leaders Call for Better Observance of Sabbath Day," News Release, 30 June 2015, http://www.mormonnewsroom.org/article/church-leaders-call-for-better-observance-of-sabbath-day.

2. Russell M. Nelson, "The Sabbath is a Delight," *Ensign*, April 2015, 129–32.

3. Brigham Young, in *Journal of Discourses* (London: Latter-day Saints' Book Depot, 1854–86), 6:277–8.

4. John W. Taylor, in *Journal of Discourses* (London: Latter-day Saints' Book Depot, 1854–86), 10:113.

5. Joseph Fielding Smith, in Conference Report, October 1916, 70.

6. "Church Leaders Call for Better Observance of Sabbath Day," 15 July 2015, www.lds.org/church/news/church-leaders-call-for-better-observance-of-sabbath-day?lang=eng.

7. James E. Faust, "The Lord's Day," *Ensign*, November 1991, 35.

8. George Albert Smith, in Conference Report, October 1935, 119–20; Smith, in Conference Report, October 1950, 7.

9. Joseph Fielding Smith, in Conference Report, October 1935, 14.

10. Sylvester Q. Cannon, in Conference Report, October 1928, 48–49; Spencer W. Kimball, "Why Call Me Lord, Lord, and Do Not the Things Which I Say?," *Ensign*,

May 1975, 7; N. Eldon Tanner, in Conference Report, April 1970, 64–65; L. Tom Perry, "Obedience to Law Is Liberty", *Ensign,* May 2013, 87; Faust, "The Lord's Day," 33–35; Russell M. Nelson, "Self-Mastery," *Ensign*, November 1985, 30.

11. Faust, "The Lord's Day," 33.

12. Perry, "Obedience to Law Is Liberty," *Ensign,* May 2013, 87.

13. J. Reuben Clark Jr., in Conference Report, October 1949, 107–8.

14. Joseph Fielding Smith, in Conference Report, October 1938, 38; LeGrand Richards, in Conference Report, October 1947, 73; George Albert Smith, in Conference Report, April 1947, 161; and

15. Gordon B. Hinckley, "An Ensign to the Nations," *Ensign*, November 1989, 51.

16. Hinckley, "An Ensign to the Nations," 51; and Young, in *Journal of Discourses*, 6:277–78.

17. Joseph Fielding Smith, in Conference Report, October 1938, 38.

18. Wilford Woodruff, in *Journal of Discourses* (London: Latter-day Saints' Book Depot, 1854–86), 21:191.

19. George Albert Smith, in Conference Report, October 1948, 188.

20. David O. McKay, in Conference Report, October 1956, 90.

21. Spencer W. Kimball, Conference Report, October 1953, 52.

22. Mark E. Petersen, "Remember the Sabbath Day," *Ensign*, May 1975, 49.

23. Joseph F. Smith in Conference Report, September 1871.

24. Joseph F. Smith, in Conference Report, October 1901, 1–2.

25. George Albert Smith, in Conference Report, April 1923, 77–78.

26. Spencer W. Kimball, "God Will Not Be Mocked," *Ensign*, November 1974, 6.

27. George A. Smith, in *Journal of Discourses*, 10:60.

28. Francis M. Lyman, in Conference Report, October 1900, 77.

29. Francis M. Lyman, in Conference Report, October 1908, 58.

30. John Henry Smith, in Conference Report, April 1906, 83–84.

31. Joseph F. Merrill, in Conference Report, April 1949, 29.

32. J. Reuben Clark Jr., in Conference Report, October 1949, 110.

33. J. Reuben Clark Jr., in Conference Report, October 1949, 110.

34. Faust, "The Lord's Day," 34, originally found in Kimball, *The Miracle of Forgiveness*, Salt Lake City: Bookcraft, 1969, 96–97.

35. Kimball, "Hold Fast to the Iron Rod," 6.

36. Spencer W. Kimball, "Rendering Service to Others," *Ensign*, May 1981, 45.

37. Hyrum M. Smith, in Conference Report, October 1906, 43.

38. George Albert Smith, in Conference Report, April 1908, 34–35.

39. Anthon H. Lund, in Conference Report, October 1907, 9.

40. Lund, in Conference Report, October 1916, 10.

41. Lund, in Conference Report, October 1916, 10.

42. Rudger J. Clawson, in Conference Report, October 1916, 36–37.

43. Richard R. Lyman, in Conference Report, April 1936, 99.

44. Spencer W. Kimball, in Conference Report, April 1944, 145.

45. Marion G. Romney, in Conference Report, April 1946, 40.

46. Joseph F. Smith, in Conference Report, April 1915, 10.

47. Francis M. Lyman, in Conference Report, October 1908, 57.

48. James E. Talmage, in Conference Report, April 1923, 141.

49. Sylvester Q. Cannon, in Conference Report, April 1926, 93.

50. Marvin J. Ashton, "Strengthen the Feeble Knees," *Ensign*, November 1991, 71.

51. L. Tom Perry, "As Now We Take the Sacrament," *Ensign*, May 2006, 41.

52. L. Tom Perry, "And Why Call Ye Me, Lord, Lord, and Do Not the Things Which I Say?," *Ensign*, November 1984, 18–19.

53. Rick Walton and Fern Oviatt, eds., *Stories for Mormons* (Salt Lake City: Bookcraft, 1983), 112, as cited in Perry, "And Why Call Ye Me, Lord, Lord, and Do Not the Things Which I Say?," 18–19.

54. Claudio R. M. Costa, "That They Do Always Remember Him," *Ensign*, November 2015, 101–3.

55. D. Todd Christofferson, "Why the Church," *Ensign,* November 2015, 109.

56. Henry B. Eyring, "The Holy Ghost as Your Companion," *Ensign*, November 2015, 104.

57. Faust, "The Lord's Day," 35.

58. Dallin H. Oaks, "Gospel Teaching," *Ensign*, November 1999, 79.

59. Quentin L. Cook, "Shipshape and Bristol Fashion: Be Temple Worthy—in Good Times and Bad Times," *Ensign*, November 2015, 41–42.

60. Russell M. Nelson, "The Sabbath Is a Delight," *Ensign*, May 2015, 130.

61. Nelson, "The Sabbath Is a Delight," 129–32.

62. Nelson, "The Sabbath Is a Delight," *Ensign*, May 2015, 132.

63. Cook, "Shipshape and Bristol Fashion," 42.

64. "Church Leaders Call for Better Observance of Sabbath Day."

65. "Church Leaders Call for Better Observance of Sabbath Day."

Index